FRACTURE

FRACTURE

Life & Culture in the West, 1918–1938

PHILIPP BLOM

Atlantic Books
LONDON

First published in hardback in the United States in 2015 by
Basic Books, a Member of the Perseus Books Group.

First published in hardback in Great Britain in 2015 by
Atlantic Books, an imprint of Atlantic Books Ltd.

1 2 3 4 5 6 7 8 9

A CIP catalogue record for this book is available
from the British Library.

Hardback ISBN: 978-0-85789-219-5
E-book ISBN: 978-0-85789-278-2
Paperback ISBN: 978-0-85789-221-8
Trade paperback ISBN: 978-0-85789-220-1

Printed and bound by CPI Group (UK) Ltd, Croydon, CR0 4YY
Design and composition by Eclipse Publishing Services

Photo and excerpt credits appear on page 415

For Manfred, Peter, and Tanja
and in memory of Jon, poet, teacher, and friend

....

God is dead. A world has collapsed. I am dynamite. World history has broken into two halves. There is a time before me. And a time after me. Religion, science, morality—phenomena originating in the fear of primitive peoples. An era collapses. A thousand-year culture collapses. . . . The world reveals itself to be a blind battle of forces unbound.

Man lost his celestial face, became matter, conglomerate, animal, an insane product of thoughts twitching abruptly and insufficiently. . . . And another element collided destructively and menacingly with the desperate search for a new order in the ruins of the past world: mass culture in the modern metropolis. Complex the thoughts and sensations assailing the brain, symphonic the feelings. Machines were created, and took the place of individuals. . . . A world of abstract demons swallowed individual expression, swallowed individual faces into towering masks, engulfed private expression, robbed individual things of their names, destroyed the ego and agitated oceans of collapsed feelings.

Hugo Ball, "Kandinksy," 1917

Contents

List of Illustrations

Introduction: 1,567 Days

ON AUGUST 10, 1920, AT NINE-THIRTY IN THE MORNING, THIRTY-SEVEN-year-old singer Mamie Smith and her musicians arrived at a recording studio close to New York's Times Square. Crowded around the large horn of the recording machine, they began improvising their way into "Crazy Blues," a song written for the occasion. Again and again they played, riffing and refining as they went. Perry Bradford, the pianist, remembered: "As we hit the introduction and Mamie started singing it gave me a lifetime thrill to hear Johnny Dunn's cornet moaning those dreaming blues and Dope Andrews making some down-home slides on his trombone, while Ernest Elliott was echoing some clarinet jive along with Leroy Parker sawing his fiddle in the groove. Man, it was too much for me."[1]

The blues dealt with disappointed love—how could it be otherwise? Smith sang with raw grief in her powerful alto voice as clarinet, violin, and trombone sighed and groaned alongside her, the musicians fortified by a steady supply of bootleg gin and blackberry juice. After thirteen takes and eight hours of work the musicians declared themselves satisfied with the result. They were tired and happy, in something of a collective trance. They saw out the day over plates of black-eyed peas and rice at Mamie's apartment.

Smith had left the grim Cincinnati neighborhood where she grew up and made a reputation for herself in vaudeville theater in Harlem before beginning to appear in bars and speakeasies. It was a life at the edge, but it had its rewards. Her expressively dark and flexible voice soon brought her a local following, and eventually even the great Victor label became interested in making a record with her. They eventually dropped the idea, however, ostensibly on artistic grounds, but more probably out of fear. Smith was black, and southern customers in particular had warned record firms that they would boycott their products if they began to record and credit black artists on their discs. Finally a smaller firm, the OKeh Phonograph Company, had decided to defy the threats and give Mamie a chance.

She had recorded her first blues song, "That Thing Called Love," on Valentine's Day 1920 with an all-white band of musicians, a compromise solution. No other African American had ever recorded a blues song before.

"That Thing Called Love" had done well for the company, and for the second record Smith was allowed to play with her regular band. When she had heard of the decision, she broke into a spontaneous dance of joy. Now, after a long day's recording, the second record, "Crazy Blues," was ready for pressing and distribution. It would sell seventy-five thousand copies in Harlem alone in just one month. Throughout the United States, sales soon topped one million—a historic achievement, and not just for a black artist. Only star tenor Enrico Caruso and Al Jolson's hit song "Swanee" sold more that year.

What made Mamie Smith's recording success so phenomenal was that both white and black households were buying "Crazy Blues." Something new had happened. Classical singers such as Caruso and professional crooners such as Jolson had begun to carry a more popular repertoire into people's lives, but always in a form as shiny and carefully arranged as Jolson's brilliantined hair. By contrast, Smith's singing conveyed unvarnished emotion. A whole culture found its voice in hers. She combined the bellow of a street hawker and the vocal punch of an angry washerwoman with the sorrow of centuries of humiliation and a young woman's sheer lust for life. It was not the first time popular singers had sung with such raw sassiness, of course, but it was the first time such a performance had been recorded. The voice of the down-and-dirty people came into the polite living rooms of the middle and upper classes, and young listeners in particular decided that it spoke for them, too.

As Mamie Smith was riding a wave of success as "Queen of the Blues," other black artists broadened the appeal of jazz in the United States and beyond. Jazz was much, much more than danceable tunes. It was the child of slavery and speakeasies, the inspiration for indecency and irresponsibility, acoustic subversion, the musical infiltration of lives lived at the margins into the center of society. In America, young black musicians such as Louis Armstrong, Jelly Roll Morton, Sidney Bechet, Bessie Smith, and Duke Ellington were often restricted to segregated or illegal clubs and bars. In Europe, which was still reeling from the nightmare of the First World War, they toured the great cities and were welcomed as heralds of a new age. Jazz somehow embodied everything that had changed, and more: it embodied the fact that nothing was the same now as it had been in 1914.

Jazz became the soundtrack of an age, the incendiary charge flung into society, igniting tensions, stoking sensuality, and sapping the old order. Even the Nazis would pay tribute to the power of its message by fighting a culture war against "degenerate nigger jazz," wary of its immense pull and eloquence yet unable to replace it with anything but cheerily sterilized swing music, military marches, and Viennese waltzes corrupted into vehicles of National Socialist feeling. But they never felt safe. Syncopation, it seemed, was lurking in every corner.

A paradox lies at the heart of this image of an all-new world suddenly risen from the war. As I have argued in *The Vertigo Years: Change and Culture in the West 1900–14*, the great shift into the modern age did not spring full-blown out of the trenches of the Western Front; rather, many of its elements were already in place well before 1914. Mass societies, consumerism, mass media, urbanization, big industry and big finance, feminism, psychoanalysis, the theory of relativity, abstract art, and atonal music all predate the beginning of the war. So why did the world suddenly seem so much more modern? Why is it that far more than a single decade seems to separate the fashions, social mores, and moral outlook of, say, 1913 and 1923?

Perhaps this apparent paradox can be resolved by another one. The First World War is generally accepted to represent a radical break for the societies concerned, followed by a new beginning. This assumption of a sudden rupture may appear to explain why the world looked different after 1918, but when studying the period one is struck time and again by the great forces of continuity originating around 1900, traversing the war years, and reaching far into the future.

In the epigraph at the beginning of this book the German poet Hugo Ball draws the apocalyptic scenario of a world ending, a "blind battle of forces unbound." Ball was writing in 1917, and while his poetic analysis appears to fit the interwar period after the supposed rupture of 1918, he is actually describing life before 1914. Even at the turn of the twentieth century, metropolitan areas had already become battlegrounds of modernity, about which he could remark: "The world became monstrous, uncanny, the relationship with reason and convention, the yardstick vanished. . . . The science of electrons caused a strange vibration in all surfaces, lines and forms."[2]

The warlike scenario of city life evoked here is strikingly similar to reports by soldiers from the front in the Great War—a hellish place of machines and technology, of constant threat and individuality

annihilated, a place ruled by abstract demons. Ball himself had volunteered for military service but had been classed as unfit for service.
His only direct confrontation with life at the front came when he
went to visit a wounded friend near Lunéville in late 1914. What
he saw behind the front lines was deeply shocking to him, and as his
lecture three years later made clear, he identified the existential rift
and the historical rupture with the "electric tingling" of modernity
and its supreme expression: the fascination and danger of life in the
big city.[3]

Even before 1914 new machines, scientific inventions, and industrial processes had been transforming the lives of city dwellers—and,
to a lesser degree, those of people in the countryside. The denizens of
the growing urban agglomerations had already come to rely on mass
transportation, mass-produced goods, food imported from across the
globe, work in factories and offices, newspapers and cinema, and
everyday technologies such as condoms, which were made from vul-
canized rubber and which facilitated easier and less risky access to
sex. These technological possibilities changed not only daily lives but
also the sense of self of those living in this way.

The social consequences and the possibilities created by these
technological changes began to transform all aspects of life. Within
less than a generation, many aspects of life such as entertainment,
education, and travel had become more democratic; women had
demanded equal rights and were fighting for them; and workers were
increasingly organized and ready to defend their interests through
trade unions and strikes. To those at the bottom, life in the metropolis
was miserable, but those who were already one rung up—those who
had enough to eat and a roof over their heads—profited from access
to cheaper goods, cheaper food, and more possibilities for learning
about and encountering different people, places, cultures, and perspectives, even if only through cinema shorts, badly reproduced
photographs in a newspaper, and a weekend third-class railway outing
for the family.

The world had grown, and it had accelerated. Clocks, conveyor
belts, timetables, telegrams, and telephones sped up daily life; racing
cars, bicycles, planes, and even trains and ships dominated the news
as new records were set and then broken every day in a contest between human mechanical ingenuity and nature. Machines extended
human abilities beyond most people's dreams.

The headlong rush of history had also caused deep anxieties. On
a philosophical level, writers of various political stripes ranging from
the fanatical and self-hating anti-Semite Otto Weininger to the left-

leaning humanist Émile Zola all emphasized the point that modernity was devouring its children, that virtue and dignity were being swallowed by the rootless, internationalized, capitalist, mass-produced life of the big city. On a societal level, the newly awakened self-confidence of disenfranchised groups such as women, workers, and people subjected to racial discrimination rebelled against their exclusion. From the colonies of all major powers came a growing wave of civil rights agitation, national pride, violent protests, and civil disobedience; from women came the campaigns of the suffragettes and the strident analysis of writers such as Rosa Mayreder, who declared traditional masculinity obsolete; and from workers came an increasing ideological and individual commitment to revolution.

This social and intellectual upheaval caused a multitude of reactions, most important those among men who saw their masculinity threatened by the changing patterns of power and by a personal and professional life marked by increasing speed and insecurity. Those who could not cope with the new demands were declared "neurasthenics" and sent to mental hospitals to recuperate away from the constant haste of city life. Others sought refuge in rituals of masculinity such as bodybuilding and a cult of health and fitness. Uniforms were in fashion, and more duels were being fought than ever before, while small advertisements in newspapers from Chicago to Berlin asked their readers to consider whether they might be suffering from a secret "manly weakness" or from "nervous exhaustion," and proposed tinctures and electric baths to stimulate virility.

For many men, the outbreak of the war was therefore a welcome opportunity to turn their backs on the "effeminate" and virility-sapping ways of city life and conquer not only enemy territory but manliness itself. As the first enthusiastic soldiers volunteered in Munich and Manchester, Linz and Lyon, their ears were ringing with sermons, lessons, and public exhortations to follow the noble call of the fatherland and find death or glory on the battlefield of honor, where they would engage in a holy fight, blessed by the Lord, that pitted man against man, saber against saber, courage against courage. For many, the war seemed the ideal remedy for life in a soulless modern world.

The enthusiasm at the outbreak of the war in the summer of 1914, what is in German simply called the "August experience," is one of the factors often used to portray the years before 1914 as naive and all too willing to rush to war. To some extent that was certainly the case. But this is only half the story, a half told and retold countless times until very recently, partly because it fitted the narrative of a war-crazed German emperor and an out-of-control military caste plunging all of Europe into misery.

Recent research paints a more nuanced picture. There was indeed enthusiasm, and there is abundant evidence for this, mainly because the most enthusiastic—often young men from middle-class backgrounds—were precisely the kind of people who were likely to leave evidence in the form of letters, diaries, poems, and memoirs. This image, however, ignores the opposition to the war coming from workers and farmers on all sides (the former because their families would go hungry and they saw the war as a capitalist plot, the latter because their fields would be left untended), and it disregards the large, usually socialist peace demonstrations in Paris, Berlin, and London, as well as the many voices declaring their shock and predicting a catastrophic end to the war even as early as August 1914.

The enthusiasm of the summer of 1914 has become a received historical truth, but that truth chooses to forget the extent to which the myth of the "August experience" was a conscious creation. More than two hundred thousand copies of the *Kriegsbriefe deutscher Studenten* (War Letters by German Students), a highly selective and propagandistic work of retrospective hero worship published in 1916 by Philipp Wittkop in Germany, were in circulation by the time Hitler came to power, and its popularity still informs the common assumption that soldiers as well as entire societies went into the war with feverish enthusiasm.

While many soldiers headed into battle torn between worry for themselves and their families, resentment at being forced to fight for a cause that was not theirs, and genuine enthusiasm for the gloriously dangerous life of a soldier and the "bath of steel" that would make them real men, their actual experience was worse than anything they might have feared. The highest hopes of heroism were dashed by the reality of mechanized warfare, in which soldiers sat in waterlogged trenches, watching their feet rot away, amid the stench of bodies decaying in no-man's-land, waiting, waiting, waiting, until at some random moment a shell would come out of the sky, hurled by a gun miles away, and obliterate all life with cruel indifference to courage and patriotism.

Modernity at War

THE FIRST WORLD WAR had many fronts, from Gallipoli in Turkey to the Isonzo River in the Alps, the terrible slaughter in eastern Europe, and satellite conflicts in the colonies. But the front experience that most clearly seared itself into the popular imagination of western European and American soldiers and societies was the Western Front, stretching between France and Belgium. This was where most of their troops were committed, and this was the scene of the most technologized, mechanized warfare humanity had seen to date. A moonlike wasteland cratered by hundreds of thousands of shells and scarred by trenches running for thousands of miles, this was modernity unhinged. Everything here was mass-produced and standardized; every human being carried a number and wore a uniform. There was no more mechanized, more industrialized, more rationalized, and at the same time more obviously insane environment than the Western Front, and the armies on all sides were gigantic machines. Men, horses, provisions, ammunition, news, secrets, ideas, and experiences were transported over thousands of miles along sophisticated road, rail, and communications networks to be consumed at their destination. Fighting had become an industrial process rather than an act of personal bravery or even heroism.

During the war countless men, especially those from rural areas, traveled to a foreign country for the first time in their lives. Yet, as soldiers in uniform, they were little more than anonymous ciphers and meticulously kept statistics in a monstrous game played between generals and politicians far away. The war had made these men modern, even if many of them resented and even hated this intrusion.

We will explore the hell that was life in the trenches and its psychological cost a little more in Chapter 1. In the present context, that of the dynamism of the vertigo years and the cultural history of technology, it is important that the soldiers' appalling experience be seen not as a negation of the urban, technological world they had known or had just encountered by enlisting but as an intensification of it. At the front they encountered an overwhelming dystopia of technology run amok, leaving in its wake a trail of mangled corpses.

Before the war, the West had been energized by an unprecedented push of economic growth, industrialization, urbanization, and culture. This combination of velocity and instability had been bearable only because the cultural foundations on which the Western project was built still seemed valid: the idea of progress, a hierarchical concept of society, and ideals such as patriotism, faith, heroic sacrifice, and honor. These pillars of a bourgeois understanding of the world were questioned only by a minority of critics. If, as Max Weber has written, the train of history was hurtling forward and the passengers didn't know where they were headed, at least the rails appeared relatively solid.

When these rails were blasted apart by the war, the immense energy driving the engine of this prewar dynamic plowed into society itself, and the war turned inward. During the armed conflict the tremendous energies of industrialization and its social and cultural consequences had been concentrated and channeled by patriotism and the need to survive, but in many ways the hostilities had been brought to no resolution. This was true even on a symbolic level. The war had not been won by a final, decisive victory that breached the opponent's lines and paved the way to the enemy capital, after which the vanquished laid down their swords in front of the victors. Instead, it had been halted by mutual exhaustion, with one side economically weaker than the opposing one, allowing German politicians to claim that the country's army was "unbeaten in the field" and "never vanquished." In fact, on all sides there was a pervasive feeling of betrayal among a majority of people whose lives had been touched by the war. The bitter and inconclusive end of the hostilities simply did not seem commensurable with the sacrifices they had made. At the same time, the values of those who had exhorted them to take up arms had been totally discredited. The postwar years were painfully experienced as a moral vacuum.

If there was any one turning point in how Europeans learned to look not only at war and sacrifice but also at Enlightenment rationality, it was the Battle of the Somme, which began on July 1, 1916, and lasted until November 18, killing more than a million men. On the first day alone, having fired 1.5 million shells at the enemy lines during the preceding week, the British Army lost sixty thousand soldiers. This was a battle of unknown and unimaginable proportions, a man-made inferno. Progress had become murderous; the Enlightenment had betrayed those who had put their trust in it. But as the full scale of the industrialized slaughter became obvious, so did the lack of ready alternatives. Patriotism and religion had been enlisted to motivate soldiers, but their rhetoric sounded hollow after untold numbers of men had been mauled and murdered by mere machines. What values were there left to live for? This would become a crucial question during the ensuing years.

There was no time to sit and ponder, however. In the war's aftermath, the immense energies of modernity continued to transform the countries of the West along the same axes as before, while political and economic crises greatly added to the prevailing sense of insecurity and anxiety. But now the optimism about technology had been crushed, the idea of a glorious and uninterrupted march of progress lay in ruins, and faith in the values underpinning society had been profoundly shaken. The great technological transformation continued unabated, but its conflicts changed in character. As the guns fell silent, battles raged on as many societies found that they were at war with themselves.

While much of the surface evidence of life after the war suggests radical change, this is actually due to the catalytic effect of accelerating a modernity that was already well established. The great social and industrial forces that had made life in the first years of the 1900s feel so vertiginous continued to exert their influence on societies and individuals. New Deal America, Weimar Germany, fascist Italy, and the early Soviet Union were all expressions of, or reactions against, the industrially driven and increasingly technologized mass societies that had already reigned in cities during the early 1900s. And the era's intellectual preoccupations—the superman, the irrational, the masses, race, health, and purity—all continued debates that had been raging long before the young Serbian nationalist Gavrilo Princip raised his gun against Archduke Franz Ferdinand in the summer of 1914.

To those with eyes to see, the war revealed the powers and structures that had been constituted by 1914. Even the conservative German writer Ernst Jünger penned a surprisingly Marxist analysis of his experiences at the front: "The war battle is a frightful competition of industries, and victory is the success of the competitor that managed to work faster and more ruthlessly. Here the era from which we come shows its cards. The domination of the machine over man, of the servant over the master, becomes apparent, and a deep discord, which in peacetime had already begun to shake the economic and social order, emerges in a deadly fashion. Here the style of a materialistic generation is uncovered, and technology celebrates a bloody triumph."[4]

This bloody triumph not only was the face of mass death in the trenches but also signaled another, deeper defeat: that of man by machine. Already a reality before the war but perceived as such only by a minority of farsighted observers, the machine age had asserted itself with its full, brutal force. The young men fighting in the trenches aged by years in a matter of weeks precisely because they understood that everything they had come to fight for, everything they had believed in, was a myth; it remained truth only for schoolmasters hopelessly out of touch with the brutal reality of their lives. The soldiers would not forget this lesson.

From now on, it seemed, most men and women would be the slaves of machines constructed to create the wealth of others, a theme recurring throughout the 1920s and 1930s, the best-known examples being films such as Fritz Lang's *Metropolis* (1926) and Charlie Chaplin's *Modern Times* (1936). "Ideas belong to human beings who have bodies," wrote the American philosopher John Dewey in 1927, "and there is no separation between the structures and processes of the part of the body that entertains ideas and the part that performs actions."[5] The war had been won not by human courage, strength, and principled endurance but by impersonal artillery, steely harbingers of industrial death miles behind the front lines. Killing was efficient and impersonal. The victims of shell shock, soldiers reduced to quivering psychological ruins by the incessant shelling at the front, became the troubling emblems of humanity.

This awakening in the disenchanted machine age, amid social unrest and political strife, created a strong sense of nostalgia and a fierce desire to reenchant the world, to find a new great vision that could replace the old and discredited ones, overcome the suffering and humiliation of the war, and point the way into a future in which human beings would subdue the machines and master new challenges with clean minds and healthy bodies. This ideology would also be the answer to the question of how to live in a broken age, how to carry on when all values remembered from home and school and rehearsed in speeches and essays seemed to have been unmasked as cynical mass manipulation.

The relationship of man and machine is one of the recurring themes of this book. Culturally, there is an arc from the trauma of the shell-shocked soldiers coming home from the Western Front with limbs shaking and twitching uncontrollably, the ultimate image of human impotence in the face of the machine age's threats, to the superhuman and steeled bodies of Fascism and Bolshevism, answers of a sort to the pervasive fears that mere flesh had become a distant second to gleaming metal. It was not for nothing that Hitler would call for Germany's youth to be "hard as Krupp steel."

Awakenings

ONLY 1,567 DAYS, from the beginning of the war on August 20, 1914, to the armistice on November 11, 1918, separated two seemingly very different worlds from each other. After the last shells had been rained down on unseen enemies, people emerged, blinking, into a harsh sun illuminating the debris around them. Four mighty empires—those of Austria-Hungary, Germany, Russia, and the Ottomans—had vanished from the map, robust economies had been ground into the dust, and political stability had been turned into civil war.

Particularly in Europe, this bleak beginning was accompanied by a deep sense of disorientation and anger toward a treacherous past and a contested future. The old order, the old values, and the old elites had all failed and no valid new ones had yet been established. In the wake of humanity's biggest slaughter, the value of rationality was being questioned. The experience of technology and modernity in people's lives had been intensified by the war, but the traumatic memories of the catastrophic events of 1914–1918 became so dominant that they solidified into national war myths—stories of heroism, sacrifice, and betrayal serving the needs of the living and turning the victims into insurmountable psychological obstacles between the present and the past.

Amid the bitterness and the urgency of the postwar years, jazz burst onto the scene like a liberating blast. In a time when anarchy and the loss of conventions had become often threatening realities, the freedom of this music and its offhand disdain for the conventional beauty of highly polished music were the ideal reply, the affirmation that expression and fulfillment were still possible.

Jazz offered new idioms for ancient questions. The infectious rhythms and electrifying improvisations of dance forms such as swing liberated listeners' feelings and bodies, while repetitive, trancelike blues laments bewailed the disillusionment and disappointment of love and of life itself. Hard on the heels of such pain came something fast, fun, and furious, a celebration of life, movement, sex, and freedom, moving the souls and feet of those who felt too young to succumb to disillusionment and asserting their right to live. The Jazz Age with its flappers in the United States, the Bright Young Things in Britain, and the androgynous, fun-loving girls and boys in the bars of Berlin and the cellar joints of Paris was a spontaneous protest against an era that was growing too serious, a time that seemed either devoid of hope or inflated with utopian dreams by the partisans of left and right.

No dictatorship has ever approved of jazz. People who drink and dance together and feel their partner's moving body on the dance floor simply find it more difficult to hate one another. Close dancing may be the best inoculation against ideology. The dictators of the age—and there were significant movements supporting dictatorship in all Western countries during the interwar years—sought to channel the hopes and energies of those courageous enough to live another day. Their promises were new versions of old religious visions. The former seminarian Stalin and the lapsed Catholic Hitler (who was never excommunicated) promised their followers a new Jerusalem, while Mussolini spoke of a new Rome. All of them preached versions of the gospel of the new man, a pseudo-Nietzschean creature so glorious and strong that he could vanquish all enemies and even technology itself to live in a future world of health and purity.

This shining city on the hill stood in stark contrast to the political realities of Europe after the war, an era designated as peacetime by the signatories of the Treaty of Versailles but in reality a state more akin to civil war and political uncertainty. In Germany alone between 1918 and 1923, more than five thousand people were killed as a result of political violence. And while other countries were not as deeply unsettled, there were also large-scale and sometimes murderous political unrest, violent strikes, rioting, and coups d'état in Italy, Austria, England, Ireland, Hungary, France, and Portugal, to say nothing of the proxy war fought after 1936 between fascists and socialists in Spain. From this perspective it is both more helpful and more accurate, as some historians have suggested, to speak of the period between 1914 and 1945 as Europe's second Thirty Years' War.

The United States seemed to be isolated from these direct consequences of the war; however, here the effects were comparable in their profound power but more mediated. There had been no battles on US soil; the country had lost fewer soldiers, both in absolute numbers and as a proportion of the population, than other major powers; and the country's economy was buoyed up by wartime production, sales of raw materials and other goods to Allied powers, and a weakening of its former competitors on the international market.

But in the United States as elsewhere, the modernity of the war transformed societies in subtle but powerful ways, working on the social and cultural fault lines within the country and turning combative energies into social ones. Mamie Smith and artists like her showed that a new culture was growing, one that would not have asserted itself, or would only have asserted itself much more slowly, without the war and the changes it brought for African Americans. Black troops had distinguished themselves in France and experienced a new respect, and they carried this attitude back home. At the same time, African American workers had taken the factory jobs of white workers who had been called up by the army. Hundreds of thousands of southern blacks had migrated to the northern industrial cities, and they were there to stay. On the back of this grew the Harlem Renaissance and a thriving jazz culture, but what also emerged was a period of increased racial hatred, with lynchings in the South and race riots in the cities of the North.

Currents and Causalities

APPROACHING THIS PERIOD of wars turned inward and its parallel and overlapping currents of fear and hope, alienation, escape, and engagement, I have chosen to investigate it through exemplary episodes designed to build up a picture out of individual components that are interlinked in many ways, often by the sense of conflict, of a war continuing not on the battlefield but in people's heads. Protagonists appear in various contexts; cultural movements and social realities, great art and great atrocities create a picture of the evolving mind-set of a rudderless time caught between hope and despair, between reconstruction and revolution.

At the heart of this history of attitudes and strategies deployed throughout the interwar years are not politicians and armies but perceptions, fears, and wishes, ways of dealing with the trauma of the war, with the energies released by industrialization, with the confusing and exhilarating identities that became possible in an industrial mass society, especially once the old values had been shattered.

Trying to capture the different resonances of past and present, this account explores the period away from its familiar great historical milestones. The chapter focusing on 1919 is not devoted the peace negotiations leading to the Treaty of Versailles, the 1923 chapter not to German hyperinflation, the one on 1929 not to the Great Crash, 1933's chapter not to Hitler's ascent to power. Instead, I have chosen less obvious and more varied themes that form a mosaic of perspectives and identities growing and evolving over time, from the initial shock of the postwar era to the growing tension after 1929, which rapidly turned into a prewar time. The chapters explore the plight of veterans and the rise of fascism, the world of speakeasies during Prohibition and a rebellion of Russian sailors, the rise of African American culture in Harlem and the discovery of galaxies beyond the Milky Way, the surrealists in Paris and evolution on trial in rural Tennessee, the doomed International Brigades in the Spanish Civil War and a historic concert in Vienna.

Dealing with the charged and changing time between 1900 and 1914, *The Vertigo Years* was based on a thought experiment: namely, to imagine that we could look at this period without the shadow of the impending First World War, without a narrow teleology. The portrait that emerged was of a time full of contradictions, optimism, friction, and vertiginous speed, looking into an open future. For the interwar period this experiment would not yield any similarly interesting results, because there was always the threat of another war, or rather of the same large conflict erupting again.

The war in 1939 did not come as a great surprise to many people. It had been predicted ever since the Treaty of Versailles had locked Germany into a state of permanent crisis. In Paris in 1919, the young Spanish portraitist José Simont was commissioned to draw the president of the Chambre des Députés, Paul Deschanel, who had been involved in the negotiation of the treaty that had officially ended the war. Deschanel would be elected president of France the following year, but for the time being he chatted with the artist who was engaged in drawing him. When Simont asked him what he thought of the Treaty of Versailles, Deschanel's analysis was succinct: "*Nous venons de signer la deuxième guerre mondiale*—we have just signed on to the Second World War."

Deschanel's pessimistic analysis of Versailles was echoed by the influential British economist John Maynard Keynes as well as others. The demands of the victorious Allies had cast Europe off balance. In particular, French president Georges Clemenceau had insisted on imposing high reparations on an already ruined Germany; while this may have appeared morally just, a country that was the central power and economic engine of the continent should not have been allowed to become unstable and teeter on the brink of revolution. The inbuilt fragility of Germany's young republic bore terrible dangers for the future.

In his great novel *The Man Without Qualities*, written mostly during the early 1920s, Robert Musil describes Vienna before the war. The ostensible plot for this comedy of morals is an attempt by a group of Habsburg officials and intellectuals to sum up the age and find a fitting tribute for the seventy-year anniversary of the emperor's reign, coming up in 1918. This grand effort, called the "Parallel Campaign," is an utter failure, however, because nobody is sure what, if anything, unifies the age, or which of the many ideologies, worldviews, and scientific achievements deserves precedence over all others. After a thousand pages and scores of grand projects and profound plans, all that remains is a modest procession in favor of world peace, with participants in traditional dress.

Musil's novel is set during the year before the war, but the confusion at its heart also describes the atmosphere of hostility during the postwar years. Amid the continuing seismic realignment of social and intellectual positions, there was no firm ground to be had, no grand unifying cause behind which everyone could rally. The surge of the new, the experience of modernity, was too replete with confusing possibilities to allow any one of them to impose itself. Consequently, the protagonist of the novel, a man called Ulrich, cannot decide what to do with his life.

As the Parallel Campaign gradually breaks apart and becomes a parody of its original ambitions, the cautious rationalist Ulrich becomes aware that all great promises are almost always false. Writing about the year 1914, Musil was commenting on the world a decade later, a world that had suffered a collective experience that appeared to have changed everything but was still pulsating with the currents and energies released during the first decade of the twentieth century—energies that continue to shape our lives today.

PART I

POSTWAR

A generation that still drove to school in horse-drawn carriages suddenly stood under the open sky in a landscape in which nothing but the clouds had remained unchanged, and in the center, in a force field of destructive currents and explosions, the tiny, fragile human body.
—Walter Benjamin, "The Storyteller," 1936

Shell Shock

Rumour had it that the constant twitching and jerking and snorting was caused by something called shell-shock, but we were not quite sure what that was. We took this to mean that an explosive object had gone off very close to him with such an enormous bang that it had made him jump high in the air and he hadn't stopped jumping since.

—Roald Dahl, *Boy*, 1984

....   ♣

CAMPBELL WILLIE MARTIN WAS ONE OF THE LUCKY ONES. HE WAS alive. He had escaped from hell after little more than a year and, despite having been wounded twice, had lost no limb. He had been a good soldier. Born in London in 1895 to a policeman and his wife, in October 1914, at age twenty-nine, he had enlisted as a volunteer private in the Royal Fusiliers, and had made lance corporal in early 1916. By then he was already serving on the Western Front, in the midst of slaughter on an industrial scale.

Then, on July 16 of that year, having been pinned down in a trench for hours during severe shelling, Martin lost consciousness. The next day, when his trench was hit by a shell, he saw eight of his comrades die in the explosion, and he lay buried under debris for an entire night before he was rescued. As a result of this, according to his personnel file, the "following day [he] felt very queer muscular

*Nameless horror: The German artist Otto Dix transformed his wartime
experiences into powerful evocations of life and death in the trenches.*

tremor set in[,] a fit of crying[,] follow[ed] by loss of consciousness
for some hours."

Lance Corporal Martin was found to be suffering from "shell
shock," as the doctors had come to name this trauma from exposure
to artillery fire and the sight of violent death, and he was graded at
25 percent disability—enough to be sent back to England for treatment at a specialized hospital. Again he was lucky: initially, the men
exhibiting such symptoms had been treated as malingerers. Some had
been simply sent back to the trenches, while others had been on the
receiving end of an old-fashioned kind of treatment that the older
officers in particular had hoped would stem the tide of the new
phenomenon:

> They were apt to be rather stern. I remember one man came
> in, big chap, six footer, and he was shaking with a shell-shock
> and I was amazed, the colonel lifted his heavy stick and
> hit him across the head on his—he had his tin hat on—hit
> him across the head to give him another shock and he used
> the words "you're a bloody fool, pull yourself together."
> But that couldn't put the man right and he could see he
> really had gone beyond, so of course he was taken care of
> and he went down. But they tried sometimes to give them a

type of reverse shock, you see, to try and reverse the process but it rarely worked.[1]

Some soldiers who had not responded to this old-fashioned method and who had run away, refused to "go over the top," or simply broken down and hidden in the muddy trenches had been court-martialed for cowardice. More than three hundred "deserters," from Britain and elsewhere in that country's empire, were executed in a miserable dawn ritual, many of them unable to stand upright, shaking and quivering even as they were bound to a wooden post to be shot by their own comrades.[2]

But by late 1916, with the war intensifying and the terrible weapons of the new century—machine guns, poison gas, and huge artillery capable of firing over distances of twenty miles in bombardments that could last for days—the British military and medical establishments had been forced to reconsider. That year's appalling four-month Battle of the Somme had resulted in more than a million casualties, and of those who emerged alive from the waterlogged trenches, many had suffered major psychological damage. Among the British forces alone, thirty thousand men were showing symptoms of the strange new condition that rendered them useless as soldiers and an ongoing burden to their units. Reluctantly the authorities began to accept that a man might be severely impaired even when he seemed to be physically unharmed, and soon these mental casualties were arriving at military hospitals by the tens of thousands.

Campbell Willie Martin was among them, and he was to remain hospitalized until after the end of the war. He is described as having been excitable and suffering from insomnia, severe headaches, recurrent panic, memory loss, and a persistent tremor in his hands. Though the doctors noted his "good physique . . . tongue clean, teeth fair," as late as 1920 his level of disability was still being graded at 20 percent; it had improved only a little since his first admission.

Unspeakable, Godless, Hopeless

MARTIN'S PATIENT FILE is one of thousands pulled from Britain's National Archives, where they are still preserved; as shell shock went, his case was not particularly severe. Contemporary film footage reveals soldier after soldier reduced to a quivering wreck by the inhumanity of what he has experienced. Faces are grotesquely distorted, etched with a permanent anguish; limbs shake or jerk violently, uncontrollably; a soldier recoils, panic-stricken, at the sight of another man in uniform. In the imaginations of these lost men, the bombard-ment has clearly never stopped.

These were the living debris of the Great War. In Britain alone, fully 10 percent of the officers and 7 percent of the ranks were even-tually diagnosed with shell shock, with some thirty-seven thousand awarded war pensions on account of it. The military doctors had learned early how to deal with the physically wounded, with legs and arms blown off or stretched out for amputation, eyes blinded by gas and eardrums burst by explosions, and faces ruined by ghastly disfigurements—but with the shell shock cases, there were no evident outward wounds.

Some of the worst cases were treated at Netley Hospital in Lon-don, among them Private Meek, confined to a wheelchair, shuddering convulsively, oblivious to the orderlies trying to relax his rigid joints; Private Preston, nineteen years of age, who had returned from the trenches mute and unable to understand any word but "bomb," at the mention of which he would dive under his hospital bed in a fit of terror; Private Smith, buried alive by shellfire in August 1917, walking stiffly, as if on wooden legs, wiping his face compulsively, as if to wash away the mud and the slime of the decomposing bodies that had sur-rounded him; Sergeant Peters, his spine distorted, his legs shuddering, making a dangerous farce of his every attempt to walk. Broken men, all of them.

Embarking as heroes and saviors of a nation's freedom, they had returned as pitiful survivors of an inhuman reality. In a 1917 letter to his wife, Margaret, the English painter Paul Nash, then stationed on the Western Front near Ypres, had described the awful scene:

> No pen or drawing can convey this country. . . . Sunset and
> sunrise are blasphemous, they are mockeries to man, only the
> black rain out of the bruised and swollen clouds all through
> the bitter black of night is fit atmosphere for such a land. The
> rain drives on, the stinking mud becomes more evilly yellow,
> the shell holes fill up with green-white water, the roads and
> tracks are covered with inches of slime, the black dying trees
> ooze and sweat and the shells never cease. . . . It is unspeak-
> able, godless, hopeless.[3]

Soldiers home on leave from this monstrous reality often found themselves more frustrated than relieved. Having lived in an ongoing butchery that had come to seem senseless, having slept alongside unburied corpses and witnessed friends and comrades ripped apart by the random, anonymous destruction of a shell fired from miles away, having lost trust in old faiths and respect for their superiors, and having come to doubt the justice of their national cause, they returned home to a world dominated by patriotic rhetoric and the wisdom of armchair warriors who continued to regard the war as just and as an opportunity for heroism and manly combat—in effect, as a kind of operetta war, a view that took no account of the savage reality and merely added insult to terrible injury. As early as 1915, a journalist for the leftist *Labour Leader*, a newspaper with pacifist leanings, had described one soldier back from the front: "[He] began laughing, a queer laugh. He went on laughing and I knew it was because the horrors he had been through were so incongruous with his experience of life till then that it seemed a joke."[4]

Wilfred Owen's "shrill, demented choirs of wailing shells" remained with the returning soldiers when they were on leave and even after their final return home. The celebrated war poet, who until 1915 had served as a vicar's assistant while studying at University College, Reading, became a victim of shell shock himself after his trench position was hit by a mortar. Flung into the air, Second Lieutenant Owen had landed among the dismembered corpses of his comrades killed by the blast. Following this horrific incident, he was trapped for days between the two enemy lines, an experience he relayed to his mother in a letter of January 1917:

> I have suffered seventh hell.
> I have not been at the front.
> I have been in front of it.
> I held an advanced post, that is, a dug-out in the middle of
> No Man's Land. . . .
> My dug-out held 25 men tightly packed. Water filled it to a
> depth of 1 or 2 feet, leaving say 4 feet of air.
> The Germans knew we were staying there and decided we
> shouldn't.
> Those fifty hours were the agony of my happy life.[5]

Rescued from his advance post, one of very few survivors, he broke down.

Recuperating at Craiglockhart Hospital in Scotland, haunted by the terrors he had endured, Owen began to cast his experience of the hell that was trench warfare in stark lines of verse. He was inspired by his encounter with another patient, the poet and officer Siegfried Sassoon.

Aristocratic, exotic, handsome, and self-possessed, Sassoon was everything that the modestly born Owen had always longed to be. Wealthy and artistic, Anglo-Catholic on his mother's side and Baghdadi Jewish on his father's, educated at Marlborough and Cambridge, Sassoon was imbued with the indestructible self-confidence of the British upper class. He had volunteered on the day war was declared and had distinguished himself at the front, being awarded the Military Cross for exceptional bravery. But the blue-blooded hero had been sent to Craiglockhart Hospital not because he had been wounded but because he had spoken his mind.

Disgusted with what he had seen during the fighting on the Western Front, in 1917 he had published a protest against the war, using his social contacts to procure a reading for it in Parliament. The previous year, under the wartime Defense of the Realm Act, the philosopher Bertrand Russell, himself an earl and the grandson of a British prime minister, had been dismissed from his fellowship at Trinity College, Cambridge, for publishing a statement of conscientious objection to the war. Russell had hoped to garner public support by being sent to prison, though as it turned out he had only to pay a fine.

For Sassoon, however, a serving officer, the stakes were much higher. Risking a court-martial and even execution, he had written an impassioned attack against those in authority. "I have seen and endured the sufferings of the troops," he declared, "and I can no longer be a party to prolonging these sufferings for ends which I believe to be evil and unjust. . . . On behalf of those who are suffering now, I make this protest against the deception which is being practised upon them; also I believe it may help to destroy the callous complacency with which the majority of those at home regard the continuance of agonies which they do not share and which they have not enough imagination to realize."[6]

There is some evidence of harsher sentencing for men of lower military and social rank, and it does seem that Sassoon's standing as a war hero and also as a gentleman saved him from a court-martial for treason. Instead of going before the judges—and possibly before a firing squad—he was declared to be suffering from neurasthenia (nervous exhaustion or neurosis) and sent to Craiglockhart Hospital, where he met the younger officer-poet Owen.

Dulce et Decorum Est Pro Patria Mori

OWEN FELL IMMEDIATELY under Sassoon's spell. Inspired by his uncompromising courage, Owen himself began to write about his feelings and experiences in a more straightforward way. In what is perhaps his most famous poem, he combines the terror of a poisonous gas attack with the bitter reflections of his comrades-in-arms, convinced now that they have been led into a slaughterhouse by the mendacious ideals of those who taught them. *Dulce et decorum est pro patria mori,* "sweet and fitting it is to die for the fatherland"—this line from Horace was inscribed on a chapel wall at the Royal Military Academy Sandhurst, and the sentiment had informed the education of generations of young officers in training. To Owen and his fellow veterans, it was no more than a cynical lie, and the line was to be quoted countless times as its own indictment. Owen himself was not to enjoy the literary glory he had wrested from the gas and blood of the Western Front. Volunteering to return to France after his discharge from the hospital, he was killed on November 4, 1918, a week before the armistice.

Owen's death at the age of twenty-five became symbolic of the fate of his whole generation—the "lost generation," as it was quickly called, though more in romantic legend than historical truth. The old men who were thought to have cheated the young generation of their hard-won victory and the ideals they had been fighting for were the generals, the politicians, the bosses, portrayed in angry articles and novels as the cynical and incompetent survivors of the Victorian age. They had sent schoolboys to their deaths, making this breed of superior young men reared on the playing fields of Eton believe that this would be a "jolly war" and that they were there to "play the game." "Lions led by donkeys," as the German general Erich von Ludendorff had called them, Britain's young men had been sacrificed on the fields of Flanders for no gain but the old men's own.

After the war, it was widely felt, the deaths of these young men meant that there was virtually no one left to carry on the work of empire, of industry, of art and science. The great bloodletting resulted in "the embarrassing spectacle of men of minor powers wrestling with major responsibilities" during the interwar years. "There is impoverishment on all levels," wrote Reginald Pound, himself a volunteer of 1914. Half a century later he would wonder whether the "strong and cultivated intelligences" of the lost generation could have "seen to it that their second-rate would not become our first-rate, or have arrested the decline of moral indignation into un-heroic tolerance."[7]

Perhaps the best-known literary chronicle of this perceived collapse was Vera Brittain's 1933 autobiographical novel *Testament of Youth*, in which the author dramatized the impact of the war on her own life and on those of the people closest to her. From 1915 until the end of the war Brittain had served as a field nurse with the

Voluntary Aid Detachment; in 1919, with her fiancé, her only brother, and many university friends now dead, she returned to Oxford, bitterly disillusioned.

Brittain's purpose in writing the book that was to make her famous was partly to counteract the impression that only men had lived and suffered through the war. "Didn't women have their war as well?" she asked herself, and then set out to answer the question. How had women experienced the war, and how had they experienced the peace that followed it? "I detached myself from the others," she wrote, describing the armistice celebrations, "and walked slowly up Whitehall, with my heart sinking in sudden cold dismay. Already this was a different world from the one I had known during four lifelong years, a world in which people would be lighthearted and forgetful. . . . And in that brightly lit, alien world I should have no part."[8]

Killing Fields

BRITTAIN'S SENSE OF ALIENATION was shared by many of the returning soldiers, particularly those who had served on the Western Front. Even if thousands of letters, diaries, and memoirs prove that the beginning of the war was not accompanied by the wave of collective enthusiasm bordering on hysteria that has often been written about, but instead drew more anxious and ambivalent responses, many young men had gone into the war with a sense of elation. In Europe and America boys in particular were educated to be patriotic and to value manly virtues such as courage, strength, and sacrifice. For many, there were paramilitary institutions such as the Officers' Training Corps and the Boy Scouts in Britain and the Commonwealth, or the collective drill in Prussian and French schoolyards. There was also testosterone and the hope of battlefield glory.

It was not easy to be a man in 1914. Traditional forms of manliness and social hierarchies had been undermined by industrialization and urbanization. Most factory work could be done by women, too, and life in the big city required working couples to bring home two wages and to have fewer children. New jobs and occupations were hard to reconcile with the ideas previous generations had had of manly virtue. Encased in anonymous buildings and wedged in front of a typewriter, pale from the lack of sunlight and nervous from the constant din of machines in the vicinity, the modern office worker looked nothing like the image of martial virility that had ruled his upbringing. The feminist writer Rosa Mayreder had even dubbed offices "coffins of masculinity."[9]

Feminism was another prewar phenomenon that did much to shake the image of what it meant to be a man. Women demanded the vote, entry into the professions, and places at schools and universities, and they were beginning to play an ever-increasing role in occupations traditionally reserved for men. A tide of male assertion had answered these demands. Scientists had vainly attempted to prove the physical and intellectual inferiority of women, and masculine rituals such as dueling had shown a sharp rise in popularity. But even before the war hundreds of thousands of men had succumbed to this new psychological pressure and fallen victim to "neurasthenia," a nervous affliction similar to today's burnout, and had been sent to recuperate in sanatoriums.

Many men had greeted the outbreak of the war as an opportunity to reconquer their questioned manliness, saber in hand, braving the firestorms to reemerge stronger and purified of the dross of weakness and complexity that characterized modern life. Their hopes had been cruelly disappointed, largely because they found themselves fighting the wrong war.

In fact, it was the very lack of real fighting that became a lasting trauma of the war. Previous wars had been decided by battles in which armies advanced against each other in a more or less skillful combination of infantry and cavalry, with artillery playing a supporting role as soldiers launched into close combat. In 1870, during the Franco-Prussian War, nine out of every ten casualties were due to wounds inflicted by bayonets, handguns, and rifles.

At the Western Front this was radically changed. Advances in artillery technology meant that powerful and accurate guns spewing shells weighing hundreds of pounds and packed with explosives, shrapnel, or gas could now be fired from many kilometers behind the front line, and for the soldiers in their trenches, every minute of every day became an agonizing wait. On the German side, where the trenches were extremely well built, two of every three soldiers killed in action died from shelling, not during combat. In the British and French units, this rate reached 75 percent. Conversely, only about 1 percent of fatal injuries on both sides were inflicted by close combat with handguns and bayonets. The soldiers were little more than sitting targets identified by reconnaissance planes and then mercilessly shelled from afar.

For the soldiers, the experience was devastating. During the first battles, as military strategies proved slow to change in the face of automated warfare, soldiers ordered to go over the top hardly stood a chance. With bayonets mounted they ran toward the enemy lines, easy targets for machine guns and artillery fire. In some instances, 80 percent of attackers were killed before reaching the enemy lines.

This dreadful death toll ripped holes not only in battle units but also in families across the world. On July 1, 1916, the very first day of the Battle of the Somme, the British and Newfoundland forces alone sustained almost fifty-eight thousand casualties (including more than nineteen thousand killed), representing some 20 percent of British combatants. The Ulster Division of Irish Protestants who fought with the British on that first day suffered more than five thousand casualties, including more than two thousand dead. And of the 801 men of the Newfoundland Regiment, only sixty-eight could answer the evening roll call, and every one of its officers was wounded or dead.[10]

Over a six-week period during the battle, ANZAC (Australian and New Zealand Army Corps) forces sustained thirty-one thousand casualties, representing for the tiny Dominion of New Zealand a loss of almost 1 percent of its entire population. As historian John Milne has noted, "The British Army's loss on that one day easily exceeds its battle casualties in the Crimean War, the Boer War and the Korean War combined."[11] The battle also claimed the life of the first American soldier in the First World War: on August 31, along with all the other men of his Royal Artillery battery, San Francisco native Private Harry Butters was killed in a massive barrage of German shellfire.

"Somme," declared Friedrich Steinbrecher, a German officer at the battle, "the whole history of the world cannot contain a more ghastly word.'" The English Tommies were to dub the debacle more earthily, and the epithet has stuck: in the Anglophone world today, the Somme is still remembered as "the Great Fuck-Up."

Having entered what they hoped would be a short, cathartic war, most soldiers who did not return were torn apart by bombs, lacerated by shrapnel, assassinated by snipers, choked by gas, or mown down by machine guns, or they perished in no-man's-land entangled in barbed wire or succumbed to gangrene, infections, typhoid, or other illnesses; as many as half of them died without ever having seen an enemy. Instead, death came out of the blue, suddenly, with devastating power. Verdun was an "academy of cubism," reflected the French painter Fernand Léger in a letter from the front, describing how around him were sights and scenes too absurd to be believed. "For example, you discover a tree with a chair perched on top of it. Normal people would treat you as a madman if you painted something like this. But here is enough you can simply copy."[12] He was right: a photograph from the front even shows half a horse wedged in the shredded branches of a tree between the trenches.

Soldiers on both sides of the conflict experienced this mechanical apocalypse as a deep betrayal of their bravery and their will to sacrifice themselves for a just cause. Their courage was no match for the industrialized slaughter; their very bodies were transformed into a raw material of death, almost indistinguishable from the grayish-brown mud around them, pounded and churned up so often by shells and grenades that it became transformed into an omnipresent slime reeking of corpses and of human excrement, and swallowing boots and whole bodies like a putrid swamp.

Rescued from this inferno, the helplessly shivering, mute, and emaciated bodies of the shell shock victims turned into wordless indictments of a war in which machines had finally and totally overpowered human beings.

A Lost Generation?

AT THE SOMME and elsewhere, the war was particularly lethal to young men from the social elite. On the British side, one-fifth of all Etonians who enlisted were killed, wounded, or listed as missing during the entire war, while the national average of casualties was one in eight men who had enlisted. But we can put an even more precise number on the lost generation: of the 26,529 students from Oxford and Cambridge universities, 4,933 were killed in the war, again roughly one-fifth. Not only was this proportion higher than the national average, but the number of those killed from these two universities alone was also greater than that from all other universities in Great Britain combined (4,920). So roughly ten thousand upper-class young men did not return from the battlefields.

While it may be true that losses among the social elite were around 20 percent, this also means that 80 percent of middle- and upper-class soldiers did return home, and it is also important to remember that 96 percent of the infantry soldiers killed were not officers and not graduates of public schools or leading universities.

But these numbers tell only half the story. Until the war, Britain had a professional army, offering careers for the younger sons of the wealthy and for working-class men with nowhere else to go. Social segregation had been maintained throughout, and much of the population had been shielded from the effects of bloody conflicts such as the Crimean War not only by sheer distance but also by unseen barriers at home. This distance held until the terrible losses among the professional soldiers at the Somme, but soon the decimation of the army meant that new soldiers would have to be found. With the introduction of conscription in 1916, young men throughout society were now affected, and their families with them. In addition to Britain's dead, 1.7 million men came home with amputated limbs, horrific disfigurements, the lasting effects of shell shock, or other war injuries. British society experienced war as it had never done before.

Despite these numbers, the lost generation is still largely a myth. In fact, with 673,375 dead or missing, according to army figures (just under 1 million if all of the Empire's forces are included), the British loss of life on the battlefield, though horrific enough, was considerably lower than that of other combatant countries, both in absolute numbers and in terms of relative population. Two million Germans had lost their lives, as did 1.1 million from the Austro-Hungarian Empire, 1.8 million Russians, and almost 600,000 Italians—numbers that speak eloquently of the suffering away from the Western Front. Vera Brittain's own brother, Edward, had been killed fighting at San Sisto Ridge, near Venice.

In proportional terms, the greatest losses by far were incurred by Serbia and by the Ottoman Empire (present-day Turkey). France was the worst-affected Western country, with 1.4 million war dead, representing 3.5 percent of the entire French population and 17 percent of all enlisted soldiers; by comparison, the British figures (excluding Empire forces) were 1.6 and 12 percent, respectively. In fact, the so-called lost generation in Britain was even more numerous than previous generations, since many young men who otherwise would have been lost to emigration, mainly to the United States, Australia, New Zealand, and Canada, chose to stay at home, often seeing action but nonetheless surviving the war.

But myths pay little heed to absolute numbers. Britain's myth of the lost generation concerned specifically the "flower of youth," the well-educated young men from middle- and upper-class families who were believed to have suffered disproportionately. Here the myth has a basis in fact. Young men of relatively affluent backgrounds were indeed more likely to volunteer, in part because they had imbibed the strongly patriotic rhetoric of their public schools and in part because they were economically more dispensable than working-class youths, whose parents and siblings were partly dependent on their income and who therefore could not simply put down their tools and go off to war.

In addition to this, in a glaring reflection of Britain's powerful class system, young graduates from "good" public schools or universities were likely to be immediately commissioned as junior officers and sent straight to the front lines with very little training and no experience at all; consequently they were more likely to be killed than the men in the ranks. This was the case even after the introduction of conscription in 1916.

Traumatized

THE NOTIONS OF "SHELL SHOCK" and the "lost generation" became deeply embedded in the British memory of the war precisely because they went some way toward explaining the feeling of betrayal and uncomprehending horror that seeped into the national consciousness after 1918. A whole continent felt shell-shocked by the events it had lived through, and the symptoms of former soldiers served as a useful shorthand, a metaphor for collective trauma.

In fact, shell shock, or what we might call today "post-traumatic stress disorder," was observed not only in Britain but also among soldiers from all parties engaged in the conflict. Germany and Austria (formerly the Austro-Hungarian Empire) had their *Kriegszitterer* (war shiverers), France its *névrosés de la guerre*; other countries with soldiers in intensely mechanized theaters of war reported similar cases. Particularly on the Western Front and on the rocky slopes of the Dolomites, in the Italian Alps, where the war had been fought in the inferno of trenches, the minds and bodies of the men subjected to this terror had simply given way under the constant strain. Some of them suffered from disorders that had symbolic force: a young Australian sniper lost the sight in his right eye, used to take aim, while others lost the use of their trigger fingers, as if their bodies had decided to refuse to work against their consciences. Most reported horrible, oppressive dreams coming to haunt them every single night.

Shell shock was new to the medical profession, and it became the reflection of a new, more intensely inhuman way of fighting. In 1919, the pioneering American psychiatrist Elmer Ernest Southard published a collection of case studies of soldiers suffering from shell shock and other injuries that left deep scars, perhaps not on their bodies (many of which were often apparently unhurt) but certainly on their minds. His work was exceptional not only because he was one of the very first specialists to recognize the phenomenon of shell shock in its severity and diversity but also because he took a truly inclusive, international outlook. Here, in the sober medical language of its time, was a catalogue of shattered minds and war-torn bodies, catalogued together with the names of the doctors treating them in their country of origin:

Case 81 (Juquelier and Quellien, May, 1917) [French]
Soldier, shell burst near him, observed in hospital: "He suddenly rose from the bench, made a few steps, seemed to be listening and anxious, as if he ought to be on guard. He looked up, seemed to be looking for something whose noise was approaching, lowered he head, made a slight jerking movement, and said 'Poum!' as if to express the noise of an explosion. He took a few more steps, the same movements were repeated, and the same 'Poum!' was uttered. This lasted for about a quarter of an hour, during which the patient was unaware of his surroundings."

"Apples in No-Man's-Land"
Case 165 (Weygandt, 1915) [German]
A soldier in November, 1914, suddenly climbed out of the trench and began to pick apples from an apple-tree between the firing lines. The idea was to get a bag of apples for his comrades, but he began to pelt the French trenches with apples. He was called back and on account of his strange conduct sent to hospital. Here he was at times given to pressure of speech and restlessness; he would climb the posts of the sleeping room and then loudly declare he wanted to get back to the trenches; he did not want to go back to Germany alive; did not want to live beyond to-morrow; was guilty of a sin; had a spot of sin, Schand [sic; German *Schande*, "shame"], on his heart.

Case 475 (Purser, October, 1917) [British]
An Englishman, 21, in a rifle regiment, arrived in May, 1915, at the Dublin University V. A. D. Hospital, being dumb, impaired in vision and hearing, having dilated pupils, tremors, restlessness and weakness, and giving the impression of visual hallucinations. Although suspicious, he was treated kindly for a few days, recovered his hearing, and wrote the few things that he remembered about home and the war, now and then tremulously and perspiringly, writing down, "Asylum; do not lock up; I am not mad."[13]

Shell-shocked soldiers were dealt with differently in different countries, according to the willingness of the medical establishments to recognize the nature of the phenomenon and to treat it with more or less innovative methods. As an ironic by-product of wholesale slaughter, the treatment of soldiers resulted in enormous advances not only in the production of anatomically correct prosthetics and in cosmetic surgery but also in the treatment of psychological trauma.

The trauma, however, was pervasive and collective. After November 1918, having endured what no one should ever endure and seen what no one should ever see, soldiers on all sides often found the demobilization they had so dreamed of in the field a painful, bewildering, and enraging experience. On their return, many of them felt abandoned in a peaceless postwar existence in which nothing seemed to be as it had been.

The war both revealed profound divisions and opened new ones—between veterans and noncombatants, those on the right and those on the left, the young and the old, those seeking to create a new world and those wishing to restore their idea of an old order. All societies became not only more impoverished but also less cohesive, less hopeful, and more unsettled. Their economies had been shattered (with the exception of the United States), and the societies themselves and their values had been shaken to their very foundations. Toward the end of the war, starting in August 1918, at the very height of the deprivations and the misery, an influenza epidemic swept through the world. This "Spanish flu" killed an estimated 3 percent of the world's population overall, but the death rate was much higher in the dense and deprived cities of Europe and in the United States. Four hundred thousand died in France alone. The end of the war saw the European countries plunged into a series of potentially devastating emergencies. There was a demographic disaster, a political disaster, and an economic disaster; they all converged in a cultural catastrophe.

A Sense of Shock

IF THERE WAS A NEW WORLD in the making, it came out of the lack of understanding of what had taken place and why, out of a sense of shock. What had been familiar before the war appeared to have become strange, what had been understood suddenly incomprehensible. Writing about shell shock victims, the highly respected medical journal The Lancet had commented: "Some men blind, some men dumb, and some crazy, and these all of them MEN, with a newly-earned meaning in the word; for there is a new meaning now in many an old word. We shall want a brand-new Dictionary."[14] But there was no such dictionary, no new and magic method for unlocking the mysteries of a world estranged.

A whole continent shared the mute, uncomprehending horror and the wide-eyed stare of the shell-shocked combatants whose experience had been too much for a human frame to bear. As millions of traumatized soldiers were demobilized and returned home, they found that there was no way of communicating what they had lived through, of understanding what had happened, and why. All they knew was that they had been betrayed and put in harm's way under false pretenses, that the thrusting, vertiginously energetic, but also fundamentally optimistic world they had inhabited only four years earlier was irrevocably lost.

The pervasive sense of dislocation and betrayal described by victors and vanquished alike was partly due to sheer numbers: Germany alone had to contend with 6 million demobilized soldiers demanding work, in addition to 2.7 million veterans who were permanently crippled. These men returned home with injuries not only to their bodies but to their minds. Most of them never spoke about the war; their children were forbidden to ask.

In France, this sense of loss and betrayal was overwhelming. The country had suffered like no other in western Europe: more than 10 percent of the population were direct casualties of the war, while civilians had also suffered greatly from food shortages, insufficient medical supplies, and the effects of the influenza epidemic. Industrial production had collapsed, as there were too few workers everywhere; in the northwestern part of the country, which had borne the brunt of the fighting, thousands of villages had been reduced to rubble, tens of thousands of businesses had vanished, and the infrastructure lay in ruins. France was deeply in debt and the value of the franc fell by half in the first year after the war.

The difficult economic environment in France was the setting for a generational conflict of particular severity. As elsewhere, particularly in Germany and the United States, for returning French servicemen it was difficult to find their way into civilian life, but even for those who had stayed behind the transition to peacetime was fraught with disappointments and disillusion. A generation of young men had been fed on a diet of patriotic rhetoric, exhorted to die a glorious death and find glory in suffering on the battlefield. Brought up to fight the *boche*, they found suddenly that the war had ended and their patriotic fervor was no longer desired; now they were supposed to be sober, settled citizens working for the reconstruction of a country that had been severely weakened by its victory and was less self-confident and less influential in the world. The vacuum left by the peace meant that many young Frenchmen lacked an orientation. "Growing up in a lost Europe of blood and hate, amidst demented or terrified men, what direction, what support could our youth find?" one of them, Marcel Arland, would write.[15]

Many young people discovered that it was difficult to acclimate to the new and unheroic life of peacetime. Before the war, as an adolescent, the French writer Pierre Drieu La Rochelle had dreamed of being strong and athletic, but he had had to accept that he was not cut out to be a sporting hero. Then, on the battlefield, he found himself leading a bayonet charge, having discovered hidden reserves of courage in his reedy, overly refined physique. He relished being a soldier and loved every moment of his experience: modern life, with all its decadent complexities and meaningless pleasures, reduced to killing or being killed. He celebrated war and was dismayed when peace broke out and with it returned the banality of bourgeois life.

Young men such as journalist and writer Jean Prévost were also bitterly disappointed by this shabby peace. "They taught us that only one thing was respectable: to fight," he wrote. "We accepted the fact that we were inferior to the combatants and that we would spend the rest of our lives admiring them. We despised civilians and had no respect for old men, teachers, women, or ourselves. . . . When the war ended, we assumed that everything would change. We would be happy; we would become a serious people like the Americans."[16] But when peace came, nothing changed. The returning soldiers were not shining heroes to look up to; they were troubled and traumatized, many of them were crippled, and they had little time for the illusions of teenagers eager to look up to someone.

A deep sense of suspicion settled between the veterans and the society they had defended. "What all self-analysts of the post-war generation could agree on was the uniqueness of their experience, their scepticism about pre-war values, their openness to new departures, and their alienation from returning veterans," writes Robert Wohl in his account of this "generation of 1914." "Their ambivalence toward returning veterans . . . was also the result of disenchantment. Brought up during the war to admire the men in horizon blue and to worship them as heroes, they found those who returned to be immature, insufficiently serious, and hopelessly old-fashioned in their values. Moreover, they were . . . put off by their apparent preoccupation with death; disappointed by their powerlessness to effect wide-ranging changes in society; and bored by their obsession with the war."[17]

The eighteen-year-old Jean Prévost described his disgust at the returning soldiers who were crippled or disfigured. These were not the heroes he had imagined encountering. In Germany and Austria, people's reactions were often very similar when confronted with those whose physical or psychological injuries were too obvious to be ignored.

These desperate figures were what had been celebrated by so many orators and writers: the conquering heroes of patriotic propaganda, the virile bodies steeled for future greatness in the furnace of war. The war was not what it was supposed to have been. Not only had it annihilated the graceful villages, forests, and meadows of Belgium and northeastern France, scarred the majestic Alpine rockscapes fought over so bitterly between Austrian and Italian units, and bloodied the lands along the Eastern Front, from Riga on the Baltic Sea down to Galicia and Czernowitz in today's Ukraine, but it had turned men into wrecks, heroes into ghostly accusers. They had been hailed as heroes, but now they were often seen as troublemakers, beggars, carriers of infections both medical and moral, dangerous subversives, ugly reminders of shame and catastrophe.

While most people preferred to look away, the depiction of the ugly face of war and its aftermath was taken up with particular fervor by expressionist artists, whose stark depictions of horror began where documentary photography stopped. Georges Grosz and Otto Dix in particular created canvases filled with the grotesque suffering of the ordinary soldiers, as the officers, monsters in uniform with shaven heads and dead-looking piglike eyes, indulge their obscene, bone-headed obsession with death and honor.

For Remembrance

ON JULY 19, 1919, as Britain marked the official end of hostilities with a victory parade, a cenotaph (literally "empty tomb") of wood and plaster had been erected in Whitehall as a monument to the millions of soldiers whose remains had been unrecognizable and whose mangled and fragmentary bodies lay in anonymous war graves. This Tomb of the Unknown Soldier was eventually replaced with a permanent structure of stone. The Unknown Soldier, a hero without a face, became the face of official remembrance of a catastrophe beyond description and comprehension.

In 1920, in addition to the symbolic cenotaph (which was indeed empty), the remains of an anonymous British combatant were buried at Westminster Abbey. Other countries also quickly erected Tombs of the Unknown Soldier: in Paris under the Arc de Triomphe, in Rome's grandiose Monumento a Vittorio Emmanuele II, and in the central place of American military memory, Arlington Cemetery.

In Germany, the city fathers of Weimar were prepared to take the nation's grief right to the country's spiritual heart, the dwelling place of Goethe, Schiller, and Nietzsche. A 1924 architectural plan envisioned an *Ehrenhain*, a grove of honor that was to house thousands of soldiers' graves, constructed on a hillside and sloping gently down behind Goethe's mythical summer home. A lack of funds prevented the project from being realized.

The ghosts of the soldiers who never returned home received central places of commemoration, foci for communal grief. But they continued to haunt the living, and many aspects of the interwar years are understandable only from the perspective of the trauma, betrayal, and disillusionment suffered during and immediately after the war. Rituals of remembrance could focus the public sense of loss, but even they and the monuments themselves were hotly disputed between political opponents. The social fracturing and fraying that had been briefly subdued during the war now reemerged with even greater force, and the shattered certainties created a powerful longing for great truths and authoritative answers. No feeling is more profoundly disturbing and corroding than that of living a senseless life.

As Europeans struggled to fathom the extent of their loss, new certainties were constructed. One of these was the nostalgic vision of an intact, almost paradisiac world before 1914, which was communicated by films, operettas, novels, and newspapers. So great was the need for some kind of truth and for a strong causality to replace the apparent chaos of the summer of 1914 that the very people who had lived through the years 1900–1914 and had described them as dizzying, frightening, hurtling too fast in an unknown direction, and profoundly disorienting were now only too willing to accept the image of a stable Indian summer of the nineteenth century, when people had lived moral lives, known their station, and devoted themselves to elaborate social rituals and the furthering of the arts.

At the beginning of the 1930s, the image of the golden world of yesterday was already firmly established and celebrated in film, fiction, and memoirs. Living somewhere in London and by now father of a family, Campbell Willie Martin may have been one of the millions indulging their nostalgia for a better world. But perhaps he knew better, faithful to the memory of the trauma that came back to him at night, in the dreams so feared by those who had seen what no human eye should ever see and lived through it all.

A Poet's Coup

We later civilizations . . . we too know that we are mortal.

   Elam, Nineveh, Babylon were but beautiful vague names, and the total ruin of those worlds had as little significance for us as their very existence. But France, England, Russia . . . these too would be beautiful names. . . . And we see now that the abyss of history is deep enough to hold us all.
   —Paul Valéry, *Crisis of the Mind* (1919)

....

NEVER HAD A CITY BEEN MORE TRIUMPHANTLY TAKEN THAN WHEN the trucks filled with volunteers poured into Fiume on September 12, 1919, to be acclaimed by thirty thousand enthusiastic people, practically the entire population of the city. At the head of the dashing occupying force rode a living legend, a war hero and the greatest living Italian poet: Gabriele d'Annunzio, who had risked everything to free the town from its occupiers and return it to the Italian motherland. From the balcony of the town hall, draped with the flags of the newly liberated town, the new master spoke to the population: "Italians of Fiume . . . here I am. . . . Today I wish to say nothing more. . . . Here is the man who has abandoned everything to be wholly at the service of your cause. . . . Here I am . . . I the volunteer, I who have fought in all arms, I the wounded and the mutilated, I reply to the deep anxiety of my country by declaring the city of Fiume today restored for ever to mother Italy."[1]

There was only one problem: mother Italy did not want the little town with its mostly Italian population on the Croatian coast. It had ceded the territory during the negotiations for the peace treaty of Saint-Germain and had received extensive lands in return. D'Annunzio's poetic escapade was unwelcome, and the prime minister pretended not to notice even after the author-turned-autocrat wrote him an effusive letter laying power at his feet.

Unperturbed by this setback, D'Annunzio created a free state on the eleven square miles of territory that were now his. He was the master of the grand gesture, after all. During the war, he had enlisted in the Italian army even though his advanced age—he was fifty-two when war broke out—would have excused him. He had flown planes, engaged in combat, led from the front. In 1918 he had even achieved a daring propaganda coup by flying to Vienna, the capital of Italy's old European adversary, and dropping hundreds of pamphlets emblazoned with the Italian tricolor and the proud claim that he could have dropped bombs instead. He was no longer flying the plane himself, however; an accident on a mission two years earlier had cost him his right eye. He was a war hero who had sacrificed for his country.

Perhaps the sacrifice was not so much for the glory of Italy as for the glory of D'Annunzio, one of the most mercurial and fascinating writers in a time full of great characters. Small, balding, and far from handsome, he was proud of having seduced, as he claimed, hundreds of women, among them some of the richest, most aristocratic, and most famous of their time. A notorious voluptuary, he had spent the past few years in Paris in order to avoid the legions of his Italian creditors, who had financed his extravagant lifestyle, which included several splendid villas and a wardrobe boasting hundreds of pairs of shoes and countless gloves in exotic leathers and delicate hues. He was famous for possessing a nightshirt with a gold-embroidered round hole in the front to facilitate congress with his current lover; for being a worthy heir of the great Casanova as well as a master of heady verse infused with passion, perfume, and allusions from antiquity; for styling himself as a modern Icarus, flying ever higher toward the sun. During his time as a fighter pilot he was seen boarding the plane in high-heeled patent leather boots polished every morning by his faithful manservant.

Even his greatest detractors had to admit that his poetry was extraordinary: sumptuous, powerful, and prescient as well as totally

amoral. He had always known how to convey in words the most refined, most avant-garde sentiments of the period. During the fin de
siècle he had been the prince of decadent poets; at the beginning of
the vertiginous twentieth century he had discovered flying and rhap-
sodized about velocity, fast machines, and seduction; when war broke
out he had become a soldier extolling the virtues of virile struggle;
and now, in Fiume, he cast himself in a new mold.

D'Annunzio had taken the city out of a feeling of outrage, using
his fame to find allies among the soldiers who felt betrayed and
disappointed at the terms of the peace, which had granted land they
regarded as Italian to other countries. Now he was determined to
use this power to create out of the energy of the moment a new
kind of movement, of community. Already during the war, as he had
attempted to push his government to enter into the conflict by
giving speeches whose passion added to his already enormous fame,
D'Annunzio had discovered a new, darkly fascinating power in his
oratory and in the experience of rousing the passion of thousands:

> Faces, faces, faces; every passion from every face runs
> through my wounded eye, innumerable as grains of warm
> sand through the fist. Is it not the Roman crowd of May, the
> evening of the Capito? Enormous, swaying, howling. I feel
> my pallor burning like a white flame. There is nothing of my-
> self left in me. I am like the demon of tumult, I am like the
> genius of the free people. . . . I see at last my Credo in blood
> and spirit. I am no longer intoxicated with myself alone, but
> with all my race. . . . They sway and are swayed. I ascend to
> crown them and I ascend to crown myself. . . . The mob
> howls and writhes to beget its destiny. . . . The mob is like an
> incandescent metal. All the mouths of the mould are open.
> A gigantic statue is being cast.[2]

The poet-turned-politician set about fashioning the statue of what
he called, against the will of his co-conspirators, not the republic but
the *impresa*—the adventure, the undertaking, the coup—of Fiume.
His inspirational and grandiloquent speeches from the balcony became daily events, eagerly listened to by his troops, who were soon
bored with life in the small harbor town; he raised his arm in a Roman
salute, which he had seen and admired in a performance at the Paris
opera; he appeared in uniform and adopted the title *duce*.

All this posturing had a strongly operatic air, as two British
travelers, the brothers Osbert and Sacheverell Sitwell, recounted. Like

Revolutionary satyr: The Italian poet and war hero Gabriele d'Annunzio was famous for his scented words and his countless affairs. Almost as an afterthought, he also invented the aesthetics of fascism.

thousands of other adventurous young people, they had been drawn to the little state and wanted to meet its commander in the town hall "built in the well-known Renaissance-elephantoid style that is the dream of every Municipal Council the world over." Being well spoken and well connected, they were admitted, though not before witnessing with a sort of baffled fascination the scenes playing themselves out on the streets: "The general animation and noisy vitality seemed to herald a new land, a new system. . . . Every man here seemed to wear a uniform designed by himself: some had beards, and had shaved their heads completely, so as to resemble the Commander himself, who was now bald; others had cultivated huge tufts of hair, half a foot long, waving out from their foreheads, and wore, balanced on the very back of their scull, a black fez."[3] Some of the freedom fighters were white-haired veterans of the campaigns of Giuseppe Garibaldi, half a century before.

D'Annunzio was an incurable romantic. He designed a constitution for his statelet that was corporatist, but also progressive in many ways: it declared the full equality of men and women and of religion and atheism, guaranteed a free and nonreligious education for children, established the strict separation of powers within the state, and provided for a strong democratic base. Many influences had shaped this work, not least the presence of the trade unionist and anarchist Alceste de Ambris, but in the end it was the poet-potentate who put his stamp on the entire work, supplementing the useful but pedestrian nine corporations (workers, teachers, seamen, and so on) with a tenth one, which he named *energia* and which was to consist entirely of artists entrusted with giving inspiration to society. One of the most important constitutional principles became music—

very appropriate for a *duce* who had brought his current lover, a moody Italian pianist, plus piano to his palace and who liked to do his political work while listening to late Beethoven sonatas.

Increasingly, however, art and reality clashed unmelodiously. Once they did so literally as D'Annunzio staged a mock battle in honor of a visiting orchestra to keep his soldiers entertained. Osbert Sitwell recounts that the list of casualties after the battle included several musicians. More frequently, however, poetry and prose were painfully at odds in the administration of the city, whose *duce* was not a man to settle down to the detailed and dull work of administration. Sometimes he would vanish into his apartments for days on end to think and seek inspiration, hardly eating and not to be spoken to under any circumstances. He was also given to sudden and grand gestures. None of this addressed the situation of a small town without an income and with a large force of bored mercenaries kicking the dust in the town square. Italy had instituted a blockade, and little food or other goods were coming in through regular channels. As lootings became more common and rapes occurred, the townspeople learned to hate their liberators. To feed the many hungry mouths and give the men something to do, the rebel state resorted to piracy.

D'Annunzio had conceived of his coup as a stepping-stone on the way to Rome, no doubt envisaging himself as a literary governor of Italy on a par with Marcus Aurelius. But his allies had other ideas. One of them, the rising fascist leader Benito Mussolini, had pledged his support but now refused to let actions follow his fraternal words. He was learning from the poet's sense of pathos and *grandezza* and began to imitate the uniforms, the Roman salute, and the rhetoric, but he had no intention whatsoever of installing his comrade-in-arms on a throne that he himself intended to occupy one day. D'Annunzio, unwilling to admit the failure of his enterprise, was stuck on his rocky outpost on the Adriatic coast, moored in the town hall built in a style as grandiloquent as its inhabitant.

In the end, the Italian government put an end to the farce in 1920. It tightened its blockade by sea and by land, drew together an invasion force, and began bombarding the city, injuring the lonely *duce* in his grandiose palace and giving him a welcome excuse to call the whole thing off. He moved out in style, as he had arrived. There was no indictment; on the contrary, Mussolini, who had been unwilling to support D'Annunzio in his political ambitions, made great use of the poet as a fighter for *la patria*. Exhausted but relieved, the author returned to his previous passions for writing, women, and increasingly the political language and style he had helped invent: Fascism.

The priapic D'Annunzio had long been smitten with virile strength, much like the futurists, though he was not as boorishly predictable as they were, with their hymns to manly violence and fast machines. His own contributions were the plot and script for the epic film *Cabiria* (1914), the most expensive made to date. The hero of this sand-and-sandals extravaganza was the immensely strong Maciste, a latter-day Hercules; the character appears in twenty-six additional films.

....

FIUME WAS THE COMIC-OPERA OVERTURE to what was to become one of the dominant and devastating tragedies of the twentieth century. Via his ally Mussolini, D'Annunzio's short-lived foray into politics was to leave a stylistic mark on many if not all dictatorships that were to follow. But beyond the salutes and the uniforms, beyond the marching and speechifying, the sense of bitterness and betrayal that was so pervasive in Europe after 1918 bred a related revolution that was far less visible but if anything more influential—a conservative revolution.

It was a backlash against disorder and disillusion, against strikes and street fighting, against the threat of Bolshevism, against the endless and dispiriting compromises of democracy and the seeming decline of morals. The inner war was reaching more deeply into societies rocked by years of bloodshed. "Citizens be prepared!" the poet had shouted at his followers in preparation for the occupation: "The battle is now beginning against everything and everybody, on behalf of our rights and our dead. We write this with blood on our banners."[4]

D'Annunzio's seductive rhetoric is a fine example of the kind of poetry that was built up as an opposition to the harsh reality of postwar Europe. The revolution he and his comrades-in-arms preached was expressed in contradictions. It was a matter of life against death, health against sickness, beauty against ugliness, youth against age, honesty against mendacity, authenticity against artificiality, strength against weakness, country against city, pure and noble nature against corrupt and corrupting city life—in short, a remedy for all the ills of modern civilization.

This revolution was to be carried out by a small, spiritual elite, but it would also be of the people and for the people, with strongly socialist traits. It was to restore the natural order and the brutal strength of primordial life forces and superior "races," wiping away the sickly veneer of weak and degenerate pleasures with which the big city lured men and women away from their racial and natural destiny, and shattering the socialist dreams of solidarity and equality. It sought to realize a utopian dream, knowing, even willing, that the way to redemption would be awash with blood.

Stories of Decline

D'ANNUNZIO AND OTHER conservative revolutionaries were determined to defend the heroic individual against the cold rule of technology and technocrats that had manifested itself beginning in 1900, and which had characterized the war. It was an attempt to rescue an idea of what it means to be human that had been rendered obsolete by modern life—if indeed it had ever existed. From his perspective the problem was not technology but decadence, the fruit of the unmanly and unnatural life now lived by tens of millions of city dwellers.

The maverick Italian poet was not alone in this opinion, which was also defended by a seductively erudite two-volume work written by a socially awkward, sickly, and myopic former high school teacher and occasional journalist, Oswald Spengler, who lived in Munich off a small inheritance and had dedicated ten years of his life to writing his magnum opus, *Der Untergang des Abendlandes (Decline of the West)*. Spengler was an eccentric polymath, with formal and informal training in a wide range of sciences and humanities, who had set himself the prodigious task of explaining history in its totality— of creating, as it were, a physiology of human life and the fate of civilizations at all times and in all regions of the globe.

His method was as eccentric as Spengler himself, and it borrowed liberally from Nietzsche, Goethe, the biologist Ernst Haeckel, and other thinkers. When the first volume of the work was published toward the end of the war, in the summer of 1918 (the second volume would appear in 1922), it received little notice, and that mainly hostile; the book seemed destined to be forgotten. Then, however, a broader public discovered it, and as sales rose steadily the influence of Spengler's ideas multiplied to a spectacular degree, spreading across languages and countries with every new translation and edition.

Decline of the West appeared in Soviet Russia in 1923; the popularity of the book had been such that in 1922, a year before the Russian translation appeared, a collection of critical articles by renowned Russian thinkers (among them the religious philosophers Nikolai Berdiaev and Semen Frank) was published in Moscow. English-speakers had to wait until 1926 to read the master's oracular prose. Even where translations were not immediately available, however, educated readers often knew German sufficiently well to understand the book. Italian intellectuals, who would not be able to read a translation until 1957, were fascinated by it and used it as a key for understanding Goethe's play *Faust*. By 1926, the book had sold a hundred thousand copies in Germany alone.

Decline of the West is not an easy read. It feels rather ponderously "German": professorial and convoluted, with rambling sentences and a parade of famous names on every page. It ranges from ancient China to twentieth-century Chicago, from Moses to Marx, and from Greek art to Goethe—not the kind of work to become a staple of everyday conversation across the Western world. But sometimes a big book carrying an apparent Big Explanation will exude a curious attraction for a particular readership, and Spengler's oracular and often opaque language ironically guaranteed that the book could be read in various ways by various people and impressively quoted even without being understood. More important, perhaps, its publication, in two parts in 1918 and 1922, resonated opportunely with readers whose postwar feelings of disillusion and resentment demanded encapsulation.

Drawing on Plato's *Republic*, Spengler divided the life span of every civilization into seasons or ages—childhood, youth, maturity, old age—to which he ascribed particular characteristics. The present, he wrote, was the dotage of the Western world, which had run the full gamut of manifestations of its genius, and which could find greatness once again only if it entered a period of "Caesarism," in which a man of destiny would emerge to eradicate the symptoms of decadent decline, namely, the rule of money, of the press, and of democracy, which Spengler regarded as mechanisms used by soulless capitalist powers to manipulate and enslave entire populations and to pervert the natural course of history.

The true nature of every civilization, Spengler thought, was determined by its "blood," a term he used freely and metaphorically to denote not so much ethnicity as the unique characteristics of a culture within a given landscape and surroundings: "A boundless mass of human Being, flowing in a stream without banks; up-stream, a dark past wherein our time-sense loses all powers of definition and restless or uneasy fancy conjures up geological periods to hide away an eternally unsolvable riddle; down-stream, a future even so dark and timeless."[5]

No individual and no civilization can escape fate, Spengler wrote, and every "strong race" would look to impose itself on others, led by an exceptional man who would maintain his power "for the duration of his personal existence or, beyond it, for that of his blood streaming on through children and grandchildren."[6] This was the fate of men, for "the Woman as Mother is, and the Man as Warrior and Politician makes, History."[7]

With the victory of contemporary Anglo-American politics, the strong and natural life force of civilization had been subdued by a huge opinion-forming machine: "Man does not speak to man; the press and its associate, the electrical news-service, keep the waking-consciousness of whole peoples and continents under a deafening drum-fire of theses, catchwords, standpoints, scenes, feelings, day by day and year by year, so that every Ego becomes a mere function of a monstrous intellectual Something."[8] This great system, Spengler believed, was doomed to fail because it would undermine itself. In the end, the "will to power" (a term borrowed from Nietzsche) would assert itself: "Through money, democracy becomes its own destroyer. . . . In the Late Democracy, race bursts forth and either makes ideals its slaves or throws them scornfully into the pit."[9]

This "conflict between money and blood" would lead to another revolution, a great rising of the naturally strong against everything that was weak and perverted. "Men are tired to disgust of money-economy," wrote Spengler. "They hope for salvation from somewhere or other, for some real thing of honour and chivalry, of inward nobility, of unselfishness and duty. And now dawns the time when the form-filled powers of the blood, which the rationalism of the Megalopolis has suppressed, reawaken in the depths . . . Caesarism grows on the soil of Democracy, but its roots thread deeply into the underground of blood tradition."[10]

For a great many readers, this curious mixture of romanticism and idealism, of acute observation and wild generalization, became a bible for the postwar age. It appeared to explain why urban life in particular felt emptied of its moral core and why Western civilization more generally seemed to be spinning senselessly around on itself, producing (apart from money) millions of wasted lives and moral decadence.

Spengler's sweeping analysis, as well as his conclusion that only a dictator could save Western civilization from its self-destruction by making it listen once more to the voice of its "blood," had many admirers and imitators, not so much among historians as among high school teachers, journalists, and politicians eager to present a coherent image of world history and national greatness to their audiences. What entranced his readers was less the intoxicating profusion of names and his forays into economics, art history, biology—wrong in many details—than a subliminal message of fate, health, and strength, which was open to many interpretations. Adolf Hitler, convinced that he was the man of destiny demanded by Spengler's theory of history, was to pay the aging author a visit in 1933. But Spengler, who abhorred violence (other than in theory) and who detested the Nazis for their plebeian manners, responded coolly. When in the same year the new regime offered him a professorial chair at the prestigious University of Leipzig, he declined.

The proponents of this conservative revolution were many, and their backgrounds were as varied as the interpretation and emphasis they gave these ideas. They included veterans of the battlefield such as writers Ernst Jünger in Germany and Pierre Drieu La Rochelle in France; Jünger's 1920 *Stahlgewittern (Storm of Steel)* was seen as glorifying the experience of war, and Drieu La Rochelle was to turn increasingly toward fascism and anti-Semitism and eventually espouse the collaborationist cause after the German invasion of France. There were philosophers, such as the existentialist and phenomenologist Martin Heidegger, later to be compromised by his links with the Nazis. Nor was D'Annunzio by any means the only poet: the influential Stefan George in Germany, the expatriate Americans T. S. Eliot and Ezra Pound, self-anointed "scientists" and prophets such as Spengler himself, and political figures such as the Frenchman Charles Maurras, a leader of the Catholic, monarchist, and nationalist Action Française; in England, the aristocratic veteran of the trenches and future founder of the British Union of Fascists, Oswald Mosley; and in Italy, the poet Giovanni Gentile and Mussolini himself.

Red Scare, Black Bolsheviks

THE CONSERVATIVE REVOLUTION was rallying its troops. On the streets, however, ideas were already clashing violently and bloodily. In Italy, fighting between militias inspired by D'Annunzio's feats of heroism and loyal to their *duce* Benito Mussolini were engaged in an intense struggle with communists and trade unionists. Violent demonstrations, strikebreaking, gun battles, and political assassinations dominated the news of the staggering state. Germany seemed practically in a state of war; Hungary saw two coups within the year and was finally subjugated to the iron fist of the winner, Admiral Miklós Horthy; Armenia was soaked in blood and the Levant was in uproar; Russia was still a vast battleground on which the Red and White armies fought a bitter war.

Among so much uncertainty, ideas took on an existential importance that they are denied during easier times. The incipient fight between the rival dreams of fascism and socialism bore hallmarks of every other social conflict, in that ideological proclamations were often used as masks for fear, greed, and envy. But at the same time this genuinely was a conflict of ideas, cultures, and aspirations. Not since the Thirty Years' War had beliefs been so vital—and so deadly.

The conservative revolution, however, with its conviction of impending conflict based on "blood" and race, was being preached not just in Europe. Indeed, in 1919, most observers forecasting racial unrest and even mass murder would have been thinking primarily of the United States. During the war the reformist and high-minded president Woodrow Wilson had promised "to make the world safe for democracy," and many of his constituents had hoped that their wartime sacrifices would advance their causes. For countless women who had to replace men in factories and businesses, that cause was suffrage; to blacks who risked their lives at the front, it was full civil rights; to Irish Americans, northern Irish independence; to Italian Americans, a recognition of Fiume as an Italian city (D'Annunzio became a hero for them); to social reformers, the end of child labor.

But the war had not made these dreams a reality. True, the demands of a war economy and the greater involvement of government in industry had bolstered workers' rights, and having to supply an entire army on foreign soil had given a boost to agriculture, but at the same time the climate in the country had turned and radical conservatives were beginning to win the argument over where society should go.

Wilson's engagement during the negotiation of the Versailles Treaty, for which he had personally traveled to Paris, was ridiculed, and the treaty he had so painstakingly put together was rejected by the Senate. This moment marked the greatest defeat in Wilson's life. The high-minded, internationalist, and somewhat Victorian president was devastated. In addition, before the treaty was voted down in the Senate, he had suffered a breakdown of his health that effectively made him an invalid. The country was turning inward, and other forces were on the rise.

Hatred and fear erupt on cultural fault lines. In Europe different ethnicities, religions, and centuries-old grudges dressed up in scientific racism fueled anti-Semitism, along with Nordic, German, Gallic, Slavic, and assorted other supremacist visions of a clean, pure future. In the United States these debates did not revolve primarily around religion (despite the discrimination endured by Catholics and Jews) or around old European memories. Instead, they were haunted by the country's original sin: a noble dream built on slavery and slaughter.

American heroes: The Harlem Hellfighters fought courageously on the Western Front. Their unit was incorporated into the French army, as their own (white) officers did not trust them in combat.

The veterans of the black battalions within the US Army had decided to risk their lives abroad for a fairer deal at home, but they had been cruelly disabused of any hopes of a better, more dignified life. During the time that one of these black units spent training in Spartanburg, South Carolina, the city's mayor, J. T. Floyd, had declared that "with their northern ideas about race equality, [these black soldiers] will probably expect to be treated like white men. I can say right here that they will not be treated like white men. I can say right here that they will not be treated as anything except negroes. We shall treat them exactly as we treat our resident negroes." Clarifying what that entailed, another citizen added, "I can tell you for certain that if any of these colored soldiers go in any of the soda stores and the like and ask to be served they'll be knocked down. Somebody will throw a bottle. We don't allow negroes to use the same glass that a white may later have to drink out of. We have our customs down here, and we aren't going to alter them." During the same month black soldiers in Houston, Texas, had rioted against the treatment meted out to them and had engaged in a gun battle with local whites that left seventeen locals dead. Thirteen black soldiers had been court-martialed and hanged.

Faced with such attitudes, black soldiers had experienced their service in Europe as a liberation. Embarking on the SS *Pocahontas*, the 369th Infantry Regiment, nicknamed the "Harlem Hellfighters," sailed in November 1917 and arrived in Brest on New Year's Day 1918. The arrival of the African Americans to the strains of the unit's band playing the most amazingly riotous, danceable march music caused a stir in the French harbor town and in the country more generally. James Reese Europe was already a famous bandleader, and General John Pershing, commander of the American Expeditionary Force, understood the publicity potential of the Hellfighters and their musicians, though he also pleaded to keep blacks away from the front, calling them "inferior" and doubting that they could ever fight as white citizens could. Between February and March 1918 the band embarked on a tour covering two thousand miles of French territory, playing in twenty-five cities. Their concerts produced scenes of intense emotion, and they were treated as stars by French citizens, who had never before heard jazz.

Meanwhile, the fighting comrades of the Hellfighters had undergone a strange transformation. Forbidden from engaging the Germans as American soldiers, the unit had simply been assigned to the 16th Division of the French army. They were feared by their enemies, and at the New York victory parade on February 17, 1919, the band proudly marched down Fifth Avenue.

Their triumph, however, was short-lived. In civilian life the former Hellfighters found themselves transformed once more into second-class citizens. They were openly segregated in the South, where the Ku Klux Klan was gaining hundreds of thousands of new members and lynchings were on the rise again, and they were treated as dangerous competition in the industrial cities of the North.

Race was a constant theme during the uncertain years following the war, and many of the concerns and interests bound up with discrimination against African Americans mirrored Europe's conservative revolution. Justifying injustice with paranoia, many whites associated the country's black population with sedition, godlessness, revolution, and Bolshevism; even President Wilson apparently told his doctor in March 1919 that "the American Negro returning from abroad would be our greatest medium in conveying bolshevism to America."[11] This was particularly painful for black Americans who had had the opportunity to see what it was like to be treated differently and to be surrounded by different ideas while fighting for their country in Europe.

The original Ku Klux Klan had emerged in the post–Civil War Reconstruction era as a movement of southern white men (and women's auxiliaries) protesting the end of slavery and the reincorporation of Confederate states into the Union. The Klan had enjoyed a brutal but brief reign in the 1860s and early 1870s before sinking into insignificance. But in 1915, director D. W. Griffith released his silent film of Thomas Dixon Jr.'s 1905 novel *The Clansman*. Dixon, a Southern Baptist minister from North Carolina, though opposed to slavery itself, had portrayed the Klan as a band of heroes fighting to defend white women against sexually aggressive and stupid blacks (who were played by white actors wearing blackface) and seeking to restore the "natural"—that is, white supremacist—order of things. The outspoken racism, transferred to Griffith's film, made it highly controversial, but the film was hugely popular nonetheless. Griffith's filming technique was innovative, and he had shrewdly cast the legendary Lillian Gish in a starring role.

The film and the book it was based on prompted a huge resurgence of the once almost defunct KKK, not only in the South but also in Detroit, Chicago, and other midwestern and northern industrial cities where blacks and whites were now competing for factory jobs. The Klan's membership was limited to native-born white Protestants, and though its main target of hatred was black Americans, it was also ready to attack anyone suspected of being "un-American," a category that included Jews, Catholics, and socialists. The Klan's first leader, or "Imperial Wizard," was William J. Simmons of Alabama, a former Methodist Episcopal minister suspended by his church for inefficiency. Directly inspired by Griffith's film, Simmons obtained a copy of the original "prescript" or rules of the Reconstruction-era Klan and promoted the group anew using modern sales tactics, including a four-dollar commission for every new member recruited. By 1920, the Klan had four million members.

Though the ensuing decades were to witness a great many Klan-directed violent attacks on black men and women, including thousands of lynchings, the activities of this second-wave KKK were not limited to violence against blacks.[12] The Klansmen began to turn on anyone who did not represent their vision of what it was to be American; they saw themselves as defenders of "pure womanhood" and guardians of morality, opposing abortion and drinking but also "loose dancing" and "roadside parking." Those accused of violating the Klan's strict moral code were abducted and subjected to a variety of tortures: flogging, branding, tarring and feathering, whipping, mutilation, or in some cases a cruel and slow death.

White supremacy? Amid the racial and political unrest in the years after 1918, the Ku Klux Klan swelled to unknown proportions, as did lynchings.

The years prior to 1919 had done much to aggravate racial tensions. During the war, the enlistment of millions of working-class white men had led to severe labor shortages in the industrial centers of the North, with some half a million southern black men being hired to take their place. Now, after the soldiers' demobilization and return, competition for jobs had become intense, and the atmosphere was further strained by the returning black soldiers' newfound confidence.

The labor situation was complicated by the unions themselves, generally white and generally unwilling to open their ranks to black workers. After a surge of growth immediately after the war, they had been swiftly beaten back by corporate interests in major industries from steel to meatpacking; when the white unions responded with strikes, businesses counterattacked by hiring black strikebreakers. "The sentiment of brotherhood can be completely discarded," declared the leftist poet Claude McKay in *Negroes in America*, lamenting this classic divide-and-rule tactic. "The American worker's movement finds itself at the crossroads. It must choose one of the following two paths: the organization of black workers separately or together with whites—or the defeat of both by the forces of the bourgeoisie."[13]

There was not much likelihood of brotherhood between black and white. In the summer of 1919, after a spring of labor unrest and strikes across the United States, racial tensions erupted in a series of race riots. In Charleston, South Carolina; Longview, Texas; Bisbee, Arizona; Norfolk, Virginia; and Knoxville, Tennessee, white mobs attacked local blacks, though only in a few cities, notably Chicago and Washington, D.C., where the local police refused to intervene, did the black population resist with violence.

All in all, there were bloody race riots in thirty-eight American cities, leaving the period of 1919 with the epithet "Red Summer." But this time the blacks fought back. Claude McKay's poem "If We Must Die" was a clarion call to the defiant New Negro:

> If we must die, let it not be like hogs
> Hunted and penned in an inglorious spot,
> While round us bark the mad and hungry dogs,
> Making their mock at our accursèd lot.
> If we must die, O let us nobly die,
> So that our precious blood may not be shed
> In vain; then even the monsters we defy
> Shall be constrained to honor us though dead!
> O kinsmen! we must meet the common foe!
> Though far outnumbered let us show us brave,
> And for their thousand blows deal one death-blow!
> What though before us lies the open grave?
> Like men we'll face the murderous, cowardly pack,
> Pressed to the wall, dying, but fighting back![14]

Though never explicitly mentioning race hatred, "If We Must Die" was recognized by McKay's readers as a defiant answer to the white lynch mobs. The poem was a call to arms, but it also staked a cultural claim. With its self-consciously traditional, almost biblical language and its strict sonnet form—the form of Petrarch and Shakespeare—it attacked the barbarity of the white mobs in an idiom that self-consciously referred back to the highest pinnacles of Western literary culture.

The rise in black defiance given expression by McKay brought on intensified fighting. On July 27 in Chicago, a black boy out swimming drifted close to a beach reserved for whites and was pelted with rocks until he drowned. The police refused to take action, and groups of black men decided to take the law into their own hands. During the ensuing thirteen days of pitched battles between African American

men (many of them veterans) and police army units supported by
vigilante groups from poor Irish neighborhoods, thirty-eight people
were killed, hundreds were injured, and hundreds of homes were ran-
sacked or burned to the ground. The government had to deploy six
thousand troops to bring the situation under control. Having been
victorious in the greatest war ever seen, America appeared to be on
the edge of a race war.

The Rising Tide

"THE BASIC FACTOR OF HISTORY is not politics, but race," wrote the
American historian Lothrop Stoddard in 1921 in his widely read
The Rising Tide of Color.[15] Like Spengler, Stoddard believed that
Western civilization was doing much to ruin itself—in this case,
though, not through capitalism, which he supported, but through the
"internecine warfare" of white peoples against one another, which
gave inferior "colored races" a golden opportunity to exploit the white
race's weakened presence on the world stage. "The war," he wrote,
"was nothing short of a headlong plunge into white race-suicide.
It was essentially a civil war between closely related white stocks;
a war wherein every physical and mental effective was gathered up
and hurled into a hell of lethal machinery which killed unerringly the
youngest, the bravest, and the best."[16]

Stoddard saw the noble "Nordic races" overrun by a stream of
Africans, Asians, "mongrels," and "ape-like aborigines," who would invariably destroy the racial purity of the white races, particularly because
the nonwhites appeared to have more "superabundant animal vitality"
than the cultured whites: "In ethnic crossings," he wrote, "the negro
strikingly displays his prepotency, for black blood, once entering a
human stock, seems never really bred out again."[17] Describing Africans
as "savage" and "addicted to cannibalism," Stoddard drew the
inevitable conclusion: "The West has justified—perhaps with some
reason—every aggression on weaker races by the doctrine of the Survival of the Fittest; on the ground that it is best for future humanity that
the unfit should be eliminated and give place to the most able race."[18]

The result of interbreeding could be observed in South America, the
author argued. "Such is the situation in mongrel-ruled America:
revolution breeding revolution, tyranny breeding tyranny, and the twain
combining to ruin their victims and force them ever deeper into the
slough of degenerate barbarism," he wrote. "The whites have lost
their grip and are rapidly disappearing. The mixed-breeds have
had their chance and have grotesquely failed."[19]

"Weakened, tired Europe" did not have an answer to this existential crisis "at the crossroads of life and death." It was part of the problem: nationalist strife between European nations (first and foremost Germany, which Stoddard believed to be inhabited mainly by inferior "Alpines" instead of the more aristocratic "Nordic stock") led to terrible wars between whites, weakening their hold on world power. America would have to deal with this question by limiting migration and segregating populations. "Migration peopled Europe with superior white stocks displacing ape-like aborigines, and settled North America with Nordics instead of nomad redskins," he opined. "But migration also bastardized the Roman world with Levantine mongrels, drowned the West Indies under a black tide, and is filling our own land with the sweepings of the European east and south."[20]

Stoddard's racial rants were highly respected and widely circulated. No university library was complete without his "scientific" disquisitions about superior Nordics; his ideas were so well known that in his 1925 novel *The Great Gatsby*, F. Scott Fitzgerald has the rich but not unduly bright Tom Buchanan say: "Civilization's going to pieces. . . . I've gotten to be a terrible pessimist about things. Have you read *The Rise of the Colored Empires* by this man Goddard? . . . Well, it's a fine book, and everybody ought to read it. The idea is if we don't look out the white race will be—will be utterly submerged. It's all scientific stuff; it's been proved."

Proved or not, the ideas of the likes of Stoddard and Spengler had wide currency, and with them came a hardening of tone, a yearning for authenticity and authoritarian strength. The KKK's brand of bigoted right-wing Protestantism was outside the law but widely tolerated for years; only toward the middle of the 1920s did it begin to be opposed effectively. This official indifference to the Klan's activities can only be explained by the assumption that there was widespread tacit sympathy for the group's brutal moral crusade, or at the very least a high degree of political opportunism: in 1919 "un-American" activities were ruthlessly suppressed.

The "Red Scare" haunted the country. Fearing a revolution on American soil, conservative politicians used a series of mail bombs sent to their homes by an anarchist splinter group as an excuse to round up hundreds of socialists, communists, and anarchists across the United States and to incarcerate them without trial. The campaign was energetically coordinated by the unforgiving young director of the Bureau of Investigations (later to be renamed the Federal Bureau of Investigation, or FBI), the twenty-four-year-old J. Edgar Hoover.

Some five hundred "undesirables," including American citizens, were arrested and held without trial; many were deported. On December 21, 1919, 249 of them—suspected anarchists, communists, or other leftists—were placed on the US Army's transport ship *Buford* (which came to be nicknamed the "Red Ark") lying in New York Harbor, with as yet no publicly known destination. The deportations were perfectly legal; under the terms of the recent Immigration Act of 1918, any noncitizen who, as a matter of principle, opposed or simply did not believe in organized government, or who discouraged any US war effort, could be deported. All 249 fell into one or another of these categories. They finally would disembark in Finland, where they were transferred to the new Soviet Union.

The Fallen Archangel

GABRIELE D'ANNUNZIO BOWED OUT of politics after his Fiume adventure, and his political fall was accompanied by a real and mysterious one. Around eleven o'clock on the evening of August 19, 1922, he fell out of a first-floor window of his villa on Lake Garda, where he had retreated into a life of self-obsessed literature and lechery. He had been sitting on the windowsill, dressed in his pajamas and slippers. Luisa Baccara, his current mistress, was playing the piano. He suddenly fell backward headfirst, fracturing his skull and becoming comatose.

A witness later described that at the time of the fall he had been closely intertwined with Luisa's sister, his hands wandering across her figure. Had she pushed him away more strongly than intended, perhaps revolted by the almost sixty-year-old faun who was by now almost hairless and had only a few greenish teeth left? Or had he fainted from overuse of his habitual cocaine? Another explanation links his almost fatal plunge to the presence in the house of Aldo Finzi, one of Mussolini's closest allies. The old master, it was said, had become dangerous competition to the *duce*'s claim to national leadership as well as an embarrassment, but he still had charisma and a reputation large enough to halt the Fascist march on Rome if his caprice led him to do so.

When he came out of his coma, the aging poet took the tumble in stride. An inveterate self-mythologizer, he labeled the incident "the archangelic fall"—his name was not for nothing Gabriel of the Annunciation—and remarked with some satisfaction that he too had now risen from the dead. But his star was indeed sinking. Mussolini had given his militias free rein to brutally eliminate the armed opposition on the streets, and they had brought him victory. The ranks of his Fascist Party had swelled to seven hundred thousand, and he felt ready to make his grab for power.

On October 22, thirty thousand blackshirts marched on Rome. Portrayed by press photographers as a charismatic leader at the head of his troops, Mussolini in fact stayed behind, watching the risky progress from afar. Power was within reach, and it was all he wanted. In Naples two days later, he intoned in front of a crowd of sixty thousand people: "Our program is simple: we want to rule Italy."[21]

Moonshine Nation

The term "War Prohibitions Act" used in this Act shall mean the provisions of any Act or Acts prohibiting the sale and manufacture of intoxicating liquors until the conclusion of the present war and thereafter until the termination of demobilization, the date of which shall be determined and proclaimed by the President of the United States.

—National Prohibition Act, 1919

....

ON JANUARY 16, 1920, IN NORFOLK, VIRGINIA, A BOISTEROUS FUNERAL cortège could be seen wending its noisy way through the streets. The funeral had been organized by the Rev. Billy Sunday, a former professional baseball player turned exuberant revivalist preacher, and the corpse the ten thousand revelers were burying was twenty feet long—an individual by the name of John Barleycorn. In towns throughout America, similar funerals were taking place, with thousands of similar churchgoers rejoicing at John Barleycorn's demise.

Billy Sunday had named the enormous effigy after Jack London's 1913 *John Barleycorn: Alcoholic Memoirs*, in which the author had described the ruination of his life of wealth and celebrity through his addiction to hard liquor. This tale of spiritual redemption was already a staple of publishing in the United States.

On the same day, in communities of a different stamp, less joyful mock funerals were also being held. Guests at Maxim's and other expensive New York restaurants downed their last glasses sorrowfully, while at the famous Reisenweber's cabaret café on Columbus Circle, every lady making an appearance at "the grave of drink" was presented with a powder compact in the shape of a coffin.

Ordinary folk by the hundreds of thousands were transporting bottles of alcohol in cars, grocery carts, and even babies' carriages, while several more hundred thousand eager drinkers stood at their doorsteps peering anxiously out, waiting for them to arrive with the merchandise. While half the country celebrated, it seemed, the other half mourned and cursed. As midnight approached, the church bells began tolling; at the stroke of twelve, the Eighteenth Amendment to the Constitution came into effect, banning the sale, manufacture, import, or export of "intoxicating liquors," and with it the Volstead Act, enforcing the provisions of the amendment. Prohibition had begun: America was officially dry.

An American Culture War

PROHIBITION HAD BEEN FOUGHT and argued over for decades. The demon drink was guilty of most social evils, said its sworn enemies, the "drys," and they had a point. Particularly among working-class families, men commonly drank away the better part of their meager wages on payday. When they came back from the saloon, many of them would vent their anger on their families. Alcohol was a social issue that made allies of suffragettes, social conservatives, socialists, fundamentalist preachers, and even the Ku Klux Klan. Billy Sunday had campaigned tirelessly against the evils of alcohol. "The saloon is the sum of all villainies," he had preached. "It is worse than war or pestilence. It is the crime of crimes. It is the parent of crimes and the mother of sins. It is the appalling source of misery and crime in the land. And to licence such an incarnate fiend of hell is the dirtiest, low-down, damnable business on top of this old earth. There is nothing to be compared to it."[1]

But drunkenness, domestic violence, poverty, and public order were not the most important issues in the fight against drinking. The real front line in this war ran between small-town rural America and the big cities, and between old and recent immigrants. It was a battle for the soul of America.

The chief ideologues of Prohibition came from the more rural areas and were strongly supported by the evangelical churches. To a large extent, such as in the case of the crusading Billy Sunday himself, this was an older wave of immigrants and their first-generation American families—many of them farming people, pioneers with strong Protestant communities in the prairie states—against new arrivals from Italy, Germany, Ireland, and Central Europe who settled in the large cities, who were often Catholic, and for whom alcohol was part of everyday life. The great campaign for renewed morality was old America fighting new America, rural America fighting urban life, the nineteenth century fighting the twentieth. It was also to some extent a case of Protestant America fighting Catholic and Jewish America, though not on religious grounds. If the breweries were monopolized by families of German origin, the distilleries were largely controlled by Jews. Prohibitionist Arkansas congressman John Newton Tillman, addressing the House of Representatives in 1917, had listed the names of important figures in the liquor business—Steinberg, Schaumberg, Hirschbaum, and so on—and confidently declared: "I am not attacking an American institution. I am attacking mainly a foreign enterprise."[2] Tillman had been happy to overlook the contribution of the Virginia-born George Washington himself to the "mainly foreign" industry: the first president's distillery can still be seen today, in excellent working condition, at his Mount Vernon estate.

The decisive push for the dry movement, however, came only with the war, as wartime prohibition laws were seen as a patriotic measure protecting the troops by reserving grain for bread and keeping soldiers and workers sober in the service of their country. As America was fighting the kaiser and his beer-swilling hordes, many of those producing America's booze could be portrayed as unpatriotic, as could their products. "Brewery products fill refrigerator cars, while potatoes rot for lack of transportation, bankrupting farmers and starving cities. The coal that they consume would keep the railroads open and the factories running. Pro-Germanism is only the froth from the German beer-saloon. . . . Total abstinence is the impassable curtain barrage which we must lay before every trench. Sobriety is the bomb that will blow kaiserism to kingdom come," proclaimed the superintendent of the Wisconsin Anti-Saloon League.[3] If you were drinking, you were drinking with the enemy.

During the war, the role of government itself had changed. Income tax and conscription had been introduced, and the gargantuan task of organizing wartime supplies, production, and logistics had been taken over by central government agencies. In this climate of government control and patriotic fervor, the Eighteenth Amendment was passed in 1917 and ratified in 1919 without encountering significant opposition. It was as if America had gone dry almost without noticing.

Early Optimism

PROPONENTS WERE CERTAIN that Prohibition would bring universal happiness with very little fuss. "There will not be any violations to speak of," opined New York's supervising revenue officer, and prominent dry politicians and campaigners agreed wholeheartedly.

It wasn't quite that easy. Perhaps out of complacency or perhaps out of a lack of political will, from the very beginning the Bureau of Prohibition was woefully underfunded and understaffed. Fifteen hundred officers were supposed to police the entire territory of the United States, including the coastline and the longest land border in the world—the 5,525-mile border with Canada. In addition, the fact that the agents were paid between $1,200 and $2,000 per year, worse than garbagemen, was a virtual guarantee that many of them could be persuaded to look the other way if encouraged with discreet donations.

To make matters worse, the law supposed to make the Eighteenth Amendment enforceable, the Volstead Act, sported a panoply of interesting exceptions and compromises that were soon exploited. Alcohol was allowed to be produced and sold for industrial, medical, and ritual purposes. In consequence, industrial ethyl alcohol was sold in ever-greater quantities, and when the government began adding lethal methyl alcohol to make it undrinkable and people died, the authorities were accused of being complicit in murder.

Doctors and apothecaries, on the other hand, found Prohibition a boon. Soon some three hundred thousand prescriptions for whisky were being issued every year, and one doctor estimated that his colleagues made roughly $40 million annually out of this new medical need. Wine producers experienced a similar blessing, as orders for communion wine skyrocketed, even if very little of it ever reached an altar. Inventive grape growers also offered thickened grape juice for home consumption; the sweet liquid might accidentally begin to ferment if left unguarded for too long.

Home brewing became a hugely popular pastime as well as a useful second income for countless families. A popular jingle of the period paints the picture neatly:

Mother's in the kitchen, washing out the jugs
Sister's in the pantry, bottling the suds

Father's in the cellar, mixing up the hops
Johnny's on the front porch, watching for the cops.

In 1921, 95,933 illicit distilleries, fermenters, and other moonshine installations were seized by the overworked authorities; by 1930, this number had almost trebled. In the same year, some forty million gallons of spirits, malt liquor, wine, cider, and other alcoholic beverages were also seized—the tip of an enormous alcohol iceberg. (The Russian experience had been similar: less than a year after the tsar's 1914 decree banning the sale of vodka "forever" in the Russian Empire, tens of thousands of illegal distilleries had started up.)

In addition to home production, liquor smuggling, known as "bootlegging," became increasingly lucrative and professionalized, the single most important factor in the growth of organized crime. Imports of whisky into Canada quadrupled after 1920, despite the fact that home consumption of whisky remained constant. Along a border that had too few agents for too much difficult and lonely terrain, smuggling booze was almost too easy. According to General Lincoln C. Andrews, assistant secretary of the treasury in charge of enforcing the Prohibition laws, his agents succeeded in intercepting only about 5 percent of the smuggled liquor.

Prohibition proved to be a farce, and a costly one. Soon a wave of prosecutions overwhelmed the courts; by 1929, half a million arrests had been made under the Volstead Act, and the prison population had swollen to double the capacity the prisons had been built for. Even a draconian five-year prison term plus a $10,000 fine for first offenses did not improve compliance. Average Americans simply did not want Prohibition.

As the saloon went the way of the dinosaur, a new kind of establishment opened its doors throughout the cities: discreet establishments behind the façade of restaurants, hairdressers' salons, or other shops. Thirsty members of the public would first undergo inspection and then would be ushered into these "speakeasies," where no wish would remain unfulfilled. Soon this arrangement was so ubiquitous that a journalist suggested that the entire history of the United States could be summed up in eleven words: "Columbus, Washington, Lincoln, Volstead, Two flights up and ask for Gus."[4]

The threat of arrest was always present, but it only served to add spice to the already lively entertainments offered in the speakeasies. Illegality was a kick, and it changed the interaction between customers. While drinking establishments had previously been a purely male domain, speakeasies also welcomed women, who would then not only drink but also smoke cigarettes, listen to jazz, and dance, sometimes with men of a different race. If convention outside these walls was against it, it simply had to be fun. In the speakeasies, millions of Americans of all classes discovered a new freedom of manners and a casual disregard for social conventions and for the law.

Mob Rule

LEGIONS OF POTENTIAL CUSTOMERS encouraged "businessmen" willing to satisfy the huge and obvious need without the sanction of government. The most famous of them advertised himself as a used furniture salesman. His name was Alphonse Capone, and he had set up shop in Chicago. Like others in the same line of work, Capone was alive to the hypocrisy of the system. "I make my money by supplying a public demand," he commented. "If I break the law, my customers, who number hundreds of the best people in Chicago, are as guilty as I am. The only difference between us is that I sell and they buy. Everybody calls me a racketeer. I call myself a business man. When I sell liquor, it's bootlegging. When my patrons serve it on a silver tray on Lake Shore Drive, it's hospitality."[5]

The spoils of this illegal trade were enormous. At the height of his success, Capone was earning between $60 million and $100 million a year from beer sales alone. In addition to this were hard liquor, gambling, and other lucrative business opportunities. As a good businessman, Capone sought to reinvest and diversify. Rackets forced owners of laundries and other businesses to buy protection from gangsters. Those who refused would be clubbed senseless or would find their businesses bombed or burned down and their staff assaulted. In some cases they were simply killed. In Chicago, the "bakers, barbers, electrical workers, garage men, shoe repairers, plumbers, garbage haulers, window cleaners, milk salesmen, confectionary dealers and undertakers" were all paying protection; any customer having his trousers pressed in a laundry was effectively paying fifty cents per pair to the Mafia.[6]

In the face of such immense commercial opportunities, Capone and the six hundred faithful associates who lent their fists, sawed-off shotguns, pistols, Thompson machine guns (or "Tommy guns"), sand-filled socks, brass knuckles, and switchblades to his service had to contend with stiff competition from other businessmen, who were invariably organized according to whichever of the great recent urban immigrant populations they belonged to: Sicilian, Irish, or Jewish. Soon Chicago alone counted about four hundred Mafia-related murders and a hundred bombings annually as the different gangs fought turf wars.

Where murders had once been cumbersome, requiring lethal skill, and getaways had been perilous and slow, hired killers wielding Tommy guns could now take their victims for a ride by luring them into cars or simply abducting them to be killed outside the city, where a body could be dumped by the roadside or encased in the concrete foundations of a new building whose contractor was almost certainly on the mob's payroll. Alternatively, murderers could carry out a drive-by shooting, spraying the victim or the building in which he was suspected to be with a shower of bullets from the passing car, and then simply blending into the traffic.

The most famous of these gangland killings, however, was more artisanal in nature. Its victim, Dean O'Banion, "a connoisseur of orchids and of manslaughter," was by day a florist and by night a bootlegger who had more than twenty kills to his name and whose operation cut painfully into Capone's profits. O'Banion always carried three guns, but on one occasion when three men he obviously knew came into his flower shop, he trusted them well enough to shake the hand of one of them in greeting. The other man did not let go and clasped O'Banion's hand while his two associates shot him repeatedly. What happened then is the stuff of Mafia legend, as Andrew Sinclair recounts: "O'Banion had a first-class funeral, gangster style: a ten-thousand-dollar casket, twenty-six truckloads of flowers, and among them a basket of flowers which bore the touching inscription 'From Al.'"[7]

Chicago was only the most famous and most brazen of territories the Mafia carved out for itself during Prohibition as police and other law-enforcement agencies looked on, always a step behind, always underfunded, dogged by corruption, and plagued by a steady stream of resignations from the service as agents found that their meager pay was not worth risking their lives for. The other side, by contrast, always had plenty of new recruits, new weapons, and new cars. Similar stories could be told about other urban centers, such as New York and Atlantic City. Prohibition had produced a new class of criminal and had led millions of ordinary citizens to casually break the law.

How could a law that had initially passed with relatively little opposition and had even enjoyed a degree of popular support be so disastrous in its implementation? First of all, the times had changed. If the Eighteenth Amendment had been passed by Congress largely because of the high patriotic feeling during the war, this emotion had now been reversed. "Spartan idealism was collapsing," wrote

Frederick Lewis Allen, a brilliantly perceptive eyewitness of the period. "People were tired of girding their loins to serve noble causes. They were tired of making the United States a land fit for heroes to live in. They wanted to relax and be themselves."[8]

But the opposition to Prohibition rested on more than just a wish to return to civilian life. It was caused by a deep suspicion of the motives of those moral guardians whose disciplined campaign had resulted in making America dry. In particular, the younger generation simply did not believe that their elders had the moral authority to force them to do anything. "The older generation had certainly pretty well ruined this world before passing it on to us," wrote John F. Carter in the *Atlantic Monthly*. "They give us this thing, knocked to pieces, leaky, red-hot, threatening to blow up; and then they are surprised that we don't accept it with the same attitude of pretty, decorous enthusiasm with which they received it, way back in the [eighteen-]eighties."[9]

But it was not only the bitter disappointment and the cynicism of a generation who found that the ideals they had been brought up with had been little more than wartime propaganda. Prohibition was also the expression of a culture war that divided the United States and, to a lesser extent, all Western countries, a war not only on alcohol but also on cigarettes, jazz, "degeneracy" and lax morals, young people and their "petting parties," women's short skirts and short hair, and close dancing. As early as 1914, the General Federation of Women's Clubs had banned all forms of dancing that sounded too little like decent, traditional entertainment and too much like fun: "tango and the hesitation waltz . . . the gunny hog, turkey trot, Texas Tommy, hug-me-tight, fox trot, shimmy dance, sea-gull swoop, camel walk, and skunk waltz."[10]

But it was too late to turn back the clock. Prohibition was changing American society profoundly, but the effects were the very opposite of what had been intended. The same wave of technological innovation that made bootleggers and Mafia killers so successful also transformed the moral outlook of society itself. Before the war, just five people in a thousand owned a car in the United States. By 1920 this figure had risen to eighty-seven per thousand, and ten years later more than 20 percent of Americans were motorized. Closed cars, it turned out, afforded valuable privacy for dates. They brought the city to the countryside. They brought not only whisky and newspapers but also travelers who previously would have had to rely on stage-coaches, trains, or horses. They brought traveling salesmen and odd bits of news, contraceptives and city ways. They took people to the movies, where they could watch Mary Pickford—who had just been granted a very public divorce in 1920 and was having an affair with the dashing Douglas Fairbanks, followed by the press with bated breath—and Charlie Chaplin and the Marx Brothers.

Cars, movies, and radios wrought more havoc with traditional morals than oceans of alcohol could have done, but they were much more difficult to hate. By turning against alcohol, however, the prohibitionists hastened their own undoing. The speakeasies did much to accelerate social change and shifts in gender roles in the big cities. People who had gotten through the door with the little grille through which a suspicious pair of eyes would examine them before turning the key knew that they were already in contempt of the law and part of a community of revelers determined to have fun anyway, and they did.

Men and women danced close together in frequently lewd dances such as the Charleston, the energetic Lindy Hop (a distant ancestor of break dancing), or the dangerously sensuous fox-trot. Outside in the law-abiding world they would not have behaved in this way, but behind the door of the speakeasy everything seemed possible. The musicians were frequently black and brought with them the rhythms and riffs of the Deep South, where their grandparents had still been slaves. Their music became the true voice of a developing counterculture in which black cool became a growing factor.

A culture war had gripped the United States. If the prohibitionists were rapidly turning out to be the losers of their own creation, a whole new culture arose out of the ruins of their moral hopes. The speakeasies changed American and finally global culture. Modern dances and ecstatic whirling were frowned upon in dry town halls and official establishments, but they were encouraged in the illegal drinking clubs; racial segregation was largely intact outside, but inside one could count on meeting not only black musicians but also intellectuals and artists; class differences kept people from talking to one another in shops and restaurants, but the bar created an almost anarchic and exhilarating equality between drinkers—including a dangerous camaraderie between men and women, who could be found drinking, smoking, and dancing the night away. The prohibitionists had wanted to change America, and they had succeeded beyond their wildest dreams—it was just that the change went in exactly the opposite direction from what they had intended.

Self-confident, sassy, and sozzled, Mae West was the ideal Hollywood heroine of this world, and her one-liners ("Is that a pistol in your pocket or are you just glad to see me?") became legendary. "Goodness, what beautiful diamonds," says a young girl to West's heroine in *Night After Night* (1932). "Goodness has nothing to do with it, dearie," comes the reply. The Roaring Twenties began in the liquor-laced speakeasies.

The big winner, however, came from the South and rapidly began to conquer the world: jazz. Originally made by and for African Americans in New Orleans and other southern cities, carrying with it the memories of slavery and the rhythms of Africa and the Caribbean, and played on instruments derived from Western classical and folk music, jazz absorbed and developed from multiple pasts. Migrants brought it to the industrial cities of the North, and soon black musicians were the hottest ticket in the permissive culture of illegal partying. Louis Armstrong, Ella Fitzgerald, Jelly Roll Morton, Duke Ellington, Hoagy Carmichael, Fats Waller, and Sidney Bechet all started their careers in this highly charged atmosphere of drink, drugs, and delirium.

From here on the victory of jazz and of black culture was unstoppable. Records and concert tours spread the fame of this new music, which more than any other encapsulated the spirit of the age. Black cool, rock and roll, soul, and ultimately rap and gangsta culture would reveal themselves to be late, unintended fruits of Prohibition.

Writers into the Breach

THE CULTURE WAR AROUND PROHIBITION was fought in literature, too. But here it was an unequal fight. Without Congress or law enforcement to call upon, the dry side could field only Upton Sinclair, a fine but moralistic novelist always moved by great causes, whose father, a liquor salesman, had drunk himself to death, and Jack London, who also took a dim view of the devil booze. On the other side was arrayed a formidable battalion of talent and wit: Ernest Hemingway, John Dos Passos, E. E. Cummings, Dorothy Parker, William Faulkner, Thomas Wolfe. The battle was not only about alcohol; "it mixed up Catholics, romantics, expatriates, libertarians, art-for-art's-sakers in a battle for free drinking, evolution, free thought, free love, Al Smith, Freud, Joyce, Karl Adam, Karl Marx, Russian movies, against traditionalists, Jew-baiters, Catholic-haters, political and social conservatives, moralists, legalists."[11]

The writer most associated with the young generation in the 1920s and their path from disillusion with society to disappointment in themselves was F. Scott Fitzgerald, whose novels *This Side of Paradise* (1920), *The Beautiful and the Damned* and *Tales of the Jazz Age* (1922), and *The Great Gatsby* (1925) were immediately acclaimed as literary monuments to this culture with its flappers, its hard-bitten young men and women, and its cult of pleasure for pleasure's sake.

"Here was a new generation," Fitzgerald wrote in *This Side of Paradise*, "shouting the old cries, learning the old creeds, through a revelry of long days and nights; destined finally to go out into that dirty gray turmoil to follow love and pride; a new generation dedicated more than the last to the fear of poverty and the worship of success; grown up to find all Gods dead, all wars fought, all faiths in man shaken."[12]

Fitzgerald's own life was uncomfortably similar to the carousel of glamorous cocktail parties, orgiastic binges, and spiritual emptiness he described in his works; indeed, it could have been a cautionary tale straight out of a prohibitionist's pamphlet. Born into a middle-class family in Minnesota in 1896 and educated at Princeton, he had left college without a degree. Drafted into the military and stationed in Alabama, he met Zelda Sayre and proposed to her. She initially accepted but then broke off the engagement, unwilling to marry a man without an income. Fitzgerald worked in an advertising agency while writing his first novel, *This Side of Paradise*. When the novel was published in 1920 and became a great success, Zelda finally agreed to marry the now famous author.

The ensuing years are the stuff of legend: the famous couple in New York, in Paris, on the French Riviera, young and glamorous, socializing and drinking and writing, writing and drinking and socializing. In Paris they met Ernest Hemingway, and the two men became close friends. Zelda resented this friendship, especially as Hemingway accused her of encouraging her husband to drink in order to stop him from writing. But Fitzgerald desperately needed to write, and not only because he had always been driven.

Despite the financial success of his novels and despite the short stories Fitzgerald turned out to keep the wolf from the door, the high life the couple led plunged them into debt. When his agent refused to advance him any more money the pressure on the author increased and he found little time to do anything but commercial work. Zelda, meanwhile, was descending into schizophrenia and was hospitalized. By now a middle-aged alcoholic and a shadow of his meteoric former self, Fitzgerald never produced anything equaling his brilliant early work and ended up in Hollywood writing short stories and screenplays, none of which were ever produced.

Going Abroad

SCOTT AND ZELDA FITZGERALD were not the only writers choosing to flee Prohibition-era America and settle in Paris during the Jazz Age. Paris was fun; it had a reputation; it had been the scene of the prewar avant-garde of Picasso, Apollinaire, Stravinsky, and Diaghilev. But most of all, it was cheap. A weak franc made it the ideal place for American artists who wanted their money to stretch further, and they came in droves. Sherwood Anderson, whose portrayal of the American provinces in the short-story collection *Winesburg, Ohio* had influenced a whole generation of younger writers; the scandalous and beautiful author Djuna Barnes; the socialist activist and novelist John Dos Passos; the deliciously explicit Anaïs Nin and her young lover Henry Miller; the lanky, eccentric poet and critic Ezra Pound—altogether some two hundred thousand English-speaking expatriates, mostly young and looking for excitement, were living in Paris in the 1920s.

"Paris was where the twentieth century was," remarked the oracle and hostess of an entire generation of artists, Gertrude Stein, who had settled in Paris permanently together with her companion, Alice B. Toklas.[13] Independently wealthy, strong-willed, and possessed by an intense desire for fame, Stein collected the works of the most daring and experimental artists of her day—Picasso, Matisse, Braque, Gris—and wrote novels and plays whose distinguishing feature was the complete absence of any kind of linear plot or apparent logic, huge, unreadable behemoths of words redeemed only by their obvious delight in punning and surreal images.

At Stein's famous open houses on Saturday evenings, one could meet artistic giants such as Picasso, Braque, and Matisse talking with expatriate writers such as James Joyce and Hemingway, Paul Bowles and the Fitzgeralds. According to Hemingway, it was Stein who gave the young American artists and wannabes flocking the streets of Paris the name by which they were to be known. When a young car mechanic was unable to repair her car, she shouted at him, "You are all a *génération perdue*." When relating the incident to Hemingway, she stuck with the phrase that had appeared to her in a moment of angry frustration: "That is what you are. That's what you all are . . . all of you young people who served in the war. You are a lost generation."[14]

The English "lost generation" may have been a myth, but the young, disillusioned, and unmoored expat bohemians in Paris were very real. Their members were aware of belonging nowhere, and expatriate life suited them. It was easier to live with the feeling of not being at home if they were in a foreign country, where they could live carefree lives. The culture war raging in the United States between drys and wets, vice and virtue, WASPy Presbyterian rectitude and "un-American" ideas and identities seemed far away here, and the refugees from these battles could ask themselves what exactly it was they had lost, or rather what they had never possessed.

Growing into adulthood after the war, they were acutely aware that they *were* lost, that they were missing a sense of themselves, of purpose, and of direction. Scott and Zelda Fitzgerald were fun in a flapperish sort of way, but their incessant partying was a little too frenetic to be innocent. Djuna Barnes had lost too much too early: raped, most likely by her father, at sixteen, she had been married off to a man almost forty years her senior, whom she left after a torturous two months. When her family fell on hard times, she had been forced to support her siblings by working as a journalist. Uncompromising in living her hard-earned freedom, she took a succession of lovers, both male and female, and finally came to Paris in 1921 on an assignment to interview James Joyce, whose novel *Ulysses*, published in 1922, she admired so intensely that for a while she thought she would never be able to write again: "Who has the nerve to after that?" She eventually managed to work up the courage to publish again. Her autobiographical novel *Ryder* (1928) would expose in graphic detail the tawdry reality behind the bourgeois façade of pre-1914 middle-class life.

Among all the artists of the lost generation, Ernest Hemingway was both one of the most utterly lost and the most penetrating analyst of this condition. His own experiences in Paris and at bullfights in Spain were distilled in *The Sun Also Rises* (1926), a novel that captured an entire generation's sense of loss and its rebellion against this hollow existence. Wounded in the war, the book's protagonist, Jake, is impotent. His life as a foreign correspondent in Paris (a position Hemingway himself had held) is a joyless succession of drunken parties and distrustful encounters with people who are equally cynical and equally lacking in orientation. To escape the emptiness, Jake makes a trip to Spain with his friend Cohn and Cohn's lover Brett, an English aristocrat whose male-sounding name indicates that she is more of a man than her companions. They live in a poisonous love triangle. Brett is very much a "new woman" and sexually liberated. She loves Jake, but because of his injury she does not commit to him, sleeping instead with Cohn and also seducing a bullfighter, the very image of traditional masculinity. In the end they all lose—their love, their hopes, and each other.

Montmartre Rag

THE CULTURE WARS between conservative values and the worldview of the postwar generation was played out throughout the European continent, and in many of these battles America became a symbol for the liberating power of the New World, far away from the stifling atmosphere of Europe's prewar ideas.

Having arrived in the French capital during the war as soldiers, African American musicians decided to stay in or return to Europe rather than trying to make a living in their homeland, where stronger competition from other black bands and the prevalent racism of the white population made life difficult. To many demobilized black musicians the memories of Europe seemed golden, despite the dangers and hardships they had encountered at the front. Now they returned to Paris with their instruments, settling in and around Montmartre, in the rue Lance, rue Pigalle, and rue des Martyrs. The city was waking up from the trauma of a war that had caused more death and suffering among the French population than in any other Western country. People wanted to forget the killing and maiming and the grimness of war.

Mitchell's Jazz Kings at the Casino de Paris in the rue de Clichy brought the sound of the American South to the Parisian public every evening, and also accompanied French singers such as Maurice Chevalier and Mistinguett. In 1924 Le Grand Duc in the rue Pigalle became another home for *le ragtime* or *la musique nègre* in the capital. Having arrived from London, where he had been on tour, the great clarinetist Sidney Bechet was astounded to find Montmartre very similar to Harlem: "Any time you walked down the streets you'd run into four or five people you knew—performers, entertainers, all kinds of people who had real talent in them . . . you'd start to go home, and you'd never get there. There was always some singer to hear or someone who was playing. You'd run into some friends and they were off to hear this or do that and you just went along. It seemed like you just *couldn't* get home before ten or eleven in the morning."[15]

From Montmartre, the syncopated rhythms of cornets, clarinets, and percussion traveled along the railway lines to Brussels and Amsterdam. A breath of black American culture brought with it a distinct aroma of freedom. London was another important destination, but here things were not so easy. Like Parisians, Londoners were seeking to forget the war and were rediscovering pleasure, but unlike France, Britain had employed black workers from the West Indies in factories to make up for the worker shortfall, a solution that seemed all the more attractive to employers as they paid black workers less than their white counterparts.

After demobilization, white British workers were competing for these jobs, resenting the blacks even more as they accused them of depressing wages. Another motive for the enmity of white working-men toward blacks was sexual jealousy, as Francis Caldwell, then head constable of Liverpool, reported: "For some time there has existed a feeling of animosity between the white and colored population in this city. This feeling has probably been engendered by the arrogant and overbearing conduct of the negro population towards the white, and by the white women who live or cohabit with the black men, boasting to the other women of the superior qualities of the negroes as compared to those of white men. Since the Armistice the demobilization of so many negroes into Liverpool has caused this feeling to develop more rapidly and actively."[16]

White workers refused to work alongside black colleagues, and factories began laying off blacks to make space for whites. In July 1919 these tensions boiled over in Liverpool when 120 black workers were laid off from a sugar refinery. Mobs of blacks and whites armed with sticks, chains, revolvers, and cutthroat razors faced each other in street battles. One man, a black sailor, was killed, and scores were wounded. It was precisely during these bloody days that Sidney Bechet and his fellow musicians of the Southern Syncopated Orchestra docked in Liverpool. They played to large audiences in London's Philharmonic Hall in Great Portland Street and were even invited— or commanded—to play at Buckingham Palace.

Culture Wars and Civil War

IN GERMANY, defeated and ostracized, it was initially more difficult to find access to the rhythms of postwar celebration. The first jazz music to reach Berlin came in 1920 in the form of a record, an awkward cover version of the "Tiger Rag" played by an otherwise unknown German band and put out by a German label. But even if the phrasing had nothing of Bechet's sensuous elegance and the musicians studiously avoided all "dirty" notes, playing the music exactly like any dance-band tune, the record caused a small sensation. Two years later original jazz records could be imported from the United States, and German musicians and bands eagerly listened, transcribed, and imitated, to the delight of their young audiences. Jazz had come, had been listened to, had conquered.

Berlin was a major battleground in the culture wars between the old world and the new, and while jazz was relatively slow to assert itself here, certainly much more so than in Paris, the battle was waged initially on different terrain, albeit also with strong references to America and the supposed freedoms to be enjoyed there.

The German architect
Ludwig Mies van der Rohe
sought to give Berlin a
modern, even futuristic, image.

It is difficult to imagine today how torn both Berlin and Germany as a whole were after the catastrophe of the war and the collapse of Wilhelm II's empire. More than in any other city (with the possible exception of Vienna), the atmosphere was marked by poverty, bitterness, social hatred, and murderous political violence. "There were speakers on every street corner and songs of hatred everywhere," the painter George Grosz would remember. "Everybody was hated: the Jews, the capitalists, the gentry, the communists, the military, the landlords, the workers, the unemployed, the Black Reichswehr, the control commissions, the politicians, the department stores, and again the Jews. It was a real orgy of incitement, and the Republic was so weak that you hardly noticed it. All this must end in an awful crash."[17]

Reeling from a defeat it was totally unprepared for, Germany was a nation split down the middle and engaged in a murderous internal battle. "On the street one group of white-shirted men was marching to the slogan of '*Deutschland, erwache! Juda, verrecke!*' (Wake up, Germany! Jew, drop dead!), while another in equally military formation hailed Moscow. That left smashed heads, broken shins, and some nasty gunshot wounds," commented Grosz.[18] "The whole city was dark, cold, and full of rumors. The streets became ravines of manslaughter and cocaine traffic, marked by steel rods and bloody, broken chair legs."

Since its inception in 1919, the Weimar Republic had been in the middle of a revolution that might have taken Germany in an entirely different direction had it been successful. This socialist revolution was led by social democrats but opposed by the party executive. The open street fighting between militias on the right and the left forced the fledgling government out of the capital and to the quiet provincial town of Weimar, where the first assembly was held in the local theater, built more than a century before by the local duke as a performance space for the plays of his minister and sometime theater director Johann Wolfgang von Goethe and his friend Friedrich Schiller, whose statues in front of the building fruitlessly invoked a spirit of classical humanism.

In early 1920, the young Weimar Republic experienced one of its most severe crises as a group of disgruntled officers staged a violent coup against the government and occupied government buildings including the chancellery, forcing the cabinet to abandon Berlin once more. This time, however, a general strike was called and the coup leaders eventually had to abandon their plan of setting up an authoritarian government in the spirit of Prussian militarism. While the republic was saved for the moment, the situation remained at the edge of civil war.

The government's fragile hold on power was secured only by a destabilizing alliance with and toleration of paramilitary forces of questionable loyalty. The problem the country's leaders faced was overwhelming: a huge accumulation of debts stemming not only from reparations under the Versailles Treaty but also from the costs of the war itself, which had been financed by the emperor almost exclusively through obligations that he had been certain would be paid back out of the reparations imposed on his crushed enemies. Now, with its economy in ruins, its politics perilous, and its population brutalized by the conflict, Germany faced a war debt of 153 billion marks (by comparison, its debt had been a total of 5 billion in 1913). Its strategy was, or was supposed to be, a managed inflation: while before the war there had been 2 billion marks in circulation, there were 45 billion in 1919. Even at this early stage, money was rapidly losing its value, and the savings and security of the middle class began to evaporate, further destabilizing an already volatile situation.

Consensus was the first casualty in the battle of extremes, and while many conservatives thought that salvation lay in a return to national greatness and to "German virtues," a large, predominantly urban left-leaning and internationalist faction opposed these dreams as a form of national suicide. The German left abhorred the legacy

Perfect posture: A German war veteran decorated with the Iron Cross is begging in the streets of Berlin.

of the empire, the world of the Prussian *Junkers* or landed nobility, and the generals and their militarist worldview.

"The city looked like a grey corpse," the painter George Grosz wrote about postwar Berlin.

> There were cracks in all the walls. . . . The dead, dirty, hollow windows seemed still to be mourning those many for whom they had looked in vain. Those were wild years. I threw myself madly into life and teamed up with people who were searching for a way out from this absolute nothingness. We wanted more. Just what this "more" was to be, we could not tell. But my friends and I saw no solution in negativism nor in the fury of having been cheated, nor in the negation of all previous values. We thus, of course, drifted further and further to the left.[19]

An unwilling soldier, Grosz was part of a new, ideologically committed generation. His name already signified his strong feelings about the ideals and politics of his country. Born Georg Ehrenfried Groß, he had invented a new, cosmopolitan-sounding identity for himself because he no longer wanted to carry a German name. A talented draftsman, he put his skills into the service of his utopian hopes:

"I considered all art senseless unless it served as a weapon in the political arena. My art was to be gun and sword."[20]

Grosz used his artistic weapons in the fight against what he and his comrades in the battle for a brave new world saw as the reactionary enemies of peace and progress. In his lost painting *Germany, a Winter's Tale*, for which a recently found preparatory study survived, he laid down his vision of old Germany. In the center of the canvas, a frightened, chubby bourgeois sits at his table clutching knife and fork, the plate in front of him empty but for a bone, a glass of beer next to him, a newspaper to one side. Around him is a world exploding: houses in ruins, a clock with hours missing, a prostitute, a revolutionary, a pallbearer—all in riotous disorder. At the bottom of the composition, a reptilian priest, a grimly brainless general, and a blind schoolteacher carrying a long cane and clutching a tome labeled "Göthe" complete the apocalyptic scenario.

His brush dedicated to class warfare, Grosz specialized in brutal officers, flabby whores, pinched bourgeois, and mutilated veterans, the last of whom could be seen begging in every Berlin street. He reflected what he saw around him: "All moral codes were abandoned. A wave of vice, pornography and prostitution enveloped the whole country. *Je m'en fous* [I don't give a damn] was the motto, at last I am going to have a good time. A few young Americans who a few days before had been playing in an army band came to Berlin, and the orchestras playing Vienna waltzes changed overnight into jazz bands. Instead of first and second violinist, you saw grinning banjo and saxophone players."[21]

Jazz became an emblem of new living and of a new generation seeking to escape the confines of the prewar world, a world whose values they no longer respected. They were the lost generation, the flappers, the new bohemians hanging around the watering holes of Paris, Chicago, London, and Berlin, of Vienna and Brussels and Atlantic City. Their days and nights seemed like a hedonistic romp, but they felt acutely that there was a terrible emptiness at the heart of their whirlwind lives; as Scott Fitzgerald described, they danced, drank, and slept around to dull their awareness of the unanswered and very possibly unanswerable questions lurking there.

But the flapper life was not for everyone. While the sense of betrayal and emptiness led some straight to the speakeasy, it motivated others to change things, to create a new Jerusalem. Despising their hedonistic counterparts, they discovered causes, ideologies, and salvation. Their enthusiasm was often real and honorable, but, as George Grosz observed in the case of Germany, their mutually contradictory hopes created a sense of menace underneath the hectic enjoyments of a time liberated from years of war:

It was a completely negative world, with gaily colored froth on top that many people mistook for the true, the happy Germany before the eruption of the new barbarism. Foreigners who visited us at that time were easily fooled by the apparent light-hearted, whirring fun on the surface, by the nightlife and the so-called freedom and flowering of the arts. But that was really nothing more than froth. Right under that short-lived, lively surface of the shimmering swamp was fratricide and general discord, and regiments were formed for the final reckoning. . . . And we knew all that; or at least we had forebodings.[22]

The End of Hope

In the fearful years of the Yezov terror I spent seventeen months in the prison queues in Leningrad. One day somebody identified me. Beside me, in the queue, there was a woman with blue lips. She had, of course, never heard of me; but she suddenly came out of that trance so common to us all and whispered in my ear (everybody spoke in whispers there): "Can you describe this?" And I said: "Yes, I can." And then something like the shadow of a smile crossed what had once been her face.

—Anna Akhmatova, *Requiem*

....

ON MARCH 7, 1921, THE SEVENTH RUSSIAN ARMY WAS COMMANDED to assault the fortress of Kronstadt, a strategically important island in the bay of St. Petersburg, or Petrograd, as it was known then. Behind the thick walls of the fortress commanding the icy expanse of the bay were thirteen thousand armed Russian soldiers and sailors. Lenin's government had declared them to be traitors and issued the command to eliminate them.

To attack the fortress over the ice was an almost suicidal undertaking, as the fortress and the battleships had numerous batteries manned by highly motivated and trained personnel, and the ice offered no shelter. In addition, many of the soldiers of the Seventh Army, most of whom were from peasant stock, were ambivalent about the attack. They would have to be encouraged, a task that was accomplished by placing a machine gun detachment behind the advancing troops, with orders to kill all deserters. A brief artillery engagement was broken off because a blizzard reduced visibility to just a few yards. The infantry was ordered to take the fortress by storm. As soon as the first soldiers, dressed in white overalls for camouflage, emerged from the driving snow they were inundated with a barrage of artillery and machine gun fire; the shells from the rebels' large guns ripped holes in the ice, drowning scores of attackers in the freezing sea.

By the next day the snowstorm had subsided. The ice around the fortress was littered with corpses. The artillery bombardment recommenced and was answered in kind. Buildings on the mainland were burning. Another assault was begun, and Lenin announced another glorious Soviet victory, the liquidation of the Kronstadt rebels. His optimism turned out to be premature. Twenty thousand advancing soldiers had refused orders, knowing that they would be trapped on the open ice, and unwilling to shoot at their comrades. The attack was a fiasco. The Kronstadt sailors in their fortress directed an appeal to workers of all countries: "Let the toilers of the whole world know that we, the defenders of soviet power, are guarding the conquests of the Social Revolution. We shall win or perish beneath the ruins of Kronstadt, fighting for the just cause of the laboring masses. The toilers of the world will be our judges. The blood of the innocent will fall upon the heads of the Communist fanatics, drunk with power. Long live the power of the soviets!"[1]

Nobody could reproach the rebels on the island for a lack of courage or loyalty to the communist ideal. Throughout the terrible years of the civil war they had fought for the rights of workers and farmers, their own people, and no deprivation, no danger had been too great for them. The navy had always been at the very heart of the revolution. In 1905 the sailors' revolt on the battleship *Potemkin* in the Black Sea had been one of the first major revolutionary incidents showing the men's determination to fight the tsar, and in 1917 the battleship *Aurora* had fired (in revolutionary mythology at least) the first shots signaling the beginning of a new, revolutionary age, sparking the glorious October Revolution.

Three gutting years of civil war had followed, three years of terror on both sides, meted out by the Red Army and the White tsarist forces, both equal terrors to the inhabitants of the countless villages in which four-fifths of Russians were still living. Areas had been conquered in punitive campaigns of plundering, burning, killing, and rape and then abandoned, a terrible cycle that was by no means new in Russia. Before 1917 the tsar's armies had engaged in the same periodic campaigns of terror in an attempt to control a population still living largely beyond the law: in a country of 160 million souls, the official police force numbered only about one hundred thousand, with everyday order maintained by the often brutal rule of village elders.

This time, however, there had been no end to the violence. Worse, the new communist masters were even less adept at ruling than the aging aristocrats and corrupt officials had been before them. Without experience in governing or even administration—historian Richard Pipes calls them a government of professional revolutionaries—they fell back on theory and extreme experiments, even to the extent of abolishing money altogether in 1920 to destroy capitalism at its root.

On the eve of 1914, Russia had been an empire of vast social, economic, ethnic, and ideological contrasts; it was as though the cities were existing in a different century than the countryside. After the disastrous First World War, which had killed some 3.5 million Russians, the destructive energies generated by these contrasts plowed into the heart of society, and Russians endured the revolution, the murderous arbitrariness of their Bolshevik masters, and then the civil war. Three hundred thousand fighting men were killed in the civil war and another 450,000 died of disease, but those numbers were only a part of the human devastation.

In a contest of cruelty, Lenin's feared secret police, the Cheka, had executed a quarter of a million people without trial, and monarchist Cossack troops shot some twenty-five thousand civilians in one province alone. Revenge was swift and terrible, as after their defeat at the hands of the Red Army some five hundred thousand to seven hundred thousand Cossacks were either shot or deported. Meanwhile, the notoriously anti-Semitic White Army murdered a hundred thousand Jews in the Ukraine; another unknown number were slaughtered during pogroms in the south of the country.

Embittered by what he believed to be resistance to his liberating policy by peasant forces loyal to the old order, Lenin had ordered grain to be impounded in villages throughout the Urals, causing the first of several artificial famines Russia was to experience within a decade. An unknown number of people starved to death—estimates range from one million to two million. A wave of typhoid followed and found easy prey among the weakened population, killing at least three million.

The navy units, the most loyal troops the communists possessed, had been isolated from this terrible epidemic of murder and death by a thick wall of propaganda. During the war they had hardly ever been able to leave their ships and visit the city, let alone their families in far-flung villages. In late 1920, however, the situation was changing.

The White Army had been pushed back and the majority of Russia was now under communist rule.

The men had borne naval discipline, meager rations, danger, and boredom for months. Now, they thought, it was time for a little repayment of their loyal services. The crews of the battleships *Petropavlovsk* and *Sevastopol*, frozen into the ice off Kronstadt next to each other, grew restive. They wanted leave to see their families, a loosening of military discipline, and a reestablishment of their famously democratic structures of decision making by ships' committees (instead of the reinstatement of the former tsarist officers, the only ones with enough technical knowledge to run a battleship). But matters only seemed to get worse as supplies deteriorated and the already bad naval rations became so meager that there was an outbreak of scurvy among the men.

Fearing a rebellion, the navy commanders allowed greater numbers of men to go on leave and visit their families. Expecting to be treated like heroes and patriots, the sailors traveled home only to be confronted with the misery of life in the countryside and the hostility of their families. "For years," recounted one sailor, "the happenings at home while we were at the front or at sea were concealed by the Bolshevik censorship. When we returned home our parents asked us why we fought for the oppressors. That set us thinking."[2]

Returning to their ships, the sailors exchanged stories and experiences: the hunger in the cities and the terrible losses in their villages, the bands of street children begging and stealing what they could, the workers laboring under armed guards of Red Army soldiers like prisoners, the Cheka units moving about menacingly. This, they concluded, was not the revolution they had fought for. Many sailors became disillusioned with the cause they had served. Thousands of them resigned their Communist Party memberships, five thousand in January 1921 alone. The Baltic fleet was turning into a liability for the Party leadership, and officials indifferent to the reasons for the sailors' disaffection blamed all problems on the actions of tsarist and imperialist agitators.

The situation on the dreadnoughts deteriorated further in February 1921, when news and rumors about unrest and strike actions in Petrograd reached the sailors. Cut off from all reliable information and fed on hearsay and propaganda, they heard stories of the army firing into crowds of demonstrators, as the tsar's troops had done in the same city (then St. Petersburg) at the start of the 1905 revolution. Strikes had broken out, and Cheka units were arresting strike leaders and summarily shooting them in secret cellars. Agitated but uncertain what to believe, the seamen decided to send a commission into the city to investigate. What they found reinforced their impression that the state of workers and peasants was turning into a remote and harsh dictatorship: striking workers were forced to work under military guard, there were army units everywhere, and roadblocks with armed detachments had been set up.

In reaction to the suppression of the strike, the Kronstadt sailors drafted a resolution demanding free speech and a free press, immediate and secret elections, the freedom to form new trade unions, the liberation of all political prisoners, and the democratic control of all parts of government, among other things. It was a list of impossible demands, as the sailors were well aware, but it was the clearest articulation yet of growing disaffection with the central government and with the revolution itself, and it came from men who had shown their loyalty and sacrificed for the cause. They were not calling for the end of the Soviet government or of revolutionary politics, but perhaps what they wanted was even more dangerous: they were attempting to take the revolution back from the Party and anchor it in a popular democracy.

Lenin's government, then still resident in Petrograd, sensed that the Kronstadt sailors were mounting a serious challenge to its authority. Initially they dispatched some of their highest-ranking commissars—Mikhail Ivanovich Kalinin, president of the Central Executive Committee and formally the head of state, and Nikolai Nikolayevich Kuzmin, political commissar of the Baltic fleet—to save the situation by talking to the men during an outside meeting held on March 1, at which fifteen thousand people were present despite the icy temperatures. Initially all went well. The delegation was met by a military band and an honor guard carrying banners, and the meeting began peacefully. But when the sailors' resolution was read and Kalinin began to speak against it, the atmosphere changed. He was heckled and jeered, his voice drowned out by whistling and taunts.

A seasoned speaker, Kuzmin next attempted to get the crowd on his side by reminding them of their heroic deeds during the revolution. But his tactic backfired when a voice from the audience called out, "Have you forgotten how you had every tenth man shot on the northern front? Away with him!" There had indeed been such atrocities during the war, and Kuzmin had been a commissar on the northern front. In one instance, a detachment of recruits attempting to flee had been intercepted, and the commander and every tenth man condemned to death and shot on Trotsky's personal orders.

Kuzmin reacted unrepentantly: "The working people have always shot traitors to the cause, and they will continue to shoot them in future!" he shouted to a howling chorus of jeers and threats.[3] When Kuzmin had finished and stepped down in front of his increasingly hostile audience, the rostrum belonged to the sailors, who one after the next decried the government and called for greater freedoms and greater equality between privileged party officials and ordinary workers. The resolution was accepted by a huge majority, and the assembly decided to send another delegation to the capital to make their demands known to the population.

During the following days the situation continued to escalate. The seamen elected their own soviet, declaring the official ruling body invalid. Kuzmin and two other officials held angry speeches and were placed under arrest by the sailors during another meeting the following day. When the rumor spread that fifteen trucks loaded with Bolshevik forces were on their way to attack the meeting, the mutiny tipped into a full-scale revolt. A Revolutionary Committee was formed to command operations, and armed men were deployed to occupy the arsenals, telephone exchange, storage depots, pumping station, Cheka headquarters, and other strategic points. The rebels decreed a curfew; all ships were under their command. With three officials in their hands as prisoners and a whole arsenal at their disposal, the Kronstadt rebellion had begun.

The government in Petrograd recognized that this challenge to its authority marked a crucial moment. After years of war the army was exhausted, and it was possible that it would not be able to control the situation if the rebellion spread to other cities and provinces, as it had done before, especially if the opponents were not White guards but soldiers who had themselves made great sacrifices to the revolution. The troops might themselves mutiny and refuse orders, endangering the very core of Soviet rule.

In what was to become an established pattern, the response of Lenin's government was two-pronged. The Party mounted a large propaganda effort to convince the people that Kronstadt had been subverted by foreign agents and counterrevolutionary forces. Meanwhile, the army on the ground was to defeat the rebels as fast as possible, attacking the fortress before the ice could melt, which would make the rebels' encampment practically impenetrable and give them control over all naval access to the capital. The Kronstadt sailors, whom Trotsky himself had called the "pride and glory" of the Russian Revolution, had become the most dangerous enemy of the Bolsheviks. Preparing for retaliation, Trotsky had ordered the arrest of the wives and children of the rebels as hostages.

During the following days news of sporadic mutinies in other army units appeared to confirm Lenin's worst fears. Railway workers at Krasnoe Selo refused to work on trains used to send soldiers against the garrison, the 27th Omsk Division refused orders, and an anti-Bolshevik plot at Peterhof Command School was discovered and quickly quashed. The rebels in their stronghold, meanwhile, appeared more determined than ever. But their stand against the Bolshevik government did not receive any substantial support. Exhausted by war and hunger, the workers of Petrograd, whose strike had set the events in motion, did not rise against the government. Moreover, supplies on the island were quickly running out. They had little fuel or ammunition left, not enough food, and almost no winter clothes, and the long watches and sleepless nights had exhausted even the most battle-hardened men. They had waited in vain for help from outside. The impregnable fortress was beginning to look like a death trap.

When the decisive assault finally came during the night of March 16 to 17, some fifty thousand soldiers advanced in thick fog against the island, a move that had been preceded by a prolonged bombardment. When the first units reached the outlying forts around 5:00 a.m., moving forward on all fours over the now waterlogged ice, the rebels illuminated the advancing soldiers with flares and searchlights and pleaded with them to join them in their fight. Only when the advancing soldiers rushed the battlements with bayonets did those in the fortress open fire, inflicting heavy casualties.

Throughout that day, wave upon wave of attackers were rebutted by the desperate rebels, who used their artillery to turn the expanse around the fort into a cold cemetery for hundreds of advancing soldiers. Retreating soldiers were shot on the spot by their own officers, who were determined to press on. Eventually the sheer number of attackers overwhelmed the defenses, and as the walls were breached, the battle in the open turned into a series of dogged street fights, with the sailors being pushed back house by house. At around 4:00 p.m., the rebels once again mustered all their forces and actually succeeded in driving the attackers off the island, but the fresh supplies of soldiers on the other side proved too much for them. Under cover of night, eight hundred defenders escaped across the ice to Finland. During the next day, ten times that number made their way to safety. The rebellion was defeated.

The human cost of the assault was dramatic. While estimates vary widely (official Communist Party figures cite seven hundred Red casualties, others twenty-five thousand), probably ten thousand Bolshevik soldiers were killed in the assault, with thousands more wounded. Among the rebels, only about six hundred were killed, and another twenty-five hundred taken prisoner. Most of these were shot without trial over the ensuing weeks, while some were sent to gulags, sometimes with their entire families, including children. The fate of Kronstadt was intended to send a signal to insurrectionaries everywhere.

The signal was received, and it changed the fledgling Soviet regime. It was perfectly clear now that Lenin's government was prepared to crush any demand for participatory government, any challenge to his power.

Death in the Forest

FOR THE GOVERNMENT, Kronstadt was an opportunity to root out opposition on all levels of society, and the rebellion itself was followed by a wave of terror, including arrests, torture, and executions. To provide an official reason for it all, Soviet propagandists once again prepared public opinion in advance for the horror that was to come. An international anti-Bolshevik conspiracy was concocted, and duly uncovered with great fanfare. Its mastermind was declared to be Vladimir Nikolaevich Tagantsev, a professor of geography and glacier expert with no interest in politics. His name had been found among dozens of others in the address book of a spy killed at the Finnish border. This was enough for the Cheka to frame Tagantsev as the mastermind of a plot to overthrow the government, a plot with connections far into the ranks of Petrograd's intelligentsia.

On May 31, 1922, barely a week after the crushing of the Kronstadt rebellion, the gentle geographer was arrested on charges of high treason and taken to a Cheka prison, where he was held in solitary confinement, interrogated frequently, and also tortured. In June he attempted to hang himself in his cell but was discovered by the guards. Soon afterward the local Cheka commander offered him a deal: leniency for him and immunity from prosecution for all members of the conspiracy he would name. The amnesty came in writing, signed by high-ranking officials. Exhausted by torture and anguish, Tagantsev relented and named names—most likely simply those of people he knew (or knew of), or names that had been suggested to him by his interrogators.

The amnesty, of course, proved to be no more than a ruse for compiling a list that effectively comprised much of Petrograd's intellectual elite, men and women who had long been suspected by the Bolsheviks of being of questionable loyalty to the Revolution. Now the arrests

Surviving the "vegetarian years": During the 1920s, the Russian poet Anna Akhmatova subsisted on bread and tea.

could begin. Eight hundred people in all were bundled away by Cheka units for questioning, among them Nikolay Gumilev, a respected poet and the former husband of Anna Akhmatova, herself a blazing star in Russia's poetic firmament. On August 25 Tagantsev and his wife, Gumilev, and some sixty others were taken from their cells and driven to the Kovalevsky Forest outside Petrograd, where they were shot. Altogether some thirty thousand men and women were executed there between 1918 and the mid-1920s, most of them without trial. It is estimated that forty-five hundred bodies still lie there in the forest, in unmarked mass graves.

Gumilev had been a well-known and influential poet who deeply influenced the poets Osip Mandelstam and the young Vladimir Nabokov, among others. But in the poisonous climate of Soviet Russia, fame could prove to be a contagious affliction. Akhmatova had been married to him for only a few years, but she had a son with him. Now her association with a man convicted of crimes against the fatherland and the revolution stifled her own life and put her in grave danger.

At the time her former husband was shot, Akhmatova was thirty-two and working as a librarian at the Agronomic Institute. What she earned there was barely enough to keep her alive; for years she lived on a diet of bread and tea, a time she would later refer to as her "vegetarian years."

Kronstadt and its repressive aftermath were in more than one way the end of the Russian Revolution. The ruthless killing of the survivors and the invented conspiracy followed by another wave of executions made it absolutely clear that the Bolshevik leadership was not interested in participative decision making by local and democratically elected soviets, but was going to rule with an iron fist.

Lenin, who had kept in the background during the rebellion itself, was shrewd enough to understand that his austerity regime of war communism needed some tempering in order to forestall further uprisings, which might prove too much for both the fighting power and the loyalty of his exhausted army. He described the rebellion as a "lightning flash" telling him what he had to do to move the regime forward, but though he loosened the reins a little, he nevertheless kept them firmly in his grip. Having conducted his policy of war communism in part as a war on the peasantry, who saw their grain impounded and whose productivity had slumped by more than a third, the regime now allowed some small-scale grain and craft production and trading, which improved the situation in the countryside and softened the population's desperation.

Lenin's grip was slipping, however, a result of his deteriorating health. He had never quite recovered from an attempt on his life in 1918, and in contrast to his former legendary energy, he now frequently felt a crippling tiredness that forced him to take extended breaks in Gorky, his country seat, away from the center of power. In 1922 he succeeded in imposing his personal protégé as Party secretary; Joseph Stalin was a hard leader and a dangerous man, but Lenin trusted him. Later that year, Lenin suffered his first stroke, and further attacks in December left him almost incapacitated. From his wheelchair he had to watch how his comrade Stalin was rebuilding the Party machine in his image. Left without the power to speak after another stroke in early 1923, Lenin nevertheless attempted to remove Stalin from power and made it known that Trotsky would be his favorite for his succession, but it was too late. When Lenin died on January 21, 1924, Stalin's power was almost absolute.

The Mummified Revolution

AS A YOUNG MAN, Joseph Stalin, the general secretary of the Party and the new leader of the revolution, had studied at an Orthodox seminary, intending to be a priest. He knew about the power and importance of religious symbols. His relationship with Lenin had been ambivalent at the best of times, and during Lenin's decline Stalin had disregarded Lenin's orders and worked to cement his own power. Now, however, Stalin saw that this was his chance to create a saint, an icon of the revolution, and a powerful myth. The body of Lenin, who had died in Gorky, was transported back to Moscow and lay in state for three days in Red Square, during which more than two million people came to pay their respects. Then, after an official funeral celebration, the body was given to scientists.

The plan to preserve Lenin's body had been conceived by two people in particular: Leonid Krasin, people's commissar for foreign trade, and Anatoly Lunacharsky, who held the position of commissar of enlightenment and who together with the writer Maksim Gorky had earlier been part of the "god builders," an offshoot of socialism seeking to convert socialist thought into a formal religion with its own rituals, observances, and dogmas. There had been serious consideration given to preserving Lenin's body cryonically, with a view to resurrecting the great leader when scientific advances would allow it, but finally Lunacharsky and Krasin, the latter a refrigeration engineer by training, decided that the body should be embalmed instead—a fitting symbol for the state of the revolution. A mausoleum was constructed on Red Square, a squat structure of cubes strongly reminiscent of a pyramid, in which the embalmed body of the leader would await eternity and the coming of the paradise of peasants and workers.

The eschatological hope inherent in the religious symbolism of Lenin's last resting place was by no means accidental. His wartime policy had been built in part on the quasi certainty that Russia was only the prelude to a worldwide revolution which appeared imminent. As a devastating war turned into an uncertain and often violent peace, however, the world revolution failed to materialize.

For the Soviet leadership the failure of a global revolution not only flew in the face of all their prophecies but also forced them to rethink their own regime, much as the church fathers had done almost two thousand years earlier, when it became clear that the imminent expectation of the Last Judgment would have to be deferred and the church be put on a more solid institutional foundation.

Even if hopes of a world revolution were fading rapidly, in 1921 they were not quite dead. As the sailors in Kronstadt rebelled against their own leadership, thousands of German workers rose against the young and still fragile Weimar Republic, which had already almost miraculously survived a series of coups and armed uprisings from the left and the right.

The uprising was part of a plan to expedite the judgment day of capitalism. To make certain that matters would run smoothly, Lenin had sent one of his most trusted lieutenants, the Galician Comintern member Karl Radek, the highest-ranking foreigner in the Soviet hierarchy. Born into a Jewish family in Lemberg (today Lviv in Ukraine), Radek was an old hand at organization and agitation. He took a leading role in the efforts to convince the workers in the Halle region in eastern Germany to rise against the capitalist yoke. The location of this effort had been carefully chosen. Nowhere else was the Communist Party as strong as in this mining district. In the 1921 county elections the party received 30 percent of the vote and was the strongest political force in Halle, a city with just under two hundred thousand inhabitants, of whom sixty-seven thousand were card-carrying Party members.

March Is the Cruelest Month

THE "MARCH ACTION" was planned in advance, with inflammatory rhetoric spread through communist and bourgeois newspapers as well as on the streets. When the police found a large unexploded bomb at the foot of the Siegessäule in Berlin, the monument commemorating victory over France in 1870, the matter seemed clear: the explosives were wrapped in pages from a local newspaper from the Halle region. The authorities decided to transfer armed police units to the area in order to keep the situation under control.

For the communist organizers, the heavy-handed police raids and roadblocks springing up in and around Halle and Merseburg were the ideal excuse for action, and soon a series of terrorist acts commenced that, according to revolutionary theory, would destabilize bourgeois power and call the workers to the cause. But the train derailments that killed innocent passengers, the bombings and arson attacks that targeted not just the houses of factory owners but also police stations and the palaces of justice in Leipzig and Dresden, the widespread lootings, and the multiple bank robberies did not cause the revolutionary masses to stream into the streets in a gigantic show of solidarity, and the general strike demanded by the communist press was implemented only patchily and halfheartedly. The revolution was refusing to take off.

In the end, only a single factory was transformed by its workers into a bastion of the armed rebellion. In a military-style operation (many of its workers had been at the front only three years earlier), the Leuna chemical works were closed off with trenches dug around the factory entrances; they even went so far as to turn a train into a mobile fortress equipped with machine guns.

On March 23, the battle between the workers and heavily armed police units commenced. It soon became clear that without outside assistance, the workers had little chance of success. Shelled by artillery fire, they had nowhere to retreat to, and after one week the factory was taken by government forces at the cost of some 150 lives. Six thousand people were arrested, with four thousand sentenced to prison by special military courts; four revolutionaries were condemned to death, and several others were shot by police, allegedly while fleeing. For the communist movement of Germany, the March Action proved a crippling disaster, as hundreds of thousands of sympathizers turned away from its two main parties. The Soviets' most explicit attempt to ferment a revolution outside Russia had resulted in abject failure.

Beyond the Soviet experiment, the shattered economies and destabilized societies of the Western world also appeared to be strained to the breaking point. In March a coal strike forced the British government to declare a state of emergency, and there was a general strike in the north of France; in the industrial cities of northern Italy, Mussolini's fascists were embroiled in violent confrontations with socialist workers' organizations in a de facto civil war. Silesia saw a bloody armed insurrection, and rioting occurred from Vienna to Reykjavik. In Hungary, Admiral Horthy installed a dictatorship, and on October 19 the Portuguese prime minister, António Granjo, was murdered during a military coup.

The Battle of Blair Mountain

THE THREAT OF REVOLUTION was felt everywhere, even in the United States. The wave of returning servicemen, a crisis in agriculture due to wartime overproduction, the racial tensions after the migration of more than a million blacks from the Deep South to the industrial cities of the North—all these had led to a period of strife. In 1919 there had been a wave of strikes involving four million workers nationwide, including Chicago policemen, who left the streets to the rule of the mob in their fight for better pay.

In the heated postwar climate, anarchists had attempted to assassinate high officials and the Red Scare had swept aside all civil rights for those in the crosshairs of Attorney General A. Mitchell Palmer and the ambitious J. Edgar Hoover, who spearheaded the campaign against undesirable foreigners, especially those with left-wing associations. That summer there had also been a deadly wave of race riots and lynchings. To a certain extent America was at war with itself, and this war was never more bitterly fought than in 1921 in Logan County, a mining district in West Virginia.

The issue at stake in what became known as the Battle of Blair Mountain was not world revolution but the cruel exploitation of the miners. Before the opening of the coal fields at the end of the nineteenth century, West Virginia had been overwhelmingly rural and agricultural. Within a generation, tens of thousands of recent immigrants had come there to work in the mines, the most productive in the United States.

The owners of the extremely lucrative coal mines had instituted a system that was in wide use. Their employees worked with company equipment which they had to lease from their employers, and they were paid by the wagonload of coal, weighed and assessed always to the company's advantage. The pay the men received was partly in tokens that could be spent only at the company store, which charged inflated prices for all goods. Wage increases were always followed by a price hike at the stores, so the employers never lost out. The workers and their families also lived in company housing, which they had to rent separately. Any form of union organization or membership was strictly forbidden, and union members were fired on the spot.

The miners effectively lived on a monetary treadmill from which there was no escape. In return they worked extremely long hours in mines with only the most rudimentary safety features. Accidents, maimings, and deaths were frequent, and in 1907 a single explosion in a mine run by the Fairmont Coal Company in Marion County had cost 361 lives. In fact, the miners' odds for survival were worse than those of soldiers at the Western Front. There had always been attempts at resistance, including strikes and outbreaks of violence that had caused the governor to send in troops more than once. In their struggle for better working conditions, the miners were faced with impossible odds.

The mine owners had employed the Pinkerton detective agency that functioned as a private army outside the law and which took appropriate measures whenever the company's authority was challenged—from mere intimidation and pistol-whipping of perpetrators to evictions of entire families and even murder. Once, in 1913, the mine guards had driven an armed train through a tent encampment in which striking miners lived. The machine guns mounted on the train fired into the tents, and it was almost miraculous that only one person was killed.

In 1921 matters were coming to a head. Another attempt at organizing the workers had resulted in the firing of dozens of workers and the eviction of their families. A year earlier, detectives who had evicted miners' families had been gunned down by embittered miners in an open shootout in the town of Matewan, whose sheriff, Sid Hatfield, was sympathetic to the miners. Hatfield was a gunman straight out of a Western. Though Prohibition was a dead letter in a southern mining town, he did not drink because he found that alcohol impaired his reactions; to deter possible opponents he would launch a potato into the air and then draw his gun and explode it in midflight with a single shot. When company detectives threatened him with arrest and reached for their guns (accounts vary according to which witness one believes), Hatfield was faster; miners positioned on roofs and behind windows finished off the job. Seven detectives and three townspeople lay dead at the end of the battle.

The opening of Hatfield's trial in January 1921 coincided with a general strike by the miners, whose level of union organization was higher than ever before despite their employers' repressive measures. Police acted largely as agents of the mining firms, harassing strikers, destroying their tents and their possessions, and brutalizing individuals at every opportunity. At the same time, imported strikebreakers weakened the force of the unionized miners, and the mines continued to work almost to capacity.

The strikers grew despondent when news spread throughout the valley that their hero, Sid Hatfield, who had been acquitted earlier that year, had been assassinated in cold blood when he arrived in a nearby town to face additional charges against him. Hatfield and a friend were walking up the steps of the courthouse unarmed on August 1 when detectives belonging to the firm involved in the Matewan massacre opened fire on the two men, killing them both. Their deaths outraged the miners, especially when the murderers appeared to be on the verge of escaping prosecution. The strikers began to organize in armed militia groups and held protest meetings at which thousands participated. Urged on by their leaders, they decided to march on Logan, the seat of a neighboring county, to force the government to take action.

With an estimated five thousand armed and angry miners wearing red bandannas marching on the small town, the authorities began to panic. They organized an army of deputies, mine guards, store clerks, and state police, twelve hundred strong, to defend the city against the invasion. Led by a colonel of the National Guard who had fought in World War I, the deputies entrenched themselves on Blair Mountain, which lay between the marchers and the town of Logan. As the miners assembled on the base of the mountain on August 30 the first sporadic skirmishes occurred between the two forces. The next days saw intense fighting with deaths on both sides. Airplanes hired for the occasion dropped bombs on the miners' positions, while US Army Air Service bombers flew reconnaissance missions against the miners. Some thirty troops and one hundred miners were killed. Hundreds more were injured.

On September 1 President Warren Harding called in the army, causing almost all the miners to surrender immediately. The battle was over, and the defeated miners were sent home. More than twelve hundred of them were indicted for treason, but only one conviction was handed down. The real consequence of the battle was elsewhere: Blair Mountain put an end to all efforts to unionize labor in the southern mining industry. Like other violent labor disputes during this period, it resulted in a significant erosion of workers' rights.

....

AFTER A MAJOR EARTHQUAKE, a multitude of aftershocks of varying intensity will continue to rock the affected area for weeks, months, or even years to come, causing more damage, more anxiety, and an immense weariness. The huge, devastating shock of the First World War was over, but its aftereffects would not cease to rumble on. While the Western world was no longer at war, it had definitely not found a state of peace. The brutalization and destabilization associated with the greatest armed conflict the world had ever seen was continuing to affect the lives of hundreds of millions of people—so much so that one could argue that the conflict was continuing, albeit on internal fronts. The social order had been rocked to its foundations, and the economic situation varied from apparently robust in the case of the United States to straitened and tense in the case of France and Britain and desperate in the case of Germany and, even more so, the Soviet Republic. It was not a time of peace but simply a cessation of organized warfare.

Even before the war, the Russian economist Ivan Bloch had argued forcefully that the kind of industrialized conflict that was to be expected if major economies engaged one another on the battlefield would not be won by anyone. It would be a war not of armies but of economic systems, and it would be decided only by which economy would be forced to its knees first. More troublingly, he had also predicted that even for the winners victory would come at a crippling price, and in the end there would be only losers.

The early 1920s showed how accurate this analysis had been. Even for the wealthiest and most triumphant of the victors, the United

States, the War entailed a vortex of social change and civil unrest that proved almost impossible to control—particularly as one ineffectual president, the ailing Woodrow Wilson, was succeeded by another one, Warren G. Harding, who freely admitted that the business of governing was far too involved and complicated for a man of his intellectual capacities.

At a moment when the United States badly needed firm and wise piloting during its transition from war to peace, from a predominantly rural economy to a predominantly urban and industrial economy, and from a predominantly white, Anglo-Saxon, Protestant society to an ethnically and religiously much more diverse one, this stewardship was lacking. As the war economy wound down, large sectors of the economy, particularly in agriculture, were struggling to cope with changing patterns of demand, while in industry there were new conflicts not only between the unions and the bosses but also between the workers themselves.

In Europe the situation was considerably worse and significantly less stable. To the orthodox dreamers on the left and the right, these conflicts were nothing but the birth pangs of a new order that would sweep away the sullied and dirty compromises of bourgeois democracy. But if the world revolution dreamed up by communist theoreticians had not followed from the war, neither had a reestablishment of the old order and its imagined firm sense of purpose and destiny. There was fighting everywhere, bitterness, and violence against or by the state. The Western world was seeking a new order.

Renaissance in Harlem

I, too, am America.
—Langston Hughes, "I, Too," 1924

....

NINETEEN TWENTY-TWO WAS A YEAR OF BEGINNINGS AND REBIRTHS.
It was a good year for modernist literature, with the publication of
James Joyce's *Ulysses* in Paris and the great poem *The Waste Land* by
T. S. Eliot in London, of Upton Sinclair's great American satire *Babbitt*
and Ludwig Wittgenstein's *Tractatus Logico-Philosophicus*.

On May 18 a group of men had made modernist history simply
by having dinner together at the Majestic Hotel in Paris. The diners
were Marcel Proust, James Joyce, the great choreographer and impre-
sario Sergei Diaghilev, composers Igor Stravinsky and Erik Satie,
Pablo Picasso, and critic Clive Bell. The men had found nothing interesting to say to one another, however. Joyce came late and Proust
even later, at half past two in the morning, by which time the Joyce
was snoring peacefully in his chair. Stravinsky was heard to say that
he detested Beethoven, and eventually Joyce woke up and admitted

to Proust that he had never read any of his works. Proust admitted he had never read Joyce, either.

Across the Atlantic, 1922 marked another kind of beginning: that of a new culture, the Harlem Renaissance. Part cultural blossoming, part political movement, part artistic statement, and part social phenomenon, the Harlem Renaissance—which owed its name to the bustling, exhilarating, and hopeful place that had given birth to it—was a truly historic moment, the awakening of a whole population to an identity that was an expression of their own bitter experiences and stubborn hopes.

In moments of excitement and uncertainty, works of art can take on great importance. This had been the case a year earlier, in 1921, when the magazine *Crisis*, the organ of the National Association for the Advancement of Colored People (NAACP), had launched one of America's most brilliant literary careers with the publication of nineteen-year-old Langston Hughes's poem "The Negro Speaks of Rivers":

> I've known rivers:
> I've known rivers ancient as the world and older than the
>   flow of human blood in human veins.
> My soul has grown deep like the rivers.
>
> I bathed in the Euphrates when dawns were young.
> I built my hut near the Congo and it lulled me to sleep.
> I looked upon the Nile and raised the pyramids above it.
> I heard the singing of the Mississippi when Abe Lincoln
>   went down to New Orleans, and I've seen its muddy
>   bosom turn all golden in the sunset.
> I've known rivers:
> Ancient, dusky rivers.
>
> My soul has grown deep like the rivers.[1]

The sense of deathless history, of a breath flowing through the centuries of what had been a brutally disrupted past for most African American families, touched a chord with many of Hughes's readers. Here was a new way of seeing history and the present.

The Afro-American Realty Company

MANY FACTORS SHAPE an extraordinary historical moment. At the beginning of the twentieth century, Harlem had been run down and all but derelict, victim of a property boom gone bust. Speculators had

New hope: Street scene in Harlem.

built apartments for middle-class families here, mostly white, but there had been too much construction, and the supply of housing had far outstripped demand. In 1908 a black real estate developer, Philip Payton, and his Afro-American Realty Company, had begun to buy or lease empty buildings and to rent them out to black tenants who had arrived in New York as part of the beginning of the mass migration northward of African Americans from the Deep South. They had responded to the need for labor in factories emptied of white Americans who had enlisted for the war, as well as to their urge to escape the bludgeoning daily racism of life in the Jim Crow states. They came mainly from Virginia, North Carolina, South Carolina, and Georgia, and from the British West Indies.

The influx of tens of thousands of black tenants around the beginning of the twentieth century had the predictable consequence of causing many of the remaining whites to leave. Between 1920 and 1930, some 120,000 white Harlem inhabitants went elsewhere and 90,000 blacks moved to the area. In 1920, 32 percent of the people living in the neighborhood were African American; ten years later, this proportion had risen to 70 percent. The wealthiest blacks lived on West 139th St., dubbed "Strivers' Row," a "block of tan brick houses, flanked by rows of trees . . . , designed in the early twentieth century by [Beaux Arts architect] Stanford White, at the time when Harlem was . . . German."[2]

It was the right moment for a new beginning. The Harlem Renaissance would not have been possible without the second and third postslavery generations, ready to rediscover their own cultural identity and to find a voice, or without the surge in black self-awareness and self-confidence engendered by the valor of black soldiers in the First World War. Another factor helped in this extraordinary cultural awakening: the adventurous cultural climate created by Prohibition.

By 1920 the cultural alchemy that was to become the Harlem Renaissance had created a bubbling, heady brew of gifted young people—poets, writers, singers, musicians, artists—seeking a new voice for themselves. They met and mingled in Harlem's businesses and jazz clubs (which were overwhelmingly owned by whites) and produced a vibrant array of literary and political magazines.

Journals for a Better World

THE MOST INFLUENTIAL PUBLICATION of the Harlem Renaissance was *The Crisis*. It was the official journal of the NAACP—"the moral and political conscience of the nation on the issue of institutional racism"—and still exists today.[3] It had been founded in 1910 by the formidable writer, civil rights activist, and visionary W. E. B. Du Bois, author of *The Souls of Black Folk* (1903), a collection of trailblazing sociological essays and sketches, and the leading black intellectual of his day.[4]

After obtaining a bachelor's degree at the historically black Fisk University in Nashville, Tennessee, Du Bois had gone on to get a second bachelor's degree, this one in history, at Harvard, where he came under the influence of the legendary philosopher William James. After further study in Berlin and wide travel in Europe, Du Bois received a doctorate from Harvard, the first African American to do so. His success provoked continuing attempts to slap him down: in 1923, in a front-page editorial, a Dallas newspaper declared of the fifty-five-year-old Du Bois: "The arrogant, ebony-head, thick-lipped, kinky-haired Negro 'educator' must be put in his place and made to stay there."[5]

Angered but not deterred by such outbursts of hostility, Du Bois chose to build a better future for blacks by attaining social acceptance through education. Even so, his magazine *The Crisis* was considered sufficiently dangerous that in 1920 a Mississippi judge had jailed a black minister for selling copies of it. Du Bois supported the idea of

Father figure: W. E. B. Du Bois was a towering figure among African American civil rights activists and advocates.

the "talented tenth," an elite group of liberally educated and socially respectable blacks who would lead their race forward to greater sociopolitical confidence, and he used *The Crisis* to present the views of NAACP leaders, including writer and diplomat James Weldon Johnson, and to promote younger black poets and intellectuals.

Charles S. Johnson's *Opportunity*, founded in 1922 as the mouthpiece for the National Urban League and also still published today, served much the same role, providing, in Johnson's words, "an outlet for young Negro writers and scholars whose work was not acceptable to other established media because it could not be believed to be of standard quality despite the superior quality of much of it."[6] Though, like *The Crisis*, in general it sought to showcase a well-educated and well-behaved black America—the "new Negro" in his Sunday best, as it were—*Opportunity* also provided a platform for black defiance.

The young Langston Hughes—the future poet laureate of the Harlem Renaissance—was a perfect example of Du Bois's talented tenth. Grandson of Mary Langston, the first black woman to graduate from Oberlin College in Ohio, Hughes was a star pupil at his Cleveland high school, had already worked as an English teacher in Mexico, and was now a student of mining engineering at New York's prestigious Columbia University. But though Du Bois had provided a vital conduit for his first literary efforts, Hughes chafed at the restraints of his expectations: Du Bois, like many of his generation, expected Hughes and other rising stars to subordinate artistic impera- tives to the political needs of the wider movement for black *equality* and, specifically, racial integration. By contrast, Hughes and his con- temporaries regarded themselves as artists first and political activists second, and even emphasized differences between the races rather than seeking to lessen or downplay them. By 1926, a new, more radical magazine was on the stands: Wallace Thurman's *Fire!!*

Thurman was just twenty-four years old when he quit his position as editor of *The Messenger*, a black socialist magazine, to start *Fire!!* Rather than presenting an impressive and unexceptionable— essentially middle-class—black elite, as *The Crisis* and *Opportunity* were seeking to do, the new journal unapologetically introduced what Thurman regarded as a more genuine picture of black America: "uneducated, crude, and scrappy black men and women depicted without tinsel or soap."[7] Thurman had recruited his contributors from the ranks of the older journals; they included Hughes, Du Bois's future son-in-law Countee Cullen, writers Gwendolyn Bennett and Zora Neale Hurston, journalist John P. Davis, painter and illustrator Aaron Douglas, and writer and painter Richard Bruce Nugent.

Though their subject matter could be daring (Nugent's short story "Smoke, Lilies, and Jade" is believed to have been the first open depiction of black homosexuality), all seven were, like Thurman himself, university-educated and very far from crude. Hurston, known as the "Queen of the Renaissance," was particularly keen on the tinseled aspects of Harlem life. She confidently referred to herself and other black intellectuals and artists as "the niggerati." Rebuked for coining such a racially charged term, she replied, "I am not tragically colored. I do not belong to the sobbing school of Negrohood. . . . I do not weep at the world—I am too busy sharpening my oyster knife."[8]

Hurston had grown up in the entirely black community of Eatonville, Florida, where all positions of authority and responsibility were filled by black people and discrimination was unknown, to the point that she was able to declare in a 1928 essay, "I remember the very day that I became colored"—namely, in 1904, at the age of thirteen, when she was sent to high school in Jacksonville, a Jim Crow stronghold. (The Massachusetts-born Du Bois had experi- enced a similar shock upon his arrival in Tennessee in 1885.) New York City, to which Hurston moved in 1925, was not Jack- sonville, but it was not Eatonville, either. "Beside the waters of the Hudson," she admitted in the same essay, "I feel my race. . . . Some- times I feel discriminated against, but it does not make me angry.

It merely astonishes me. How can anyone deny themselves the pleasure of my company?"[9]

Hurston's dismissive urbanity, a witty pretense that there was no problem anyway, was an unusual line of opposition to the efforts of Du Bois and other older blacks for social respectability and racial integration. More common was the view of Hurston's close friend Hughes, who, in a celebrated 1926 essay, described "the mountain standing in the way of any true Negro art in America—this urge within the race toward whiteness, the desire to pour racial individuality into the mold of American standardization, and to be as little Negro and as much American as possible."[10]

Some young intellectuals were prepared to go further. Artist Aaron Douglas, in tones reminiscent of the black separatist Marcus Garvey, went so far as to declare: "We believe that the Negro is fundamentally, essentially different from their Nordic neighbors. We are proud of that difference. We believe these differences to be greater spiritual endowment, greater sensitivity, greater power for artistic expression and appreciation. We believe Negro art should be trained and developed rather than capitalized and exploited."[11]

Douglas created several powerful illustrations for the first issue of *Fire!!* in November 1926, and it helped to make his name as the leading visual artist of the Harlem Renaissance. But this was to be the only issue that made it to the stands—the journal quickly folded for lack of financial support.

Not that there were no backers for the talented tenth, even if they rejected that epithet. Having fallen out with his wealthy father, Hughes, for example, would soon benefit for several years from the largesse of Charlotte Osgood Mason, a white heiress in her seventies, known to her many Harlem beneficiaries as "Mother." Though herself a long-term recipient of their help, the irrepressible Zora Neale Hurston cheekily dubbed Mason and other white supporters of the Harlem Renaissance "negrotarians."

Identity Games

IN THE WIDER WORLD, the prolific output of black writers was easily overshadowed by the publication of Carl Van Vechten's controversial 1926 roman à clef, *Nigger Heaven*. Van Vechten, a photographer as well as a journalist and writer, was one of Hurston's "negrotarians"; his novel described a love affair between a prim young black librarian and an aspiring but undisciplined black writer in "the great black walled city" of Harlem.

A white, middle-class boy with a taste for opera, modern dance, beautiful young men, and artistic rebellion, Van Vechten was attracted to outsiders and soon began to play an important part in the Harlem Renaissance. As black writers had done before him, Van Vechten made use of the idiom and rhythms of black speech among the young "sheiks" and "shebas": "Dis place," says Rose, who both pays and is paid for sex, "where Ah met you—Harlem. Ah calls et, specherly tonight, Ah calls et Nigger Heaven! I jes' nacherly think dis heah is Nigger Heaven!"[12]

But Van Vechten did not spend much time describing the lives of the working poor or any kind of underclass; instead, he dwelled on the black rich, or rather two distinct groups of them: on the one hand, the hard-drinking, cocaine-sniffing decadent rich, and their sordid and often violent world; and on the other, those of the bourgeois "blue vein club," well-educated, lighter-skinned blacks who distanced themselves from the darker-skinned, even occasionally passing for white.

Despite some supportive characters, lack of black solidarity was a marked feature of Van Vechten's novel. "Don't [Negroes] want a member of their race to get on?" asks the would-be writer, Byron. "Where have you been living?" answers his fair-skinned black friend Dick, who is about to "cross the line" and live as a white man. "They *do* not. You'll have to fight your own race harder than you do the other. . . . If they're in trouble they go to white lawyers, and they go to white banks and white insurance companies. . . . Most of 'em . . . pray to a white God. You won't get much help from the race."[13] As for white people, "I believe," says the prim young librarian, "that they actually prefer us when we're not respectable."[14]

Du Bois, always anxious to present a "respectable" picture of his race, slammed Van Vechten's book as "an affront to the hospitality of black folk and to the intelligence of whites."[15] Other black intellectuals, however, defended it as a product of artistic freedom and anyway true to life, and white middle-class readers responded enthusiastically, with the book igniting a fashionable interest in Harlem culture, both high and low.

Though Du Bois was taking a more and more conservative stance toward literary Harlem, his political stance was moving further to the left. In 1927, increasingly interested in the economics of class distinctions, he paid a visit to Soviet Russia.

....

THE BLACK CULTURAL REVIVAL had many facets. There was Du Bois with his Pan-African Congress, petitioning major powers not only to grant a greater number of enforceable civil rights to blacks everywhere but also to decolonize Africa; there was Marcus Garvey, a forceful Jamaican orator and politician who sought to repatriate all African Americans to Africa in a movement appropriately named Black Zionism; and there was everything in between. It was a climate marked by bitterness and determination to break out of the racial boundaries set by white America—but, most important, it featured an incredible optimism that a new beginning might be possible. "For generations in the mind of America, the Negro has been more of a formula than a human being—a something to be argued about, condemned or defended, to be 'kept down,' or 'in his place,' or 'helped up,' to be worried with or worried over, harassed or patronized, a social bogey or a social burden," wrote Alain Locke, one of the greatest exponents of the spiritual rebirth of black culture, in an essay entitled "Enter the New Negro." "Harlem, as we shall see, is . . . the home of the Negro's 'Zionism.' The pulse of the Negro world has begun to beat in Harlem."[16]

The majority of the inhabitants of the new Harlem, however, simply wanted a decent life without the humiliating daily experiences constantly meted out to people of color. They also wanted to have fun, and it was this aspect of the great Harlem Renaissance that was to make it famous beyond the boundaries of the district and a small circle of literature lovers who admired young black poets whose works were only just beginning to hit the literary mainstream.

For most whites, Harlem meant entertainment, and principally jazz, "the most significant, the most indigenous and unprecedented American music of the 1920s."[17] Before the 1920s, jazz, like blues, had existed as black music only, almost unknown to white Americans. But at the beginning of the decade commercial radio stations spread the new sound, with popular white entertainers such as bandleader Paul Whiteman, the "King of Jazz," helping to bring it a little closer to the mainstream. (It was Whiteman who, in 1923, was to commission George Gershwin's *Rhapsody in Blue*.)

White audiences were ready to pay to see black musicals, too. And when the theaters closed, they streamed uptown into the late-night bars and clubs of Harlem to feel the beat, however muffled in their presence, of the Negro pulse. By 1923 many were heading for the Cotton Club, a whites-only establishment run from his cell in Sing Sing prison by the English-born gangster Owney "The Killer"

Madden. All the waiters and most of the entertainers at the Cotton Club were black, though the leggy chorus girls were expected to be lighter-skinned ("tall, tan and terrific"), and some whites, including Gershwin, Irving Berlin, Mae West, and Judy Garland, did perform on "celebrity Sunday nights."

Standard fare for the white guests, however, were reassuring scenes from the "Old South" or "darkest Africa": a cheerful band of "darkies" on the veranda of a cotton baron's mansion, their slave quarters painted into the backdrop, or a troupe of painted "savages" gyrating to frenzied drums. But beneath the crystal chandeliers, among the tables covered with red-and-white gingham, first-rate entertainment was also to be had: Duke Ellington, Bessie Smith, Louis Armstrong, Lena Horne, and a whole firmament of other black stars made their show business debut, or their name, at the Cotton Club—and made its owner a fortune into the bargain.

With the opening of the Savoy Ballroom in 1926, black music took another step forward. The now familiar Cotton Club "hot jazz"—which "vomited, neighed, barked, and snorted"—was meta-morphosing.[18] The dancing it accompanied, ever less restrained, turned into jitterbugging or Lindy Hopping—the latter named, surprisingly enough, for the aviator Charles Lindbergh. It was at the elegant, pink-walled Savoy that the new style was to find its most enthusiastic exponents, including pianist and composer Duke Ellington, drummer Chick Webb, and, later, singer Ella Fitzgerald and pianist and orchestra leader Count Basie. With his 1931 hit "It Don't Mean a Thing," Ellington was to give the new music its last-ing name: swing.

Unlike the Cotton Club, the Savoy was not segregated; under white ownership (reputedly that of Chicago mobster Al Capone) but black management, it welcomed patrons of both races. The only re-stricted area of its vast ballroom, which could accommodate up to four thousand people, was the famed northeast corner, where the very best dancers, most of them black professionals, competed for the laurels of the evening, cheered on by hundreds of the less proficient. "The music shivered and broke, cracked and smashed. Jungle land. Hottentots and Bantus under the amber moon."[19]

Despite the lack of formal segregation, the young poet Langston Hughes had nothing but contempt for the "corner" phenomenon of exceptional black dancers being gaped at, as he saw it, by white onlookers, as if they were visiting a zoo: "The lindy-hoppers at the Savoy even began to practice acrobatic routines," he wrote, "and to do absurd things for the entertainment of the whites, that probably never would have entered their heads to attempt for their own effort-less amusement. Some of the lindy-hoppers had cards printed with their names on them and became dance professors teaching the tourists. Then Harlem nights became show nights for the Nordics."[20]

Hughes, himself the son of a well-to-do family, may have been overlooking the importance of the "show nights" as a source of income for the Harlem dancers. But it was impossible to escape the intrinsic ambivalence, if not outright hostility, at the base of race re-lations in almost every walk of life.

Harlem Shadows

A YOUNGER GENERATION OF BLACKS was tired of staying where white prejudice had put them, and 1922 witnessed articulations of a newly confident African American culture, among them the publication of *Harlem Shadows*, a slim book of poetry. It was one of the first books by a black author to bear the imprint of a prestigious mainstream publisher, Harcourt, Brace, whose authors included T. S. Eliot and Virginia Woolf. The author's name was Claude McKay.

The poem that gave the collection its title described the author's deep ambivalence about life in Negro Harlem, where young black women reduced to prostitution were wearily haunting the streets at night in their "slippered feet" in search of clients, distraction, and per-haps redemption. It culminated in an indictment of the society that gave them no other choice:

> Ah, stern harsh world, that in the wretched way
> Of poverty, dishonor and disgrace,
> Has pushed the timid little feet of clay.
> The sacred brown feet of my fallen race!
> Ah, heart of me, the weary, weary feet
> In Harlem wandering from street to street.

McKay was one of the thousands of recent arrivals in Harlem who had come to make a different life for himself, but he was more for-tunate than most. The youngest of a comfortable farming family in Clarendon, Jamaica, he had not been subject to the savagery of southern racism as a child. In 1912, at age twenty-three, he had come to the United States to study agronomy at the Tuskegee Institute in Alabama, a former teachers' college founded by Booker T. Washington in the previous century as part of the drive for higher education for black Americans.

Rebelling against the regimented teaching style at Tuskegee, and shocked by the experience of racial segregation and daily discrimination in Alabama and other American states, McKay had eventually abandoned his university studies and had moved north. In New York he had opened a restaurant, and closed it, bankrupt; he had worked as a waiter on the railways; and he had become involved in left-wing politics. All the while he had been writing poetry. His lyric gift and the passion evident in his writing brought McKay quick recognition as one of the most promising voices of his generation.

The poet, meanwhile, had decided not to stay in a country in which black people like himself could be hunted through the streets. McKay sailed for Britain, armed with a letter of introduction to George Bernard Shaw. In London, however, he encountered a different but still pervasive form of social exclusion. He found it difficult to make a connection with white British society, whose members he described as "a strangely unsympathetic people, as coldly chilling as their English fog."[21]

McKay quickly found that as a dark-skinned foreigner he was more or less explicitly expected to remain among his kind, and he found company in a club for "Coloured Servicemen" whose members, many of them from Britain's colonies, related stories that sharpened his own outlook on the British Empire and the position of its subjects. Eventually McKay found other welcoming niches in the vast edifice of London society. Even in the United States, he had been keenly interested in left-wing politics. Now, at the International Socialist Club, he became immersed in the fervent ideological debates between British Communists and Russians or Poles of Jewish descent, "dogmatists and doctrinaires of radical left ideas: Socialists, Communists, anarchists, syndicalists, one-big-unionists, and trade unionists, soapboxers, poetasters, scribblers, editors of little radical sheets which flourish in London."[22]

Once back from England, Claude McKay had intensified his political activism. He briefly became co-editor of the Marxist magazine *The Liberator* but soon left the job because of political differences with other members of the staff. He was also restless, and in 1922, the year of the publication of his collection *Harlem Shadows*, he set off again, this time bound for Moscow, where he was to meet Trotsky and attend the Fourth Congress of the Communist International.

After his visit to Russia, McKay remained in Europe for another twelve years. He traveled to Germany, then to France, where he settled for several years in the Paris expat community; after that he continued to Spain and Morocco. His restlessness may have been accentuated by his homosexuality, which also made him feel like a pariah, a man who could never take for granted that he would not be viciously attacked. But in contrast to older intellectuals such as Du Bois, who were full of hope for a better future, McKay felt that the war had shattered many of the ideals he had grown up to love: "And now this great catastrophe has come upon the world, proving the real hollowness of nationhood, patriotism, racial pride, and most of the things one was taught to respect and reverence."[23]

To McKay and his generation, respect and reverence were yesterday's virtues. A new and very different culture was celebrated in Harlem, and it attracted not only tourists but also other artists who were ready to understand the rhythms of the "new Negro" as the heartbeat of their own time. Their interest was not so much in the political debates within the black community but in its vibrant, defiant, and joyous cultural life.

The Creation of the World

BLACK MUSIC, HOWEVER, did not remain in a cultural ghetto. It was already being played on Broadway as well as uptown in Harlem, with Noble Sissle and the great ragtime pianist Eubie Blake producing highly popular black musicals as early as 1921. The 1920s musical was something quite different from its predecessor of earlier decades, the Viennese-style operetta; rather than "a play dotted with occasional songs . . . [it] was essentially a garland of songs and dances strung on a thin plot line, with occasional spectacular 'production numbers' planned at strategic points."[24]

Although the field was dominated by white composers such as Jerome Kern, Irving Berlin, and George and Ira Gershwin, the traffic-jam success of Sissle and Blake's *Shuffle Along* and *Chocolate Dandies* had launched some legendary careers, including those of singer Paul Robeson and dancer Josephine Baker, at the time a teenage chorus girl.

Shuffle Along, described by Langston Hughes as "a honey of a show, bright, funny, rollicking, and gay, with a dozen danceable, singable tunes," was the first production with black writers and an all-black cast to run in the heart of New York's entertainment mile.[25] During its phenomenal run of 484 nights, black audience members were no longer relegated to the balcony but sat in the main-floor seats, following a story whose characters were not burlesque minstrels but people with emotional complexity and depth, and whose music was inspired not by white vaudeville but by jazz bands.

The composer George Gershwin had first heard jazz when he was a child—he had roller-skated past a club and been spellbound by the sounds emanating from within. He came back time and again to immerse himself in the syncopations, unfamiliar harmonies, and song lines of this music, which he himself would later help to make famous with works such as *Rhapsody in Blue* (premiered 1924), which announced a new era from its very first tones, a drawn-out, dirty glissando on a solo clarinet that continues to cackle and laugh and eventually is joined by a muted trumpet and then by a piano.

There are still original recordings and piano rolls on which Gershwin himself plays the piece—his style not grand and symphonic but playful, fast-paced, and punctuated by stomps and whirls, conjuring up the image of exuberant revelers on a late-night dance floor somewhere in Harlem. The way was open for other composers to assimilate elements of jazz into their work, be it Maurice Ravel in the wonderful blues movement of his violin sonata (1923–1927), William Walton in his *Façades* extravaganza for voice and band (1923), or French composer Darius Milhaud, who had come across jazz on a visit to Harlem a year before the 1923 premiere of his ballet suite *La création du monde*.

Jazz was fun and new, but it could also send a political message. Opera composers began to use jazz elements as a signature of the new era, an era of universal human rights and of stories belonging to the little people, whether in Gershwin's *Porgy and Bess* (1935), in Ernst Krenek's *Johny spielt auf* (1927), whose protagonist is a black jazz musician and which created a political scandal and was picketed by hordes of angry Nazis in front of the theaters, or in the early stage works of Kurt Weill, who would eventually go on to write *Mahagonny* (1927) and *The Threepenny Opera* (1930).

The range and complexity of black culture in a wider cultural sphere is epitomized by two stars of the stage whose character and ambitions could not have been more different. Born in St. Louis, Missouri, in 1906, Josephine Baker had learned her musical craft in *Shuffle Along* but soon felt ready to strike out on her own, and in 1925 she starred in *La Revue Nègre* at the Théâtre des Champs-Élysées in Paris. The show was a wild success and went on tour through Europe.

Globe-trotting aesthete and diarist Harry Graf Kessler met Baker in Berlin the next year, at the home of playwright Karl Vollmoeller. Having been promised that "fabulous things" would happen that night, the cosmopolitan count recorded in his diary that he found the men "surrounded by half a dozen of naked girls and Miss Baker, stark naked but for a red gauze loincloth and the little Landshoff girl . . . as

The American dancer Josephine Baker became an international star, causing scandal and sensation wherever she went.

a boy in a dinner jacket. . . . The naked girls were lounging or dancing in between the four or five men in their dinner jacket, and the Landshoff girl, who really looks a picture of a boy, was dancing modern jazz dances with Baker to the sounds of the gramophone."[26] Berlin decadence had arrived.

Baker's skyrocketing fame rested in equal parts on her uninhibited sex appeal and her uncomplicated willingness to play to colonialist and racist stereotypes. Her most famous outfit consisted of nothing but a banana skirt combined with heavy, "oriental" necklaces and earrings and perfectly slicked-back hair, and occasionally offset with a huge tail of ostrich feathers. Her carefully honed appearance was a perfect mix of an imaginary Africa where all inhibitions stayed behind and a sophisticated, ultramodern sensibility of sleek, abstract stage sets and jazz rhythms. Her wildly ecstatic dances were sufficiently indecent to see her appearances banned in Vienna, Prague, Budapest, and Munich, which only increased her magnetic appeal to a public for whom she had become an orientalist erotic fantasy incarnate.

Like Baker, the actor and singer Paul Robeson owed his success to the stage and to his skill at portraying black characters in a predominantly white theater, but that is where the similarities end. Robeson was a college football star and class valedictorian who went on to graduate from Columbia Law School—an astonishingly accomplished young man who had drifted into acting as an extracurricular pastime and soon found himself starring in an off-Broadway production of *Shuffle Along*, as well as other plays. He had not intended to become an actor and actually worked as a lawyer for a while, but the racism he encountered in the legal profession, on the one hand, and his handsome physique, his phenomenally resonant bass-baritone voice, and the natural dignity of his appearance, on the other, made him an almost instant star at a time when many "African" roles were still played by white actors in blackface.

Robeson's breakthrough came with Eugene O'Neill's *The Emperor Jones*, effectively a one-man play telling the story of an escaped convict who becomes emperor of a Caribbean island, only to be killed by the superstitious islanders. His success in that play led him to appear in the musical *Showboat* and to become one of the first black actors to play Othello, in London. Despite his distinguished career, Robeson constantly had to battle with racist attitudes and, in the United States, segregation. He became increasingly uneasy performing of a heritage that was not his own, and eventually enrolled at the University of London to study African languages and recover the historical roots of his identity. His interest in the cultural background of African Americans went hand in hand with a political awakening and gradual radicalization, which would eventually lead him to visit the Soviet Union and to become actively involved in politics.

"The world broke in two in 1922 or thereabouts," wrote Willa Cather in her essay collection *Not Under Forty*.[27] The two parts resulting from this breakup were "the forward-goers" and "the backward," the latter essentially those born before the last decade of the nineteenth century, with Cather herself "one of their number." "The backward" showed little sustained interest in the Harlem Renaissance—O'Neill's *The Emperor Jones* notwithstanding—but neither did America's younger white writers, Cather's "forward-goers." Progressives such as John Dos Passos and John Steinbeck stuck to what they knew, and the decadents and cynics and experimenters—Scott and Zelda Fitzgerald, Henry Miller, Ernest Hemingway, E. E. Cummings, Thomas Wolfe, and even, briefly, William Faulkner—were all in Paris, in the middle of their "summer of 1,000 parties."[28]

· 1923 ·

Beyond the Milky Way

On this plate (H335H), three stars were found, 2 of which were novae, and 1 proved to be a variable, later identified as a Cepheid—the first to be recognized in M31.

—Edwin Hubble, 1923

....

ON OCTOBER 5, 1923, ON MOUNT WILSON IN PASADENA, CALIFORNIA, our place in the universe was overturned forever. Edwin Hubble, a thirty-three-year-old astronomer and former high school teacher who had been working at the Mount Wilson Observatory for four years, wrote that he had discovered a Cepheid variable star within the galaxy known as M31 or Andromeda. Self-confident and ebullient, Hubble knew the importance of his discovery and could not wait to notify his predecessor at Mount Wilson, the astronomer Harlow Shapley, with whom he was engaged in a professional but not always very cordial rivalry.

Shapley had made a name for himself five years earlier with a series of papers on the size and architecture of our galaxy, the Milky Way. In contrast to received opinion, he had argued that it was larger by a factor of ten than the span of thirty thousand light-years that had been previously estimated. He had also made another startling claim: in this larger galaxy, containing uncounted stars and planets, our sun was not at the center—in fact, it was not anywhere near the center. Our solar system, one of a vast number of solar systems, was positioned on the sidelines of the immense Milky Way, sixty-five thousand light-years away from the galaxy's center.

Though only a comparatively junior staff astronomer at Mount Wilson, Shapley was aware of the psychological implications of his discovery, as he wrote to his employer, George Ellery Hale: "The first man, away back in the later Pliocene, who knocked out a hairy elephant with his club, or saw his pretty reflection, or received a compliment, became suddenly conceited (it was a mutation) and there immediately evolved the first reflective thought in the world. It was: 'I am the center of the Universe!' Whereupon he took himself a wife, transmitted this bigotry of his germ plasm, and through hundreds of thousands of years the same thought without much alteration has been our heritage."[1] With his confident assertion, Shapley demolished the delusion to which a whole species had been subject.

A brilliant author with a robust sense of his own abilities, Shapley had seen his great chance when he was invited to present his opinions to an audience of specialists in "The Great Debate," a confrontation in 1920 between the two most important but as yet unprovable views of the nature of the universe. While his opponent had argued that the Milky Way was not the only galaxy in space and that other nebulae that had been observed were in fact independent galaxies, Shapley had taken the position that most astronomers then agreed on: that there were no stars, nothing at all, outside the Milky Way and that our galaxy effectively constituted the entire universe. His fellow astronomers had duly taken note of the thirty-five-year-old Shapley and rewarded him the same year with the directorship of Harvard College Observatory.

A New Eye into Space

IN 1923, EDWIN HUBBLE was still a relative beginner in professional astronomy, but like Shapley, he was possessed of a firm belief in his own powers. Having studied mathematics, astronomy, and philosophy in Chicago and jurisprudence, Spanish, and literature at Oxford, he had returned from Britain after his father's death in 1913 in order to help support his mother and siblings. After a year of high school teaching, however, he had gone back to school at the age of twenty-five to work toward a doctorate in astronomy. He spent the war years in the army but did not see active service, remaining in the United States with the rank of major. In 1919 Hubble was offered his first position as an astronomer, at Mount Wilson Observatory. He would continue to work there for the rest of his life.

Two years before Hubble's arrival, the observatory had been fitted with the new Hooker telescope, the most powerful then in operation. It was a gigantic technological achievement. The 100-inch mirror at its center was ground in California from an enormous glass disc cast at the Saint-Gobain plant in Paris, then transported up a perilous dirt road to the observatory on the back of an early Mack truck. Installed with immense care, it saw first light in November 1919, giving California astronomers an instrument whose resolution and precision were unrivaled anywhere in the world.

Hubble set out to test the hypothesis that the universe might consist of multiple galaxies and that the Milky Way is only one among many. To reach a conclusion, he needed to have a reliable means of measuring the distance between Earth and any celestial object captured by his telescope. In the case of relatively close astronomical objects, the method involved fairly simple trigonometry: scientists measured the apparent change in position of a star at both extremes of Earth's orbit around the sun, and then inserted that figure into a simple equation.

For very distant objects, however, the difference between the two observation points was not large enough to provide a useful result, and a different method was needed. It was found in a paper written twenty years earlier by a little-known but brilliant astronomer, Henrietta Swan Leavitt, who had worked at the Harvard College Observatory as a "computer" for her male colleagues, cataloguing celestial data collected on photographic plates—a slow, painstaking, and boring job far below her intellectual capacities.

Leavitt had posited that a particular class of celestial objects, the so-called Cepheids, which were characterized by a periodic change in their brightness, might be used for such distance measurements. The full cycle of the dimming and intensifying of the light emanating from the star could vary from a few days to a few weeks depending on the object, but it was always stable in any single object. She assumed that the length of the cycle was determined by the size of the star, and that stars of the same size would have the same brightness and periodicity. By determining the period of a star, it was possible to draw conclusions about its size and therefore its maximum brightness. The further away a star was, the less bright it would seem from Earth. But if the period of a distant object was known, its distance could be determined by measuring its apparent brightness and contrasting that with its actual brightness according to its periodicity. The loss in luminosity became a measure of the distance.

Harlow Shapley had used Leavitt's technique in his observations, which resulted in a vastly larger Milky Way than previously thought. Hubble, however, wanted to go much further. The new 100-inch telescope enabled him to find objects that had been all but impossible to identify and describe before. By measuring their period and brightness, he would be able to calculate their distance from Earth. The work took many long and cool nights in the observatory, its roof opened to the stars and the telescope moving almost imperceptibly slowly to keep up with Earth's rotation. Hubble and his assistant would train the telescope on a spot in the night sky and take photographs with exposure times ranging from a few minutes to several hours. He needed to identify some faint signal that had not been analyzed before, evidence of a star that was too far away to be part of the Milky Way.

On October 5, 1923, Hubble recorded in his notebook that he had identified a Cepheid that was part of the Andromeda nebula, known to astronomers as M31. Shapley had calculated that Andromeda was a distant part of our own galaxy and that nothing lay behind it. But Hubble's photographic plate of the Andromeda nebula, which to the untrained eye appears as a large smudge with fuzzy edges surrounded by irregular specks of stars, revealed a Cepheid that he calculated had a period of 31,415 days, making it a giant star seven thousand times brighter than the Sun.

The recorded star was so dim that it could not have been measured without Mount Wilson's powerful new telescope. Its faintness and the length of its period indicated that the star must be one million light-years away from Earth, far outside the confines of Shapley's Milky Way. The only possible conclusion was that there were stars and entire galaxies outside our own. "Dear Shapley," he wrote with deceptive friendliness when his calculations were concluded in February of the following year, "You will be interested to hear that I have found a Cepheid variable in the Andromeda Nebula (M31). I have followed the nebula this season as closely as the weather permitted and in the last five months have netted nine novae and two variables."[2] Driving home his victory, he appended extensive data that proved his point.

Hubble went on to make further discoveries, the most important among which was his explanation for the redshift in the color of distant galaxies. It had already been assumed that the observable color shift in the appearance of celestial objects had some relation to their motion relative to Earth, namely, that the light waves of bodies moving toward Earth at great speed would be compressed and therefore appear slightly shifted toward the blue end of the spectrum, while objects moving away from the observer would have their light waves effectively lengthened and would appear redder than they would if they were stationary. Hubble could show that all distant celestial objects showed some redshift and that the change is more marked the further away the objects are, indicating that the more distant objects are traveling at greater speeds.

Through his observations, Hubble could express the distance and speed of a star in relation to its redshift in a mathematical formula, but he failed to grasp the last implication: if galaxies are moving away from one another, they must once have been closer together, much closer, and an event of immense force billions of years ago must have hurled them into space. It fell to the Belgian astronomer and priest Georges Lemaître to make the obvious connection in 1927: a universe that was still expanding away from a central point must have emerged from a "Cosmic Egg exploding at the moment of the creation."[3] The Big Bang was born in all but name.

Hubble's discovery had revolutionized humanity's conception of its place in the world, and it is difficult to overestimate its long-term effects. Over three millennia, from an essentially local idea of Earth as a disc, the planet had become round and had been dislodged from its position at the center of the universe to be a mere satellite of a sun, which in turn had been found to be one of many in a galaxy of suns, the Milky Way. Now this galaxy was no longer a universe—the only universe—but merely one among countless galaxies in the immense, fathomless, and expanding darkness of space, and Earth had become an infinitesimal dot in a world of unimaginable magnitude. It was the last and perhaps greatest blow to humanity's narcissism, which Shapley had identified in his letter, writing about the caveman who believes himself to be the center of the universe. Humanity was not at the center, and not even prominently placed in the periphery; it appeared to be lost, cast into the darkness and void of deep space as a tiny speck inside the vast apparent emptiness of the universe.

Alice-in-Wonderland Physics

WHILE IN CALIFORNIA the world was shown to be infinitely larger than previously thought possible, scientists in Europe were investigating the strange world of matter at the subatomic level. Their findings and theoretical models of the smallest building blocks of our material reality were disorienting, even deeply shocking.

Perhaps for the first time in modern history, these findings were more of a collaborative endeavor than a story of individual intellectual heroism, as it had been up to Einstein's formulation of the theory of relativity. Several scientists throughout Germany and elsewhere in Europe discussed and elaborated hypotheses that would change the very nature of how we look at the physical universe. One of them, the German professor Werner Heisenberg, was still in his twenties when he made his revolutionary contributions to quantum physics, the next frontier of science after relativity.

Physicists had long been puzzled by the fact that light appeared not only to behave as a smooth, immaterial wave, as expected, but also under certain circumstances to show characteristics expected from particles, despite the fact that according to classical, Newtonian physics it could only be either one or the other, never both wave and particle at the same time. As early as 1900 the German theoretical physicist Max Planck had posited that electromagnetic energy such as ultraviolet radiation, X-rays, or visible light was composed of multiples of a discrete and indivisible energy unit, the quantum. Against all appearances, light had to be looked at not as an immaterial wave but as a wave pattern consisting of individual units of energy.

Planck's hypothesis provided an explanation for some of the questions that were being discussed at the time, but it failed to address others. A new solution came from a revolutionary suggestion by Heisenberg, whose ideas completely upended the traditional understanding of physics. The brilliant young scientist worked with Max Born in Göttingen and Niels Bohr in Copenhagen, where he developed crucial aspects of a new model of the world at the atomic and subatomic levels.

A light quantum (or electron), Heisenberg claimed, was neither a particle nor a wave; rather, it could behave like either, depending on the circumstances and on the moment of observation. It had no fixed observable identity. Indeed, the role of the observer became paramount in physics, as the natural world at once revealed itself and shrouded itself in impenetrable mystery. "Modern atomic physics does not deal with the essence and structure of atoms," he wrote in 1931, "but with what we perceive when we observe them; the emphasis always lies on the concept of the 'process of observation.' The process of observation can no longer be simply objectified, and its result cannot be directly made into a real thing."[4]

The scientist as observer could do no more than record his or her perceptions, but in doing so was further limited by the eccentricities of nature. The act of observation itself, Heisenberg argued, altered the system observed, and to some degree even created it. What was more, at the subatomic level the movement of individual particles (or waves) was essentially random and could not be predicted with any degree of certainty. Even causality, the cornerstone of Newtonian physics, was rejected in favor of mere probability.

The trajectory of an electron around the nucleus of an atom is not a stable path, and in measuring it one can only determine either its position or its impulse, never both. It is not possible to ascribe a particular speed *and* a particular location to any subatomic particle. Any prediction made about its behavior is therefore based purely on probability. At the macroscopic level—the level of human experience—this makes no difference to the prediction of future events because the aggregation of an immense number of probable outcomes at the subatomic level results in near certainty, but at the level of individual particles no outcome is ever certain from one moment to the next.

Germany's strong culture of public lectures by scientists as well as popular scientific literature, much of it written by leading research scientists, meant that Heisenberg's theses were hotly debated among physicists as well as in a wider context. The disturbing implications of his ideas were clear, and they attacked the very foundations of science and of Western thought.

It is worth staying with this idea for a moment. In the seventeenth century, Sir Isaac Newton formulated a series of laws that ever since had been regarded as an accurate and objective description of the physical universe. According to this set of principles, every object had a clearly definable identity and behaved lawfully under all circumstances, according to its motion, its inertia, its gravity, its energy. Everything was either one thing or another, either here or there, either wave or particle. The world functioned like a gigantic clockwork mechanism, chiming the hours with unerring precision.

The concept at the core of Newton's physics, however, was much older and reaches via the Middle Ages straight to ancient Greek philosophy, the authors of the Bible, and the mythical narratives of Mesopotamia. The ideas at stake were identity and duality, the irreducible bedrock of Western thought. Biblical symbolism is dualist, with its heaven and hell, sun and moon, day and night, good and evil, clean and unclean. This had been the matrix of a way of thinking that divided the world into lords and servants, believers and infidels, and it was just as essential that every element in this chain had a

fixed identity that might be transformable but would always be one
or the other. Christian thought had enthusiastically made use of this
principle, which was compromised only by the doctrine of the Holy
Trinity, in which a single being was supposed to be both three and
one, depending on the perspective and the situation—a quantum God,
in a way.

Perhaps the stubbornly illogical doctrine of the Trinity (from its
inception nothing but a theological compromise) kept open intellectual windows for a more flexible kind of logic in the medieval
monks struggling to understand how three could be one. This was
church doctrine, but it flatly contradicted the basic three laws of logic
coming down from Plato: the law of identity (everything is identical
to itself and nothing else), the law of the excluded middle (of any
proposition it must be true that either it or its negation is true), and
the law of noncontradiction (nothing can be true and not true at the
same time). An entire philosophical canon had been constructed on
these laws, and what Newton had done was simply apply them to
nature. As an ethical principle, this exclusive and dualist logic had
been at the heart of the self-perception of people in the West. As a
philosophical principle, this had blossomed into scholasticism, the
Renaissance, and the Enlightenment. As a scientific and finally also
economic principle, it proved capable of creating a new world within
less than four centuries.

Quantum physics and other theoretical developments overturned
the cumulative result of a millennium-old tradition by claiming
that the very matter of the universe was unlike anything Newton had
imagined, and that at its heart lay states of radical uncertainty in
which particles could be two different things, had no fixed identity,
had contradictory characteristics, and were governed not by laws but
by simple chance. The new physics argued that there are no absolute
laws in nature, only statistical probabilities.

Before the war, Einstein had shown Newtonian physics to be a subset of laws he had described in his theory of relativity, a subset that
was valid only within a small spectrum of physical phenomena
that happened to coincide with human experience. The closer any
object approached the speed of light and the longer the distances it
traveled, the more Newton's laws appeared to be no more than
approximations. To understand this cosmic dimension, the observer
had to understand that no position was ever fixed, that every movement was relative to others.

Even physicists balked at such a radical abolition of the laws that
seemed to describe the universe so well. Albert Einstein was the most

famous opponent of Heisenberg's radical conclusions, just as he opposed the idea of an expanding universe and the conclusions it invited. "Quantum mechanics is certainly imposing," he wrote in 1926 in a letter to Max Born. "But an inner voice tells me that it is not yet the real thing. The theory says a lot, but does not really bring us closer to the secret of the 'Old One.' I, at any rate, am convinced that He is not playing dice."[5] Other eminent physicists, Max Planck among them, agreed with him.

How German Is Real Science?

THE DEEP PROBLEM underlying both quantum physics and cosmology was the loss of any intuitive understanding of the world. With every new advance, science made the universe a more unfamiliar, less home-like place in which countless galaxies are hurtling through eternal darkness while the building blocks of matter are mysterious units of no certain identity, ruled only by chance, and objective knowledge becomes an impossible aspiration.

Einstein and Planck were among the most prominent scientists to revolt against this alien and counterintuitive understanding of physics, but while their aversion to the probability-based approach of quantum physics originated in their ultimately religious worldview, which could not reconcile the idea of the "Old One" with a universe built on random events, German scientists soon found themselves embroiled in a very different debate concerned with the supposedly racial character of such a theory. Could it be that scientific theories had become so disorienting simply because so many Jews had had a hand in formulating them?

This jump may seem surprising, as ethnicity does not appear to have any causal link with higher mathematics, but a disproportionately high number of theoretical physicists, from Max Born to Einstein and others, were of Jewish descent. Sociologically, the reason for this lay simply in the fact that during the late nineteenth century, standard physics (which was still overwhelmingly Newtonian) was believed to be a theoretical model of the world that had almost reached completion. Theoretical physics, by contrast, was a marginal research area for cranks and lonely eccentrics, and it offered little funding, little prestige, and few career opportunities. While ethnic Germans were commonly allotted the most prestigious chairs and research positions in standard physics, work in theoretical physics was often left to Jews, or to women such as the brilliant Lise Meitner.

As often in the history of anti-Semitism, the result of social need and pressure was turned against those who had successfully accommodated to it. During the nineteenth century, Jews had been accused of possessing a sharp and "corrosive" intellect, but no creative genius. Now modern science was portrayed as a Jewish invention designed to sap the lifeblood from German culture. Even Heisenberg, who refused to emigrate when Hitler came to power and whose role during the Third Reich continues to be hotly debated, would be attacked as a "white Jew," a gentile carrying the "bacillus" of Jewish thinking, in a 1937 article in the SS newspaper *Das schwarze Korps*.

During the 1920s the debate about "Aryan physics" was in full swing, as its main proponent, the Nobel Prize–winning physicist Philipp Lenard, was to explain in his four-volume *Deutsche Physik* (1936):

> "German physics?" one will ask.—I could equally have spoken of Aryan physics or the physics of peoples of Nordic character. . . . The current literature suggest that we may already be able to speak of the physics of the Japanese; in the past there was a physics of the Arabs. A physics of the negroes is unknown to me; but there has been a broad development of a particularly Jewish physics, . . . Jews are everywhere, and if anyone still defends the idea of an inter-nationalism of the natural sciences, he must subconsciously mean the Jewish ones, which the Jews are creating every-where and in an interchangeable way.[6]

The noble German physics was to be built on *Anschaulichkeit*, on the intuitive understanding of physical processes with a basis in classical, Newtonian physics. While "Jewish physics" was decried as rationalistic and dogmatic, its Aryan counterpart was to privilege an investigation focusing on the categories of "energy" and "force." More than a scientific disagreement, this was a moralizing crusade against the intellectual freedom and speculative creativity associated with some outstanding Jewish scientists.

Lenard was not alone in his rabid anti-Semitism, but the debate about a "German physics" also stood for a wider concern: a revolt by a traditional concept of physics against the counterintuitive arrogance and opacity of modern physical thinking. Quantum physics came to symbolize a modern world that was becoming uncanny to its inhabi-tants, a world that had abandoned empirical evidence and immediate understanding for arcane theory. This revolt went beyond the image of the sciences—throughout Europe and particularly in Germany the advocates of *Lebensphilosophie*, a holistic "philosophy of life," attacked what they saw as the coldly mechanistic rationalist world-view underpinning society.

Being and Time

TERMS SUCH AS "energy," "power," and "life" were at the very heart of a cultural debate that went far beyond the confines of science. It was framed by the oracular Oswald Spengler, whose own thought on the dichotomy between pulsating, primeval life and dead, abstract reason owed much to the father of all antirationalist thought of this period, Friedrich Nietzsche. Nietzsche's subtle, poetic, and entirely unsystematic attacks on academic style and thinking were predestined to be quoted out of context, and his pithy and often sarcastic observations could be put in the service of a wider assault on rationality itself. To Spengler, the domination of scientific thinking was nothing less than a sign of cultural decadence, as he outlined in his immensely influential *Decline of the West*: "All art, all religion and science, become slowly intellectualized, alien to the land, incomprehensible to the peasant of the soil. With civilization, decline begins. The unfathomably old roots of Being are dried up in the stone-masses of its cities."[7]

A rational, theoretical understanding of the world, Spengler claimed, was possible only at the price of deadening the world and by "forcing the voices of the blood to be silent," voices that connected every individual to the chain of ancestry and to destiny. Abstract thought, by contrast, was chronically unable to grasp what is truly important, namely, "the when and wherefore, Destiny, blood, all that our intuitive processes touch in our depths."[8] Modernity, then, was a race toward death, a sign of a culture having reached the end of its term. "Cinema, Expressionism, Theosophy, boxing contests, nigger dances, poker, and racing—one can find it all in [ancient] Rome," he wrote, somewhat improbably. "The last man of the world-city no longer wants to live."[9]

Spengler's very German conception of history and culture stood in a context of broadly similar ideas. With the notable exception of the Vienna Circle, which devoted itself to exactly the kind of positivist philosophy so despised by Spengler, philosophers at German-speaking universities turned away from the clarity and rationalism of thinking in the tradition of the Enlightenment and toward different forms of exploration of lived experience and immediacy, be it in

Edmund Husserl's phenomenology, Wilhelm Dilthey's philosophy of life, the impenetrable grammatical games of Martin Heidegger's ontology, or the works of the many disciples of Henri Bergson, a French thinker whose distinction between duration as lived experience and clock time as mechanized measurement divorced from life made him one of the most widely read philosophical authors of his generation.

To a considerable extent this rejection of rationalism was a consequence of experiencing the war. For the postwar generation, reason was no longer the beacon of great things to come, extolled since the Enlightenment; it had darkened, turned against its creators, and shown its potential for utter destruction and insanity. The results of rational inquiry had rocked the civilized world to its foundation and turned men into savages. All values appeared debased, all certainties shaken, all hope perverted. As reason had failed to create the glorious future it had promised, it was time to turn elsewhere. "We are generally experiencing today a full rejection of positivism," wrote the sociologist Alfred Vierkandt in 1920. "We are experiencing a new need for unity . . . a type of thinking which primarily emphasizes the organic rather than the mechanical, the living instead of the dead, the concepts of value, purpose, and goal instead of causality."[10]

This rejection of reason seems almost willfully opposed to science, but it quite arguably played an important role in shaping some of the most creative scientific ideas of its time, notably quantum mechanics, as Werner Heisenberg himself would later write: "It is not by chance that the development that led to this end no longer took place in a time of belief in progress. After the catastrophe of the First World War one understood outside of scholarship as well that there were no firm foundations for our existence, secure for all time."[11]

Weimar Physics

THE SHADOW OF THE WAR and the social climate of the 1920s may indeed have contributed to the conception and formulation of a physics in which the main tenets of logical, scientific thought—identity, causality, objectivity—are dethroned and their place usurped by ambivalence, chance, and uncertainty. While the years before the war had been a period of immense transformation and destabilization, the robustly positivist idea of nineteenth-century science continued to be a strong presence in universities, schools, and newspaper offices. After 1918, this "rationalistic dogmatism" was decried even by mathematicians. One of them, Gustav Doetsch, believed it to be "sinking with violent convulsions into its grave in order to make room for a new spirit, a new life-feeling."[12]

The debate about a "German physics" ran its course and would soon die out. But there is another, more plausible and more intriguing hypothesis about the discomforting world described by mainly German physicists after 1918, an intriguing thesis put forward by the historian Paul Forman. The subatomic world described by Heisenberg and others, Forman argued, was an unpredictable and hybrid world of perspective, chance, and probable outcomes. In his view this disconcerting scenario, governed by the principle of uncertainty, had a great deal in common with the social and political realities of Weimar Germany. Science seemed to mirror society.

Forman fielded some impressive witnesses for his thesis, among others the eminent physicist Erwin Schrödinger (he of the famous cat), who wrote in 1932: "In a word, we all are members of our cultural milieu. So soon as the orientation of our interest plays any role whatsoever in a matter, the milieu, the cultural complex, the Zeitgeist, or whatever one wishes to call it, must exert its influence. In all areas of a culture there will exist common features deriving from the world view and, much more numerous still, common stylistic features—in politics, in art, in science."[13]

Scientists were not outside of their society, they were part of it, and the game of perspectives continued. Seen from the vantage point of its being embedded in its cultural context, the new and puzzling quantum physics was the exact opposite of a coldly abstract theoretical game and indeed approached the intuitive qualities of the vitalist philosophy that was so fashionable after the war. If the mechanistic and rationalist worldview of the old order had led straight to the killing machines of the Western Front, the philosophy of irrational life forces created a counterbalance to this deadly rationality, and the new physics mirrored its cult of energy, willpower, and life. Nature, the younger generation of physicists seemed to claim, is not a giant clockwork, and God does play dice, after all.

The Universe Around Us

TO THE WIDER GENERAL PUBLIC, these debates about science were as irresistibly fascinating and as impenetrably opaque as the results the scientists produced. At a time when there seemed to be little left to believe in, when values and hierarchies had been swept away by the great disillusionment that followed the war, the calm arguments and mathematical formulas of science appealed hugely to the popular imagination, which was fed by a steady stream of articles and books, as well as a growing number of films focusing on scary science and mad scientists, such as Harry Pollard's US release *The Invisible Ray* (1920, now lost), the 1921 Italian production *L'Uomo Meccanico* (The Mechanical Man), *The Power God* by Francis Ford (1925), and the extraordinary Soviet Martian extravaganza *Aelita* (1924).

While movies and novels exploited the unlimited imaginative possibilities of the new scientific magic, books by scientists did their best to explain the actual theories to an ever-wider audience. The British physicist and astronomer James Jeans made popular science books his specialty; they garnered him a great deal more fame than did his scientific work at Cambridge University. His 1929 introduction to cosmology, *The Universe Around Us*, sold out within a month of its publication and went through seven editions within a decade. A second book, *The Mysterious Universe*, published one year later, sold ten thousand copies on the day of publication and went through fifteen editions before 1939.

Science became a metaphor for society. With Germany and France in crisis and shaken by violence on the streets, Russia in the aftermath of its revolution embroiled in a horrific civil war, Italy paralyzed by the conflict between socialists and Fascists, and Austria only beginning to wake up from the loss of its huge empire, a degree of pessimism and foreboding was understandable in continental Europe, but it also, and especially, prevailed in Britain. The historian Richard Overy has pointed out that much of the scientific interest in the United Kingdom was focused on the idea of entropy, "a physical state which tended towards stasis, degeneration and extinction."[14]

In Cambridge, the philosopher and mathematician Bertrand Russell and his Austrian counterpart Ludwig Wittgenstein were famously advocating a combination of intellectual rigor and epistemological modesty; both men were renowned, indeed legendary, for not suffering fools gladly. But two other authors also engaged the intellectual dilemma of a time increasingly and painfully caught between a scientific approach, whose intellectual advances went counter to any intuitive understanding of the world, and the ideological vacuum created by the Great War. Both bore the same surname, Haldane, and they were in fact uncle and nephew.

Richard Burton Haldane was a distinguished politician who had served as secretary of state for war and as lord chancellor, but his busy career had not dissuaded him from also translating and writing on philosophy and science. In his book *The Reign of Relativity* (1921) he tackled head-on the vast implications of Einstein's theory and the new understanding of the natural sciences for the broader realm of culture. He recognized that a new culture of skepticism had developed as a direct result of the war, and that it was accompanied by a new search for big answers that proved dangerously wanting, for "without a permeating faith of some kind, a faith that can compel in ordinary times as well as those of emergency, a people can hardly remain great."[15]

The problem was that truth itself had been shown to be relative, depending on the perspective of the observer. Whereas previous generations had been more or less certain of an objective truth, an objectively knowable world, science, culture, and politics had conspired to destroy this certainty. Building on his reading of Einstein and of the British philosopher of mathematics Alfred North Whitehead, Haldane came to a conclusion that went far beyond the theory of science: "Every particular form of knowledge is relative, and is destined in the end to recognize the boundaries of its own apparent order, and to demand that we should pass over to conceptions of a new character."[16]

To a time looking for answers, Haldane's account of science and philosophy as transitory and bound to the horizon of the observer was a bitter pill to swallow, and it was not sweetened by an analysis authored by his nephew J. B. S. Haldane, an enthusiastic advocate and public defender of Darwinism, even if his strangely prophetic look at the future of science opened up great possibilities. Like his uncle, Jack Haldane was a product of his aristocratic background, but he also carried with him the experience of his generation. Commissioned into the Black Watch after having studied mathematics and classics at Oxford, he had served on the Western Front, as he related in his *Daedalus, or Science and the Future*, published in 1923, which begins:

> As I sit down to write these pages I can see before me two scenes from my experience of the late war. The first is a glimpse of a forgotten battle of 1915. It has a curious suggestion of a rather bad cinema film. Through a blur of dust and fumes there appear, quite suddenly, great black and yellow masses of smoke which seem to be tearing up the surface of the earth and disintegrating the works of man with an almost visible hatred. These form the chief part of the picture, but somewhere in the middle distance one can see a few irrelevant looking human figures, and soon there are

fewer. It is hard to believe that these are the protagonists in the battle. One would rather choose those huge substantive oily black masses which are so much more conspicuous, and suppose that the men are in reality their servants, and playing an inglorious, subordinate, and fatal part in the combat. It is possible, after all, that this view is correct.[17]

This scenario, Haldane writes, is "part of the case against science," and it leads him to ask,

Is Samuel Butler's . . . horrible vision correct, in which man becomes a mere parasite of machinery, an appendage of the reproductive system of huge and complicated engines which will successively usurp his activities, and end by ousting him from the mastery of this planet? Is the machine-minder engaged on repetition-work the goal and ideal to which humanity is tending? Perhaps a survey of the present trend of science may throw some light on these questions.[18]

The trends Haldane foresaw for humanity are striking in many ways. In four hundred years, he wrote, Britain would be covered with windmills producing its energy, which would be stored using liquid hydrogen; contraception would profoundly change sexual morality; the reproduction of plants and animals, including humans, would finally be revolutionized by science. All this was disquieting, even alarming, but

the chemical or physical inventor is always a Prometheus. There is no great invention, from fire to flying, which has not been hailed as an insult to some god. But if every physical and chemical invention is a blasphemy, every biological invention is a perversion. There is hardly one which, on first being brought to the notice of an observer from any nation which has not previously heard of their existence, would not appear to him as indecent and unnatural.[19]

The rule of the natural sciences was as compelling as it was disquieting. To many people the world appeared to have lost its metaphysical anchor, the ultimate pivot of their existence.

No author gave a sharper and more coolly despairing analysis of this than the Prague insurance clerk Franz Kafka, who died of tuberculosis in an Austrian sanatorium in 1924. In his story "The Hunger

A quiet citizen: Many of the characters in Franz Kafka's fiction are overwhelmed by nefarious and anonymous machinery.

Artist" Kafka pens a deviously compelling portrait of what has happened. The hunger artist was famous in the great days of his art, when entire cities followed every day of his fasts with frenzied curiosity. His manager knew to make him break off his fast after forty days, when interest was bound to wane. Much to his annoyance (he would have liked to go on fasting), the artist would then be led out of his cage and given a carefully chosen meal in front of the adoring crowd, complete with military band, only to start fasting again after a rest period. But the great days of the art of hunger are over, people stop coming to his performances, and the artist has been reduced to working in a circus, where the crowds on the way to seeing the wild animals simply lose interest in him, and eventually no one notices that he has simply fasted himself to death. The animal keeper buries the hunger artist without ceremony, relieved because now he can put a young panther, a magnificent animal, in the artist's cage.

On a very obvious level the hunger artist is the proverbial German *Hungerkünstler*, a poor artist who feeds greedily off the adulation his suffering creates and who dies as soon as his public loses interest. But the hunger artist who fasts for forty days, whose fame rests on his martyrdom, and who lives on "in seeming glory, honored by the world," is also the pathetic brother of the Savior himself, a grubby messiah of the fairground whose dubious feats of self-denial have lost their appeal. He dies not heroically but out of lack of public interest. The art of hunger belonged to the spectacles of the past, we are told, but nowadays people have discovered other attractions. Reduced to a marginal place in the circus, the emaciated hunger artist who once commanded universal adoration tries to force people to notice him by fasting on and on, but the best he can hope for are fathers who point him out to their children, telling of times past, and in their eyes he can see "something of the new, coming, more merciful times." In the end, however, his place is taken by a savage feline hunter, the embodiment of strength, freedom, and joy.

Demonstrating his miracles and his suffering on a fairground, Christ himself would not stand a chance against the indifference of a crowd hungry for novelty and sensation. The great self-denier whose agony once transfixed entire peoples has been unceremoniously swept away, and in his place has been put a panther, the very image of a pure, sinuous, pitiless will to live.

In Hubble's world, a world that was no longer at the center of the universe and in which even matter had become at once better understood and more opaque to the human mind, old prophecies were relegated to a forgotten corner of the fairground. The conflict between faith and reason, between the knowledge of experience and the knowledge of science, and between a rationalist approach to the world as represented by the science of the nineteenth century and a new, intuitive grasp on life itself was present in the scientific debates of the day and was carried into a public debate marked by pessimism and bafflement. As the hunger artist ceased being adored after the "great turnaround," people were looking for new attractions, new explanations, new messiahs. Amid fear and hope, the fight for a very different future was beginning to take shape.

Men Behaving Badly

I attach no importance to life
I pin not the least of life's butterflies to importance
I do not matter to life
But the branches of salt the white branches
All the shadow bubbles
And the sea-anemones
Come down and breathe within my thoughts
  —André Breton, "The Spectral Attitudes," 1926

....

WHAT IS A RATIONAL RESPONSE TO LIVING IN A WORLD THAT NO longer makes sense? In Europe, a marginal but growing and highly publicized movement believed it had found the answer: nonsense. Aggressive, subversive, gleefully celebrated nonsense. Nonsense used as a weapon.

It was all art for art's sake in the beginning, a relieved assertion of newfound freedom after the hellish experience of war—and a rejection of the beauty, the conventions, and the art of a society that had sent men to the trenches in the name of some edifying lie. An act of anarchistic and artistic opposition to the war, it had started in Zürich, in the safety of neutral Switzerland, the temporary home of, among many others, James Joyce, Jorge Luis Borges, Romain Rolland, and Lenin.

Here, in a watering hole ambitiously named Cabaret Voltaire, a group of exiles and revolutionaries met, debated, drank, played chess, and amused themselves. Their pastimes were becoming stranger by the day: they would mount shows in which they appeared onstage in bizarre costumes, howling and singing and declaiming words that they had invented on the spot and which referred to nothing. They were proud partisans of everything improvised, messy, and meaningless. Even the name of their group had been chosen precisely because it sounded like baby language and was empty of all significance: Dada.

Together with like-minded artists in Germany, the Zürich friends had the highest hopes for their new way of seeing, of chanting the world. "How does one achieve eternal bliss? By saying dada," wrote Hugo Ball, one of its intellectual fathers, in 1916. "How does one become famous? By saying dada. With a noble gesture and delicate propriety. Till one goes crazy. Till one loses consciousness. How can one get rid of everything that smacks of journalism, worms, everything nice and right, blinkered, moralistic, Europeanized, enervated? By saying dada. Dada is the world soul, dada is the pawnshop. Dada is the world's best lily-milk soap."[1]

This "pawnshop" contained a variety of fragments of lives, images, and mislaid beliefs, all lovingly watched over and publicized by a young man from Romania who had been born Samy Rosenstock but now went by the more mysterious and alluring name Tristan Tzara, and who made it his life's calling to spread the new gospel throughout the world via poems, essays, and manifestos. Dada spread to German cities and finally even to Paris, where it was thankfully, even greedily received by a handful of young men in search of an idiom for their rejection of the world they had grown up in. "Dada gave the Venus de Milo an enema and permitted Laocoon and his sons to relieve themselves after thousands of years of struggle with the good sausage Python," wrote the painter Hans Arp, one of the spiritual fathers of the new idiom.[2]

In Tzara's words they found the force they were seeking. "Dada does not mean anything," he had announced in his "Dada Manifesto 1918." "How can anyone hope to order the chaos that constitutes that infinite, formless variation: man? . . . Order = disorder; ego = non-ego; affirmation = negation . . . We are not afraid; we aren't sentimental. We are like a raging wind that rips up the clothes of clouds and prayers, we are preparing the great spectacle of disaster, conflagration, and decomposition. . . . Every man must shout: there is a great destructive, negative work to be done. To sweep, to clean."[3]

Dr. Breton Loses His Patients

THE MOST DETERMINED and most intransigent of this group of young men was André Breton, a medical student who had worked with shell-shocked soldiers during the war and who was now casting around for a way to make his mark. Born in 1896 in the Paris suburb of Pantin, Breton hated the lives and values of the petty bourgeoisie with the intimate hatred of experience. He had always wanted to break out. At school, before the war, he had been drawn to the bad boys of French literature, particularly Baudelaire and Rimbaud, and a little later also to the arch-experimentalist Apollinaire. The young man began to write poetry himself, but his poetic career was interrupted when he was drafted into the army and sent for basic training to a barracks that he would later describe as "a sewer of blood, idiocy, and mud."

Working as a medical intern at a military hospital in Nantes, Breton, then barely twenty, encountered his first shell-shock victims, as well as the writings of Sigmund Freud, which fascinated him. In 1916 he also met a convalescing soldier whose uncompromising attitudes would give his life a new direction. Jacques-Pierre Vaché, an arts student, had been injured on the Western Front and passed his time at the hospital by drawing grotesque figures on postcards. He was remarkably handsome but seemed to disdain everyone and everything around him, reason enough for Breton to be spellbound by this patient, who was one year his senior. Vaché introduced the aspiring doctor to a life of intellectual revolt against society, and their friendship grew even more intense after Vaché's release from the hospital. Together, the two young men talked and drank at local bars and went to the cinema. They would movie-hop for hours on end, seeing fragments of many different films, out of which they would reconstruct a narrative all their own.

When Vaché was sent back to do active service, the intense relationship between the young men was continued by correspondence. Vaché was an excellent and eccentric writer whose missives were charged with anarchic poetry and who reveled in the "theatrical (and joyless) pointlessness of it all."[4] Breton's close relationship with the alluring Pierre Vaché came to an end with horrible suddenness when Vaché was found in a hotel room lying naked on the bed with two other men, all dead from an overdose of opium.

After the end of the war, Breton worked at the Val-de-Grâce hospital in Paris as an assistant doctor in the closed psychiatric ward. Here, during the lonely night watches, alone in the dark corridors of the hospital and listening to the ravings and cries of his patients, he experienced the force of irrational expression, of insanity and despair, and here he delved once again into the writings of Sigmund Freud.

The idea of the subconscious fascinated and frightened Breton, because his own brief experience of fighting and suffering had made a smooth return to civilian life difficult for him and, he observed, for society at large. "You came back from the War," he wrote, "but what you could not come back from was what you then called the head-stuffing [*bourrage de crânes*] which within four years had turned beings who want nothing but to live and . . . get along with their like into beings who are distraught and frenzied, and not only exploited, but liable to be decimated at whim."[5] Four years of fear, inhumanity, and military propaganda had left indelible traces, he concluded, and it had debased people more than ever before.

Holed up in Breton's flat and in a drugless trance, Breton and his friend the writer Philippe Soupault decided to collaborate on a literary work like none other. It was to be the result of automatic writing, tapping the subconscious with as little interference as possible from their conscious thoughts. The experimental setup was simplicity itself: for one week they would write down everything that came into their heads, without revision, writing until they were exhausted, until their minds started to swim in a sea of words and spontaneous images, adding new and wondrously nonsensical phrases to the text as they attempted to give free rein to their subconscious.

Writing their work of half-conscious, ecstatic prose revealed itself to be as exhilarating as it was dangerous. No literary judgment, no conscious filter of any sort was to be applied, but they would write with "a praiseworthy disdain for what might result from a literary point of view," as Breton would later remember. "The ease of execution did the rest."[6] The result of their collaboration, *Les Champs Magnétiques* (The Magnetic Fields), was published in several installments in the journal *Littérature*, and as a book one year later, in 1920. The automatic writing contained in it was a sequence of images akin to walking through a series of paintings by Hans Arp:

> The cave is cold and one feels that it is time to go; the water calls us, it is red and the smile is stronger than the fissures running like plants over the house, O magnificent and tender day like this extraordinary little hoop. The sea we love cannot carry men as skinny as us. We need elephants with women's heads and flying lions. The cage is open and the hotel is closed for the second time; what a heat! In the

main place one notices a beautiful lioness who claws the lion tamer on the sand and lies down from time to time to lick him. The large phosphorescent swamps create pretty dreams and the crocodiles take back the suitcase made of their skin.[7]

After *The Magnetic Fields*, Breton did not continue his explorations of automatic writing. The exhaustion of his week with Soupault had brought them both to the brink of insanity, he felt, and during his work in the psychiatric ward he had encountered too many men who had been pushed over this brink. He had finished with this and was pushing for alternative routes to an art that would strike a fatal blow to the petty bourgeois world, the world he himself had grown up in and which he held responsible for the catastrophe of the war. Gifted with great rhetorical talent as well as an apparently limitless capacity for striking poses and convincing himself of the epoch-making importance of whatever he happened to be thinking and doing, he was a leader in the making. Restless as ever, he was ready for something new, and he prepared to meet the harbinger of a revolution that would, Breton believed, transform not just literature but all other areas of life as well.

Tristan in Paris

THIS CHANGE WOULD COME from Zürich, the young poet thought, for it was there that he had found his most astounding poetic master and soul mate yet, the enigmatic and fearless Tristan Tzara, the prophet of Dada and its demolition of all certainties. Breton had begun to correspond with him the previous year, and now, in 1920, the arch-Dadaist himself was bound for Paris. Breton could hardly wait, and his expectations were heightened further by repeated announcements of Tzara's imminent arrival in the capital—all false alarms.

When Dada finally came to the French capital, it did so suddenly. On January 17, 1919, Germaine Everling, mistress of the painter Francis Picabia, who had invited Tzara to come see him in Paris if ever he was in town, heard a knock at the door of Picabia's apartment, where she was looking after her two-year-old daughter. She asked her nanny to send the inopportune visitor away, but he would not budge and finally entered the bedroom. There he stood, Everling remembered later,

> small, slightly stooped, swinging two short arms at the ends of which hung chubby, but certainly sensitive, hands. His skin was waxy, like a candle: behind his pince-nez his myopic eyes

seemed to be searching for a fixed point on which to alight. He hesitated at the doorway, and mainly seemed very embarrassed to be there. . . . Constantly, automatically brushing a long shock of black hair from his forehead, he said in a thick Slavic accent: "I am very sorry to bother you, Madame, but I don't know where to put my bags." . . . I realized that he intended to settle into my home.[8]

And so he did. The penniless master simply commandeered the living room, used a Louis XV console as a table on which he would write on a huge typewriter, refused the maid access to the room because he deemed his possessions too important for her to touch, and had all his correspondence sent to the Picabia home. He stayed for almost a year.

Unconcerned about issues of domestic comfort, Breton could hardly contain his excitement at meeting the man who could transform European literature, whose revolutionary energy might revolutionize society itself. When he finally clapped eyes on the short, nearsighted Romanian, he was utterly nonplussed, but soon he was won over by Tzara's other qualities. "They had expected Tzarathustra, not the waxen-faced homunculus fidgeting before them," writes historian Mark Polizzotti, but "included in his Zürich baggage was three years' experience in getting the public's attention, not to say its goat."[9] With an arsenal of poetic provocations that included staging simultaneous readings of several works interrupted by shrill shrieks, sobbing, and loud banging on all sorts of objects, Breton believed that he had finally struck gold. "For Tzara, performance should be as loud as a gun burst, and as irritating as a pebble in the shoe," notes Polizzotti.

At the first public performance it fell to Louis Aragon to recite Tzara's poem "The White Leprous Giant in the Countryside," which contained these memorable lines:

> The salt collects in a constellation of birds on the padded
>   tumor
> In his lungs the starfish and bugs sway
> The microbes crystallize into palms of swaying muscles
> Good morning without a cigarette tzantzantza ganga
> Boozdc zdooc nfoonfa mbaah nfoonfa.[10]

The audience was predictably and deliciously outraged. For lack of other projectiles, some of those who had paid to hear all this hurled their house keys at the stage in fury.

But for Breton, this brand of provocation soon lost its appeal. He wanted to move something forward, and he wanted a movement. Dada with all its anarchic antics, he began to feel, could not provide him with this. He was too serious by temperament and perhaps too controlling by disposition for mere explosions of festive nonsense. More public events followed, more outrage was generated in the press, but Breton began to cast his net wider. During his honeymoon he took his new wife, Simone Kahn, to Vienna to visit Sigmund Freud, only to be disappointed once again. The aging psychoanalyst had little time to sacrifice to the young French assistant doctor who appeared on his doorstep unannounced and whose interest in psychoanalysis was mainly artistic, not scientific. Coming from very different backgrounds and generations (not to mention opposite sides in the war), the two men had very little to say to each other, and Breton, needless to say, was bitterly disenchanted by the fact that his former idol failed to see the deep significance of his work. Despite this personal disappointment, however, Breton continued to be fascinated by Freudian ideas.

Back in Paris, Breton continued to cast around for a role of importance in the literary world. In 1922 he organized the International Congress for the Determination and Defense of the Modern Spirit, to which he invited Europe's leading writers and artists. This kind of event—sober, ordered, and above all important—was more to his taste than Dada antics. In an attempt to forestall any spontaneous and unwelcome interventions, he demanded security measures, including the option of withdrawing the right to speak from any speaker and the freedom to restore order by all means necessary, even by calling the police.

Having recently fallen out with Tzara, who did not like the direction Breton's activities were taking, he also published a statement denouncing "a publicity-mongering imposter . . . a person best known as the promoter of a 'movement' that comes from Zürich, whom it is pointless to name more specifically, and who no longer corresponds to any current reality."[11] Dignified and not at all anarchistic for once, the Romanian replied, "An 'international' Congress that reprimands someone for being a foreigner has no right to exist." Those invited to the congress themselves disowned the dictatorial antics of its convener.

Breton was bruised by this disastrous turn of affairs, but far from deterred. It was time to move on, as he wrote in a prose poem in the pages of *Littérature*:

> I can only assure you that I don't give a damn about any of
>   this and repeat:
> Leave everything.

Leave Dada.
Leave your wife, leave your mistress.
Leave your hopes and fears.
Drop your kids in the middle of nowhere.
Leave the substance for the shadow.
Leave behind, if need be, your comfortable life and
    promising future.
Take to the highways.[12]

His self-imposed exile took the form of further experimentation. Together with a group of friends, he engaged in sessions of hypnosis at his apartment in the rue de Fontaine, during which René Crevel, the most gifted subject of them all, would fall into a trance and recite his visions, as Breton's wife, Simone, would write to a cousin: "It's dark. We are all around a table, silent, hands stretched out. Barely three minutes go by and already Crevel heaves hoarse sighs and vague exclamations. Then he begins telling a gruesome story in a forced, declamatory tone. A woman has drowned her husband, but *he* had asked her to. 'Ah! The frogs! Poor madwoman. Maaaaadd. . . .' Painful, cruel accents. Savagery in the slightest images. Some obscenity as well. . . . Nothing can match the horror of it."[13]

By 1924, Breton's constant and headstrong (and occasionally inspired) interventions, his provocative writing (which by now included two published prose works), and the sheer allure of the severe intellectual persona he had crafted for himself had made him a real presence on the Paris cultural scene. At twenty-eight years of age, he appeared to have achieved his ambition of becoming the leader of an artistic movement. Having been unable to co-opt Dadaism for his purposes, he now proceeded to invent his own, and in 1924 he published a *Surrealist Manifesto*, a truly remarkable document in which he summoned a young lifetime's experience as a seeker for great truths and, arguably, even greater gestures.

In his manifesto, Breton railed against realism not so much as a style but as an attitude toward life: "I loathe it, for it is made up of mediocrity, hate, and dull conceit. . . . It constantly feeds on and derives strength from the newspapers and stultifies both science and art by . . . flattering the lowest of tastes; clarity bordering on stupidity, a dog's life." Instead, he wrote, the banal and deadly world of waking and of rationality had to be fused with the reality of dreams "into a kind of absolute reality, a *surreality*, if one may so speak." For those blockheaded enough to need a dictionary definition, he duly supplied one:

> SURREALISM, *n*. Psychic automatism in its pure state, by which one proposes to express—verbally, by means of the written word, or in any other manner—the actual functioning of thought. Dictated by the thought, in the absence of any control exercised by reason, exempt from any aesthetic or moral concern.[14]

Breton's surrealism was born out of rejection—of former friends, of bourgeois reality, of artistic realism, and of the carefree anarchy of Dadaism. What the world needed, he thought, was a disciplined movement, a collective assault on bourgeois culture in an effort to subvert and finally topple it altogether.

With its assertive tone and its apparent explanation of the motivation behind an artistic craze that had already attracted a good deal of publicity, the manifesto was a considerable success because it achieved what was most important: public attention. As the rebuttals, discussions, and controversies blossomed, Breton's statue as the "pope of surrealism" became unassailable. Not yet thirty, the young man from the suburbs had quite simply invented a movement for himself to lead and turned himself into a public figure. He took to his new role with a Jacobin zeal, which led him to sanction all infractions of his unquestioned authority by cutting dissenters out of the surrealist fold and out of his life.

Members of his group were required to be disciplined and to toe the ideological party line, and Breton even forbade other surrealists to publish in any magazine other than *La Révolution Surréaliste*, which he controlled. As Mussolini's Italy was turning into a Fascist state, the pope of surrealism in Paris began to look disconcertingly like a pint-sized, poetic version of *Il Duce*. Breton himself was not shy about admitting this. In early 1925, he published an article entitled "Why I Am Taking Charge of *La Révolution Surréaliste*." He meant more than just the journal, whose editor he had sacked.

What had begun as angry rejection by a few young men, many of them former soldiers, of the society of their parents and of the rationality that had made possible the slaughter at the front had by now blossomed into a new kind of art, some (but not all) of which was assembled around Breton. Especially in and around Paris, surrealist artists and others with similar aesthetic ideas but no stomach for ideological discussions created works that found a visual language for portraying psychological, half-conscious states and processes. Among these artists were Francis Picabia (the onetime involuntary host of Tristan Tzara) and the German Max Ernst, who had moved in with a close friend of Breton's, the poet Paul Éluard, who shared with Ernst his large house and his alluring wife, Gala, a Russian émigré who would later marry Salvador Dalí, then still an art student in Madrid.

While poets and painters were engaged in vigorous experiments in living (similar emotional and marital constellations were to be found in the Bloomsbury Circle around Virginia Woolf), some of the most innovative surrealist works embraced not only the sensibility of the new period but also its technology. This dismayed Breton, who was acutely suspicious of aspects of surrealist production beyond his control and who rejected anything that could or would result in "cozying up to the establishment" by accepting money for art, being shown or performed in regular venues, and being produced with a professional budget.

One of the productions drawing the master's wrath was a 1924 collaboration between Picabia, the composer Eric Satie (he of the dreamy *Gymnopédie*), and the Swedish Royal Ballet. Satie had written the music for a new choreography, with Picabia designing the sets. For the intermission, Picabia and the filmmaker René Clair had produced a short movie, fittingly entitled *Entr'acte*, a wonderfully inventive tableau of images and scenes that used new and unsettling visual effects. In one of the most arresting and recurring sequences, a ballerina is filmed dancing—from underneath, through a glass floor. The second part of the film is the funeral procession of a hunter who has been killed by another hunter on the roofs of Paris. The hearse is drawn by a camel, and the mourners follow the coffin hopping and jumping en masse. Eventually the hearse rolls off on its own, gathering speed, and sending the entire group of mourners off in a mad pursuit through the French countryside.

Entr'acte was an amusingly provocative piece of work that succeeded in exploiting the technical and artistic possibilities of film. Another short movie shown for the first time during the same year and also ostensibly dealing with dance offered a different dimension of artistic accomplishment. *Ballet Mécanique* was written by the painter Fernand Léger, who was considerably older than the surrealist firebrands who were drawing so much attention. Before the war, Léger had been a cubist whose compositions were less haunted and foreboding than those of his colleagues and whose use of bright colors and graceful forms was more reminiscent of Kandinsky than of Picasso. After three years at the front and a gas attack he only narrowly survived; however, the optimism had seeped out of his paintings.

Ballet Mécanique is a surrealist masterwork, an abstract film whose finely orchestrated use of shapes, movements, and rhythms

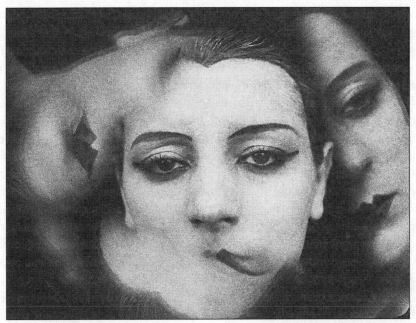

Dreams and trauma: The French painter Fernand Léger dramatized his experiences in his experimental film Ballet Mécanique, *1924.*

lends coherence and dramatic development to this succession of strange images, kaleidoscopic effects, superimpositions, and fast cuts, accompanied by a savage score, famous in its own right and written for sixteen pianos, percussion, and street sirens by Georges Antheil. The real force of this fifteen-minute dreamscape, however, is its exploration of experiences and impressions Léger had been carrying around with him since his return from the trenches.

It begins, seemingly innocent enough, with a woman swinging on a swing like a little girl. Soon, however, the backward-and-forward movement of the swing becomes insistent, filmed from unusual angles and mirrored in the mechanical swinging of a pendulum and in images of machine parts in action, distorted and multiplied by the camera. The woman's lips and eyes appear, and a man's head emerges from a hiding place, images that are always interrupted and intercut with the pitiless swing and thrust of technological images. We see the legs of marching soldiers, people on a speeded-up merry-go-round, pistons, racing shapes, and cars seemingly running over the camera. The whole creates a sense of dislocation, claustrophobia, and insistent movement, almost cutting into the viewer's head. The woman's lips, her heavily made-up eyes, and the incessant thrusting have an obvious sexual dimension, but the imagery also vividly exemplifies the widespread sensation of human bodies becoming machine parts, swallowed up by technology and enslaved by machines.

As the tempo of the cuts speeds up, the sentence *On a volé un collier de perles de 5 millions* (someone stole a pearl necklace worth five million) becomes almost obsessively dissected, dismembered, and repeated, as the words' meanings break down and are shattered into the individual letters, as in the fractured perception of a traumatized patient. The face of another woman, a vamp this time, smiles alluringly into the camera but is broken up into various cubist facets. The entire film dramatizes a world without meaning, shattered and broken apart (another sequence focuses on mannequin legs, eerily similar to the prosthetic limbs so common after the war), a perception deranged and distorted by a traumatized mind that sees masks where there are faces, nonsensical shapes in words, bizarre and threatening shapes in everyday scenes, mutilation in beauty, and artillery shells in the shape of bottles.

Léger's work was not so much a mechanical ballet as a machine-made nightmare of mental disintegration, an unparalleled visual dramatization of fragmented mindscapes. Despite the fact that its creator did not officially belong to the surrealist movement, he had used the same techniques and the same artistic vocabulary to create one of the psychologically and poetically most incisive works of the period.

The Surrealist World Revolution

FOR BRETON, SUCH CREATIONS outside his tight control were irritations and wasted opportunities for publicity. But he was already moving on to the next stage. Impatient with Dada's anarchic exuberance, dissatisfied with the aesthetic and personal squabbles within the surrealist fold, and exasperated at what he saw as the ideological confusion of his fellow artists, he decided to seek another direction. If, as he believed, surrealism really had the potential to subvert and ultimately bring down the values of a decayed society and to build something fresh in their place, then there was only one possible route: political action. "Communism alone among organized systems permits the accomplishment of the greatest social transformation," Breton wrote in 1925. "Good or mediocre in itself, defensible or not from the moral point of view, how can we forget its role as the instrument by which ancient buildings are destroyed?"[15]

Breton threw himself into political activities. He signed petitions and wrote his own, penned one article after another, declared his solidarity with the suffering peasants of Bessarabia and the workers of Hungary along with the oppressed everywhere, discussed the end of the bourgeoisie on the terrace of the Café de Flore, read Marx and Hegel, drafted proclamations in support of the working class, and wrote disavowals, doctrinal clarifications, and revolutionary slogans. Among his artist friends, some were interested in this political turn, while others were bored or even horrified but did not want (or did not dare) to incur the famous wrath of the man who had put surrealism on the cultural map practically single-handedly.

Breton himself was torn, as always, between his sudden, overwhelming infatuations with ideas and people and the inevitable disillusionment that followed: "I am extremely tired, morally fatigued . . . Either because the tendencies I've recently had to adopt for myself run too counter to my previous tendencies, or because in trying to break down others' resistances I've momentarily killed my own."[16]

The irreverence and ideological insouciance of his friends made disciplined work all but impossible, Breton concluded. The official communists, however, did nothing to make his life easier. For three years, he vacillated, sought contact, declared his loyalty, and sought to distance himself again. Finally, in 1927, he decided to apply for membership in the French Communist Party in order to work for world revolution from the inside. As a famous left-wing intellectual, he expected to make policy, take part in discussions at the highest level, and be recognized as one of the leading minds of the revolution. He thought his own tactic, surrealism, could do as much to shatter the citadel of the bourgeoisie as any general strike or a whole army of armed peasants could.

The Party, however, remained cool. The top brass distrusted the mad antics of these young, middle-class men who refused to work with their own hands and instead spent their time with poetry, hypnotism, and weird public performances. This was not the kind of revolution they had in mind. When Breton finally got his membership card after an extended and by all accounts almost hostile series of interviews with Party functionaries, he was not invited into the general secretariat as secretary for culture, but instead assigned to a cell of workers at a gasworks.

C'est la Vie

AS ANDRÉ BRETON IN PARIS was succumbing to the totalitarian temptation, the fame of surrealist and Dadaist works spread. Germany had had highly active and rebellious Dada groups since before the war, Zürich had been a sanctuary for experimental artists and social revolutionaries, and in Belgium, too, the influence of Dada was present in paintings, in print, in public performances, and in poetry. But while this avant-garde landscape on the European continent was vibrant and varied, Dada and surrealism had surprisingly little resonance in the Anglo-Saxon world, and particularly in the United States.

A solitary artist with an aversion to groups and dogmatic artist's manifestos, Marcel Duchamp had moved to New York before the war and had created a huge and controversial success with his *Nude Descending a Staircase*, a dynamic image capturing a sequence of movement on a single canvas. The work had been exhibited at the now legendary Armory Show of 1913 in New York and had been purchased on the very last day of the exhibition by Walter and Louise Arensberg, an eccentric and wealthy couple whose collection concentrated on avant-garde works long before they became fashionable in the United States. The Arensbergs' home on New York's Upper West Side became a meeting point for many artists and intellectuals interested in new ways of seeing, among them Duchamp himself, and after the war also Francis Picabia, the controversial photographer and novelist Carl van Vechten, the composer Edgard Varèse, the writer William Carlos Williams, and the photographer Charles Demuth.

The dynamic paintings of futurism and the broken perspectives of cubism had been key to Duchamp's aesthetics, but they proved nothing more than a phase for the artist, who would subsequently invent his very own brand of surrealism with seminal works such as *Fountain* (1917), a urinal he had signed and exhibited in a gallery, and his cryptic masterwork *The Bride Stripped Bare by Her Bachelors, Even* (1915–1923), to which he devoted a large part of his career. Never content to stand still and settle into a routine, and horrified by the idea of being subsumed into any movement, Duchamp reinvented himself in drag as Rrose Sélavy, a pseudonym that can be read as "Eros, c'est la vie" (Eros is life) or as "arroser la vie" (making a toast to life), and eventually ceased producing art altogether, preferring to invest his immense subversive energy into playing chess and composing chess problems.

Though not part of Breton's cohort, Duchamp formed a direct connection between Paris and New York, as did another artist, the American Man Ray, who had repeatedly photographed Duchamp as Rrose Sélavy and who soon found himself at the heart of the Paris surrealist crowd. Born Emmanuel Radnitzky to Russian Jewish immigrants, Ray had moved to Paris in 1921 and had fallen in love with

Kiki de Montparnasse, one of the emblematic female protagonists of the almost exclusively male surrealists (whose attitudes toward sex and women, incidentally, were remarkably archaic).

Kiki, whose actual name was Alice Prin, had been raised in dire poverty and had started to work in factories at the age of twelve. Her gamine, almost doll-like beauty was soon discovered by Montparnasse artists frequenting the same cheap cafés as she did, and she was soon modeling for, among others, Chaim Soutine, Amedeo Modigliani, Francis Picabia, and Fernand Léger, who also used her as the female seductress in his short film *Ballet Mécanique*. Man Ray fell in love with this young woman who did not let her poverty destroy her spirit of independence or her determination to have fun. They became lovers, and Ray used her as subject of hundreds of photographic portraits, among them such iconic images as *Le Violon d'Ingre* (the famous nude seen from behind with the f holes of a cello superimposed) and *Noir et Blanc*, in which a highly made-up Kiki seems to be lost in contemplation of a small African mask she is holding in her hand.

Man Ray was to stay in Paris for twenty years, during which he met and photographed the entire intellectual and artistic avant-garde, from André Breton to Gertrude Stein. The French capital provided a context for him in which he was understood and appreciated. In his native United States, interest in this kind of art was still very weak, and only with the advent of Nazism would there be a massive influx into New York of surrealist artists such as Picabia, Breton, Ernst, and the young Dalí, creating a critical mass that would inspire and influence a younger generation of American artists.

"There is no progress in art, any more than there is progress in making love. There are simply different ways of doing it," Man Ray would write in 1948, and this statement curiously bridges the gap between artists on both sides of the Atlantic. The point was that for many of them art was an act of love, of instinct, the expression of an erotic relationship with the present. Surrealists and Dadaists in Europe, drawing on cubism and Freud, on the destructive abandon of futurism, had found a way of giving voice to the feeling of their generation, to the anger and disillusionment with values that had not been able to prevent the world from collapsing around them.

The war was present in the work of the surrealists, but mainly as a background attitude, a disillusionment with all values of bourgeois society, from its morality, its rationality, and its idea of objective truth to its concepts of beauty. In Germany the experience of the war was used in a more immediate form, if fueled by a similar anger. The painters George Grosz and Otto Dix had initially used the devastated faces and amputated bodies of veterans as an expression of their anger. Both had served at the front, and both had been traumatized by the experience.

Dix chose to immerse himself in a cathartic process when he began work on a cycle of etchings and a large triptych, both entitled *Der Krieg* (The War). As an immediate inspiration he used drawings he himself had made at the front as well as his war diary, which chronicled the brutal awakening and disillusionment of a young man who had gone to war hoping for adventure. One jotting from late 1914 reads: "In the past wars were led for the sake of religion; today for the sake of trade and industry (money)—a step backward."[17] There was nothing left to believe in; naked greed was all that was left. Another note reads simply, "Jeremiah 20:14." The Bible verse it refers to is "Cursed be the day wherein I was born: let not the day wherein my mother bare me be blessed."

Especially in his etchings, Dix created a stunning panorama of the conflict as experienced by common soldiers. Corpses, twisted limbs, grinning skulls, and uniformed skeletons form the backdrop for the monotonous routine of the living, one of whom can be seen wolfing down his food next to a dead comrade. The landscape around is nothing but a pockmarked expanse of putrid mud. Soldiers whose faces are distorted in anguish seek distraction with local whores. A distraught mother is trying to feed her baby's corpse. The faces of the fighting men are turned into identically monstrous insects by gas masks or transformed into grotesque masks of suffering by shrapnel.

It took the artist six years to find the graphic language in which he could tell this tale. The black and white of the etchings heightens the bleakness of the experience and lends added depth to its overwhelming darkness. To find the appropriate technique, however, Dix had not looked at new forms of expression. He had chosen styles and ways of working the printing plates that alternately used fine, free lines and atmospheric acid washes reminiscent of the two great masters of the medium: Rembrandt, with his subtly explored depths of darkness and light and his freedom of line, and Francisco Goya, whose cycle *The Horrors of War* was a direct inspiration in many ways. Dix was not the only artist to turn to the masters of the past in search of a language adequate to capture an experience that initially passed all bounds of expression. A similar return to classical molds and models could be observed in a wide range of artists, from Picasso to Léger.

Analyzing the American Way of Life

IN MANY WAYS the surrealist guerrilla tactics and the expressionist detonations of anger were less interesting to American artists because they were dealing with a different set of questions. The impact of the immediate war was far less present in the buoyant economy of the early 1920s. Instead, the United States presented a burgeoning immigrant society with apparently infinite improvements in living standards. Here, a critical generation of artists and intellectuals faced other challenges.

What connected artists on both sides of the Atlantic was Breton's idol Sigmund Freud, whose teachings not only had been the most important influence behind surrealist interest in the creativity of the subconscious and its liberation from bourgeois repression but also were enthusiastically received and discussed by East Coast intellectuals eager for a new vocabulary with which to understand the galloping changes society was undergoing.

Freud had accepted an invitation to lecture at Clark University in 1909, and despite the fact that he himself remained cool toward American culture, his teaching was received with genuine enthusiasm. It inspired doctors and educators, social thinkers and self-help gurus. In 1924, the legendary movie executive Samuel Goldwyn even made the arduous journey to Vienna to convince Freud to write a movie that was to be a great love story, a proposal he sweetened with a fee of $100,000. Freud declined. He disliked the United States, hated to be addressed as "Sigmund" instead of "Herr Professor," and felt humiliated by the offer.

Despite the master's aversion to the United States, Freud's teachings lent themselves wonderfully to a very American gospel of self-improvement, even self-transformation, which for the first time was also tapped into by professional advertisers, who studied their targets, the consumers, not only from a social point of view but also from a psychological one. "The growth of popular magazines and national advertising . . . is concentrating increasingly upon a type of copy aiming to make the reader emotionally uneasy, to bludgeon him with the fact that decent people don't live the way *he* does," an influential 1929 study into city life concluded.[18]

Both prompted and repulsed by this commercial pressure, artists and writers were trying to understand the relationship between individuals and society in a time increasingly dominated by mass production, media, advertising, conspicuous consumption, and convenience. As the economy picked up after the unsettled years directly following the war, these developments accelerated, and they raised fundamental questions for artists and their art. How should they deal with this new world? Should they embrace it or retreat from it into a more individual, more traditional, and more conventionally pleasing aesthetics?

Psychoanalysis provided a framework for asking these questions because it contained not only an idea of self-transformation but also a critique of social conventions. If society demanded that sexual impulses were to be suppressed, and if this resulted in people being stunted and unhappy, then Americans had to develop a new relationship with their own bodies and emotional lives and a rejection of the frantic, commercialized society that made these demands. "Something oppressed them," wrote the novelist Malcolm Cowley. "It was the stupidity of the crowd, it was hurry and haste, it was Mass Production, Babbittry, Our Business Civilization; or perhaps it was the Machine, which had been developed to satisfy men's needs, but which was now controlling those needs and forcing its standardized products upon us by means of omnipresent advertising and omnipresent vulgarity."[19]

Plumes of Saffron Smoke

ONE ANTIDOTE TO THIS DULLNESS lay in the magnificence of art. Painters such as Joseph Stella devoted themselves to exploring and showing the magical, dreamlike beauty of human bodies freed from social constraints, as in his *Birth of Venus*, a work radiating color and a curiously prim, stylized nakedness. Other painters went down the same road, concentrating on portraits, heroic nudity, grand landscapes, or the intimacy of still lifes.

But the rejection of modernity seemed helpless and deeply inadequate in the face of the awakening of a great civilization and of new if ambiguous forms of living. Writing about an exhibition of new paintings, the art critic James N. Rosenberg commented:

> [It] seems to me that American art shrinks from contact with American life. . . . And this gigantic life of capitalism, of the machine that has become a Frankenstein, has it nothing for art? Vast furnaces with plumes of saffron smoke; naked men sweating at the forge; turbines, motors, engines, power, water-falls, vessels in the harbor, dock-hands, sweat shops, cabarets, midnight follies, politicians, towering buildings lost in steam, crowds on the city streets; grain elevators, wharves, battle ships—is there no food in these for art? Yet

the American painter turns his back on stuff of such a sort, seeks refuge at Woodstock or Gloucester, and buries himself in Cezanne.[20]

One artist particularly alive to the inherent contradiction of American painting was Georgia O'Keeffe. Born into a farming family in 1887, she had earned a meager living as a schoolteacher and might not have made the transition to living and working as an artist had not a friend of hers, the photographer Anita Pollitzer, secretly sent some of her drawings to Alfred Stieglitz in New York, where he managed a gallery for modern artists, called simply 291. Stieglitz, himself one of the most influential photographers of the twentieth century, was impressed by the abstract compositions he had received and included them in a 1916 exhibition without consulting O'Keeffe. When she learned about the show she was taken aback at first, but eventually she consented to the exhibition and even did a solo show at the gallery during the following year. In 1918, O'Keeffe agreed to move to New York to paint full-time. Soon Stieglitz became more than just her dealer and representative, and they formed an intimate relationship that was to last for the rest of their lives. They were married after Stieglitz's divorce from his wife in 1924.

At the time of her arrival in New York, O'Keeffe had painted mainly floral subjects and abstract compositions, and her work was deeply introspective. Now, however, she discovered the exhilaration and the drama of a modern city, and by the mid-1920s she was filling canvases with the huge, geometric forms of skyscrapers, the bewitching geometry of the Brooklyn Bridge, or the dazzle of reflections of sunlight caught in high-up window panes.

Another painter, Edward Hopper, treated not the intrinsic beauty of city life but its dystopian potential. His paintings were imaginary snapshots of everyday moments: of loneliness among millions, of small human tragedies played out under the harsh light of commercial premises or in the half-shade of private dwellings.

Like O'Keeffe and Hopper, many artists were experimenting and debating whether traditional art could conquer the big city as a subject, or whether such art was even an appropriate means for treating it. This was an urgent issue, because the landscape of strutting towers of concrete and brick, rail transport, streets swarming with cars and pedestrians, billboards, and illuminated advertising changed not only the traditional face of urban life but also arguably the range of human experience, as the critic Edmund Wilson remarked, with a sly reference to the pleasures of the speakeasy: "Do we not, between the office and the night-club, in the excitement of winning and spending, and slightly poisoned by the absorption of bad alcohol, succeed in experiencing sensations which humanity has never yet known? May we not, under this pressure, in constant collision, be proud at least of striking off flashes of a novel repercussion and color?"[21]

These novel repercussions of color, the everyday drama of light and shade, the abstractions of shape, the sheer exhilaration of scale, and the faces of the millions inhabiting this new world offered themselves to a medium that was itself a child of the rampant progress of technology: photography. Photography was to painting what jazz was to classical music—a contemporary idiom, born out of the social and technological realities of a new era. The apparent directness of the medium allowed a complex play with expectations: a face in the crowd could shine with the immediacy and universality of the human condition, while a shift in perspective or a technical sleight of hand rendered the familiar strange and forced the public to look at their world with new eyes. Unknown realities and possibilities were revealed by artists working between straight reportage and abstraction. Faces became icons; urban spaces blossomed into fascinating geometric vortexes of light and shade. Alfred Stieglitz, Charles Demuth, Edward Weston, Imogen Cunningham, and Walker Evans were among those who created the new face of the United States and established a new aesthetic stance toward a world that was new in every sense of the word, even if the dramas and the comedies played out on this grand stage set were as old as humanity itself. It was, as Lewis Mumford wrote, "a stripped, athletic, classical style of architecture . . . all that is good in the Machine Age: its precision, its cleanliness, its hard illumination, its unflinching logic."[22]

From illustrations in the daily papers to artworks in galleries, photography was changing how people looked at the world and how their interest could be manipulated. But the medium also made possible other discoveries. Scientists had used photography since its inception. Now the systematic documentation of the night skies was about to reveal new secrets.

Monkey Business

If evolution wins, Christianity goes.
—William Jennings Bryan, 1925

....

JOHNNY SCOPES WAS AN UNLIKELY HERO IN WHAT WAS TO BE DESCRIBED as the trial of the century. A handsome, unassuming Texas farm boy, twenty-four years old, a popular high school teacher and football coach, he sat in the courtroom and did not speak unless spoken to. But it was not about him; the trial was a clash of titans and of principles, a spectacular confrontation of two visions of society staged in the summer of 1925 in the little town of Dayton, in rural Tennessee, before the eager eyes of more than two hundred journalists.

The misdemeanor with which the young teacher stood charged had been effectively fabricated by a handful of local citizens sitting around a soda fountain. Only weeks before, at Robinson's drugstore, they had been discussing an article in the *Chattanooga Times* in which it was reported that the New York–based American Civil Liberties Union (ACLU), founded only five years before, was looking for a way to challenge the constitutionality of a recently passed Tennessee state law forbidding the teaching of evolution in all public schools. The men assembled at Robinson's decided they could provide a precedent that would serve the ACLU's needs and in the process create publicity—and business opportunities—for their own obscure town in Rhea County. One of the leaders of the "drugstore conspirators," as they came to be known, was a local (male) state prosecutor named Sue K. Hicks; the other, George Rappleyea, a metallurgical engineer, was originally from New York.

They sent for the local science teacher, Johnny Scopes, a friend of Hicks's, who appeared fresh from a tennis match with one of his pupils. Though without much real interest himself in the principle at stake, he agreed to serve as sacrificial lamb in a test case to be brought against him by Hicks himself. "I was simply teaching to get money to go back to school again," Scopes said later. "I did see it was a big important issue. . . . I don't know if I'm a Christian. I do believe in the ethical teachings of Christ, and I believe there is a God. . . . But all of biology and most other sciences are basically the story of the evolution of matter and of life. I was hired to teach science, and I went ahead and taught it. . . . Many of the men teaching science were married and so tied up they couldn't take chances. So I stepped in."[1]

A warrant was issued for Scopes's arrest, and he admitted to having taught the theory of evolution in a high school biology class where he had been filling in for another teacher who had fallen sick; he was then released on bail. Hicks and Rappleyea were delighted at this opportunity to strike a blow for intellectual freedom and put their little county on the map in the process. One of the strangest trials of the century had begun; in a satirical report, the famous Baltimore critic H. L. Mencken, who denounced his religiously inclined compatriots as "boobus Americanus," dubbed it "the monkey trial."

Like the Red Scare and Prohibition, the anti-evolution law had been a consequence of the prescriptive atmosphere prevailing in the United States after the War. The law's sponsor, George Washington Butler, a local farmer and member of the Tennessee state House of Representatives, believed that modern education was alienating young people from the teachings of the Bible. The law he had introduced was succinct and forthright:

> Section 1. *Be it enacted by the General Assembly of the State of Tennessee,* That it shall be unlawful for any teacher in any of the Universities, Normals and all other public schools of the State which are supported in whole or in part by the

public school funds of the State, to teach any theory that denies the story of the Divine Creation of man as taught in the Bible, and to teach instead that man has descended from a lower order of animals.

Section 2. *Be it further enacted,* That any teacher found guilty of the violation of this Act, Shall be guilty of a misdemeanor and upon conviction, shall be fined not less than One Hundred ($100.00) Dollars nor more than Five Hundred ($500.00) Dollars for each offense.

Section 3. *Be it further enacted,* That this Act take effect from and after its passage, the public welfare requiring it.

Butler had drawn up the bill after listening to a speech given by a man who was to be one of the protagonists of the Scopes trial: William Jennings Bryan, a prominent Nebraska Democratic Party politician and a fervent evangelical Christian. He had spent the years after the war crisscrossing the United States, giving an average of two hundred speeches a year, in which he denounced the godless ways of modern society and in particular the teaching of evolution, which, he believed, was directly responsible not only for the current plague of immoral behavior but also for the war itself. The Germans, he reasoned, had taken Darwinian teachings to their extreme and decided that their wealth and influence entitled them to rule the world: might made right.

An instinctive populist abundantly blessed with the gift of persuasion, Bryan had risen to national prominence in 1896, polemicizing against the gold standard with a fine flourish of the kind of religiously inspired rhetoric that was to make him famous: "You shall not press down upon the brow of labor this crown of thorns; you shall not crucify mankind upon a cross of gold." The "Cross of Gold" speech earned Bryan a nomination as candidate for the presidency in the first of three campaigns, all of which he was to lose. His talents as an orator, however, had made him a man of wealth, much of which he had invested in the Florida land boom.

To Bryan, who had been President Woodrow Wilson's secretary of state in 1915, the war had been a test of the moral fiber of the United States, with the battle lines clearly drawn not in Flanders but in Washington. They ran between the modernists, who advocated American intervention in the war, and the conservatives, who wanted to keep the country from intervening in a conflict that they considered a direct result of European godlessness and decadence. The religious dimension

Best enemies: Clarence Darrow and William Jennings Bryan sweating it out at the Scopes trial.

of the argument was not tied to Darwinism alone: American religious moderates and intellectuals had long adopted an approach to the Bible that emphasized probing textual criticism, which had revealed the sacred text to be composed of different layers and traditions, created at different times and by different authors. This form of biblical scholarship had been pioneered at German universities.

Christian conservatives were squarely opposed to what they perceived as a weakening of the biblical message. When war broke out in 1914, the evangelical journal *Our Hope* exclaimed: "The new theology has led Germany into barbarism and will lead any nation into the same demoralization."[2] Some millenarian evangelicals even supported a strictly isolationist stance on the grounds that the European war not only was the natural consequence of secularism but also heralded the Second Coming of Christ.

The Bible and Its Enemies

LIKE OTHER CONSERVATIVE CHRISTIANS, Secretary Bryan had been opposed to American intervention in Europe—so much so that he had staked his career on it. "As long as I am in office there will be no war," he had declared, a promise he had eventually managed to keep only by resigning as President Wilson moved toward intervention. Bryan had continued his campaign against it in speeches, articles, and books.

As Europe plunged into the political and socioeconomic crisis of the early postwar years, Bryan saw the social unrest, strikes, and economic woes, as well as the Russian Revolution, as vindication of his view that without religion, humanity was tottering on the edge of the abyss. Driven by the force of his unshakable convictions, in speeches with titles such as "The Menace of Darwinism" and "The Bible and Its Enemies," he had used his vast public speaking experience to campaign against the teaching of evolution in schools, and to attempt to turn Christians and all Americans away from science in general.

The battle between evolution and theology had been raging since publication in London of Charles Darwin's *Origin of Species* in 1859. Formidable scientifically minded pugilists had squared off against clergymen and other indignant or anxious believers in a barrage of articles and speeches and debates on both sides of the Atlantic. The former included the anatomist Thomas Huxley—"Darwin's Bulldog"—who in an Oxford debate of 1860 with the intellectually evasive Bishop "Soapy Sam" Wilberforce declared that while he himself was not ashamed to have a monkey as an ancestor, he would be ashamed to be connected with a man—such as Wilberforce, for instance—who was using his great mental gifts only to obscure the truth. In the absence of final evidence, the debate between the two had been no more than a series of clever point-scoring opportunities, but as the scientific record solidified over the ensuing decades, defenders of the truth of the biblical account of creation had only hardened their position and their resolve.

After the war, Protestant Christian organizations in the United States had begun to form a united front in the battle, drawing part of their weaponry from a series of volumes published by the Bible Institute of Los Angeles, which had been founded in 1908 by California oil magnate Lyman Stewart. The institute's volumes were entitled *The Fundamentals: A Testament to the Truth*, and in them theologians attacked scientific and other critical perspectives on the Bible, developing instead a literalist understanding of it. The ninety chapters provided an intellectual foundation and a formal name for the newly influential American phenomenon: Christian fundamentalism.

The message was eagerly received. In the early years of the decade, the evangelist preacher Billy Sunday, following on from the success of his campaign for Prohibition, had been drawing crowds of five thousand and more to his near-hysterical sermons, in which he regularly condemned "the old bastard theory of evolution," wished all "modernists" to hell, and said gruesomely of teachers who taught evolution that their hands were "dripping with innocent blood." His carnivalesque Billy Sunday Crusades drew up to two hundred thousand people, marching and singing, accompanied by bands and even Ku Klux Klansmen in full white-hooded regalia.

When in 1921 the Kentucky Baptist State Board of Missions passed a resolution calling for a state law banning the teaching of evolution in schools, William Jennings Bryan had immediately seized on the idea, hoping to start a movement that would sweep the entire United States. His own rural state of Tennessee, whose population was pious, poor, and less well educated on average than the populations of other states, seemed a promising point of departure. Failure to act would be disastrous, he argued: "A scientific soviet is attempting to dictate what is taught in our schools."[3] With the Red Scare of 1919–1921 still fresh in American minds, Bryan's reference to a "scientific soviet" was enough to awaken many religious and political slumberers.

In 1924, the Canadian-born creationist and amateur geologist George McCready Price dismissed finds of hominid remains in the Neanderthal Valley in Germany as "degenerate offshoots which had separated from the main stock both ethnically and geographically."[4] Others, including Bryan, quickly followed his lead. Neither man allowed his own rudimentary understanding of the natural sciences to stop him from ridiculing any scientific principles that appeared to be in conflict with his Christian faith. "If they find a stray tooth in a gravel pit, they hold a conclave and fashion a creature such as they suppose the possessor of the tooth to have been, and then they shout derisively at Moses," Bryan scoffed. "Men who would not cross the street to save a soul have traveled across the world in search of skeletons."[5]

Bryan in particular was not a man to be swayed from his point by the inconvenient dictates of logic: reduced to paper, his speeches often read like angry ranting, but he was an outstanding speaker with a commanding baritone voice, and he used his talents to convince Butler that the teaching of Darwinism—"the monkey entering the school room," as he put it—was one of the chief moral dangers threatening America. Butler, with only a few years of primary education to his name, was easily swayed by the mighty orator, and duly lent his political weight to the campaign against the teaching of evolution. When the Butler Act was finally passed, many Tennessee lawmakers admitted they had voted for it less out of conviction than because they had feared being portrayed as godless themselves. But motives no longer mattered: the law was on the books, a victory for antiscientific forces in general and Christian fundamentalism in particular.

Mr. Darrow Comes to Town

THE YOUNG SCIENCE TEACHER John Scopes was no more than a willing pawn in what the ACLU viewed as a single battle in the great conflict between religion and science—in effect, a battle for America's soul. As with Prohibition, the lines were being drawn between Christian fundamentalists, on the one hand, and moderate believers and secularists, on the other. It was in essence a battle between rural and urban, and between states' rights supporters and federal rights supporters; symbolically, if not strictly geographically, it was a battle between South and North.

With big constitutional principles at stake, the trial could not remain a local affair, conducted away from the eyes of the world in a tiny Tennessee town, and the heavyweights duly arrived. The recently founded World Christian Fundamentals Association (WCFA) secured William Jennings Bryan as counsel for the prosecution, in the hope that his powerful oratory would sway the jurors. The two local lawyers originally assigned to defend Scopes quickly stepped aside to allow a more famous colleague to plead for him: Chicago's star performer Clarence Darrow, a lion of the courtroom, master of every oratorical trick in the book, and at this time perhaps America's most famous defense counsel, who had volunteered his services.

Darrow had two reasons to throw his hat into the ring: while the case chimed with his personal agnosticism and his lifelong advocacy of individual rights, he may also have sought the brief in an attempt to clear his own name, which was ambiguously associated with the most sensational criminal trial of the decade, held only one year earlier. In the Leopold and Loeb case, two affluent and educated young men had brutally murdered a fourteen-year-old boy from their neighborhood, simply to see whether they could get away with it.

Leopold and Loeb confessed, and Darrow took on their defense in a trial in which their guilt was no longer in question. Their amateurish approach to committing the perfect crime and a trail of clues leading straight to them had been outlined at the beginning of a trial that kept the newspapers and their readers breathlessly excited for weeks. In his twelve-hour closing statement, Darrow argued that the two defendants were clearly mentally ill, and that as neither had reached the age of twenty-one, they were too young to be sentenced to death. The judge agreed with the eloquent defense lawyer, much to the irritation of the popular press, which had called for the defendants' execution. As a result of that trial, the sixty-eight-year-old lawyer had become a household name nationwide, and so he could pick and choose the cases that interested him.

Another reason he did not hesitate to offer his services in the Scopes trial was that it gave him the opportunity to confront Bryan, his political and ideological antithesis. Darrow's father had been a freethinker known locally as "the village agnostic," and Darrow himself had given fiery speeches against the "slave morality" of Christianity. As a board member of the American Civil Liberties Union, founded in 1920 with the goal of defending individual rights and freedom of speech, he saw a great opportunity for his cause in the publicity generated by the Dayton trial.

Like the Christian fundamentalists, the civil rights activists had also coalesced due to the war, and the ACLU was the successor of an organization set up in 1917 to protect conscientious objectors and antiwar protesters. While Bryan and his allies considered it the right of every state to determine its own laws, the civil liberties advocates saw the outlawing of the teaching of evolution not only as scientifically wrong and educationally unsound but also as a dramatic infringement of teachers' freedom of speech. The absolute certainty in one's own righteousness and the truth of one's beliefs that comes with faith was a great danger, Darrow believed. "The origin of what we call civilization is not due to religion but to skepticism," he argued. "The modern world is the child of doubt and inquiry, as the ancient world was the child of fear and faith."[6]

The ACLU, however, was initially not pleased that Darrow had taken the case. Though not opposed to him personally (their National Committee had been preparing to invite him to join them), they were annoyed not to have been consulted about his appointment. They also feared the negative publicity that the Leopold and Loeb case had garnered for Darrow in the South.

The Circus

FOR DAYTON, the preparations for the trial were a mixture of national emergency and the circus coming to town. With dozens if not hundreds of journalists expected to cover the proceedings, many hospitable townspeople moved out of their houses to give them to the reporters for the duration, and the journalists themselves were amazed by what they found. "The town, I confess, greatly surprised me," wrote the polemical journalist H. L. Mencken, in town to cover the trial. "I expected to find a squalid Southern village, with darkies snoozing on the horse blocks, pigs rooting under the houses and the inhabitants full of hookworm and malaria. What I found was a country town full of charm and even beauty."[7] He also reported, with almost palpable regret, that Daytonians were by no means Bible-thumping hillbillies, but friendly and intelligent people who fully realized that as far as they were concerned, the most important thing about the trial was the publicity it brought to their town.

Scopes was duly indicted by a grand jury, and the trial was set for July 10, during the summer holidays, to allow scholars and scientists to attend as witnesses, as the presiding judge explained. Both prosecution and defense began a period of intense preparation. Bryan in particular began a barrage of pretrial publicity, arguing that it "isn't proper to bring experts in here to try to defeat the purpose of the people of the state" and bellowing his usual arguments against the wickedness of Darwin and godlessness.

As the trial began, the public interest was extraordinary. More than two hundred reporters crowded into the little courthouse. The center of the courtroom was given over to microphones, and the proceedings were relayed to four outside auditoriums and, by special telephone line, to a Chicago radio station, which broadcast the entire trial live. A nearby pasture was marked out as an airstrip to transport exposed photographic plates to the big cities, where they were incorporated into the reporters' wired and telephoned reports. Despite the fact that the world-renowned British novelist H. G. Wells had declined an invitation to appear as a witness for the defense, there was little doubt that the trial and its international coverage would put Dayton on the map.

On the morning of the first day of the trial, the temperature inside the freshly painted courtroom was stifling. A publicity-savvy firm for dental hygiene products had distributed free fans with the slogan "Do Your Gums Bleed?" printed on them, and the tightly packed reporters, members of the public, legal teams, jury members, and other attendants fanned themselves furiously during the proceedings. A photo shows the two opponents, Darrow and Bryan, sitting at a table in their shirtsleeves and suspenders, looking each other in the eye as if they could win their contest by staring down the other side. It was a strangely intimate scene between two men who were so similar in age, character, and background and so very different in outlook. (In the photograph, Bryan is holding a fan.)

The trial began with a long prayer delivered by a local minister. Darrow objected, calling a religious observance in a trial about religion a strong bias. His intervention lost him sympathy with both the judge and the assembled townspeople. He plowed on, undeterred.

As the defense made its case in front of the packed court, the *New York Times* reported in sensational tones: "Clarence Darrow bearded the lion of Fundamentalism today, faced William Jennings Bryan and a court room filled with believers of the literal word of the Bible and with a hunch of shoulders and a thumb in his suspenders defied every belief they hold sacred."[8] Darrow's main argument was simple: by effectively making one interpretation of the Bible the basis of the school curriculum, the state had violated its own constitution, which granted to all men "a natural and indefeasible right to worship Almighty God according to the dictates of their conscience." That, he stated, "takes care even of the despised modernist, who dares to be intelligent," but it certainly meant that no holy scripture, including "the Koran . . . , the Book of Mormon . . . , or the Essays of Emerson," could be privileged over others.

The *Times* had bowed in admiration of Darrow's eloquence and passion, but those in the courtroom did not. "The net effect of Clarence Darrow's great speech yesterday seems to be precisely the same as if he had bawled it up a rainspout in the interior of Afghanistan," wrote Mencken; though the journalist had found the little town of Dayton beautiful, he was growing increasingly impatient with its inhabitants. It was the purpose of the defense team to turn the trial into a trial of evolution, not of a modest high school teacher. "Scopes himself was quickly overshadowed by the eminent characters who heaved and howled in the courtroom. . . . Once, after he had been unseen and unheard for two or three days, the judge stopped the proceedings to inquire what had become of him. He was found—in his shirtsleeves like everyone else—sitting in the middle of a dense mass of lawyers, infidels, theologians, biologists and reporters, and after he had risen and identified himself the uproar was resumed."[9]

The defense team called in expert witnesses to explain the science behind the theory of evolution, but the judge consistently attempted to limit the lawyers' opportunities for grandstanding and tried instead to keep the trial focused on determining whether Scopes had indeed taught evolution to his pupils. The witnesses, three boys from his class (no girls were allowed to testify), stated that he had. They had been carefully coached by Scopes himself, who, as he admitted after the trial's end, had not actually said anything about evolution during the class in question, but was willing to pretend he had done so for the sake of testing the law.

Finally it was Bryan's turn to speak. Dripping with sweat, his bald pate glistening, the portly old warrior rose to his feet to deliver his address and defend the literal truth of the Bible. "The Christian believes man came from above, but the evolutionist believes he must have come from below," he thundered. The audience lapped up his every word. The truth, he asserted, does not require experts and difficult scientific concepts: "The one beauty about the Word of God is, it does not take an expert to understand it."[10]

"The whole course of the trial of Scopes was marked by gorgeous oratory," Mencken recorded.[11] But as the dramatic arguments flew back and forth it became increasingly clear that there were no opinions to be swayed. "All that remains in the great cause of the State of Tennessee against the infidel Scopes is the final business of bumping off the defendant," noted a pessimistic Mencken. "There may be some legal jousting on Monday and some gaudy oratory on Tuesday, but the main battle is over, with Genesis completely triumphant."[12]

Darrow had kept his greatest weapon for last: calling his opponent, Bryan, as a hostile witness, he tried to put fundamentalism on the stand. But despite his sharp questioning Bryan would not budge from his literalist position, and the jury was no more convinced by the cross-examination than it had been by the expert witnesses or by Darrow's speech. The case, the seasoned lawyer began to realize, was lost. The jury found Scopes guilty of having broken the law as it stood, and fined him one hundred dollars. The event that many papers had dubbed the "trial of the century" had ended without the spectacular rhetorical victory of either side.

Despite being exhausted by the trial and severely diabetic, William Jennings Bryan immediately set off to give more speeches, traveling hundreds of miles, working relentlessly, and eating like a horse. He returned to Dayton five days after the end of the trial, took a large meal at his hotel, went to his room to rest, and died in his sleep. Christian conservatives saw him as a martyr to the cause and began collecting funds for a college in his name, which would open in 1930.

In 1927, the Tennessee Supreme Court quashed Scopes's conviction on a technicality: the fine had been set by the jury, not by the judge. In his ruling, the presiding judge added: "The court is informed that the plaintiff in error is no longer in the service of the state. We see nothing to be gained by prolonging the life of this bizarre case.

On the contrary, we think that the peace and dignity of the state, which all criminal prosecutions are brought to redress, will be the better conserved by the entry of a *nolle prosequi* herein."[13]

....

THE "MONKEY TRIAL" was followed closely and publicized by the international press, partly out of simple sensationalism and partly because it resonated strongly with the discussions between faith and science that were being conducted in many countries around the globe. In Europe, the case for evolution had been decided three decades earlier, but it touched on other issues that were very much alive and raw. Those issues focused on the two individuals William Jennings Bryan had regarded as the archenemies of religion and of all morality: Charles Darwin and Friedrich Nietzsche.

If it is almost impossible to fathom the profound influence these two thinkers had on the culture of the first half of the twentieth century, it is only because their influence is still so deeply ingrained in our culture that we can hardly imagine it without their presence. It is only possible to understand modernity and its ideological expression, modernism—or communism and fascism, or other social, political, and artistic movements—if one begins to realize the profound and seminal importance these two deeply private and often deeply misunderstood thinkers had on the generations that came after them.

It is an intellectual curse that individuals are rarely ever remembered for more than what fits into one or two short slogans, regardless of how complex and subtle their work is. In Darwin's case, these were "survival of the fittest" and "natural selection"; in Nietzsche's, they were "will to power" and "beyond good and evil," if not simply "superman," a term so easily distorted that it was hardly ever used as anything but a caricature of its original meaning.

Even before the war, these two quite unrelated theoretical edifices—one strictly scientific, the other more poetry than philosophy—had been fused into a single monstrosity, usually known as social Darwinism. The idea was almost distressingly simple: if Darwin says that the fittest are destined by nature to survive and if Nietzsche says that only the fittest should survive and that ideas such as empathy or solidarity are nothing but "slave morality," then the only natural and moral result is rule by a race of strong and ruthless supermen, weeding out everything that is, or is perceived to be, weak and unable to impose itself on others.

Of course, neither thinker had said any such thing. Darwin's "survival of the fittest" (a term coined not by him but by his admirer Herbert Spencer) in no way precluded altruism and cooperation, and Nietzsche's superman was not a rampant proto-Nazi but an ideal of self-transcendence more akin to Buddhist teachings than to anything his followers made it out to be. It did not help that Darwin's theories appeared to raise as many questions as they settled (a fact eagerly exploited by his creationist opponents) and that Nietzsche's genius circled the core of his philosophical ideas apparently unconcerned by the occasional contradiction and was understandable only by reading the entirety of his works, such as his immensely popular but easily misunderstood *Thus Spake Zarathustra*. To aggravate this already almost impossibly confused situation, Nietzsche's sister, Elisabeth Förster-Nietzsche, not only cared for the philosopher after his complete mental breakdown but also took to editing his works, effectively rewriting them in the light of her own great admiration for the rising star of German politics, Adolf Hitler.

If social Darwinism was a monstrous deformity born out of ill-digested ideas, it became hugely popular not despite but because of its simplistic message of total domination by a race of ideal humans (the particular race magically always coincided with the imagined race of whoever was promoting the idea). It was made all the more attractive by the apparent degeneration engendered by modernity, and by the apparent superiority of Western civilization over other cultures, particularly in the colonial empires of the European countries.

Even before the war, a whole scientific industry had been generated by the need to prove racial superiority over others. Lectures were given, systems devised, skulls measured, ideal features described, brains weighed, Greek sculptures analyzed as ideals of beauty, and spurious archeological artifacts passed off as proof of racial purity and superiority of the Germans, the French, the Italians, the Russians, or whoever else happened to be conducting and financing the research.

The results of this activity not only had been used by all sides to justify the war itself (apart from the Bible, *Thus Spake Zarathustra* was the book most frequently read by German soldiers at the front) but also had inspired political theories and social programs, particularly eugenics, the theory of breeding biologically perfect human beings by encouraging those of "superior stock" to breed while others, believed to be inferior, were either to be discouraged from having children or even prevented from doing so through programs of mass sterilization, or worse.

Eugenics was widely accepted and promoted across the political spectrum, and it is worth remembering that from a purely biological perspective, eugenic ideas appeared justified at the time. Even toward the end of the nineteenth century, Jean-Baptiste Lamarck's theory of heredity claiming that learned characteristics can be passed on genetically to future generations had significant support in the scientific community, and the research conducted with peas by the Austrian monk Gregor Mendel had shown that traits were indeed passed on through the generations. In the light of these findings and ideas it seemed reasonable to look at Europe's urban slums with their alcoholism, rickets, high crime rates, poverty, and misery and conclude that these "traits" should not be passed on to future generations.

Theories about the nature of heredity and of evolution were hotly discussed in the scientific community, and the existence of random mutations was as yet only one among several competing concepts. Amid this welter of ideas, eugenicists captured not only the public imagination but also to a large degree the attention of those in power. Many members of the social elite, across the entire political spectrum, were active supporters of eugenic ideas.

In Britain, the Galton Institute, named after the nineteenth-century eugenicist Francis Galton, counted among its members economist John Maynard Keynes, future prime minister Arthur Neville Chamberlain and former prime minister Arthur Balfour, Charles Darwin's son Leonard and his grandson Charles Galton Darwin, the sexologist Havelock Ellis, the American doctor and cereal magnate John Harvey Kellogg, and the birth control activists Margaret Sanger and Marie Stopes. Other prominent supporters were George Bernard Shaw, Virginia Woolf, philosopher Bertrand Russell, and novelist H. G. Wells; the list goes on to form a virtual who's who of British intellectual life.

Less efficiently organized in France but nevertheless very vociferous, the eugenics movement had strong supporters there, too. In a lecture at the Sorbonne given in 1932, eugenicist Just Sicard de Pauzole summed up the purpose of his work: "The lower classes, the poorer classes, have a much higher birthrate than the upper, richer classes. . . . Misery, along with alcoholism, syphilis and tuberculosis, is a powerful factor in degeneration . . . and children of poorer classes compared to children of rich classes show an inferiority of physical, intellectual and moral development . . . caused by fatigue and deprivation of the mother during gestation, by insufficient feeding in early years, by poor housing conditions and by working at an early age."[14]

This degradation, Sicard believed, was passed on to the next generation, and the solution was therefore not an insistence on greater social justice but a concerted effort to prevent "inferior" men and women from having children. In the United States, where immigration was continually changing the demographic makeup of society through a steady influx of poor arrivals (during this era, often from southern or eastern Europe), the Anglo-Saxon elite did its very best to defend its position and to envision a future created along eugenic—particularly "Nordic"—lines.

The Second International Congress of Eugenics was held in 1921 and hosted by the American Museum of Natural History in New York. The list of attendees included Alexander Graham Bell, the congress's honorary president; Charles Darwin's son Leonard; future US president Herbert Hoover; Henry Fairfield Osborn, director of the museum and president of the congress; and the noted racist author Lothrop Stoddard, whose *The Rising Tide of Color Against White Supremacy* (1920) was selling strongly a year after publication.

During his opening address, Osborn emphasized the urgency of the task:

> I doubt if there has ever been a moment in the world's history when an international conference on race character and betterment has been more important than the present. Europe, in patriotic self-sacrifice on both sides of the World War, has lost much of the heritage of centuries of civilization which never can be regained. . . . In the United States . . . we are engaged in a serious struggle to maintain our historic republican institutions through barring the entrance of those who are unfit to share the duties and responsibilities of our well-founded government. The true spirit of American democracy that *all men are born with equal rights and duties* has been confused with the political sophistry that *all men are born with equal character and ability to govern themselves and others*, and with the education sophistry that education and environment will offset the handicap of heredity.[15]

At the conference, delegates were alarmed at the sight of a plaster statue labeled as "the average American male." He was a product of statistics. Derived from data gleaned from US Army recruits during the war, this composite man was anything but heroic; the average American, it seemed, was already genetically a degenerate. His shoulders were narrow and sloping, his figure unathletic, his

THE AVERAGE AMERICAN MALE

Statuette of man having the average proportions of 100,000 white soldiers at demobilization as determined by the United States War Department. By Jane Davenport.

Not so heroic:
The "average American male"
according to statistical data.

arms hanging weakly by his sides. He was white, and the very whiteness of the plaster invoked not only the color of his skin but also
the marble of Greek sculpture, representing the aesthetic ideal of
human development, but *this* white man, the subliminal message ran,
was in no state to defend his wife and children against Stoddard's
rising tide of color, against the hordes of other races coming for them.
To drive home the point, the average male was exhibited next to
the heroic figure of an idealized Harvard athlete. Something had
to be done.

Eugenics spoke to a determination to defend privilege as well as
a genuine idea of bettering society and a very American hope of personal and social transformation through technology and a grand
narrative of US history. An official poster for the 1933 Chicago
World's Fair made this point when it showed the head of a noble
white female, clearly inspired by classical Greek sculpture, crowned
by a tiara composed of an American eagle and the words "I will" with
the year, 1933, next to her superimposed over the face of a Native
American chief with feather headdress and the year 1833. The white
figure simply effaced her colored American predecessor, and she
did so proudly. The legend at the top of the poster read: "A century
of progress." The exhibition also featured a Thrill House of Crime
replete with the alleged faces of criminal types such as "coke
addict," "bomber," "maniac," and "kidnapper." From 1934 to 1943,

the American Public Health Association regularly invited the German government to present a eugenics exhibition in different parts of the United States.

Not only official exhibitions were used to popularize the eugenics message. With great alliterative aplomb, two women, Mary T. Watts and Florence Brown Sherbon, founded the Fitter Families for Future Firesides contests, in which members of the public could have themselves examined by doctors and compete in categories such as "most perfect baby," "average family," or "best couple."

In the Shadow of the Superman

WHILE EUGENICS enjoyed broad popular support, the ugly ideological concoction that was social Darwinism could be looked at from a more philosophical standpoint, emphasizing Nietzsche's importance over that of Darwin and culture over biology. Hardly any thinker was immune to this, and no author could avoid dealing with Nietzsche and his legacy in some more or less bastardized form. During his defense of Chicago child murderers Nathan Leopold and Albert Loeb in 1924, only a year before defending John Scopes at the Tennessee "monkey trial," Clarence Darrow claimed that their crime had been inspired by Nietzsche—a clever move, as after the war all things German were still automatically suspicious. The suspects, law students from wealthy families, had killed a neighborhood boy simply because they were convinced that they were too intelligent and too superior to be caught.

In his summation at the end of the trial, Darrow spoke of how the hearts of men had been "calloused by war" and of a pervasive atmosphere of cruelty that misled his young clients into believing murder to be a glorious act. Speaking of Nathan "Babe" Leopold, the lawyer noted that he was "a boy without emotions, a boy obsessed of philosophy, a boy obsessed of learning." This learning, however, had led his client astray:

> Babe took to philosophy. . . . He became enamoured of the philosophy of Nietzsche. Your Honor, I have read almost everything that Nietzsche ever wrote. He was a man of a wonderful intellect; the most original philosopher of the last century. A man who probably had made a deeper imprint on philosophy than any other man within a hundred years, whether right or wrong . . . a philosopher of what we might call the intellectual cult. Nietzsche believed that some time

the superman would be born, that evolution was working toward the superman. He wrote one book, "Beyond Good and Evil" . . . a treatise holding that the intelligent man is beyond good and evil; that the laws for good and the laws for evil do not apply to those who approach the superman.

. . . Babe was obsessed of it, and here are some of the things which Nietzsche taught: Become hard . . . It was not a casual bit of philosophy with [Leopold]; it was his life. He believed in a superman. He and Dickie Loeb were the supermen. . . . The ordinary commands of society were not for him. Many of us read this philosophy but know that it has no actual application to life; but not he. It became a part of his being. It was his philosophy.[16]

Darrow had persuaded his young clients to enter a guilty plea, believing that he could save them from the electric chair only if he could avoid a jury trial. Both were sentenced to life imprisonment, a sensational victory for the defense counsel, whose clients were clearly guilty of a terrible crime and reviled by the press, which had repeatedly called for their execution. Nietzsche had won the day. The sway this "most original philosopher of the last century" held over their impressionable minds was seen to be so great that they had practically no chance of escaping his enchantment.

If Nietzsche could be portrayed as a corrosive influence on young minds in Chicago, the unfolding debate about values, crisis, and civilization after the war on both sides of the Atlantic would have been unthinkable without his reverberating voice and the inspiration it gave to followers on the European continent. In Germany, Oswald Spengler's ideas were saturated by Nietzsche, as was the poetry of Stefan George and the novels of Thomas Mann, while the rising revolutionary conservative movement around Adolf Hitler saw itself as an avant-garde of supermen. But the influence went much further. It made itself felt in France as well as in Mussolini's Italy, from north to south, and from the political right to the far left.

Lone Prophet

ONE OF THE MOST TELLING and perhaps strangest biographies among all of Zarathustra's followers was that of Oscar Levy, Nietzsche's chief apostle in Britain and the editor of the first edition of his collected works in English, who devoted his entire career to translating, writing prefaces for new editions, and generally popularizing Nietzsche. In every way, Levy, a German Jew who had left his native country in 1894 on account of his disgust with Germany's militaristic culture for the more civilized atmosphere of England, had made it his mission to spread the word in his adopted country, which had traditionally looked askance at continental philosophy in general and at Nietzsche in particular.

For Levy, this healthy empirical skepticism toward the poetic utterings and occasional ravings of Germany's most German philosopher was simply a challenge to work harder against nearly overwhelming odds. Perhaps unsurprisingly, Levy was particularly exercised about Nietzsche's apparent anti-Semitism, which he had come to share wholeheartedly and with a mixture of self-loathing and megalomania. The Jews, as he believed he understood from Nietzsche, had been the agents of humanity's greatness and also of its imminent downfall, from which only the Jews could save it.

At the beginning of this extraordinary idea stood, appropriately enough, a conversion, which in Levy's case had taken place at the British Museum. Surrounded by the great art of previous civilizations—evidence of other ways of seeing the world, of other ideas of beauty and human fulfillment—he felt moved to question the values of his own society: "I have the sudden thought that Monotheism etc. may not be 'Progress' after all, as I had been taught in school and life under the (unconscious) influence of Hegel. My Damascus: 'But then the Jews were wrong!?' The Chosen People not chosen for Beauty like the Greeks? Only for Morality, and what a Morality: the curses of J. C.!"[17]

This sudden revelation brought Levy to a position that had strong similarities with that of the eugenicists, if from a philosophical perspective. Christianity had infected the great civilizations of antiquity with what Nietzsche had called the Jewish "slave morality" of guilt and groveling. This had to be reversed. Aiding and supporting "the feeble, commonplace, pitiable, unsound, and helpless" was not doing humanity a favor but only turning it into "a flock of sheep . . . mutually innocuous and useless." Instead, he believed he had found the answer to the great crisis of civilization in a new aristocracy of Nietzschean supermen, strong, proudly immoral, and weeding out everything that was weak.

Levy had worked tirelessly to pave the way for a wider reception of his idol in Britain, but during the war he had had his right of residence revoked and had been obliged to leave. After a sojourn in Switzerland he had returned, apparently undaunted, in 1920, only to find that most of his former acquaintances were now giving him a wide berth as an enemy alien. In spite of such obstacles, he had plowed on, spreading the gospel of his curious anti-Semitism, which was generous enough to include Christianity and to call for a new, if decidedly idiosyncratic, mission for the Jewish people: "The world still needs Israel, for the world has fallen prey to democracy and needs the example of a people which has always acted contrary to democracy, which has always upheld the principle of race. The world still needs Israel, for terrible wars, of which the present one is only the beginning, are in store for it; and the world needs a race of good Europeans who stand above national bigotry and national hypocrisy, national mysticism and national blackguardism."[18]

With his idea of a people faithful to race but disdainful of nationalism, Levy's moral crusade led him to keep strange company. He admired blatantly racist and virulently anti-Semitic writers such as Arthur de Gobineau and George Lane-Fox Pitt-Rivers, who made use of him without sharing any of his confused but magnanimous feelings toward his fellow humans. Instead, they could quote his tirades about the historical role of the Jews, which still make shocking reading: "We who have posed as the saviours of the world, we, who have even boasted of having given it 'the' Saviour, we are today nothing else but the world's seducers, its destroyers, its incendiaries, its executioners. We who have promised to lead you to a new Heaven, we have finally succeeded in landing you in a new Hell."[19]

To Levy this polemic was only the preface to a world revolution led by Jewish intelligence, but to many who read him it was exactly the kind of argument that had been put forward in the notorious *Protocols of the Elders of Zion* and which was being eagerly studied and propagated by politicians such as Adolf Hitler, who had just finished a stint of imprisonment at Landsberg—a valuable pause in his political career that had allowed him to commit his own, remarkably similar ravings to paper, and to posterity, in his notorious *Mein Kampf*.

In England, Levy's racial theories met an increasingly frosty reception, and in 1921, only one year after his return to the country he had chosen a quarter of a century earlier, he was deported as an enemy alien by the Home Office, which viewed his enthusiasm for Nietzsche as flagrant pro-German propaganda. Levy was dismayed but not silenced. He protested against his expulsion and was informed that only those Germans who were of unequivocal use to British commerce were allowed to stay. "Alas! I was only the importer of a few new but very odd and doubtful ideas!" he commented. He moved to France and from there back to Germany, where he was to remain until 1933.

In 1924 he traveled to Italy to meet Mussolini, his new political idol. "Fascism is not only an antidote, but likewise a remedy against Bolshevism," he had written in 1921. "For Bolshevism is not so much a revolutionary as a reactionary creed. Bolshevism wishes to put the clock back to the old principles of the French Revolution: it even stands up most shamelessly for Liberty, Equality and Fraternity. These ideas, however, have decayed, nay, have become idols which are as good as dead: it is for the new fascistic movement to bury them altogether and to enthrone in their place other ideas and living aspirations for the guidance and progress of mankind."[20]

As a writer, Levy received applause almost exclusively from the historically "wrong" side, but when Hitler came to power in 1933 Levy left Germany for France, and finally returned to England on the eve of the Second World War. He was to remain there until his death in 1946. Misguided as he had been about the historic potential of fascism, he was not alone in believing it to be a solution to the malaise of his own day, and it is to his credit that he eventually understood his error. In November 1933, true to his Nietzschean beliefs, he offered a bracing perspective on the ideology of National Socialism that might have surprised its adherents:

> The modern Germans are less a civilized than a religious people. Their religion comes, strange to say, right out of the Old Testament. The Chosen Race idea, which is at the root of the German mentality, springs from the soil of Israel. Israel likewise produced, long before Hitler and Göbbels [sic], its "Ahnenprüfer" (ancestor examiners) in the historical figures of Ezra and Nehemia. They forbade all intercourse with foreign women. . . . They, too, were all for the purity of Race, for pride of Race, for power of Race. The Germans, following in their footsteps, do not know how reactionary they are and how akin, spiritually, to those, whom they detest. . . . This Hitlerism is nothing but a Jewish Heresy.[21]

Debates about Darwin and Nietzsche, about evolution and radical moral doubt, echoed through this deeply unsettled period. They represented the two most important ways to conjure up the spirit of the age and its great ideal: the New Man, the answer to the trauma of the war and the reign of anonymous technology. New Men could be bred selectively, and they could create themselves through an act of heroic self-transcendence. It was a great but ambiguous dream, and the image of this great hero was enlisted to serve ideas on both the right and the left, pursued by scientists and occultists alike, venerated in many forms and rituals. The dream of the New Man was evident in the work of artists and the earnest idealism of nudist associations venerating sun and air, in the public fascination with competitive sport, fashion for new body lines, and scientific advances. But it was an ambiguous dream now, teetering on the verge of nightmare. The experience of the First World War had shown that technological progress was no longer inherently positive, that machines could become malign, and that, like Goethe's sorcerer's apprentice, humanity could no longer rid itself of the spirits it had called. The New Man was simultaneously the era's most potent promise and its greatest threat.

Metropolis

*Man has, as it were, become a kind of prosthetic God. When he
puts on all his auxiliary organs he is truly magnificent; but those
organs have not grown on to him and they still give him much
trouble at times.*
 —Sigmund Freud, *Civilization and Its Discontents*, 1930

Hear the evangel of the new era—
The machine has no inhibitions
Man invented the machine in order to discover himself
Yet I have heard a lady say "Il fait l'amour comme
une machine à coudre," with no inflection of approval.
 —Mina Loy, "The Oil in the Machine," 1923

....

IT WAS NOT AN IDEAL START FOR THE US RELEASE OF A MAJOR
European movie. "I have recently seen the silliest film," the review
began. "I do not believe it would be possible to make one sillier. . . .
It is called 'Metropolis,' it comes from the great Ufa studios in
Germany, and the public is given to understand that it has been produced at enormous cost. It gives in one eddying concentration almost
every possible foolishness, cliché, platitude, and muddlement about
mechanical progress and progress in general served up with a sauce
of sentimentality that is all its own."[1] The damning review appeared
in the *New York Times*. Its author was none other than a master of
science fiction writing, the British novelist H. G. Wells.

Wells was clearly more than a little annoyed about the work,
which had been advertised as the greatest German film of all time,
as well as the most expensive. With *Metropolis*, the UFA studios

wanted to rival Hollywood and demonstrate to the world that they had all the technology, know-how, trick photography, and other niceties Hollywood had to offer, but could in addition give their films real cultural import, not to say spiritual content. It was here that they went wrong, as Wells pointed out with obvious glee. The problem, as he saw it, was that there was too much murky, Faustian romanticism in what was supposed to be a thoroughly modern fable: "Perhaps Germans will never get right away from the Brocken. Walpurgis Night is the name day of the German poetic imagination, and the national fantasy capers insecurely forever with a broomstick between its legs."

Metropolis was artistically a mess and commercially a disaster. Its pharaonic cost, five million marks, though modest by today's standards, drove UFA to the brink of bankruptcy and forced them to collaborate with US studios, making them financially dependent on their transatlantic partners and putting an end to their dreams of challenging Hollywood's dominant position. But even though the film flopped at the box office even in the severely cut rerelease concocted after the difficult German premiere, it is still an important historical and artistic document. Furthermore, its very failure is fascinating.

Directed by Fritz Lang after a script by his wife and collaborator, Thea von Harbou, the movie tells a fable of love and redemption in a dictatorship "some hundred years in the future," in which society is split sharply into two classes, the haves and the have-nots. On the higher levels of the dazzling futurist city with its seventy-floor skyscrapers, multilevel roads, and planes floating between buildings lives a class of rich and leisured beautiful people whose lives are dedicated to sport and lavish celebrations, while in the lightless catacombs below, an army of slave workers is stoking the gigantic machines that keep the huge city running. Above it all, in an office in the "new tower of Babel," is Joh Fredersen, the undisputed ruler of Metropolis, whose technological vision and authority have created this futurist world.

What happens next is almost inevitable. Freder, the dictator's son, wanders into the lower city because he has spotted an attractive girl, Maria, who is one of the work slaves. There he witnesses an accident when an exhausted worker breaks down and a machine explodes, killing some of his colleagues. Shocked by the accident and by the general hardship he has witnessed, he decides to help, and eventually the workers revolt, egged on not by the noble Freder but by a robot built to resemble Maria and sent by the wicked Joh Fredersen to lead them astray while the real Maria, the spiritual leader of the workers, is imprisoned. Eventually the workers burn the false Maria at the stake, young Freder appears as their champion, and the real Maria is liberated. The father relents and shakes hands with the leader of the rebellion. "The heart must mediate between brain and hands," as the film declares.

Ambitious and endlessly imaginative, Lang was not much interested in the moral of the story, or indeed in any part of the story, which may account for its patchy realization and sentimental end. To him, *Metropolis* was an opportunity to create a new cinematic world composed of gigantic sets, innovative trick filming, and thousands of extras, who often had to work under terrible conditions, lining up for take after take until the director was satisfied. One scene, in which the workers have to struggle with a flood, was shot with an army of extras—altogether the film would use twenty-seven thousand men, women, and children—who had to brave the icy water time and again. In the quest to realize his artistic vision, Lang was pitiless, and during the 310 days and 60 nights of filming, usually for more than twelve hours per day, the crew, not to mention the shivering extras, came to resent him bitterly.

If the film flopped in spite of its impressive technical wizardry, the creation of an entire futurist city, dramatic crowd scenes, and amazing sequences, Lang's indifference and the script had a great deal to do with it. As Wells had so caustically remarked, von Harbou had created a scenario that was prophetic in many ways, not all of them intentional.

Apart from the obvious Christian allusions—the cruel father, the son as mediator between him and the desperate mortals, the tower of Babel, the holy virgin Maria, and so on—there were other, more disturbingly contemporary resonances. The oppressed workers were waiting for a leader, a *Führer*, to rise up against the injustice of their lot; the masses are whipped up by speeches given by the false Maria, and they break the city's "heart machine" in order to force things to a total standstill. The public is invited to sympathize with their quest and with the idea that only a charismatic figure can save the day and rescue the people from the dictatorship of a decadent elite.

Another obvious strand was, paradoxically, the blatant anti-modernism lying at the heart of the sci-fi narrative. Ultimately, the huge, gleaming city is nothing but a new Babel, and its creature, the false Maria, is the ultimate temptress, the Whore of Babylon in action. Brigitte Helm, who played both the flesh-and-blood Maria and the automatic, false one, was careful to portray the real heroine as chaste and motherly, while the machine Maria was a harlot in human form, wantonly sensual and seductive as she dances semi-naked for

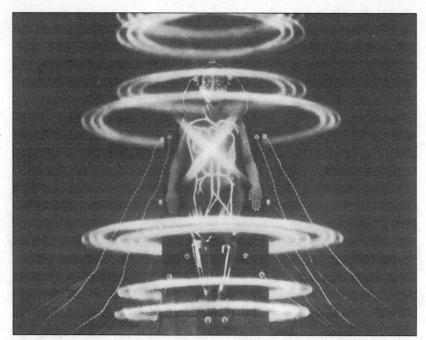

Man and machine: still from the transformation scene in Metropolis.

the privileged young men, who fall into a collective frenzy over her
desirable body.

Maria, who can be seen celebrating candlelit masses for the
masses in the lower city, is the ideal German woman, and she looks
conspicuously medieval. Wells, who did not suffer fools gladly, was
particularly scornful of this anti-technological utopia, in which
machines and innovation stood for a soulless dictatorship, while salvation apparently lies in turning to the past. "That reversion to torches
is quite typical of the spirit of this show," he scoffed in his review.
"Torches are Christian, we are asked to suppose; torches are human.
Torches have hearts. But electric hand-lamps are wicked, mechanical,
heartless things. The bad, bad inventor uses quite a big one."

While the film portrayed the ideal of womanhood as chaste, pious,
and rooted in the soil of history, the false Maria can also be read as a
cipher for many of the anti-Semitic stereotypes of the time. Like the
Jews of contemporary anti-Semitic caricature, she is quite literally a
product of an urban, technological, ultramodern world of industry
and capitalism, devoid of feelings and originality, and dedicated to
corrupting the purity of the people. She is not rooted in anything and
merely mimics the soulfulness of those around her while in reality

seducing them with her neurotic sexuality and leading them to their destruction. These were all accusations leveled at the Jews by anti-Semitic writers, and it is no accident that von Harbou would go on to have a successful career under the Nazi regime.

Metropolis was to be a metaphor of the threat of a world ruled by soulless technology, a theme that was particularly popular among conservative and right-wing thinkers and politicians. The anti-Semitic dimension of the story, which is not immediately obvious anymore, is all the more disturbing in that the liberation of the enslaved people becomes possible only when the false Maria is burned at the stake and the flames sear off the simulacrum of flesh to reveal the automaton's iron physique.

Half high-tech tale and half medieval legend, *Metropolis* betrays a very German ambivalence toward the rush of modernization that had swept the country along for a generation and had covered more ground in less time than anywhere else. Europe's technologically most highly developed and most highly industrialized country, the home of the avant-garde aesthetics of the Bauhaus as well as a hub of scientific research, Germany was obviously not at ease with the rapid unfolding of the new. The city of Metropolis and its rulers are decadent, cruel, and technocratic, while true spirituality and indeed salvation lie in the quasi-medieval piety of Maria and her followers.

Mechanical Golems

WITH THEIR GREATEST FILM TO DATE, Lang and von Harbou had given the popular discussions about progress and its perils a distinctly German spin, despite the fact that their ideas were not necessarily German in origin. Not only is the mechanical Maria a seemingly innocuous metaphor for the anti-Semitic fantasy of a Jewish world conspiracy, but the figure touches a nerve of this highly body-conscious period, in which the image of the automaton had become an important part of the popular imagination. As Wells pointed out in his review, the writer and director had plagiarized not only his own futurist novels but also a play by the Czech author KarelČapek that had premiered six years before the release of *Metropolis*.

Enigmatically entitled *R.U.R.*, Čapek's drama was another very conventional love story in technological garb, though this time without a happy end. In the play, an inventor on an island invents human-like robots out of a synthetic protoplasm, and his son, who is in it only for the money, launches mass production. Soon a race of useful automata in human form populates the earth. Because they do humanity's dirty work, they are referred to as "robots," after a Czech word indicating hard labor. Eventually the robots rebel against their masters, begin a bloody war against mankind, and finally extinguish almost all human life on earth.

Both helpful and potentially threatening, robots were everywhere in the culture of the 1920s. In the United States, the view of these technological helpmates was generally optimistic. Newspapers carried stories about thousand-foot-high robots secretly being developed by governments around the world to fight humanity's wars. In a 1930 advertisement for Westinghouse's "mechanical wonder maid," Katrina Van Televox, the marketers of the $22,000 machine promised, apparently without irony: "Katrina talks . . . answers the phone . . . runs a vacuum cleaner . . . makes coffee and toast . . . turns the lights on and off and does it all willingly at command from Mr. T. Barnard the Westinghouse Electric & Manufacturing Expert who is accompanying her on her tour." In the same year, the scientist Samuel Montgomery Kintner introduced the world to a robot of his own devising, Rastus, a laborer who was, rather significantly, a "mechanical negro."

Robots had commercial potential. While the real contraptions of steel and tubes were still too primitive to do significantly more than automata had done for centuries, the possibilities were endlessly exciting. When would it be possible, as the *San Antonio Light* asked in 1928, that a "romantic old maid" could keep a fully functioning robot under her bed for sentimental moments—and, by implication, even for amorous hours? The writer hoped that this day would not be too far away. "In this happy future, no old maid need look under the bed for a man, in vain," the article explained. "He would always be there and such a nice man, a perfect imitation of her favorite matinee idol or film star, with blond or dark hair, moustache or clean shaven, anything her heart desired. These would be stock models, turned out in quantity production and quite reasonable in price."[2]

Stories such as these made good copy and were entertaining without being scientific. At the same time, however, the real and progressing mechanization of factory work was a source of anxiety. Utopian writers had sketched a future in which all work would be done by machines that would have to be only occasionally supervised or repaired by humans, a golden dream. As the Depression began to bite after 1929, however, it began to look more like a nightmare, a competition between man and machine for the few precious jobs left. The mood of the press changed together with the anxieties of its readership, and now robot stories began to take a nasty turn verging on hysteria. When in 1932 the British inventor Harry May gave a demonstration of a robot he had constructed to be able to shoot a gun, he accidentally fired the weapon while putting it in the automaton's hand. The story was immediately reported in the United States, where it took on a life of its own, with various sources writing that the robot had intentionally shot and wounded May, or even killed him—the first robot to rise against its maker and attack it.

The fact that the story of the murdering robot was an invention did nothing to stop it from spreading. This was a time when more and more people felt vulnerable to the huge success of machines. "Is Man Doomed by the Machine Age?" asked the magazine *Modern Mechanics and Inventions* in 1931, illustrating its story with the image of a huge robot at a switchboard, menacingly glowering down at the tiny human figures toiling below. In the same publication, boxing champion Jack Dempsey promised to come to the rescue, claiming that "I can whip any mechanical robot." The terrible and treacherous false Maria in *Metropolis* had simply come too early to tap into the fears of the public.

The Iron Fist of Progress

IF ROBOTS CLAIMED such a large part of the popular imagination in the 1920s and 1930s, it was not just because technological progress appeared to bring a dream as old as humanity almost within reach. In Europe at least, bodies enhanced and to some extent created by science were already part of everyday life. Tens of thousands of mutilated veterans had received reconstructive surgery for their horrific and often disfiguring injuries or were forced to wear masks covering part of their face to give a naturalistic imitation of their previous appearance, and hundreds of thousands lived with increasingly sophisticated prosthetic limbs replacing their hands or even entire arms and legs. The fusion of biology and technology was already taking place.

The medical establishment bandaged, cut, grafted, shaped, re-educated, and experimented, all in an effort to enable their mutilated patients to lead a life as close to normal as possible. But in doing so, doctors were steering close to what was still widely considered the inviolable border between human ingenuity and divine creation. To the public, this was irresistible, as it provoked age-old superstitions as well as ageless curiosity. Again, films were ideally placed to capitalize on the thirst for sensational stories arising from this situation. The 1924 Austrian movie *Orlacs Hände* (The Hands of Orlac) adapted a 1920 novel by the French writer Maurice Renard in which a concert pianist loses his hands in a train crash and receives the hands of a freshly executed murderer by transplantation. Soon afterward, the otherwise gentle Orlac finds himself irresistibly drawn to knives and feels an intense desire to kill. In 1935 the film was remade in Hollywood under the title *Mad Love*, starring Peter Lorre.

During the war and in its immediate aftermath, victims of shell shock had been successfully treated not only with hypnosis but also with electric shocks to reactivate bodies rendered painfully useless by the trauma of bombardment and butchery. The British actor and director James Whale, a veteran of the Western Front, had directed the war drama *Journey's End* in London in 1928 to great acclaim. Soon after, he was invited to Hollywood, signed to a contract by Universal Studios, and given the choice of any story he wanted to make. He picked Mary Shelley's classic tale *Frankenstein* and selected as his leading man another Englishman, William Henry Pratt, whose dramatic features meant that he was often hired to play oriental villains. Pratt had emphasized this exotic appeal by choosing a more alluring stage name, Boris Karloff.

Released in 1931, *Frankenstein* immediately established itself as a paradigmatic film. The story of a mad scientist using body parts reclaimed from the grave and exposing them to electricity and mysterious rays to create a monster that turns into a murderous nightmare when awakened obviously struck a chord with the thrilled audience. The ill-begotten creature, it was revealed, had the brain of a criminal but was not malicious from the outset. Instead, Dr. Frankenstein's misunderstanding and ill treatment of the monster make it more and more angry and desperate until at last it breaks free from its dungeon and inadvertently kills a young girl. In the end, the monster is being burned alive—much like the false Maria in *Metropolis*—by an angry mob, restoring the balance of nature.

The expiatory ritual of a public burning is profoundly disturbing, but it also reflected a psychological truth dramatized by another film released in 1931, Rouben Mamoulian's *Dr. Jekyll and Mr. Hyde*, starring Fredric March, in which yet another scientist turns bad, this time by imbibing a potion that allows him to live out his primitive instincts without any moral restraint by transforming him into the ruthless and lecherous Mr. Hyde, who does not stop at murder to get his way. When Dr. Jekyll finds that he is no longer able to control his violent alter ego, the situation deteriorates, and he is finally, as Hyde, shot by the police.

Based on a classic story by Robert Louis Stevenson, *Dr. Jekyll and Mr. Hyde* has always lent itself to Freudian readings, which were certainly popular at the time. But popular movie villains such as

Jekyll/Hyde, Orlac, Frankenstein's monster, the terrifying Nosferatu, and characters such as Dr. Jack Griffin in *The Invisible Man*, a 1933 film based on a story by H. G. Wells, also spoke to their audience in a different way. Millions of soldiers had gone into the war believing that they were fighting for a good cause, only to be terribly disillusioned once they reached the trenches. The war had not only shattered, mutilated, and disfigured their bodies but also made them kill as horribly, anonymously, and senselessly as the men on the other side were killing them. Like Frankenstein's initially meek monster or the false Maria, they had been made into something abhorrent by their masters, and now they had blood on their hands.

The dead on both sides still haunted the war's veterans, as the Swiss-French poet Blaise Cendrars, who had lost an arm on the Western Front in 1915, described in his story "J'ai Tué" (I Have Killed), written in 1918. The tale is a moving and masterful evocation of the experience of warfare in dense, modernist prose, a deeply disturbing verbal approximation of the unsayable:

> Total conflagration. Lightning's striking. Fires, blazes, explosions. Avalanches of cannon shells. Rollings. Barrages. Rock-drills. In this shivering electric glow frantic profiles of swerving men, a finger on a billboard, a lunatic horse. . . . We're right in the arc of the falling shells. We can hear the big Granddaddies coming home. There are locomotives in the air, invisible freight trains, collisions, smash-ups. . . . Sounds come out of it in couples, male and female. Gnashings. Shooooshings. Creakings. Yowlings. Coughs, spits, yells, grunts, whines. Terrific chimeras of steel, mastodons in heat. Apocalyptic mouth, slit pouch from which indistinct syllables come lurching downward, enormous as cavorting whales.[3]

Running through the raped countryside of bomb craters, rotting limbs, and half-mummified corpses, the narrator finds himself with a bayonet and is confronted by a German soldier. At this moment, moral considerations count for nothing:

> I've risked grenades, cannons, mines, fire, poison gas, machine guns, the whole anonymous, demoniac, precise, blind machinery. I'm going to kill a man. *Mon semblable*. A monkey. Eye for eye, tooth for tooth. Just the two of us now. Just fists, just knives. No feeling. I jump at the enemy. I slash him, slash him, slash deep in the neck. Bloody butter. The head's

almost ripped out of place. Windpipe's tough as nails. I've killed the Kraut. I was livelier and quicker than he. More skilled. I struck first. I've a greater sense of reality, being a poet. I've acted. I've killed. Just a shit that wants to live.

A war that made murderers out of poets, rendering them not fighting heroes but simply shits who want to live, without higher goal, without any greater justification than naked survival, could and did turn honest men into monstrous alter egos of themselves. When they returned, they found it almost impossible to talk about their experiences, about the change that had taken place within themselves, and they continued to live in fear that their brain might be the brain of a criminal, their hands the hands of a murderer, that they would wake up one day and find that Mr. Hyde had won, that Jekyll could no longer turn back into his former self.

While Hollywood horror struck the fear of God into its viewers with visions of a creation that was not divinely sanctioned and the terrible consequences that followed, serious scientists were also interested in the metaphor of the body as machine. In 1919, the Scottish anthropologist and anatomist Arthur Keith had published *The Engines of the Human Body*, in which he described the human machine as a system of levers (bones), internal combustion engines, and a "telephone exchange" (the central nervous system). But the idea of mechanizing humans was popularized most energetically by Fritz Kahn, a German doctor who lived a peripatetic life between the United States, Germany, and Palestine. Having grown up partly in Hoboken, New Jersey, and in New York, Kahn went to school in Hamburg, Bonn, and Berlin, where he also studied medicine. During the war, the young doctor served on the Western Front and in the Alps, the scene of entrenched battles and particularly vicious shelling. In early 1918 he suffered a breakdown and was sent to recuperate with a farming family in the Tyrol.

Returning from a prolonged trip to Algeria, Kahn became engaged in social projects. An ardent Zionist since his student days, he was active on behalf of Jewish charities and traveled to Palestine in 1921. In the following year, he opened a gynecological practice in Berlin and also began writing popular medical books in which he consistently described the human body as "the most highly performing machine in the world." His works owed their considerable success in part to their lavish illustrations, striking plates showing the inner workings of the human machine, complete with a command center in the brain, where little men in white coats ran operations; the arteries

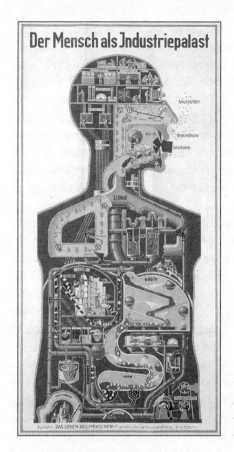

Der Mensch als Industriepalast

Man as machine: Fritz Kahn's explanation of the workings of the human body, 1922.

as a system of pipes; the liver transforming sugar and cleansing the plant on a conveyor belt system with attentive workers; and so on. As a metaphor, not only was man the machine easily understood, but its determinism also lent itself to being applied to social and political questions.

By now a popular figure, Kahn was invited in 1926 to become scientific advisor to a large exhibition in Düsseldorf devoted to health, social questions, and physical fitness, where he was responsible for questions surrounding "the hygiene of the Jews"—a testimony to the organizers' inherently racist way of thinking. Kahn himself, incidentally, was not immune to biological determinism. In his book *Unser Geschlechtsleben* (1937; English trans., *Our Sex Life*, 1942), he introduced the sexual characteristics of a "normal man" and "normal woman," noting that men had high foreheads indicating intelligence and decisiveness, whereas women's low foreheads were testimony to their sentimental nature and readiness for self-sacrifice.

Cogs in the Machine

HUMANS AS MACHINES, either metaphorically or literally as mechanically enhanced cyborgs, haunted the imagination of the interwar years. It was a very modern nightmare, born not only out of the experience of the war but also of city life and the Taylorized work in the factories. In 1936 Charlie Chaplin's *Modern Times* would go one step further and tell the story of a worker whose humanity rebels against the mechanization of his existence and who is eventually swallowed whole by the huge machine of which he has become a tiny, organic part.

Mechanization was frightening, but not for everyone. The heartland of these dreams of a perfect plan for a flawless society of the future was revolutionary Russia, known as the Soviet Union after uniting with some of the smaller former tsarist states in 1922. After the terrible bloodletting of the civil war, after the executions and the famines and the epidemics, after the constant hunger and the disastrous early government initiatives, the new empire appeared to some to be settling down to hope, and to thinking about how to realize a dream of justice and equality that was as old as humanity itself.

Not everyone took so optimistic a view of the developments in the new state. The crushing of the Kronstadt rebellion had appalled many sympathizers in the West, and even in Russia itself many idealistic socialists had become disillusioned. But while Comrade Stalin secured his hold on power with an ever-widening net of secret police spies, jails, torture cellars, gulags, and executions, many committed younger intellectuals and artists still thought that they could realize utopia—and often continued to think so until the Cheka knocked at their own doors in the small hours of the morning.

Among those keeping faith with the revolutionary idea and the possibility of utopian renewal was an engineer and poet, Alexei Gastev, who had been a communist activist since his student days. His engagement had led him to be excluded from the Moscow Pedagogical Academy and had caused him to be banished to Siberia three times, until he finally emigrated to France in 1907. In Paris, he had worked at the Renault car factory and had observed first hand the introduction of Taylorism, the gospel of efficiency and labor optimization preached by the American pioneer Frederick Winslow Taylor, who had analyzed product streams down to individual sequences of movements executed by the workers on the factory floor and had propagated a series of changes designed to save effort and time and thus increase productivity. Taylor viewed the individual workers in a

Swallowed by the big machine: Charlie Chaplin as a deranged worker in Modern Times, *which was seen by many as too critical of modern capitalism.*

factory as little more than parts of a machine, and improved on their efficiency not by making their work pleasanter or safer but simply by making them more efficient.

On his return to Russia on the eve of the Revolution, Gastev became a trade unionist and made himself the prophet of Taylorism, and he found an interested listener in Lenin, with whom he corresponded. After the establishment of the Soviet state, Lenin made the rapid industrialization of the huge but hugely backward empire his greatest priority, and he turned to the engineer to introduce the miracle of labor saving to the factories. "The war taught us much," Lenin wrote, "not only that people suffered, but especially the fact that those who have the best technology, organization, discipline and the best machines emerge on top; it is this the war has taught us. It is essential to learn that without machines, without discipline, it is impossible to live in modern society. It is necessary to master the highest technology or be crushed."[4]

In 1920, as a step toward the realization of the dream of a fully industrialized Soviet Union, Lenin had helped Gastev to set up the Central Institute of Work, which was devoted to analyzing work practices and training workers in how to work more efficiently. Gastev threw himself into his task like a man possessed, his goal the realization of the total, machine-like efficiency of factory work and ultimately of every aspect of life in the new society.

Gastev's veneration of the "iron messiah" knew no bounds. He thought of machines as his "iron friends" and saw the crashing, whistling, grating, and screaming of the factory as the music of the future. Eventually, he believed, even the cumbersome process of democratic decision making would be taken over by competent automata, able to evaluate facts far more objectively than humans. His shining example of transformation at the workplace and its social implications was arch-capitalist Henry Ford, the founder of the Ford Motor Company and the man who introduced the moving assembly line in his factories. Ford not only had written *My Life*, an auto-biography that went through multiple editions in its Russian trans-lation, but also had expounded on the hidden morality of work in other books.

In his *Machinery, the New Messiah*, Gastev sang the praises of his new gospel of Fordism, which not only was a way of increasing productivity but also introduced clean, moral living to the workers. "A clean factory, clean tools, accurate gauges, and precise methods of manufacture produce a smooth working, efficient machine," Ford had written, while "clean thinking, clean living, and square dealing" would produce a good home life.[5] At the time, however, Ford's factories were no Sunday schools, but arenas of ruthless competition in which the workers were but cogs in a machine honed to perfection. "A great business is really too big to be human," Ford opined. Gastev admired this pitiless determination and its hugely successful outcome. The Soviet Union was importing Ford cars and tractors by the tens of thousands, and he was convinced that the communists must learn from their ideological adversary. *Amerikanizatsii*, "Americanization," became the watchword of the day.

The goal of this process was nothing less than a total transfor-mation of society. In the new order, Gastev wrote enthusiastically, machines would set the course and people would follow, performing standardized gestures and living standardized lives. All aspects of life would be optimized for efficiency and uniformity, including not just housing and education but also language, food, thoughts, and sex. The ideal person was to be regarded as a production unit, evaluated only according to its efficiency and named with a combination of neutral letters and numbers, "soulless and devoid of personality, emotion, and lyricism—no longer expressing himself through screams of pain or joyful laughter, but rather through a manometer or taxi-meter. Mass engineering will make man a social automation."[6]

At the Central Institute of Labor, workers had to learn to perform their tasks strapped to machines that ensured maximum efficiency of their movements. Every task was photographed and described in diagrams and "cyclograms," and the resulting improvements were transmitted to factories around the Soviet Union. Battling shortages of tools and scientific instruments as well as food and heating fuel for his institutes, Gastev tirelessly pushed forward the gospel of an eventual total mechanization of society, regardless of opposition from the workers and of other Bolsheviks. When the German writer Ernst Toller visited the institute, he described rows upon rows of trainees in identical work clothes standing at identical work benches and being taught to obey the electric signals of a machine, repetitively, day after day, for up to six months per course.

To the enthusiasts of revolutionary planning, such daily monotony was nothing less than a social ideal. The Society of Contemporary Architects was founded in 1928, and its members saw their mission as something much larger than just putting up houses for the prole-tariat. Their aim was to "alter radically the structure of human life—productive, social, and personal," by imagining and constructing structures that were "social condensers" in a great surge of Soviet urbanism. The workers' houses were to be arranged in communes, each of which was to have its own dining hall, club, wash house, kindergartens, cultural spaces, and parks. In contrast to the petty bourgeois habits of the past, property and the tasks of daily living were to be shared freely, and life was to be organized according to scientific principles. One architect helpfully drew up a "graph of life" intended to regulate the daily routine of workers, as well as the planning priorities of urbanists:

1. Lights out. 10:00 P.M.
2. Eight hours of sleep. Reveille. 6:00 A.M.
3. Calisthenics—5 min. 6:05 A.M.
4. Toilet—10 min. 6:15 A.M.
5. Shower (optional 5 min.) 6:20 A.M.
6. Dress—5 min 6:25 A.M.
7. To the dining room—3 min. 6:28 A.M.
8. Breakfast—15 min. 6:43 A.M.
9. To the cloakrooms—2 min. 6:45 A.M.
10. Put on outdoor clothing—5 min. 6:50 A.M.
11. To the mine—10 min. 7:00 A.M.

12. Work in the mine—8 hours. 3:00 P.M.
13. To the commune—10 min. 3:10 P.M.
14. Take off outdoor clothing—7 min. 3:17 P.M.
15. Wash—8 min. 3:25 P.M.
16. Dinner—30 min. 3:55 P.M.
17. To the rest room for free hour—3 min. 3:58 P.M.
18. Free time. Those who wish may nap. In this case they retire to the bedrooms. 4:58 P.M.
19. Toilet and change—10 min. 5:08 P.M.
20. To the dining room—2 min. 5:10 P.M.
21. Tea—15 min. 5:25 P.M.
22. To the club. Recreation. Cultural development. Gymnastics. Perhaps a bath or swim. Here it is life itself that will determine how time is spent, that will draw up the plan. Allotted time: four hours. 9:25 P.M.
23. To dining room, supper, eat, and to bedrooms—25 min. 9:50 P.M.
24. Prepare to retire (a shower may be taken)—10 min. 10:00 P.M.[7]

By 1938, the institute and its seventeen hundred branches had trained more than half a million workers according to the new system. Gastev was awarded the Order of the Red Flag for his work, one of the highest decorations of the Soviet Union. He was even allocated an apartment in a Moscow building housing many of the most famous writers and intellectuals of the Soviet Union. There, on September 8, 1938, agents of the secret police arrested him and took him away. Accused of being a counterrevolutionary conspirator and condemned to death during a half-hour hearing on April 14, 1939, he was shot the following day.

Gastev's fate was shared by tens of thousands of enthusiastic revolutionaries who suddenly found themselves on the wrong side of internal Kremlin power struggles or policy changes, or simply were chosen to fill execution quotas imposed from above. His faith in a technological future in which the entire Soviet Union would be one enormous, gleaming machine animated by anonymous production units of flesh and blood, a vast landscape of steel, concrete, and asphalt glorifying the world revolution, would live on, if not in the way he himself had hoped. His writings and beliefs animated a swath of science fiction novels. The most famous of these, Yevgenii Zamyatin's *We*, was written in 1921 but not published until 1927, after the author had managed to have the manuscript smuggled out of the country. The novel is set in One State, a police dictatorship

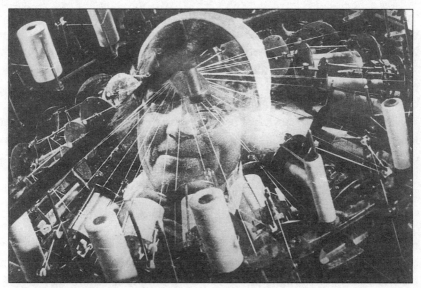

Spinning out of control: Tsiga Vertov's utopian vision of Homo sovieticus *as a perfect machine part.*

in the future, in which individuals are known only by a combination of letters and numbers. The narrator and the chief engineer of One State is D-503, who initially lives a comfortable life enhanced by occasional visits from his lover, O-90, assigned to him for impersonal sex visits. In One State, people live out their utterly uniform lives in glass houses to facilitate supervision by the secret police and do exactly as they are told.

When D-503 is confronted with a woman who breaks the strict rules and shows signs of personal traits and desires, he is appalled but strangely fascinated. Shortly afterward he begins to dream in his sleep—a sure sign of mental trouble, according to the state authorities. He becomes involved in an illicit love affair that results not only in a pregnancy that was not sanctioned by the all-knowing administration but also in his lover's being smuggled out to another life, where she will be able to keep her child rather than be forced to give it up for adoption. D-503 has to pay a high price for this act of foolish individualism, as his last diary entry reveals. He is overpowered, tied to a table, and subjected to a "great operation" on his brain, after which he will function "like a tractor in human form," like thousands of his fellow citizens who have also been operated on.

Another fictional treatment of Gastev's soulless utopia was Yakov Protazanov's 1924 film *Aelita, Queen of Mars*, in which the queen

malfunctions and diverges from her strictly laid-out aristocratic existence after watching a dashing young Russian engineer on Earth
through her telescope. In the futurist world on Mars evoked in the
film through striking constructivist sets, love is not supposed to be
part of the system, and Aelita falls afoul of other members of the elite,
only to be rescued by her interplanetary sweetheart, who has built a
spaceship and flown over. In Protazanov's rendering, the distant planet
looks remarkably like Gastev's imagined future Russia, only on Mars
the shiny world of the elite is supported by an army of slave workers
much like those who would appear in *Metropolis* two years later.

Concrete Utopias

IN GERMANY, THE IDIOM OF A NEW WAY of living very consciously
opposed to the heavy drapes and knickknacks of the Wilhelminian
time and its war-mongering ethos had one name: Bauhaus. Like the
torn, contradictory country full of new beginnings that housed it,
the Bauhaus art school was in many ways pursuing ideals that were
mutually exclusive. Remembered today mainly for its functional
design and architecture, the ancestor of the huge wave of often
blandly functional buildings of the 1960s and 1970s that used
Bauhaus methods without its spirit, the school's ambitions were much
more comprehensive and aimed at nothing less than a revolution of
all areas of life.

The Bauhaus was founded in Weimar by Walter Gropius, a visionary architect whose elegant Fagus shoe-last factory in the German
town of Alfeld was erected in 1911 and is one of the earliest examples
of the new style of architecture, which almost ostentatiously eschewed
all ornament. With its emphasis on straight lines and materials such
as glass, concrete, and steel, its functionality and industrial efficiency
were as indebted to Taylor and Ford as Gastev's dreams of a mechanized society in the USSR were.

Before the war, Gropius had been working in the office of Peter
Behrens, a proponent of a new, unornamented style of architecture.
Among his colleagues at Behrens's firm were Ludwig Mies van der
Rohe and the young Swiss architect Charles-Édouard Jeanneret-Gris,
who would later become famous under his adopted name, Le Corbusier.
In 1915 Gropius married Gustav Mahler's widow, Alma, with whom
he had had an extramarital relationship since before the composer's
death in 1911.

Invited to become director of the Weimar arts school by its former
head, Henry van de Velde, Gropius threw himself into the task of

conceiving of a new way of teaching and producing art, objects of daily use, houses, and urban spaces. To help him build an institution that he hoped would become a center for a new kind of aesthetics, he invited some of the most prominent artists of the day to teach there, among them Wassily Kandinsky, Lyonel Feininger, Paul Klee, and Oskar Schlemmer.

The ideas underpinning the Bauhaus project were utopian, and they evolved together with the cultural debates in Germany and beyond. Initially, the leading lights of the Bauhaus school were inspired by the British Arts and Crafts movement, with its emphasis on freeing objects from the factory, reclaiming functional beauty, and promoting craftsmanship over soulless mass production. "The artist is an intensification of the craftsman," wrote founder-member Walter Gropius. Iconic objects conceived by Bauhaus designers and built in its workshops—Marcel Breuer's steel-and-leather easy chair or the Bauhaus building in Dessau and the masters' houses surrounding it—have left an indelible mark on modernist aesthetics, precisely because they form an intersection between craft and art, utility and beauty.

This early vision eventually began to shift, following the pull of ideas fashionable at the time. The Bauhaus had always had authoritarian aspects, with its "masters" and its inflexibility in aesthetic questions. Indeed, the majority of Bauhaus teachers pursued a very German, almost Wagnerian idea of a total work of art, an all-encompassing approach to aesthetics that went beyond objects and buildings and moved into dance, music, and social concerns, creating an integrated vision of life. While ideas of craftsmanship and social engineering continued to play an important role, some of the teachers and students were clearly interested in a purely mechanical aesthetics inspired by the idea of the human body as machine, as attested by their robotic stage productions and by movements and proportional studies by Oskar Schlemmer and his students. The benign artistic dictatorship of truth and beauty that was the Bauhaus school began to make its own contribution to the great theme of man and machine.

The Bauhaus experiment was to last only until 1933, when the Nazi government, which considered it both suspect and an ideological rival, forced it to close down. Even before then, however, it had changed significantly. So many big, artistic personalities in so small a space and often forced together in a curious mixture of socialist experiment and German academy had always presented plenty of problems, but eventually, and partly in response to commercial pressures on the school, the designs increasingly gravitated toward mass production. The great attention to proportion, volumes, and detail that constitutes the secret of the beauty of Bauhaus design was often trumped by more mundane concerns.

Gropius had left the Bauhaus in 1928 to pursue an independent career, which was also increasingly oriented toward large-scale settlements and housing for the working classes. In doing so he abandoned much of his earlier insistence on craft and individuality and turned to prefabricated components as the quickest and easiest way of alleviating the housing shortage. Even the layout of the buildings themselves was partly determined not by the needs of their future inhabitants but by the most efficient ways of utilizing building machines, materials, and workers during the construction process.

If Walter Gropius came to compromise his earlier ideas, the same could not be said for the second great proponent of rationalist building, Le Corbusier, whose enthusiasm for building on a huge scale and according to industrial necessities was so boundless that he simply defined a house as "a machine for living in." While the majority of his architectural output consisted of individual houses, Le Corbusier's real passion was for designing or redesigning whole cities according to his own principles, which revolved around efficiency, clean lines, and meticulously planned intersecting zones of life, work, and transport. Earlier than most of his colleagues, he had understood that cars would change the way cities were planned, built, and inhabited, and he fully embraced the new means of transport, which would emancipate individuals and make them infinitely mobile.

In 1922, Le Corbusier presented his Contemporary City, a plan for a huge new metropolis for three million people built around cruciform towers surrounded by streets on multiple levels, much like the Metropolis in Fritz Lang's film was to be. When the architect found that his project did not excite the general enthusiasm he had hoped for, he went a step further and publicized an initiative that was certain to attract publicity. Financed by a French manufacturer of cars and airplanes, he developed the Plan Voisin, a grand scheme for rebuilding Paris by simply tearing down most of the buildings on the Right Bank and replacing them with a series of eighteen high-rise buildings arranged like so many building blocks.

When Le Corbusier introduced his Plan Voisin at an exhibition in 1925 by exhibiting a sixty-foot diorama of the new, imaginary Paris, the response from responsible politicians was a mixture of genuine horror and derision. Paris, that most graceful of cities, was not to make way for a modernist nightmare, even if it would rid the inner city of its small, cluttered streets, much as Baron Hausmann had done in other parts of the city two generations earlier. The architect was

Brutalist modernism: The Swiss architect Le Corbusier proposed razing Paris to the ground and building a series of skyscrapers and highways in its place.

undaunted by this predictable reaction to his elaborate pipe dream; his self-confidence was apparently as indestructible as his zeal for grand projects.

Pushing for a realization of his dreams, Le Corbusier sought alliances wherever they appeared most promising. His sweeping architectural ideas and his emphasis on discipline and radical, rationalist solutions attracted the applause of the French journalist and writer Georges Valois, founder of Le Faisceau, a fascist organization whose journal, *Nouveau Siècle*, not only distinguished itself though its strident anti-Semitism and nationalism but also reprinted Le Corbusier's plan and ideas. The architect cultivated this promising connection. In 1934 he would lecture in Italy, as Mussolini's guest.

In Britain, the modernism of the metropolis with its machines and robots was seen with considerable skepticism. Some enthusiastic intellectuals such as George Bernard Shaw were ardent supporters of what they saw as the great Soviet experiment for the future of humankind, but grand solutions have never found favor in a country and a culture so quintessentially empirical, individualist, and attached to custom. There were also other, more pressing concerns at hand. In 1926, a general strike paralyzed the country, and the economy was ailing. But the almost universal enthusiasm for a new, automated world as well as the Soviet excesses already becoming apparent did not go unnoticed.

Aldous Huxley had read Yevgeny Zamyatin's *We*—or at least George Orwell would later claim he had. In 1931, while living in Italy, Huxley began work on a novel about a future world state whose population is universally happy. People are divided into castes. Everyone knows his or her place, functions reliably, and is policed, just in case. There is no jealousy, sex serves only for recreation, and everyone is free to consume soma, a happy-making drug. The idyll is disturbed when a boy from a faraway land, whose mother used to be part of this somnambulist society, is brought to London and is unable to cope with this world empty of emotions, individuality, and personal attachment. Eventually the relentless and merciless happiness of the majority breaks him. The novel, published in 1932, was called *Brave New World*.

From Frankenstein's monster to the unhappy Aelita, Queen of Mars, from the demonic false Maria in *Metropolis* to *R.U.R.*'s murderous robots, the technological utopias of the interwar years and their visions of New Men were fraught with deep anxieties about the future. Fear and suspicion poisoned the political climate, too, as no utopia but one's own was deemed innocent, rational, or even moral. In many societies, particularly those whose borders had been redrawn and whose institutions were deeply weakened, this climate of simmering hatred erupted into violent conflicts. Neighbor was pitted against neighbor and brother against brother in Europe's civil wars—nowhere more so than right at the heart of the continent, in Austria.

· 1927 ·

A Palace in Flames

It was an unsettled time. You never knew which party was the strongest. You never knew which one to join.
—Helmut Qualtinger, *Der Herr Karl*, 1963

....

"THE FILES ARE BURNING!" THE MAN REPEATED AGAIN AND AGAIN, "all the files!"

"Better than people!" a young man in the crowd shouted back at him angrily before being swept along by the rush of bodies and the shouts warning of renewed attacks by police shooting into the crowd.

The young man was Elias Canetti, then a student, who recounted this episode in his autobiography. It was July 15, 1927, and the crowd had converged from all sides on the Palace of Justice in Vienna. They had arrived with grim determination in front of the grand building. Nothing would stop them. Fearing the worst, the social democratic mayor of Vienna had clambered atop a fire truck and implored the angry crowd to disperse. Instead, they broke through the gates of the building and started ripping up files and throwing them out of the windows, smashing furniture, and destroying whatever else they could lay their hands on.

The burning Palace of Justice in Vienna became a symbol of Austria's fratricidal internal conflicts.

Then a new plan swept around the crowd, whispered or shouted from one angry mouth to the next: "We'll smoke them out!" Someone laid the fire. Soon the windows were bursting with the heat, and dark smoke billowed into the street. The fire brigade, already on standby, attempted to intervene, but their path was blocked by the demonstrators. The firemen were forced to watch helplessly as the first red flames leaped through the roof and the draft of the fire swept up thousands of sheets of paper like so many confused birds. The Palace of Justice was burning.

The reaction was swift and cruel. With the express consent of the chancellor of the young republic, Ignaz Seipel, police were ordered to shoot into the crowd. Mounted officers and platoons armed with rifles turned the ensuing skirmishes into a bloodbath. Fleeing demonstrators were shot in the back; the crowd melted away but formed anew; angry demonstrators jeered at their pursuers before running off; one man beat his chest with his fists and shouted, "Right here! That's where you have to shoot!" At the end of the day, eighty-nine demonstrators lay dead, and hundreds more were injured.

The deadly confrontation of July 15 was the consequence of a different, earlier shooting, during which an eight-year-old boy and a war veteran had been killed. On July 14 their murderers, two men belonging to a paramilitary organization, had been acquitted of all charges, a decision that provoked the march on the Palace of Justice. For the young Canetti, this day as part of a crowd, this experience of being swept along, of belonging to something bigger, stronger, and strangely impersonal, was life-changing. In his later work, he would return to this defining day over and over, including in his study *Masse und Macht* (Crowds and Power) and in his novel *Auto da Fé*, in which a library is burned by a mentally unhinged scholar.

Canetti was not alone in seeing the blaze as a powerful symbol for a social and political catastrophe. The great Austrian novelist Heimito von Doderer, still almost unknown today in the English-speaking world, was deeply moved by the events surrounding the burning of the Palace of Justice, as was the famously acerbic publicist Karl Kraus. So, too, were thousands of others, most of whom would not commit their locked-up feelings to paper but would carry them into the following years like so many incendiary bombs.

Not for decades had the Austrian capital been as close to full-blown civil war as on this hot summer's day. The events leading up to it bolster the claim made by Karl Kraus that Vienna was "an experimental station for the apocalypse," a political and cultural microcosm of societies torn between recovery and collapse, between hope and hatred, and between socialism and fascism.

Two factions, both with armed paramilitary wings, confronted each other with implacable hatred in Vienna and throughout the country: a largely urban movement comprising social democrats, socialists, communists, and various splinter groups, and a conservative, Catholic, and often fascist faction with particularly strong support in rural areas and among the petty bourgeoisie.

The conflict was nothing less than a battle for the country's soul. Its origins lay in the dissolution of the Habsburg Empire after the defeat of the Central Powers a decade earlier. Until 1918, the empire had covered 20 percent of Europe's territory, from the deep forests of Transylvania to the Swiss border, and from the northern regions of Bohemia, just south of Dresden, to the Adriatic coast of Bosnia and Montenegro. Largely rural and in many places economically backward, the empire had always been a problematic political entity, often caught up in internecine warfare between different ethnic groups struggling for more influence, more recognition, or outright independence, but this difficult legacy had also been the source of its cultural richness in such cities as Vienna, Prague, Budapest, Czernowitz, Trieste, and Lemberg (now Lviv in Ukraine).

Habsburg culture was as multifaceted as the ethnicities contributing to it, and in each of the cultural centers a variety of languages, religious and cultural practices, geographic origins, historical identities, and political allegiances created a cultural life of almost unparalleled diversity, as groups and individuals not only competed with one another but also enriched the common cultural sphere and created new forms of expression. Prague, for instance, despite its relatively modest two hundred thousand inhabitants, of whom only a very small percentage had ever gone on to higher education, boasted two universities, one teaching in German and one in Czech, and a general cultural landscape doubled along the language divide.

Economically, the Habsburg Empire was unable to compete with its neighbor Germany, but nonetheless it was expanding rapidly. Coal and steel from mines in Silesia (in today's Czech Republic) fueled industrialization, while the eastern territories of Hungary and modern Romania were mainly agricultural, so much so that during the early twentieth century the Habsburg Empire was the only European producer actually exporting grain—all others had been relying on imports, mainly from Russia and Canada, since before the Great War.

When the empire was dissolved after the war, this economic system was shattered. Comprising territory that was a mere 12 percent of the former empire, Austria no longer had access to the rich deposits of coal and ore in what was now the independent state of Czechoslovakia, and it had also lost its breadbasket in the east. What remained, the Austrian First Republic, was a sparsely populated alpine land with a capital, Vienna, designed to rule an empire, but with no empire now to rule.

The young republic faced a mountain of problems: the war had been ruinously expensive as well as cruel, and the state was practically bankrupt—so much so that the reparation payments demanded of Austria in the Treaty of Versailles were tiny in comparison to the sums demanded from Germany, despite the fact that guilt could be laid at the feet of the Habsburg military just as much as at those of the warmongers in Berlin.

But there were problems greater than economic uncertainty. Nobody had wanted this Austria. For monarchists, and to some degree for the educated bourgeoisie who were partly monarchist and partly international, Habsburg's greatness lay in its authority over the vast variety of cultures it had administered and controlled, a situation that had many similarities with Britain's colonial empire. The bourgeoisie had no interest in a small, national state called Austria, and neither had the more internationally oriented educated elite, particularly if they were assimilated Jews.

German-speaking nationalists, on the other hand, had traditionally looked toward Germany, dreaming of a unification of German-
speaking peoples; they wanted no separate Austrian nationality at
all. Finally, the workers and the left-leaning elements of the middle
classes had hoped for a revolutionary state with an international
orientation.

All of these groups were now disappointed. The new state of Austria was seen as little more than a sad and truncated fragment of the
former Habsburg lands, an administrative area without any real identity. The school maps from which Austrians had learned their geography before 1918 had not even shown an "Austria," but only the
individual states and duchies—Upper Austria, Lower Austria, Tyrol,
Carinthia, Salzburg, et cetera. All they had in common was that most
of them had predominantly German-speaking populations, despite
the fact that the border regions were often mixed and riven by
nationalist strife: Tyrol had a large Italian minority, Carinthia was
home to many Slovenes, and a large, mainly German-speaking part
of western Hungary was to become part of Austria by referendum
in 1921.

The obvious challenge for the postwar republic was to provide
the new country with a national identity, to invent what it meant to
be an Austrian. The two main political forces had very different ideas
about this. The socialists, who held a solid majority in Vienna and
who had been gaining in strength elsewhere, particularly in industrial
areas in upper Austria, wished to transform the new nation into a
modern socialist republic with an international outlook, allied with
the Soviet Union. For conservatives this was anathema. Austria in its
modern form, they argued, might be a tragedy and a travesty of history, but its people must be faithful to their historical identity, which
had emerged from Catholicism and was rooted in the rural areas,
where the peasants lived—or so it was claimed—according to the age-
old virtues and traditions of an authentic Austrian life.

Red Vienna

IN THE PERILOUS AFTERMATH OF THE WAR, hope and fear were closely
linked. For socialists and social democrats, the collapse of the empire
was an opportunity to start anew and to realize the dreams of social
justice that animated their movement. When Vienna itself became a
socialist-led federal state in 1922, the city government embarked on
a hugely ambitious program of social reform in education, health care,
and public housing. In spite of the economic difficulties, a whole series

A utopia in stone: Built between 1927 and 1930, the Karl-Marx-Hof in Vienna was a vast housing project representing the hope for a better life for all.

of large housing projects were constructed. These *Gemeindebauten* (municipal buildings), however, were designed to provide far more than clean, dry apartments with running water and central heating at a price affordable to workers: they were to be elements of a social utopia.

The largest of the new projects, the Karl-Marx-Hof, constructed between 1927 and 1930, is still a monument to these ambitions, and still the largest contiguous housing complex in the world, consisting of some fourteen hundred apartments sheltering five thousand inhabitants. But it was not the sheer numbers that made this vast enterprise so astonishing. The huge structure of the Karl-Marx-Hof, with its imposing, sculptural façade more than half a mile long, also contained kindergartens and laundries, shops and medical offices, community rooms, baths, and a lending library. Other housing complexes also had their own theaters. Everything here was a statement of faith in the dignity of workers, the little people who formed the constituency of the city government. The housing complexes were generous and light: the Karl-Marx-Hof covered a vast area, but only one-fifth of the ground was built up, the rest being left for spacious courtyards, playing fields, and playgrounds, all adorned by sculptures, frescoes, and mosaics.

During the interwar period the Vienna city government provided new apartments for more than 220,000 people on modest incomes. Such public largesse, financed by a special housing tax, created a great loyalty among the left-leaning electorate; it was part of a flourishing socialist public culture with its own newspapers, sports clubs, workers' education associations, theaters, savings banks, cooperative stores, night schools, soup kitchens, children's organizations, garden collectives, and publishing houses.

On May 1 of every year, the socialist movement demonstrated its power with a huge procession attended by hundreds of thousands of workers, parading with banners, brass bands, and decorated floats, marching along the Ringstrasse past the historicist buildings and the imperial palace built only a few years earlier to celebrate a very different past.

Conservatives watched these parades with horror and regarded the city's socialist culture in general with a suspicion bordering on hatred. While the city government was firmly in social democratic hands, the federal government, elected by the entire, largely rural country, was controlled by the Christian democrats under the leadership of "the pitiless prelate," Ignaz Seipel, a Catholic priest who had taught theology before becoming first imperial minister of social affairs and then, after the war, chancellor of Austria from 1922 to 1924 and again from 1926 to 1929.

Seipel's Austria looked very different from the collectivist utopia propagated in Vienna's public housing projects. His vision for the country was faith-based and authoritarian. Despite his birth in Vienna, where his father had been a coachman, the Christian democratic chancellor stood firmly on the side of the conservative countryside—the winning side, as it seemed to him. Vienna, which before 1914 had been not only the fifth-largest city in the world but also one of the world's main cultural centers, was now atrophying. Until 1918, the city at the heart of a multinational and notably multicultural empire had been home to 2.1 million people, but after the war almost four hundred thousand of them left the capital of the now much smaller, almost exclusively German-speaking country. "Vienna by the Danube has become Vienna by the Alps," sighed one of its most famous journalists, Anton Kuh.[1]

To conservative Austrian nationalists the Alpine connection could not be strong enough. In their search for a national identity, they promoted the *Trachten*, the traditional dress of the Upper Austrian, Styrian, and Tyrolian peasants, which had already enjoyed considerable popularity among townspeople before the war, when it had been adopted as a trendy form of vacation clothing for the lawyers, busi-nessmen, journalists, and municipal administrators who could afford to take their families away from the city during the summer for a few weeks of carefree rambling and vacationing. Now, however, yester-day's slightly affected holiday gesture of dressing up in dirndls with tight bodices and flowery aprons or lederhosen and green felt jackets with deer-horn buttons—even Sigmund Freud was photographed wearing them—was becoming an ideological statement. With politics, the *Trachten* came into the cities. Official associations and style guides made certain that the clothing was authentic enough to pass muster.

The metropolitan intellectuals were horrified by what they saw as the progressive provincializing of an erstwhile European cultural hub, particularly as nationalists of all stripes propagated their ideas with increasingly strident anti-Semitic overtones. Vienna was home to just under two hundred thousand Jews, most of whom had moved there from other parts of the empire during the second half of the nineteenth century. They formed some 10 percent of the city's popu-lation, but with their traditional respect for education and a great new eagerness to assimilate, they were quickly overrepresented in second-ary schools, in universities, and in journalism, law, medicine, and other professions. Having been challenged to discard the kaftans and long beards of their forebears, to stop speaking Yiddish, and to become good Habsburg citizens and, later, Austrian patriots, most had suc-ceeded beyond all expectations.

Even before the war, the assimilatory success of Vienna's Jews had turned against them, as the resentful losers of modernity looked for an object on which to vent their anger. Anti-Semitism, of course, had a long tradition in central Europe, but its nature had been changing with an increasingly industrial, complex, and capitalist social reality. Jews were among the winners of this transformation, which had taken them out of the humiliation of the ghetto and into the heart of bour-geois society. Like the demonic machine Maria in Fritz Lang's film *Metropolis*, they were now caricatured as the epitome of a new urban, rootless, soulless, sexualized, neurotic, money-grabbing present.

Even toward the end of the nineteenth century, as the social trans-formations resulting from industrialization had begun to bite, writers in Germany, France, the Habsburg Empire, Russia, and elsewhere in Europe had fulminated against Jews, singling them out not on reli-gious grounds, as once would have been the case, but on "scientific" and "racial" grounds, and particularly as the embodiment of inter-national capitalism, which appeared to be destroying the certainties of the old ways. Now, after the war, anti-Semitism was being plied with renewed force. In prewar Vienna, it had been carried into the very heart of politics by the highly successful mayor Karl Lueger, who had manipulated the prejudices of his electorate with virtuosic brio. As a society without orientation or identity began to look about for scapegoats, the Jews were singled out in a new wave of contempt.

City Without Jews?

IN THE CAPITAL OF THE NEW REPUBLIC, the perceived drift toward a provincial Vienna-by-the-Alps was creating feelings of claustrophobia for some. The city was still home to a flourishing Jewish community, ranging from the Orthodox denizens of the Leopoldstadt district, the "matzo island," to liberal religious practitioners and totally assimilated families intolerant of anything reminding them of the religion and the historical humiliations of their ancestors. Many of these latter had changed their names along with their faith and would not allow even a word of Yiddish to be spoken in their presence. This very determined assimilation was countered by the many equally determined Zionist associations—from youth clubs and sports associations such as the iconic football team of the Vienna Hakoah Football Club to the quasi-Masonic lodges of B'nai B'rith—whose activities testified to the feeling of many Jews that they had no future in an increasingly hostile Europe.

True, Vienna was still home to great Jewish intellectuals—Sigmund Freud; the writer and dramatist Arthur Schnitzler, and other authors such as Josef Roth, Franz Werfel, and Stefan Zweig; Karl Kraus and a host of distinguished journalists; social democratic or socialist politicians such as Otto Bauer and Julius Tandler; actors and stage satirists commenting on the country's varying fates and political climates; and scientists and civic leaders—a vibrant society gathering and debating in cafés and private salons, in theaters, and on the pages of the great newspapers. But as the debate about Austrian identity became more restrictive and more removed from the Habsburg embrace of variety, the visions for the future became less optimistic. In 1922, the novelist Hugo Bettauer published his *Stadt ohne Juden* (City Without Jews), imagining a future in which ethnic Austrians would expel all Jews and rapidly decline into a yokelish Catholic provincialism so shocking that in the end the yokels would be obliged to call back the people they had banished.

Two novelists who witnessed the events of July 15 and who would return to the image of the burning Palace of Justice in their work exemplify the tensions within Vienna's population and reveal the importance the event had in the imagination of people of very different backgrounds and outlooks. Elias Canetti is the first of them. Born in 1905 in Ruse in today's Bulgaria, then part of the Habsburg Empire, he belonged to a Ladino-speaking Jewish family that had been part of the forced exodus from Spain in 1492, and which had relatively recently moved from the city of Edirne in the Ottoman Empire. Having been taken at the age of six from the richly oriental atmosphere of Ruse to Manchester, where his father was pursuing a business opportunity, Canetti was soon moved again, first to Lausanne and Vienna, then to Zürich and Frankfurt, then back to Vienna, where at the time of the 1927 riots he was a student in chemistry.

Canetti was a quintessential cosmopolitan, comfortable in five languages (Ladino, Romanian, German, English, and French) and in different environments, passionate about literature, and eternally unsure of himself. The events he witnessed that July left a deep impression on him, giving rise to his principal philosophical work, *Masse und Macht* (*Crowds and Power*), the initial spark of which he explicitly traced back to that summer's day when he himself was caught up in the surge of bodies, voices, and sheer atavistic instinct, feeling himself become part of the ecstatic, collective, and ever-hungry organism that is a crowd.

The other witness who devoted an entire novel to the events of July 15 was a very different man, Heimito von Doderer. Born into a family of the minor nobility, Heimito's curious first name was inspired by his mother's infatuation with Spain and, very possibly, with a Spanish gentleman by the name of Jaime. The boy spent his entire childhood and youth in Vienna, where he received a conservative, class-conscious education. After a listless stab at studying law, in 1915 he enlisted in a cavalry regiment and was sent to the front, first to Galicia and then to Bukovina, where he became a Russian prisoner of war.

During his time in a Siberian prison camp, Doderer had decided to become a writer, and after his return to Vienna in 1918 he worked hard, but largely without success, to realize his ambition. His first novels found hardly any readers, and the young author struggled to make a living through journalism and various literary odd jobs. Times had changed, and the world he had been educated for had vanished. In many of his narrative works, Doderer ruefully reflected on this transformation and on his sense of living outside of his own time. He was as much an exile from the epoch of his birth as Canetti was an exile from the place of his childhood. Neither of them now "belonged."

Vienna, however, was now a city for people who did not belong. In fact, nobody felt at home in the new state that was post-Habsburg Austria. Doderer's seismographic sensibility charted the many ways of being lost in this new world, along with nostalgia for a former world that memory and longing made appear idyllic. To him, July 15 was a moment of original sin, when violence seized the heart of what had once been a tolerant and benevolent empire.

Indeed, for Doderer the entire year 1927 was both eventful and traumatic. Without any real enthusiasm, he married his Jewish girlfriend of many years; it was a torturous and tortured relationship between a gifted pianist from a worldly and intellectual background and a struggling writer whose deeply wounding anti-Semitic tirades were frequently used as weapons against her. The marriage ended with their final separation in 1932, with Doderer joining the NSDAP, the Nazi party, then still illegal in Austria, the following year. After Austria's annexation by the German Reich in 1938, he would sue for divorce, thus removing the last layer of relative safety shielding his wife from persecution.

Though personally unappealing, Doderer as a writer was a virtuoso of plot and characterization. His powerful, highly idiosyncratic language, with its use of dialect and frequent Viennese allusions, resists the efforts of even the ablest translators. In his monumental *Die Dämonen* (The Demons), he charted his city's fall from grace as the "seam" connecting Gentile and Jewish Vienna began to split, a split symbolized by the burning of the Palace of Justice. As always, Doderer's own attitude was profoundly contradictory, snobbish, and laced with self-loathing. He was a Nazi who despised Nazism, an anti-Semite who admired Jews, a racist who believed that the concept of race was fraudulent ("in Vienna, the concierges form an entire race apart," he remarked), a man too weighed down by his own contradictions to regard as true the things he believed in. In other words, as many noted, he was an archetypal Viennese of his day.

Opposing Forces

THE TENSIONS BETWEEN the visions and forces of the left and right in Austria increased with each year. In 1920, the conservatives had founded the Heimwehr (Home Defense), an armed militia that functioned as the military wing of the Christian Democratic Party, which was tolerated and at times actively assisted by army officers and the police. Political leaders of the Heimwehr identified Marxism and all left-wing groups and ideas as their particular enemy. Their demonstrations of power eventually led the social democrats to create the Republikanischer Schutzbund (Republican Protection League), which was also armed.

Sporadic confrontations between members of the Heimwehr and the Schutzbund were part of life during the First Republic, creating a constant atmosphere of menace in Vienna and other parts of the country. When on January 30, 1927, the two rival organizations held meetings in the village of Schattendorf, in the eastern province of Burgenland, defiantly congregating in inns only a few hundred yards from each other, the threat of violence was heavy in the air. Leftist Schutzbund adherents were in the majority. They shouted menacing slogans: "Down with the [Heimwehr] veterans! Down with the Christian dogs! Down with the monarchist murderers!" There were isolated scuffles as some Schutzbund members crossed the threshold of the rival inn. Then the Schutzbund left, all of them, marching triumphantly down the street.

Two of the Heimwehr men, armed with rifles, were standing by the iron-grated window of their inn, watching the hated leftist crowd depart. Aiming at their enemies' backs, they opened fire, emptying their magazines. A Croatian demonstrator, Matthias Csmarits, fell to the ground, mortally wounded. An eight-year-old boy was also killed. Five others were injured.

When the case against the two Schattendorf shooters, together with one accomplice, was finally heard in July 1927, Austrian workers expected justice for the callous murders of two of their own. But the members of the jury—a butcher's apprentice, a carpenter, a carpenter's apprentice, a civil servant, a landlord, a secretary, a printer's apprentice, a hairdresser, a pensioner, a plumber's apprentice, a farmer, and a housewife—found that they could not reach a verdict on account of the contradictory witness statements. When the judgment was read on July 14, the defendants were acquitted of all charges and fully rehabilitated as "honorable men." The news was in the papers the next morning.

Elias Canetti described his own reaction when reading of the acquittal of the men who had shot unarmed workers in the back. On the morning of July 15, he was sitting in a café in a comfortable suburb, reading the papers. Incensed by the news he learned from the front page, he took his bicycle and made his way to the city center, where thousands of workers were already gathering in protest. It was not an organized gathering. The Socialist Party leadership had tried not to inflame an already tense situation even further and refrained from scheduling protest marches and strikes, with the result that the workers coming together in spontaneous anger had no leadership and no official route for any demonstration. Apparently without direction, they converged on the Palace of Justice, where the judgment had been handed down. The events unfolding there were to haunt the republic for years; they would later be seen as a bloody prelude to the country's full-blown civil war seven years later.

The Hatred of Patriots

LIKE AUSTRIA, POSTWAR FRANCE SUFFERED a lacerating and traumatic postwar legacy that the intervening decade had done little to heal. The country's losses had been horrifying, with 1.7 million dead, almost 4.3 percent of the total population—a higher death toll than any other western European nation. A further 4.2 million soldiers had been wounded or maimed, and an untold number of the returning soldiers had been psychologically scarred by their experiences. In addition to the human tragedy, the structural damage caused by trench warfare and intense bombardments had left deep marks on the landscape of northern France, an area that not only had once been rich in historical sites but had been one of the country's most fertile areas, crucial to prewar agricultural production.

Trench warfare and millions of grenades and bombs had made this garden of France into a *région dévastée* of some six thousand square miles, a huge wasteland bare of all familiar landmarks, a poisonous moonscape of craters, trenches, tree trunks, and ruins, in which even locals could find their way only by compass through over a thousand razed villages. More than five hundred thousand houses had been destroyed, and the cities of Arras, Cambrai, Laon, Lille, Saint-Quentin, Soissons, Verdun, and Reims had been severely damaged. Even the great and historic cathedral of Reims, the sacred coronation place of French kings, had been gutted by shelling.

Reconstructing this devastated region was not just a question of national pride but also one of economic necessity. Resources were scarce, however, and the demands gigantic. As in all countries primarily involved in the fighting, the war had depleted the national coffers, drained the supply of raw materials and labor, and created a lopsided wartime economy that now needed to be reoriented to peacetime needs. Just as in Austria, the country's character, civilization, and future—its soul, as it were—were contested in a series of battles fought in newspapers, debating chambers, and the streets.

A country with highly industrialized regions, especially around Paris and in the north, and with a strong revolutionary tradition,

France was home to a vigorous communist and socialist movement that had emerged from the war with renewed force. During the early 1920s, in a situation dominated by social unrest, economic hardship, and large-scale strikes, the atmosphere had become so poisonous that France had appeared to stand on the brink of a new revolution. Looking toward the Soviet Union, radical members of the socialist movement had dreamed of overthrowing the government, which appeared too weak and too conservative to address the problems of the nation effectively.

Despite several violent general strikes, bloody confrontations between workers and police, and the foundation of short-lived "workers' soviets" in Paris factories, the revolution had not occurred, but the climate of visceral distrust between left and right had persisted, even after the government had succeeded in stabilizing the plummeting franc at one-fifth of its prewar value. Opposing the socialists, communists, and trade unions was a vigorous monarchist movement seeking to return France to its former grandeur by installing a new Bourbon king, along with militant Catholics and fascist admirers of Mussolini—the latter three overlapping in various constellations and associations. It was, as often in recent French history, a struggle of identities between the Catholic emblem Jeanne d'Arc and the republican symbol Marianne.

The towering figure of ultraconservative France was a man with a perfect intellectual pedigree for this position: Charles Maurras, the son of a tax collector and a deeply devout mother. Born in 1863 and educated by his mother, Maurras had lost his faith early on, but he had maintained a strong attachment to the Catholic Church, which he regarded as one of the great pillars of order and morality. France, he believed, had reached its apogee in the seventeenth century under the Sun King, Louis XIV, when its pure, Latinate culture had flourished. Afterward it had fallen prey to the evil influence of Germanic Romanticism and had lost its way; its infatuation with egalitarianism, democracy, and other "foreign" ideas had led, in Maurras's view, to the catastrophe of the Revolution of 1789, a conspiracy of Germans, Jews, and Freemasons against all that was glorious about France.

In his newspaper, *L'Action Française*, Maurras fulminated against everything he despised, and as his hatred was all-encompassing and easily incurred, he had much to write about. This was never more apparent than in the case of Léon Blum, the Jewish leader of the Socialist Party (also known as the French Section of the Workers' International). Blum was a gentle-tempered man, a former literary critic who had been moved to go into politics because he wanted to make a contribution to his country's war effort (his myopia had prevented him from serving in uniform), and he was now working for a reconciliation between the party's revolutionary radical wing, which was seeking a dictatorship of the proletariat, and its more moderate members, whose commitment to social justice without political violence he shared. For Maurras, Blum was the perfect hate object; in the pages of *L'Action Française* he was described as "the circumcised [deputy] of Narbonne" and "the belligerent Hebrew."

Maurras did not hesitate to insult. In 1935 he was to write of Blum: "He is a monster of the democratic republic. He is a mirage of the dialectic of the *'heimatlos'* [without homeland]. Human garbage and to be treated as such ... He is a man who must be shot, but in the back."[2] In February of the following year, when fanatical members of the Camelots du Roi (the King's Hucksters—an appellation coined by a scornful journalist), a rightist youth organization originally founded to hawk *L'Action Française* on the streets and to spread its message, would drag Léon Blum from a car and beat him almost to death, Maurras would express no regrets. When Blum became prime minister in 1936, Maurras vented his feelings once again: "It is as a Jew that we must see, comprehend, understand, fight, and kill this Blum."[3] Indicted for incitement to murder, Maurras was given eight months in prison.

Antidemocratic, nationalist, and anti-Semitic as he was, Maurras was nonetheless no friend of fascism, mainly because he distrusted its totalitarian impulses. He wanted to turn back the clock to a time before the 1789 revolution, before democracy, individualism, and liberalism had sullied what he regarded as the French genius. His dream was a revival of a French monarchy, supplanting the Third Republic and restoring a sense of greatness and moral purpose to the nation. To this end, he needed the Catholic Church (in whose doctrines he did not believe) as a guarantor of stability and to encourage a sense of sacrifice in the population, just as he wished for an aristocratic elite willing to fight and a social order inspired by the estates of the Middle Ages.

This muddled and to some extent contradictory vision (though a rabid anti-Semite, Maurras despised other kinds of racism, regarding them as too German) exerted a considerable intellectual pull, not only on French thinkers of the right but also on conservatives as diverse as Charles de Gaulle, Spain's Francisco Franco, King Albert of Belgium, the Portuguese dictator António Salazar, and even the Anglo-American poet T. S. Eliot.

While Maurras was idiosyncratic in his generous hatred of modernity and everything associated with it, some other intellectuals in France were more immediately in step with the grand fascist march toward a brighter, cleaner future. Writers such as Pierre Drieu La Rochelle went from a flirtation with the left (and a close friendship with the surrealists around André Breton) to propagating a socialist fascism that would lead ever closer to Hitler; Robert Brasillach became editor in chief of the virulently anti-Semitic newspaper *Je Suis Partout* (I Am Everywhere).

Incendiary books and newspaper articles from left and right whipped up hatred and were instrumental in creating an atmosphere of crisis, much as they did in Germany and Austria, in Ireland, Belgium, and Spain, and elsewhere in Europe. Real power, however, appeared to need a strong arm, and even in France, armed militias began to be a factor in daily politics. Maurras, *L'Action Française*, and the Camelots du Roi were already an established force belonging to the Catholic and royalist wing. In 1927, the Croix-de-Feu (Fiery Cross), originally a veterans' association, also entered the fray, as did the Ligue des Patriotes (Patriots' League, financed by Champagne producer Pierre Taittinger), the overtly fascist Ligue des Jeunesses Patriotes (Young Patriots' League), and the Faisceau (Sheaf), which openly imitated Mussolini's Fascist rituals. All of these right-wing organizations marched in uniform; several had access to firearms, and many waited for an opportunity to use them against the hated socialists.

Beautiful Sacha

THAT MOMENT WOULD ARRIVE in 1934, after the suspicious death of Serge Stavisky, "Beautiful Sacha," a French con man of Ukrainian Jewish origin, who had used his excellent connections within the government to organize a Ponzi scheme fronted by the bank Crédit Communal, which allowed him to steal two hundred million francs from small investors. Pursued by the police, Stavisky had gone underground and had finally been tracked down at his Alpine chalet near Chamonix, France. According to police testimony, two shots were fired when the agents entered the building; they found the suspect dead, killed by his own hand. Soon, however, doubts were raised about this version of events. It was difficult for even the most determined man, critics remarked, to kill himself with two shots to the head.

When the left-liberal government refused to set up a parliamentary commission to look into the involvement of politicians in Stavisky's death, both right-wing and communist associations called for their members to take to the streets. After a chaotic January, during which more than two thousand policemen were injured in clashes with demonstrators, the government was forced to resign.

But the troubles were not over. As the full consequences of the Stavisky affair became known, and Édouard Daladier, the designated prime minister, clumsily attempted to limit the political fallout, bills appeared on the streets of Paris calling for rival demonstrations on February 6, the day of the swearing-in of the new government. The largest demonstration was planned at the Place de la Concorde, directly across the Seine from the Chamber of Deputies at the Palais-Bourbon.

In the small hours of this freezing February day, the demonstrators assembled like members of an army. *L'Action Française* had urged its readers to participate, and Croix-de-Feu, Jeunesses Patriotes, Union Nationale des Combattants (a veterans' association), and Union des Contribuables (a taxpayers' association) had all mobilized their members, as had the Communist Party and its militant wing, the Association Républicaine des Anciens Combattants, which was hostile to the assembled rightist groups. Some thirty thousand determined and embittered demonstrators braved the cold at the Place de la Concorde alone.

While some of the demonstrators had come merely to voice their outrage, others planned to prevent the government from being formed by storming the Palais-Bourbon. But the commander of the Croix-de-Feu shied away from taking the poorly defended heart of French democracy by force. With this hesitation, the militant wing of the demonstrators lost their impetus, and soon what had begun as an orderly march degenerated into a series of pitched battles between rightists, communists, Catholics, socialists, and police, who had erected barricades on the bridge linking the Place de la Concorde and the Palais-Bourbon and who were now fighting off angry and determined but uncoordinated demonstrators armed with sticks, stones, and some small firearms.

The battle for the Solférino Bridge continued throughout the night. As the demonstrators attacked time and again, policemen were ordered to fire into the crowd. As dawn broke over the smoking barricades, revealing burned-out buses and cars and smashed shop windows, the harvest of battle became obvious. Among the police and other defenders of the Palais—firemen, gendarmes, republican guards—one soldier was mortally wounded, while 1,664 had sustained lighter injuries. Among the attackers, sixteen men had been killed and 657 wounded.

A Dream Besieged

ACROSS THE EUROPEAN CONTINENT, ideologically opposing factions were engulfed in bloody clashes about ideology, and more specifically about the role modernity was to play in their societies. This simmering state of war was gripping almost all European countries, with the possible exception of Britain, where Oswald Mosley's fascist Blackshirts, at a self-declared (and contested) peak of some fifty thousand members, never rose to become a genuine popular movement.

In Austria, where the 1927 burning of the Palace of Justice had become a symbol of the country's desperate and increasingly deadly battle for a new identity, events would not stop at a single bloody riot, as they had done in France. In 1934, only two weeks after the siege of the Palais-Bourbon that had cost seventeen lives, the tensions in Vienna erupted into a civil war.

The confrontation was almost inevitable. By 1934, Austria was no longer a democracy. After his election in 1929, the conservative Catholic chancellor Engelbert Dollfuss had taken advantage of a hitch in the democratic protocol—one after another, all three presidents of the parliament had resigned for procedural reasons, leaving that body technically unable to vote—to simply declare that the assembly had "rendered itself defunct." Not willing to wait until members of parliament could elect three new presidents and assume their normal duties, Dollfuss had the police stop the next parliamentary sessions by force; he then simply assumed power and proceeded to govern by decree.

The front lines in the Austrian struggle for nationhood were drawn mainly between socialists and conservative Catholics, between visions of a modern workers' paradise and a rigid, rightist autocracy of national virtue. With Dollfuss, the latter had won by what amounted to a coup d'état.

A new, dictatorial Austria rapidly took shape. Dollfuss introduced censorship of the press, prohibited political assemblies, and outlawed the paramilitary wing of the socialist party, the Republikanischer Schutzbund. Political opponents were arrested and sent to prison camps, and the death penalty was reintroduced for even usually non-capital offenses, including "public violence and malicious damage to foreign property."

From the very beginning of his dictatorship, Dollfuss was particularly concerned to reverse the secular reforms of previous governments and to make his homeland into an obedient daughter of the Catholic Church. By official decree, posts in higher education were to be filled with "men of Christian principles" as well as good patriots; religion became a compulsory subject at school, and in a particularly spectacular piece of legislation, anyone wishing to leave the Catholic Church had to be examined by a neurologist at the state's behest. The bishops showed themselves appreciative. In a letter to the faithful they purred: "The year 1933 has brought rich blessings to all of Christianity, and has brought special joys to our fatherland Austria."[4]

Not all Austrians were grateful for these blessings. By early 1934, thousands of socialists were interned in camps or prisons for political reasons, and members of the now-illegal Schutzbund were stockpiling weapons. When on February 12 one of their arsenals in Linz was raided by police as part of a campaign to disarm all socialist and social-democrat organizations, the local Schutzbund commander refused to hand in his cache and gave orders to fire.

News of the incident quickly proved to be the spark that ignited an already highly volatile situation. As police and army units tried to move in, in a series of preventive strikes, they encountered stiff resistance, and soon fighting had spread through the country, though it did not reach all provinces: some social democratic leaders preferred to resign from their party rather than risk bloodshed, and rural areas were almost unaffected by the violence.

In Vienna, pitched battles between government forces and Schutzbund militias were intense. Resistance was focused on the great showcase project of socialist utopian living, the splendid Karl-Marx-Hof to the north of the city, while people in the cafés and offices in the center were all but oblivious to the fighting and simply continued their lives, as the writer Stefan Zweig would remember. Meanwhile, the army brought in artillery and was shelling the Karl-Marx-Hof, which socialist workers had transformed into an improvised fortress.

Faced with overwhelming force and unable to mobilize a larger rebellion, the Schutzbund capitulated after three days of fighting, on February 15. More than two hundred of them had been killed and hundreds more injured, while government forces had lost 128 men. For the government, this moment of triumph was also a chance to dismantle the socialist leadership. Nine Schutzbund commanders were condemned to death and executed at the garrote, with one of them, who had been badly wounded, carried to the place of execution on a stretcher. Members of the civilian leadership of the Social Democratic Party did not wait to be arrested; they fled to neighboring Czechoslovakia.

The writing on the wall in 1927 had spelled out bitter conflicts. Only seven years later, the battle in Austria between a secular, social democratic, and progressive vision and one that was Catholic, corporate, and rural had been fought, and won decisively by the latter. Fueled by a real conflict of social visions and cultural identities, Europe's political map was rapidly changing.

Boop-Boop-a-Doop!

To the woman of the period thus set forth, restless, seductive,
greedy, discontented, craving sensation, unrestrained, a little mor-
bid, more than a little selfish, slack of mind as she is trim of body,
neurotic and vigorous, a worshiper of tinsel gods at perfumed
altars, fit mate for the hurried, reckless and cynical man of the
age, predestined mother of—what manner of being?
—Walter Fabian (Samuel Hopkins Adams), *Flaming Youth*, 1923

....

HELEN KANE WAS AN UNLIKELY BROADWAY STAR. SHORT AND PLUMP, a curvaceous and self-confident girl from the Bronx, she did not conform to the boyish, languid flapper figure that was then fashionable. A seemingly ungovernable mop of brown hair gave her a precious few more inches of height. But then there was her voice: cute, sexy, with an almost cartoonish New York twang. Outlined in black, her huge eyes appeared to wink at every man in the audience; her puckered crimson lips were a heart-shaped promise.

When Kane came onstage in 1928 in Oscar Hammerstein's revue *Good Boy*, she peered out into the audience and launched into her newest number, "I Wanna Be Loved by You" (later famously resurrected by Marilyn Monroe), and she was. Her fans waited almost breathlessly as she worked toward her trademark line, a coy afterthought to the lyrics, a barely sung *boop-boop-a-doop*.

Oh so cute: Betty Boop became an ironic symbol of femininity during the Great Depression.

While never a great singer or actress, Helen Kane commanded immense attention and even greater fees. There were Helen Kane look-alike contests, dolls, and eventually a cartoon that would immortalize her, taking her catchphrase as the character's name: Betty Boop. To a young generation of Americans, the ingénue glamourpuss was a symbol of their own determination to get out, get away from their parents, and enjoy life.

The shadow of the war was no longer hanging over them. They had no interest in the solemnity, anxiety, trauma, and tension of their elders. While others debated the crisis of society and fought for a great future, they answered with a coy *boop-boop-a-doop* and a sidelong glance at the next attractive person in the room. Politics was not for them, and their ideology was the Charleston.

"It Was Fun to Flirt"

FLAPPERS WERE FABULOUS. They had taken their life into their own hands and away from their parents. The girls wore short hair and scandalously short dresses, smoked in public and drank with men, were sophisticated about sex and blasé about marriage and other old-fashioned ideas, went to parties and made out in cars.

"I do not want to be respectable because respectable girls are not attractive," announced Zelda Fitzgerald, herself a goddess of flapperdom, summing up the attitude of this dangerously independent young generation. "Boys do dance most with the girls they kiss most. . . . Perceiving these things, the Flapper awoke from her lethargy of sub-deb-ism, bobbed her hair, put on the choicest pair of earrings and a great deal of audacity and rouge and went into the battle. She flirted because it was fun to flirt."[1]

The cheerful nihilism of the flappers was a child of economic success and general escapism. After the first unsettled postwar years, with their violent strikes, race riots, Red Scare, and social strife, the peace economy had taken off and a new sense of optimism was making itself felt. "The chief business of the American people is business," President Coolidge had said in a speech to newspaper editors in 1925, and this pragmatic outlook on life articulated what many people felt and wanted. After a decade of strife, it seemed, they had gotten away with it and things were becoming right again.

As Coolidge had made clear, the emphasis in the United States was on business, not justice. The income of the top 0.1 percent of the population equaled the total income of the bottom 42 percent, and those on the wrong side of the tracks were on their own, but there were jobs again and manufacturing was booming.

Nowhere was the new freedom more obvious than in the production of automobiles, the archetypal American product—a guarantee of prestige for some and mobility for all. They were also a crucial stimulus for a whole raft of associated industries: the construction of roads and bridges, the production and refining of crude oil, and an ever-vaster network of gas stations, tire manufacturers, auto repair shops, and tourist cabins and motels. America was taking to the streets. Around 1920, twenty-three out of every twenty-four cars built in the world were manufactured in the United States, and some ten million automobiles were registered in America; by the end of the decade this number had tripled, reaching just under one car per family. Almost half of them were Model T Fords, available for a mere $290 in 1924.

By 1929, American drivers would clock up a collective two hundred billion miles during a single year. Cars transformed the lives of isolated farmers who had previously had a much harder time reaching the next town, of office workers who could now choose to live in the suburbs, and of millions of teenagers who could get away from home to go to the movies or to parties, or to simply discreetly park their vehicles at dimly lit roadside spots and engage in the kind of devotedly nonverbal communication their parents would have never countenanced under their roof. "Petting" entered the vocabulary during the mid-1920s.

As manufacturing boomed, factories were producing things nobody had ever thought they needed: household appliances such as toasters and vacuum cleaners, cars and radios, cosmetics and lingerie, perfumed soaps and cigarettes and cameras. The decisive weapon in this war for people's dollars was the transformation of citizens into consumers and the usurpation of their attention by the sleek and sexy seduction of advertising.

As early as 1920, a respected behavioral psychologist, John B. Watson, had resigned his position as chair of psychology at Johns Hopkins University in Baltimore and accepted a job at the J. Walter Thompson advertising agency. Watson was a specialist in animal behavior and had written a dissertation on the learning ability of rats. An admirer of Russian psychologist Ivan Pavlov, he was convinced that conditioning was the key to the human psyche. "Give me a dozen healthy infants, well-formed, and my own specified world to bring them up in and I'll guarantee to take any one at random and train him to become any type of specialist I might select—doctor, lawyer, artist, merchant-chief and, yes, even beggar-man and thief," he famously claimed, adding that talents and race had little or no power over social and cognitive conditioning.[2] As an advertising man, he put his ideas into practice by arguing that a successful ad had to access the fundamental emotions of its customers—love, fear, rage, shame—and associate them with branded products by means of ceaseless repetition.

"Through the turnstile to a land of ADVENTURE!" trumpeted a 1929 ad for the grocery store Piggly Wiggly, the first self-service supermarket chain, with more than two thousand outlets throughout the United States. Others followed this logic. J. C. Penney had one thousand stores in 1928, and branded goods became a staple, offering not only predictable quality but also extended marketing opportunities. The Curtis Candy Company in Chicago sent out a fleet of planes to drop its Baby Ruth candy bars over forty American cities, and in 1926, after the sweet manna from heaven had come floating down with little parachutes, Curtis was selling five million candy bars a day.

Starstruck

IF CANDY BARS COULD BE SOLD according to this logic, so could movies and the dreams they projected onto the silver screen. Charlie Chaplin had transformed himself into a branded product as the universally recognizable Little Tramp, and Hollywood executives were quick to understand that the public wanted to live with their stars, or rather, that they wanted to live with a projection, a public image that could be created and carefully groomed. Movies, after all, were becoming seriously big business. In the mid-1920s, fifty million movie tickets were sold each week in America; by 1929, this number had risen to eighty million.

Before the war, the center of the film industry had been in France, but as French films were struggling to find the means of financing big-budget productions in a depressed economy and as the German and Italian film industries had failed to establish a strong position for very similar reasons (see *Metropolis*), Hollywood had become the place to be as well as the producer of the biggest and most successful movies, with stars such as Buster Keaton, Greta Garbo, John Gilbert, Mary Pickford, and Douglas Fairbanks Sr. and Jr.

One of the greatest and most carefully managed movie stars, and one of the first to be broken by this system, was the radiant Clara Bow, the original It Girl. Bow's beginnings certainly did not predestine her for a great career. The only surviving child of three (the first one, a girl, had died two days after birth and was dumped in the trash can by her distraught mother), she was born in 1905 or 1906 in the tenement slums of Brooklyn to an alcoholic father and a mentally unstable mother who was at times reduced to prostitution. As a child, Clara was lonely, hungry, and ashamed of her tattered clothes. She stuttered and had few friends, but whenever she could lay hands on a nickel she was off to the movies, her one escape from the poverty and the dirt surrounding her.

When the young girl announced her wish to go into acting, her mother was horrified. Waking up one night, Clara found her mother kneeling over her, holding a carving knife to her throat. She managed to fight her mother off and lock her in a room, and then did not dare to come home for three days. Bow made it into the movies by sheer determination, winning a talent contest and then making the rounds of agents until she was given a few small roles. By 1924 she was working in Hollywood. Her mother, meanwhile, had been committed to an asylum.

Working in the Hollywood studio system, which tended to view its actors as slaves, Bow was in front of the camera from dawn to dusk: in 1925 alone, she starred in fifteen feature films. The camera loved her. A vivacious girl from Brooklyn with no formal training but an immense presence and mesmerizing eyes, she could apparently play anything. The 1926 release *Mantrap* proved her breakthrough: "Clara

Bow! And how! What a 'mantrap' she is! And how this picture is going to make her!" the *Variety* review shrieked. Bow had found her character in the role of a flirtatious everyday girl who makes her own decisions. Not for her the polite reticence of a young lady who waits to be spoken to. Seeing a man she finds interesting, it is she who pursues him, and it is she who slaps him when he makes an advance—not because it is unwelcome but because otherwise it would simply be too easy for him.

Despite her long hair and curves, Clara Bow was the perfect incarnation of the flapper, that mythical postwar creature consisting of equal parts fun, fashion, self-determination, and bootleg liquor. Her public loved her for it, and in a single month she received as many as forty-five thousand letters from her fans—more mail than an average town of five thousand inhabitants got.

The carefree Roaring Twenties needed their own star, and their designation for it. When English novelist Elinor Glyn, who specialized in risqué fiction for a broad market, published *It* in 1927, the word seemed perfect. Glyn herself was a surprising candidate to give the flapper generation an identity: born in 1864, overbearingly aristocratic in her manner, and with an impossibly exaggerated upper-class English accent, she seemed more like an unloved governess, whose charges' low waistlines and loose morals were calculated to offend old folks everywhere.

But the prolific author, who was known for publishing up to three saucy novels per year, was savvy enough to invent a concept that sounded mysteriously alluring and yet empty of any definite content—the ideal marketing tool. In her novel, she defined the elusive quality as follows: "To have 'It,' the fortunate possessor must have that strange magnetism which attracts both sexes. . . . In the animal world 'It' demonstrates in tigers and cats—both animals being fascinating and mysterious, and quite unbiddable."[3]

"The flapperism of today, with its jazz, necker-dances, its petting parties and its utter disregard of the conventions," as one review described it, was ideal fodder for Hollywood.[4] And so the fascinating and quite unbiddable Clara Bow was cast as the It Girl in a 1927 film based on Glyn's novel, which styled her as the ultimate flapper.

Flapperdom was a universal fad and quickly spread abroad through movies, illustrated magazines, and jazz recordings. The Charleston swept Berlin and set London a-jitter. Flappers were celebrated by films and newspapers as part of a tide of an irresistible and irresistibly scandalous social and sexual liberation. The cosmopolitan Harry Graf Kessler noticed this when he visited a party in Berlin, where the new, nihilist freedom was celebrated with even more abandon—and with an American guest: "I reached [the] apartment past midnight. Once more the company was a weird collection, with nobody knowing anyone else. . . . The names of the women, in every stage of undress, were unintelligible and it was impossible to tell whether they were lovers, tarts, or ladies. . . . The gramophone ground out popular hits all the time, but Josephine Baker sat on a couch and ate 'hot dogs' instead of dancing. So it continued until three, when I took my leave."[5]

While flapper culture took place mainly in bars (legal or otherwise) and other dubious haunts frequented by the young and wealthy for the hell of it, the new jazzy feeling received its hymn from a young American composer who in 1928 went to see France's most famous composition teacher, Nadia Boulanger, a formidable presence in the European music world. A composer, teacher, and conductor, Boulanger was sought out by the most talented young composition students because she was known not only for her brilliance but also for her capacity to understand and support her student's individual voice while working on the technical aspects of composition. The young man from New York who sat down at the piano and began playing some of his own pieces hoped to get a gloss of European sophistication because he self-consciously assumed his music lacked structure and intellectual depth. When he stopped, she simply told him that she had nothing to teach him. His name was George Gershwin.

On his return from Europe, Gershwin worked his new ideas into a large-scale piece for orchestra, *An American in Paris* (1928). With its syncopations, car horns, and surprising turns, the idiom is decidedly more American than Parisian, but very possibly the title was intended less as a direct evocation than as a whimsical reference to Gershwin's journey, on which he went to delve into a grand musical tradition and instead found his own orchestral voice. Paris, after all, was also Europe's jazz capital, and black American musicians had made their home there.

While flapperdom never quite made it in Paris, it found there someone who would elevate aspects of it to an art. Like Clara Bow, Coco Chanel came from the wrong side of the tracks. Born in 1883, she was the illegitimate daughter of a laundrywoman and a street vendor, and was educated at a strict and joyless convent after her mother's death when Coco was only twelve. The nuns taught her to sew so that the orphaned girl would have some income. With enormous, single-minded energy, she worked her way up from seamstress to head of an international fashion empire, financed in part by her judicious choice of lovers, most notably the vastly wealthy Duke of Westminster.

Chanel had understood that high fashion needed to learn from the flappers and their impatience with corsets, long dresses, high collars, and general sense of stifling rigidity. She sought her inspiration not in the grand attire of famous women of the world but in the clothes of sportsmen, riders, sailors, and fishermen. Elegant and understated but at the same time vastly more practical than the designs worn by women before the war, her creations had a daring simplicity that made them de rigueur with the new urban elite. Perhaps her most lasting contribution to fashion was a stylish staple introduced in 1926, a piece of clothing so fundamental to a woman's wardrobe that it became known by its acronym, LBD—little black dress.

The Teddy Bears' Picnic

FLAPPERS WERE A DISTINCTLY AMERICAN phenomenon, perhaps the first wave of youth culture comprising fashion, music, behavior, language, and cultural icons that spread across the world. In totalitarian societies such as the Soviet Union or Italy or in very conservative ones such as Spain, flapperdom never properly took hold, but its influence made itself felt from Dublin to Tokyo and from Shanghai to Berlin. Still, some very distinctive variations existed. In London, flapper fashions were on display in fashionable shops (at Selfridge's they were worn by live mannequins lounging behind the glass), but the press was fascinated by a different craze: the Bright Young Things.

Perhaps the riot of irresponsible glamor and willful childishness could have happened only in England, and only as a reaction to the solemnity and the grief of the immediate postwar years, during which these fashionable young people reached their adolescence. While the nation was recovering from the collective shell shock of the casualties and the undermining of the social order, from the economic crisis, the strikes and the riots, and the terrible feeling that Britannia no longer ruled the waves as effortlessly as it might have done before, a privileged few fresh out of school or university simply giggled, put on silly costumes, and poured themselves another cocktail.

The years of postwar austerity were over, and times had changed, apparently for good. To many of the young people of 1928 the moral world of their parents seemed antediluvian. Virginia Woolf had observed that human nature changed in 1910. Her example had been her cook: "The Victorian cook lived like a leviathan in the lower depths, formidable, silent, obscure, inscrutable; the Georgian cook is a creature of sunshine and fresh air; in and out of the drawing-room, now to borrow the *Daily Herald*, now to ask advice about a hat. Do you ask for more solemn instances of the power of the human race to change?"[6]

The idea that a domestic employee could talk to the mistress of the house as one woman to another, that the cook suddenly looked at herself as a sexual equal to her employer, had appeared revolutionary to Woolf. Now, twenty years and one war later, the entire game had changed again. Nietzsche had buried God; the Dadaists, the surrealists, the fascists, and the communists had proclaimed bourgeois values dead; Freudians had declared middle-class decency a dangerous illness. The flapper generation carried on this great campaign, not sitting at writing desks or in newspaper offices, nor angrily demonstrating on the streets and in factories, but partying in night-clubs, alluringly seedy cabarets, and the homes of the wealthy.

Not everyone was so approvingly matter-of-fact about changing attitudes. Back in 1920, Dr. R. Murray-Leslie had scoffed that a lack of eligible young men had created "the social butterfly type; the frivolous, scantily clad, jazzing flapper, irresponsible and un-disciplined, to whom a dance, a new hat, or a man with a car, were of more importance than the fate of nations." Another arbiter of taste decried suffragettes and other feminist activists as mannish and ugly: "Many of our young women have become desexed and masculinized, with short hair, skirts no longer than kilts, narrow hips, insignificant breasts," wrote Arabella Kenealy in the *Daily Mail* in 1920.[7]

The young women thus insulted simply did not care. Their busy social calendars hardly ever left them the time to pick up a paper. Some of these enviable youths were the very incarnations of wealth and privilege. Among the prominent members of the Bright Young Things were Bryan Guinness, heir to a beer fortune, who was said to earn one-twelfth of a penny from every bottle sold; the fabulously wealthy and ineffably exotic American-Italian-English aesthete Harold Acton, famous at Oxford for declaiming T. S. Eliot's poem *The Waste Land* over Christ Church Meadows with a megaphone; Elisabeth Ponsonby, the daughter of Arthur Ponsonby, a senior Labour minister and antiwar campaigner; Henry Yorke, son of an industrialist and later better known by his pen name Henry Green; the archly eccentric Sitwell siblings Edith, Osbert, and Sacheverell; the aristocratic but cash-strapped Mitford sisters, whose life choices would tear them apart; and Stephen Tennant, the gayest of the gay members of the set, whose costumes and general

demeanor went down in legend and song and who would appear
even at an ordinary soirée with gold powder adorning his wavy
blond locks.

Some of these young people were fabulously rich, while others
were subsisting in what was then still called genteel poverty, but all
of them had considerable social standing and were themselves members of the aristocracy or related to them. But their exploits would
have remained utterly conventional and would not have inspired
so much brilliant writing had it not been for some less well-born
hangers-on who compensated for their lack of pedigree with sheer
talent and outrageousness.

The American actress Tallulah Bankhead became a favored Bright
Young Thing during her stay in London in the late twenties. She did
not tolerate a single dull minute, frequently enlivening as well as confusing proceedings with her vigorous, immediate, and, as she put it,
"ambisextrous" hunger for erotic encounters. Other hopefuls included
the up-and-coming photographer Cecil Beaton, who did anything he
could to win commissions and accolades from the beautiful people
he so envied, people he made even more beautiful in his elaborately
arranged portraits; the travel writer Robert Byron, who was expelled
from Oxford for refusing to behave himself and study; the brilliant,
surly, and hard-drinking novelist Evelyn Waugh, forever trying to
negotiate a path between his monumental snobbery and his even
greater desire to belong in the right kind of environment; Noël
Coward, already a star of the theater and never truly part of any set,
but always on hand to imbibe, amuse, and observe; and the young
poet John Betjeman, just down from Oxford, where he had failed for
a second time to receive his degree in divinity. Betjeman remembered
one night's entertainments:

> The spurt of soda as the whisky rose
> Bringing its heady scent to memory's nose
> Along with Smells one otherwise forgets:
> Hairwash from Delhez, Turkish cigarettes,
> The reek of Ronuk on a parquet floor
> As parties came cascading through the door:
> Elisabeth Ponsonby in leopard-skins
> And Robert Byron and the Ruthven twins.

Being a Bright Young Thing was all about cascading through doors
in leopard skins, being outrageous and amusing. There was an endless
succession of pajama parties, a swimming pool party with orchestra,

endless weekends at the country houses of rich—and often outraged—parents, legendary costume balls, puckish practical jokes, and nocturnal car races through the streets of London.

The pervading atmosphere of these amusements was reminiscent of Peter Pan with cocktails—in 1926 there had even been a party on this very theme. It was all so willed in its innocence, its refusal to see the world from an adult perspective. The themed parties led straight back to the childhood obsession with dressing up, and it was as if the life at boarding school (which almost all members of this charmed circle had attended), with its quest for fun, defiance of school rules, and nocturnal expeditions sneaking out of windows and across rooftops, had never ended.

One of the favorite hangouts of the brightest of the Bright Young Things was the Gargoyle Club at 69 Dean Street in Soho, founded by David Tennant, brother of the gold-locked Stephen. The club breathed the air of a new era with its walls covered in mosaics of mirror shards and two paintings by Matisse on display. The owner said that he had opened the establishment simply to have a convenient place to dance with his girlfriend.

Here, in 1926, members of the fashionable set were invited to an "Edwardian Party" and asked to "come as you were twenty years ago." In April 1930, some five thousand revelers congregated in eighteenth-century costumes to celebrate Mozart. The whole extravagance was supposed to have cost more than £3,000—roughly $100,000 in today's money. The menu of the exclusive dinner preceding the dancing had been taken straight from a historical recipe book of dishes served at the court of Louis XVI, and later an orchestra in period clothes and wigs as well as a jazz band entertained the party-goers into the small hours of the morning. Returning home, a high-spirited crowd encountered some street workers and posed, pneumatic drill in hand, with the astonished workmen for a commemorative photograph.

The fun and games of this privileged set would have evaporated with the alcoholic haze surrounding them had it not been for the abiding fascination of the press, who saw that there was great copy to be had from their antics as well as from their blasé attitude. Papers such as the *Daily Express* and magazines such as *Punch* and *Tatler* followed every party, every extravaganza, and every mini scandal, and no event was deemed complete without the requisite gaggle of press photographers and reporters. This media attention magnified the importance and the resonance of the entertainments of what was, after all, a relatively small, charmed circle of more or less aristocratic youngsters and their hangers-on, making them into a national phenomenon.

For the general reader who lived on £200 a year—an office clerk, say, or a minor civil servant—stories about the Bright Young Things allowed glimpses of a life of privilege and leisure. Perhaps they aspired to a similar lifestyle; perhaps they felt envy and dissimulated by expressing it as moral disapproval. But in a wider context, stories about champagne, Pimm's, and beautiful people were part of a change in social tides. Despite the fact that not all of the Bright Young Things were either young or bright, they stood for the generational divide between those who had lived through and often served in the war and those who had been too young to do so. While the difference in years was often slight, the contrast in outlook, could be enormous.

Eventually the cheerful nihilism and the occasionally forced indifference to everything political began to wear thin, the alcohol haze lifted, and the young party-goers began to cast around for answers, and for a faith. In the case of the Mitford sisters this search would famously lead in divergent directions. Nancy became an expat living in France and a novelist concentrating on social mores; Diana would divorce the millionaire brewery heir Bryan Guinness to marry the British fascist leader Oswald Mosley; Unity would surrender herself entirely to an adulation of Hitler that left even her family speechless and that would culminate in her attempted suicide when her idol's case seemed lost; Jessica became a communist and would later go to work for the Republican side in the Spanish Civil War; and Deborah married Andrew Cavendish, becoming the Duchess of Devonshire.

The search for ideological certainty also infected other members of the seemingly charmed circle of Roaring Twenties indulgence as their heedless hedonism soured in an increasingly menacing political atmosphere. Evelyn Waugh, one of the sharpest observers of social mores among his hard-drinking friends, turned to Roman Catholicism; Tom Driberg intensified his engagement with communism; Brian Howard would travel to Germany and Austria to study the rise of Hitler's National Socialists. Using Unity Mitford to gain access to the Nazi hierarchy, he became an important voice informing British readers about the menace of fascism, and later also writing about the Spanish Civil War. Others failed to make a successful transition from the heyday of youth to a more engaged adulthood. Elisabeth Ponsonby would drink herself to death at the age of thirty-nine, and as for the beautiful and gold-locked Stephen Tennant, he simply took to his bed and hardly ever got up again until his death in 1987.

Flappin' Outrage

WHILE FLAPPERS AND BRIGHT YOUNG THINGS dominated the gossip pages and the exasperated minds of many parents in 1920s New York and Chicago as well as in London—places in which a growing and apparently robust economy appeared to be firmly married to political stability—in other, less stable countries, the values of a rebellious and inherently apolitical younger generation would themselves come under fire. This was never made clearer than during Josephine Baker's dance engagement in Vienna in February 1928.

Baker was the epitome of a bright and breezy new entertainment culture mixing jazz and the music hall with orientalist fantasy and sex, leaving almost nothing to the imagination of her delighted and largely male audiences. Janet Flanner, correspondent for the *New Yorker* (itself a novel and always up-to-the-minute product of sophisticated urbanity), breathlessly recounted to her readers an appearance in Paris, the city that had made Baker famous:

> She made her entry entirely nude except for a pink flamingo feather between her limbs; she was being carried upside down and doing the splits on the shoulder of a black giant. Mid-stage he paused, and with his long fingers holding her basket-wise around the waist, swung her in a slow cartwheel to the stage floor, where she stood. . . . She was an unforgettable female ebony statue. A scream of salutation spread through the theatre. Whatever happened next was unimportant. The two specific elements had been established and were unforgettable—her magnificent dark body, a new model that to the French proved for the first time that black was beautiful, and the acute response of the white masculine public in the capital of hedonism of all Europe—Paris.

The announcement of Baker's imminent arrival caused a storm in the Austrian capital, where rival political factions were competing for the moral high ground, and while the socialist city fathers were uneasy about a spectacle that was widely decried as immoral, the Catholic conservatives and the fascists were practically foaming at the mouth at the idea of a black woman accompanied by an all-black jazz orchestra performing erotically suggestive dances onstage in Vienna.

The city of Mozart and Schubert, it seemed, would not survive this insult. The previous year the performance of Ernst Krenek's opera *Johnny Spielt Auf*, featuring a jazz musician in blackface, had caused a political scandal and led to violent confrontations in the streets. Now, however, the stakes seemed even higher. The *Neues Wiener Tagblatt*, a major conservative newspaper, predicted nothing less than cultural apocalypse: "Literature and music, dance and socializing have become black arts, the negrofication [*Vernegerung*] is the last and lowest development of the European. The cacophony of the jazz band plays the *danse macabre* of European culture, and its arhythmical gyrations of Charleston and Black Bottom proceed at the pace of a movie."[8] Not only black culture but American culture in general was the death of the classical tradition, it seemed. Another journalist described Baker's dancing as "the last stop on the ride into the immense, immeasurable depth of the abyss."

After wrangling about venues and threatened demonstrations, Josephine Baker finally did appear onstage in Vienna, though only as part of a larger show that flanked some of her tamer moments with routines by Viennese actors in blackface, which even the audience found embarrassing.

The reaction to Josephine Baker rehearsed many of the arguments conservative critics habitually trotted out against the hedonism of the Roaring Twenties and its emphasis on youth culture, which had never before been so assertively and so unapologetically present in public life. In Berlin, where Baker had performed her notorious banana dance in 1925, journalists were less inclined to moralize and more ready to see her for the phenomenon she was, writing about her band: "They are a cross between primeval forests and skyscrapers; likewise their music, jazz, in its color and rhythms. Ultramodern and ultraprimitive."[9]

As Vienna was shrinking into provincialism, Berlin had taken over as the German-speaking capital of cosmopolitan culture. For a precious few years it would become the place to be for the daring and the sophisticated, from the English writer Stephen Spender to Viennese theater director Max Reinhardt and many more. Berlin's artistic life and youth culture were second to none as Berliners enjoyed their "golden twenties" (*die goldenen zwanziger Jahre*) of economic recovery, apparent political stabilization, and a hesitant but real growth in confidence in the future. In bars and beer gardens, young people were dancing the Charleston and German musicians copied jazz riffs from records imported from the United States.

The spirit of frivolity and celebration spread on the wings of song, carried by the words of the musical sensation of 1928, the Comedian Harmonists, a male vocal sextet made up of singers whose inspiration came from an American vocal ensemble, the Revelers.

Initially the members of the young group, all relatively young and entirely unemployed, met and rehearsed without payment, calling themselves the Melody Makers. After a rocky start, they established themselves with cheeky lyrics and cheery arrangements, prepared with masterly verve. Almost all their texts were indecent, though this was not always apparent at first listening. In the classic "Veronica der Lenz Ist Da" (Veronica, Spring Is Here) the singer's beloved is informed that it must be springtime because "the asparagus is growing," and young people should seek happiness and freedom in the forest—a particularly lovely take on the sanctity of the German woods in Romantic lore. Indeed, spring finally seemed to have arrived, and the Weimar Republic appeared to breathe a collective sigh of relief.

Not everyone took part in the fun and games. Politically, the tensions had eased but not vanished; socially, however, they were still painfully acute. For the deliciously dangerous culture of the Berlin demimonde, this mixture of carefree winners and scroungers, prostitutes and petty criminals, was what made life interesting. But there were also those who understood the potential danger of so many people living at the edge of what could be described as a decent life, and even further below.

The official face of the newly glamorous metropolis did not show the misery—"those in the dark remain unseen," as the leftist poet Bertolt Brecht wrote. The line occurred in his most famous ballad, "Mack the Knife," describing in ominous tones the murderous practices of a career criminal who is an expert at assassination. It was the first number of Brecht's *Threepenny Opera*, which had been set to music by Kurt Weill and premiered on August 31, 1928, at Berlin's Theater am Schiffbauerdamm.

The Threepenny Opera tells a sordid story of small people and their dreams crushed by an equally seedy and workaday capitalism, represented by Jonathan Jeremiah Peachum, called the "king of beggars" and in reality a kind of pimp for beggars, and Mack the Knife, who makes a good living by theft, extortion, and murder. Masquerading as a love story between Peachum's daughter Polly and the ruthless Mack, the opera describes a capitalist power struggle in which Peachum attempts to get rid of his competitor by betraying him to the police and seeing him hanged. His plan backfires as the newly crowned queen of England not only pardons Mack but also ennobles him. The most ruthless gangster wins.

Musically innovative and shot through with elements from popular music, jazz, and tango as well as classical forms, inspired in its cynically smooth message, *The Threepenny Opera* became a huge success on the stage, predictably loved by those on the left and hated by the Nazis with equal intensity. Ostensibly simple, folksy, and without artifice, it was the coolest and most sophisticated thing going, but while its melodies were mesmerizing, its eminently quotable lyrics implied that the party would soon be over.

PART TWO

PREWAR

The Magnetic City

What is Magnitostroi? It is a grandiose factory for remaking people. Yesterday's peasant . . . becomes a genuine proletarian . . . fighting for the quickest possible completion of the laying of socialism's foundation. You are an unfortunate person, my dear reader, if you have not been to Magnitostroi. I feel sorry for you.
— R. Roman, *Krokodil v Magnitogorske*, 1931

....

AN ANGRY, ICY WIND WAS BLOWING OVER THE BARREN LANDSCAPE, tugging at the clothes of a group of riders moving among the foothills on the eastern slopes of the Ural Mountains, far away from civilization. It was March, and winters were long. This place could only be reached on horseback or on foot. They surveyed the barren landscape in front of them. Within a matter of years, even months, they would build a factory here, and not just any factory, but the largest steelworks in Europe and perhaps in the world.

The place the small group of riders had reached was called Magnitnaia Gora, the magnetic mountain. Centuries earlier, settlers had noticed that their compasses were behaving strangely around these hills. The rocks were full of iron ore, and the leadership in Moscow was determined to exploit this resource, setting in motion a vast project on a par with the building of the pyramids. They would build a huge socialist city where there had been nothing.

"To transform our country from an agrarian one into an industrial one capable with its own powers of producing essential machinery—that is the essence, the basis of our general line," Stalin had declared in 1925, and now this ambition was to become a concrete policy.[1] It was true: recovering from a terrible and bloody civil war, the huge Soviet empire needed to make a rapid transition from a country of peasant villages in which little had changed for centuries to a fully modern, industrial society. The war had damaged much of Russia's already small industrial base—factories had been destroyed, workers displaced or murdered, engineers, administrators, and factory owners exiled.

Stalin's industrial push was not just about feeding the population and defending a country weakened by years of fratricidal warfare; at the heart of the Party's ambition to industrialize the Soviet Union in record time was the desire to demonstrate to the entire world the inherent superiority of socialism over capitalism. Only if they could achieve the impossible could the Bolsheviks prove that the future belonged to them.

To create this miracle, Stalin had announced the first Five-Year Plan, designed to transform industry and manufacturing in one huge leap of faith and to forge a truly Soviet society through a comprehensive program of collectivization. "We are advancing full steam ahead along the path of industrialization—to socialism, leaving behind the age-old Russian backwardness," he had proclaimed. "We are becoming a country of metal, an automobilized country, a tractorized country. And when we have put the USSR on an automobile, and the *muzhik* [Russian peasant] on a tractor, let the esteemed capitalists, who boast of their 'civilization,' try to overtake us."[2]

The City of the Five-Year Plan

MAGNITOGORSK, LITERALLY THE MAGNETIC CITY, was to be the microcosm of these vast ambitions. When the decision was made in 1927 to build a plant here that would double the Soviet Union's production of pig iron and steel, not only was the remote site in the Urals lacking infrastructure, but there were also no engineers in the Soviet Union capable of designing and building such a huge plant. The Soviet leadership therefore engaged the services of Henry Freyn and Co. in Chicago, a firm specializing in the design and implementation of large industrial structures.

In fact, and in spite of Stalin's wishes, the "esteemed capitalists" played a major role in Russia's push to jump centuries of development within a mere half decade. The inspiration for Magnitogorsk stood in the United States itself, on the shores of Lake Michigan, about twenty-five miles from Chicago: the steel town of Gary, Indiana. Built in 1906, Gary was in many ways a perfect template for the Soviet model, as it, too, was the result of a concerted and at times despotic act of will. What made its story truly American, however, was that the founder and master of this city that was to have a hundred thousand inhabitants was not the state but a private capitalist concern: the United States Steel Corporation.

Gary had been created by a stroke of the pen. It was a gleaming utopia that had become not only a flourishing town but also a powerful steelworks producing more than four thousand tons of steel a day. "An amazing feature of Gary, built as it is on shifting sands, is that it is actually so solid, so permanent, so strong. There is nothing suggestive of the shoddy or the temporary," commented an observer in 1920. "Schools, libraries, clubs, commercial buildings, homes, churches, meeting places, all have the aspect as if having been built for permanence. This city has arisen so swiftly, so solidly, just because a great Corporation ordered it! It is vastly more of an achievement than as if it had been ordered by an arbitrary monarch, with absolute control of the nation and of its resources."[3]

Laid out on a grid, the prosperous and hardworking town was a genuine result of America's entrepreneurial spirit and seemed to many to be the very incarnation of the United States. Not everybody loved it; President Woodrow Wilson had campaigned against it, going so far as to call it un-American, because it was the private fiefdom of a corporation and not the fruit of truly American democracy. But his was a minority opinion, as a rabbi living and working in the town made clear: "Gary is America. Every American city is Gary writ large and small."[4]

Russian Communist leaders were impressed by the idea that an industrial city could be simply invented at the drawing board. They would build a city that was bigger, more efficient, and altogether grander than its American counterpart, and it would be located directly adjacent to one of the largest and most easily accessible deposits of iron ore within the Soviet empire. The steel it would produce would be used in industry, but it would do much more than that, as a pamphlet advertising the town described: "Metal is not produced simply for its own usage. . . . Metal draws all industry along with it, all spheres of human life, beginning with the production of turbines, tractors, harvester combines, textiles, food, and ending with books. Metal is the basis of modern civilization."[5]

It was only a matter of time until the lofty dreams of a new and proud proletariat producing steel in an ideal Soviet city would run into the reality of communist bureaucracy. Chicago engineers drew up plans only to find them altered by commissars and committees eager to prove their patriotic usefulness and suspicious of the designs of the capitalist outsiders. Production targets and working capacities were increased arbitrarily, keeping pace not with the technological possibilities but with the ever greater demands of propaganda. The facilities were originally conceived for an annual capacity of 656,000 metric tons of pig iron, but in 1929 this number was raised several times, winding up at 1.6 million metric tons, and then in 1930 it rose again, to 2.5 million metric tons.

The small group of settlers arriving in March 1929 had the task of building barracks and other essential structures. A railway line had been promised for years but still existed only in part. So far, the gigantic plant and the town supplying it consisted of nothing but strings stretched along the windswept, thawing soil to designate where barracks and factory buildings were to be erected. By May, work had begun on a brick factory, and with the help of the Red Army the last few miles of railway lines were being laid. Work on the great socialist project could finally begin in earnest.

At the same time, there was nothing on the ground, and planning was bedeviled by incompetence and fraud. The railway had been built so shoddily that trains could go no faster than six miles an hour, so at times some of the passengers simply walked next to the rail cars. Traveling the 540-mile route from Moscow to Magnitogorsk took more than a week. The Russian state corporation entrusted with the building and oversight of the plant was called, appropriately enough for a steel-producing company, Stalstroi—but only weeks earlier it had been called Tekstilstroi and had specialized in the production of textiles. The only change to prepare it for its gigantic new task had been to rename it. The American subcontractors began to understand that their task would be incomparably greater than just building the world's largest steelworks. "The fundamental thing that sharply struck us," its chief of construction noted, "was that among those who work at the site, there was no clue as to what a steel plant was."[6]

When the American engineers finally arrived at the construction site in summer, they did not trust their eyes. What had been described to them as a town consisted of little more than tents, and there were no roads, very few tools, and no heavy machinery. To make matters worse, the workers now being brought to the site by railway were overwhelmingly untrained and resentful at their forced move, for very few had come of their own free will. Many of the new arrivals were in fact the victims of the new policy of collectivization and of the prosecution of kulaks decreed by Stalin.

Portrayed by Soviet propaganda as large landowners and capitalist bloodsuckers, the kulaks were in reality not much more than freehold farmers owning a little more land than other peasants. Now, hundreds of thousands of them were forced to surrender their livestock and leave their land or work in collective farms. Predictably, the results were catastrophic. The farmers would rather kill their cattle than hand them over to the new masters, and during 1929 and 1930 millions of farm animals were slaughtered by their owners.

Expropriated kulaks formed part of the new population of Magnitogorsk and were soon arriving by the trainload at the dirt track that served as a station, as a communist activist would remember:

> An extraordinary plenipotentiary arrived. They called for me. A car came at 1 a.m., and I rode to them. Comrade Gugel Iakov Semenovich, the chief of the construction, was there. The plenipotentiary turned to me and asked my name. Then he asked: "Do you know who you're speaking with?" I said, "I don't know you." He answered: "Here's how you can help me. In three days there will be no fewer than 25,000 people. You served in the army? We need barracks built by that time." . . . They herded in not 25,000 but 40,000. It was raining, children were crying, as you walked by, you didn't want to look.[7]

A Symphony of Sirens

THE CONSTRUCTION OF THE CITY was being driven forward relentlessly, despite a lack of almost all basic provisions. The party had set a date by which the factory would have to start production, and the °responsible officials knew that their lives were on the line. As the hot continental summer was slowly tipping into a bitter winter with temperatures as low as –40°C, the workers were constantly driven to their limits. "At that time the slogan was: 'Blast Furnace by the Deadline!'" remembered one worker. "You would see this slogan literally everywhere. . . . You'd go to the toilet, to take care of your natural needs, and even there you'd see it: 'The Blast Furnace by the Deadline!' . . . The only thing they didn't do was to write it in the heavens."[8]

Steel ovens in the steppes:
Magnitogorsk.

Toiling under constant pressure and with primitive tools and materials, the often untrained workers frequently produced results that were unusable and even dangerous, and accidents were a daily problem. The entire gigantic building site sometimes seemed to be in a state of emergency: "As soon as the phone rang, you knew it was a breakdown somewhere," wrote Iakov Shmidt, one of several short-term directors. "The switchboard operator notified me immediately of all emergencies. Simultaneously, on the site, in the event of a fire, warning signals on all train engines were sounded, along with the siren on the electrical station. This unusual 'symphony' made disturbing impressions on all those living in Magnitka."[9]

Another eyewitness saw the events in an altogether brighter light. Born in Philadelphia in 1912, John Scott was a communist and an idealist and emigrated to the Soviet Union in 1932 to help build a better future for mankind. One of the few people to actually volunteer to work in Magnitogorsk, he suffered the same deprivation as his fellow workers—and loved it. "I was very happy," he wrote in his memoir, *Behind the Urals*. "The Bolsheviks planned their economy and gave opportunities to younger men and women. Furthermore, they had got away from the fetishization of material possessions, which ... was one of the basic ills of our American civilization. I saw that most Russians ate only black bread, wore one suit until it disintegrated, and used old newspapers for writing letters and office memoranda, rolling cigarettes, making envelopes, and for various personal functions."[10]

Reading Scott's account of his experiences in Soviet Russia, one can get a sense of the often genuine enthusiasm of young activists willing to endure anything for the sake of the greatest dream ever dreamed. Just like the party officials, he saw the motley crowds of former peasants, workers in other industries, and prisoners as nothing but raw material to be purified, forged, and shaped into new Soviet men, just like the metal would be processed in the blast furnaces they were erecting. "Khaibulin, the Tartar, had never seen a staircase, locomotive, or an electric light until he had come to Magnitogorsk a year before," Scott recounted.

> His ancestors for centuries had raised stock on the flat plains of Kazakhstan. They had been dimly conscious of the czarist government; they had had to pay taxes. They had heard stories of the October Revolution; I even saw the Red Army come and drive out a few rich landlords. They had attended meetings of the Soviet, without understanding very clearly what it was all about, but through all this their lives had gone on more or less than before. Now Shaimat Khaibulin was building a blast furnace bigger than any in Europe. He had learned to read and was attending an evening school, learning the trade of the electrician. He had learned to speak Russian, he read newspapers. His life had changed more in a year than that of his antecedents since the time of Tamerlane.[11]

Scott was one of the few Westerners to make his life in Russia out of idealism, but many leftists looked east with the keenest interest. "Intellectuals, social workers, professional men and women are welcome most cordially in Russia," an advertisement in *The Nation* read in January 1929, pointing out that this was the country "where the world's most gigantic social experiment is being made—amidst a galaxy of picturesque nationalities, wondrous scenery, splendid architecture, and exotic civilizations."

The Sound of Things Falling

AS THE ROARING TWENTIES WERE HURTLING toward the next decade, which promised to bring more stability, more growth, and more wealth for all, an increasing number of economists and other observers began to believe that the good times could not last forever. And in the decade's last year, the enthusiasm felt by many committed socialists and communists in Russia and elsewhere about building a new world was suddenly galvanized by an event that, they believed, they had predicted all along.

What precisely happened on October 29, 1929, has been exhaustively researched, but *why* it happened is still a subject of lively debate. Following a period of unprecedented growth that saw the value of the Dow Jones stock index increase tenfold, the market suddenly and catastrophically slumped over a period of five chaotic days. There was no immediate hard and fast reason for this collapse: a fraud case involving a London investor had created nervousness, but nothing that had not been seen before; an oversupply of wheat had created a volatile futures market in grain, but that in itself would certainly not have precipitated financial apocalypse. The real reason was most likely the roaring engine of the Twenties itself: an exuberant and rapid industrial and economic development that saw industry profits rise by more than 30 percent in the United States and brought returns on investment of more than 20 percent.

In this financial feeding frenzy, many investors had thrown caution to the wind in order to cash in. As always happens in moments such as this, many small investors had come along for the ride, acknowledging that things could not go up indefinitely but convinced that they would get out in time. In this atmosphere of heady uncertainty, a small but pervasive doubt, a plausible rumor, was enough to bring the entire immense castle in the clouds crashing down to earth. On October 29, shares traded on the New York Stock Exchange lost 12 percent of their value in a day of chaotic and panic-driven selling. All attempts by big investors such as John D. Rockefeller to restore confidence by buying shares failed as the markets spiraled out of control.

During the next days and months the downward trend continued, and by 1932 the Dow Jones index had lost 89 percent of its value compared to the eve of the crash. Only 16 percent of private households in America had their money invested in the stock market, but the effects of the chaos were much wider and more devastating. The destruction of huge fortunes in the market sapped the optimism that had fueled the great upward trend of the twenties. Workers were laid off, and at the height of what was to be called the Great Depression, twelve thousand American men and women lost their jobs every day; a quarter of the US workforce found themselves on the street with nothing to sustain them but bread lines and soup kitchens.

The Depression was much more than just the end of an economic era of robust, self-confident capitalism and a strong middle class. Karl Marx had predicted decades earlier that the capitalist system would eventually end up destroying itself, and he had continued to argue that a world revolution and ultimately a more peaceful, socialist society would result from this catastrophe. In 1929, this prediction appeared to have become reality, and socialists across the world regarded the crash as nothing less than the historic proof of the accuracy and scientific nature of Marxism.

The Budapest-born author and journalist Arthur Koestler was one of the millions of hopefuls in the West who would come to be known as "fellow travelers," believing that the only just future for humanity would be in socialism and looking to the Soviet model both for inspiration and also often for ideological guidance and financial support. Growing up in a prosperous middle-class Jewish family reduced to penury during the First World War, Koestler had lived through the brutal early days of Miklós Horthy's regime in Hungary, had been forced to interrupt his studies in Vienna because he could no longer pay the university fees, and had been driven to look for alternatives to the social order that had treated him and his family so harshly.

Koestler had gone to Palestine to be part of the huge surge of idealism as young Zionists tried to build a new homeland for the Jews, practicing socialism in kibbutzim (agricultural communes) and creating an intellectual culture to which he himself wanted to contribute. Initially forced to support himself as a day laborer, he had managed to publish his first articles and eventually became Middle East correspondent for a prestigious German publication. From Jerusalem he moved to Paris in 1929, where he witnessed the effects of the crash and the change in social climate as the Great Depression took hold. From his perspective it seemed inevitable that Marx's forecast had been right, and he joined the Communist Party in 1931. "If History herself were a fellow-traveler," Koestler would later note, "she could not have arranged a more clever timing of events than this coincidence of the gravest crisis of the Western World with the initial phase of Russia's Industrial Revolution. . . . The contrast . . . was so striking and so obvious that it led to the equally obvious conclusion: They are the future—we, the past."[12]

The Soviet authorities did their very best to foster this impression, particularly among intellectuals and artists, whose high social profile could help them spread the good news. This diffusion took two routes: through cultural activity (both open and covert) abroad and by inviting influential visitors to the USSR.

Ballets Russes

SOVIET CULTURE PROVED TO BE a crucial asset in the attempt to capture the Western imagination. During the postwar years, a period of artistic retrenchment in the West, when neoclassicism triumphed over artistic experimentation, some of the most exciting and most innovative works of art came from the Soviet Union. Before the revolution, there had been Diaghilev's Ballets Russes. Now there were films by Sergei Eisenstein and Dziga Vertov, along with stunning constructivist paintings, posters, and collages by Malevich, El Lissitzky, and Aleksandr Rodchenko, as well as other forms of experimental art. This led the British writer Stephen Spender, then living in Berlin, to rhapsodize: "We went to see those Russian films which were shown often in Berlin at this period: *Earth, The General Line, The Mother, But Tim King, Ten Days That Shook The World, Their Way Into Life,* etc. These films . . . excited us because they had the modernism, the poetic sensibility, the satire, the visual beauty, all those qualities we found most exciting in other forms of modern art, but they also conveyed a message of hope."[13]

Of even more propagandistic value than the message carried by the works of Soviet artists were sympathetic eyewitness accounts published by Western intellectuals who had traveled throughout the USSR to form their own opinion. These visits, of course, were not unsupervised impromptu journeys. Instead, writers and artists of sufficient standing who were judged by Soviet officials to be amenable to giving the right kind of opinion were cordially invited over. Depending on their rank and perceived importance, some or all of their trip would be paid for. During the 1920s and 1930s, some one hundred thousand cultural visitors made this ritual journey at the invitation of the Party, usually strictly controlled by Intourist guides, translators, official visits, rigid itineraries, and spies. Nothing was to be left to chance.

A procession of prominent writers and intellectuals from different Western countries, including such luminaries as H. G. Wells, André Gide, Theodore Dreiser, Romain Rolland, George Bernard Shaw, and Lion Feuchtwanger, visited the Soviet Union on minutely managed trips. "I came back from the USSR a different man," confessed a deeply moved Louis Aragon, who had been André Breton's brother-in-arms and a cofounder of surrealism in Paris. Like Breton, Aragon had turned to communism, and the two prominent surrealists were not alone. Even Pierre Drieu La Rochelle, then already well on his journey toward fascism, was so deeply fascinated and preoccupied by the Soviet Union and its apparent ability to realize the dreams of humanity that he wrote: "Now, the fire from Moscow. From now on, within each man there is an inner dialogue in which Moscow is inevitably one of the interlocutors."[14]

The cultural tourism of Western intellectuals became so important that it spawned a minor Soviet industry, which might be best described as a factory for Potemkin villages. According to legend, Count Potemkin, a favorite of Catherine the Great, had tried to impress his empress by building a series of phantom villages consisting only of façades in a region she had commanded him to develop. The story is likely apocryphal, but it showed a remarkable longevity, not least because it appeared to describe a salient feature of Russian culture: a combination of rank incompetence and a gift for keeping up appearances. A team of dedicated Soviet officials worked tirelessly to ensure that the experiences of the invited writers would exceed their highest expectations.

As of 1927, tour guides assigned to foreign dignitaries received special training not only in standard subjects such as political economy, Lenin and Leninism, and revolutionary history, but also in the history and constitutional arrangements of the major guest countries, world geography, and foreign languages. They were also drilled on common talking points. Child poverty and child homelessness were shocking, it was true, but this was a hangover from tsarist times. The speed of improvement and transformation, on the other hand, was truly staggering. To prove this, visitors were taken to a series of factories, orphanages, universities, *kolkhoz* farms, and other large projects where they could see for themselves the huge steps being made toward a happier, more humane future. Officials at these institutions had been issued an ever-evolving catalogue of taboo subjects, informally referred to as "the Talmud."

Visits under these conditions could be very comfortable affairs indeed. In 1927, star American journalist Theodore Dreiser, who was increasingly popular in Russian translation thanks to his controversial views on his home country, made his first all-expenses-paid trip to the USSR. He was deeply ambivalent about the experience but quickly captivated by some aspects. Arriving in Moscow, he stayed at the Grand Hotel and witnessed a parade on Red Square from his hotel window. His diary captures his surprised delight. "They are marching to show the world how great is their faith in red Russia. And here, where so recently was only poverty, ignorance & blind faith are now more or less educated & trained men & women, boys & girls."[15]

At the Leningrad train station, a quite unexpected welcome was prepared for the visitor. "There was an automobile waiting and I was carried off in grand style to the Hotel Europe. En route I was struck by the beauty of the city, the broad streets and fine buildings, the air of smartness and alertness which Moscow lacks. The hotel proved to be much more imposing and comfortable than the notorious Bolshaya Moskovskaya in Moscow. Lackeys opened the car doors. . . . There was an air of grandeur and obsequiousness and order soothing to a soul harassed by the shabby lobbies, wretched service and leaky plumbing."[16]

Dreiser's taste for luxury was well known to the Soviet authorities, who kept detailed files on all visitors. Dreiser himself was described as "typically bourgeois . . . with a specific petit bourgeois individualist ideology" and treated accordingly.[17] The final report on his stay concluded that "Dreiser will still present the situation in such a way that his readers will understand that under the Soviet regime, the broad working and peasant masses have been given and are enjoying a freedom that never existed before, either under the czar or elsewhere."[18]

The infectious enthusiasm for the great cause of Bolshevism could make uncritical admirers out of people who had never before been defenders of dictatorship. The French novelist Henri Barbusse, the author of the popular antimilitarist novel *Under Fire*, found authoritarian methods surprisingly unproblematic when they were used in the name of a "dictatorship of Reason." He argued that the Bolsheviks needed to use violence: "Not only are they right in their orthodoxy, they are also right to impose their authoritarian means. . . . Every revolution imposes a constitution by force. . . . They are right in saying that if you want to abolish classes you should want to impose the dictatorship of the proletariat. To believe that there is a different way of realizing social equality for all is not only mad but criminal."[19]

George Bernard Shaw became another prominent apologist for the Soviet dictatorship. Always eager to chastise social injustices in his plays and active in the Fabian movement, led by Beatrice and Sidney Webb, Shaw saw no reason to justify Soviet atrocities—he simply declared them just and necessary. He had traveled through the Soviet Union in 1931 together with Conservative MP Lady Nancy Astor, who during their special audience with Stalin had asked the Soviet leader why he kept ruling like a tsar and killing his own people. "I think you are all awful!" Astor exclaimed at one point. In her rather Victorian manner she showed more understanding of the situation than the staunchly socialist Shaw, who was adamant and aggressive about the purity and virtue of the communist revolution

in Russia. Having been shown happy peasants and contented, productive factory workers, Shaw lapped it all up, believing the show put
on for him to be evidence of the final victory of socialism. He would
continue to defend Stalin and to deny Soviet atrocities for many years
to come.

Back in Britain, Shaw managed to convert the Webbs to Stalin's
cause. They, too, allowed themselves to be taken in all too readily.
Their political opponent Winston Churchill was scathing in his considerably more realistic assessment of the dramatist's trip to the heart
of Soviet power:

> The Russians have always been fond of circuses and travel-
> ling shows. Since they had imprisoned, shot or starved most
> of their best comedians, their visitors might fill . . . a notice-
> able void. And here was the World's most famous intellectual
> Clown and Pantaloon in one, and the charming Columbine
> of the capitalist pantomime . . . Arch Commissar Stalin, "the
> man of steel," flung open the closely guarded sanctuaries of
> the Kremlin, and pushing aside his morning's budget of death
> warrants, and *lettres de cachet*, received his guests with
> smiles of overflowing comradeship.[20]

Not all distinguished visitors were taken in so easily. Amid this
chorus of near-unanimous praise some skeptical voices stood out. As
early as 1920, the British philosopher Bertrand Russell, never afraid
to give a dissenting opinion, had visited Moscow and met Lenin. On
his return he described the Soviet Union as a "continually increasing
nightmare."[21] In the 1930s, the French novelist André Gide would
play a similar role, denouncing Stalin's gulags, the show trials, and
the general oppression, particularly after his own Russian journey.

Life in Amerikanka

THE CONTROVERSIES ABOUT STALINIST OPPRESSION—indeed, full
knowledge of the extent of that oppression—was still some way
in the future in 1929, despite the questions asked by Lady Astor.
After the Wall Street crash, it really did seem as if socialism had won
a historic and predicted victory over capitalism and the future belonged to the workers of Magnitogorsk. Arriving there in 1932, John
Scott reveled in the feeling of hope and comradeship amid the deprivation. "In Magnitogorsk I was precipitated into battle. I was
deployed on the iron and steel front. Tens of thousands of people

were enduring the most intense hardships in order to build blast furnaces, and many of them did it willingly, with boundless enthusiasm, which infected me from the day of my arrival."[22]

By then, the Magnetic City was indeed operating a huge steelworks, one of the largest in the world and the pride of the Soviet leadership. The hectic choir of emergency calls and sirens announcing fires had been replaced by the epic song of the factory of factories. Socialism had wrought the miracle it had promised, and collective effort and true enthusiasm had transformed the most arid steppe into a thriving and productive socialist city inhabited by vigorous proletarians. The entire story was a homage to the new Soviet man and to the great machine that was communism—a machine in which people had value only as cogs that either functioned or had to be replaced.

The day-to-day reality, however, was very different. There had been trouble from the start, but the accidents, acts of sabotage, and thefts at the gigantic building site had been replaced by an oceanic routine of smaller and larger calamities. Built close to a vast reservoir of iron ore, Magnitogorsk was hundreds of miles away from the nearest coal mine, and the railways were always prone to breaking down, which would slow production to a snail's pace for lack of fuel or other materials. The management wrote a steady stream of begging telegrams and letters to the central administration in Moscow, but the responses were predictably sluggish and often negative.

In addition to the constant problems at the factory, the town was still little more than an assembly of tents, barracks, and a few brick buildings, despite the fact that the winters could be perishingly cold. Inside these primitive dwellings, Stalin's policy of collectivization was realized further than Moscow cadres had imagined possible. Living with four times as many people as intended, the inhabitants found that all privacy and all possibilities of retreat had simply vanished. "In the barracks, mud and ceaseless noise," one of them remembered. "Not enough light to read. The library is poor, newspapers are few. They are stolen to roll cigarettes. . . . Gossip, obscene anecdotes, and songs emerge from the mud-filled corners. At night drunks return to the barracks, stupid from boredom. They disturb the sleep of the others. From time to time traveling artists drop in to Magnitogorsk: sword swallowers, jugglers, comedians."[23]

The location of the future settlement turned out to be a particularly thorny issue, as poisonous fumes from the steel factory and smoke from the ironworks drifted across the central portion, which had originally been set aside as a living area. The only other residential site was situated nearly two miles away across a river—a long trek to work on a subzero morning in a city that had as yet few motor vehicles and no trams.

Construction of the new buildings proved a miserably drawn-out affair, beset by incompetence, graft, and systematic thievery. Property crime was so high that an attrition rate of 30 percent or more of all materials and goods ordered was assumed to be simply a matter of course. Even years later, there were pitifully few improvements. "The construction was begun in 1935," reported a local journalist in 1937. "Last year, the walls of four buildings were erected. Now the only thing they are doing is building a single school. There is a night watchman on the site, but in the daytime construction materials are carried off by whoever bothers to take the trouble."[24] The workers left without houses would not have been able to buy furniture for their apartments anyway. The woodworking shop at the factory, charged with producing furniture for factory and domestic use, usually had neither wood nor nails in sufficient quantities.

One of the few buildings already standing was a circus arena, which doubled as a courtroom for public trials, usually open-and-shut cases offering the accused little or no chance of defending themselves. But the prosecutions conducted in this location were mainly part of the political theater of intimidation; all other cases in this city of one hundred thousand were heard by three judges with little or no experience. A true microcosm of the Soviet Union, Magnitogorsk even had its own prison camp, in which mainly political prisoners were interned behind barbed wire. Meanwhile, the prison for common criminals, built to hold four hundred, was filled with nineteen hundred inmates.

In his great novel *The Foundation Pit*, the Soviet writer Andrei Platonov describes the digging of a gigantic foundation, an undertaking so vast that the workers eventually forget why they are digging and what the eventual goal of their work is. To Platonov, himself formerly an idealistic young engineer burning to build the revolution and to sacrifice his best years for the construction of a shining socialist future, the foundation pit became a symbol of Soviet life, just as the magnetic city became a microcosm of life in the Soviet Union. In 1937, Magnitogorsk was declared a closed site and foreigners were ordered to leave.

Before this exodus, however, the capitalist experts without whom there would have been no Soviet utopia had a conspicuously comfortable life. The American engineers brought in to construct the factory were not living with the Russian workers but were housed in an idyllic settlement outside the main city, an elegant suburb with spacious houses surrounded by lush gardens that could have been anywhere in New England. "Amerikanka" was a comfortable place, sporting such luxuries as indoor toilets, wood-burning stoves, and hot water. The settlement also had a tennis court along with a dining room in which clients were served by waitresses. Soon the top brass of the Soviet administration discovered the comforts of American-style suburban living and took some houses for themselves and their families. "All animals are equal, but some animals are more equal than others," George Orwell would observe in his 1945 novel *Animal Farm*. In the Soviet Union, this fiction had already become reality.

· 1930 ·
Lili and the Blue Angel

Falling in love again, never wanted to
What am I to do? I can't help it.
—"Falling in Love Again" from *The Blue Angel*, 1930

....

IMMANUEL RAAT IS A HIGH SCHOOL TEACHER IN A PROVINCIAL GERMAN
town. Behind his back, his pupils call him "Professor Unrath"—
Professor Garbage. Not that any of them would dare to say it to his
face, because in the classroom he is a tyrant, ruling his adolescent subjects with an iron fist. He commands and humiliates, threatens and
punishes at will, and the teenage boys in his class stand at attention
when he enters the room, as was customary in German high schools.
This military theme dominates his approach to education, as he sees
his pupils as enemies who must be humiliated and defeated.

Professor Raat's private life is similarly ruled by discipline. On
a meager teacher's salary, he cannot afford more than two rooms in a
garret stuffed with books, a desk overflowing with papers, and
a globe, a hint to his status as master of his own small universe. His
emotional life is channeled into the heroes and heroines of world

249

literature and his affection for the songbird he keeps in a cage and feeds with sugar every morning. Limited, pompous, and pedantic, he is the incarnation of the old Germany of discipline and *Bildung* (education), in which the title of professor transforms a schoolteacher into a minor deity in the provincial firmament, despite the fact that he is too poor even to get married.

The character of Professor Raat was the creation of Heinrich Mann, brother of the more famous Thomas Mann and an outstanding novelist in his own right. His novella *Professor Unrath* chronicled the decline and fall of an honorable man in impossible circumstances and was made into a film by Josef von Sternberg in 1930. When the teacher, played by the Oscar-winning actor Emil Jannings, discovers that his pupils frequent a disreputable bar where they listen to racy cabaret songs performed by an alluring singer called Lola, he decides to confront the woman who is endangering his pupils' virtue. At the bar, however, he is overwhelmed by the force of the new, a world he had not known existed.

Stumbling into the dressing room of the scandalous soubrette, whose daring costumes appear to drive the teenage boys into a frenzy, the middle-aged professor finds that neither his title nor his status carries any weight in this demimonde of clowns, freaks, titillation, and alcohol. Only the show's director and magician, a tyrant like himself if a less subtle one, is impressed by being visited by one of the leading citizens of the town.

Sternberg had confided the role of Lola to a young up-and-coming actress who had experienced life in a traveling variety troupe herself at the beginning of her career: Marlene Dietrich. With her sex appeal and deliciously offhand, off-key singing, Dietrich made her character, and herself, immortal. "Ich Bin von Kopf bis Fuss auf Liebe Eingestellt" (in English, "Falling in Love Again"), her most famous number, became an instant hit, as did the film.

Jannings brilliantly portrays a man whose guiding principles have been oppression and repression and who now completely falls under the spell of the unashamedly sexy, unashamedly ignorant Lola, a typical creature of interwar hardship who does not give a damn about titles and bourgeois rituals and is only interested in making a buck, having a little fun, and living to see tomorrow. Unable to resist Lola and her dangerously seductive life, the high and mighty schoolteacher is finally disgraced and literally turned into a clown, trawling through bars and nightclubs with Lola's troupe.

Raat's undoing was a young woman's shameless twentieth-century appeal; it shattered his nineteenth-century-style emotional personality.

No angel: Marlene Dietrich in her first great role, in Der blaue Engel, *1930.*

What made it a story with much wider resonances in Germany, however, was a powerful political and social context. The professor's downfall was also a consequence of the 1929 crash and the ensuing Great Depression. For many decades, roughly since the middle of the nineteenth century, German society had been dominated by a tacit deal. In effect, the nation's cultural capital as well as large parts of its social capital was placed in the hands of the middle class, which had established a hierarchy of its own through titles and qualifications rivaling those of the aristocracy.

Whereas under the ancien régime the only things that counted were aristocratic titles and the land wealth that went with them, the new, bourgeois culture with its doctors, professors, mayors, and councilmen created new titles resting, in theory at least, not on money and family but on education, competence, and good character. It was this new middle class that had made Germany great, developing its cities, peopling its universities, creating its industries, and bringing forth the poets and thinkers the Germans were so proud of. Their virtues had been described by Max Weber's characterization of the Protestant work ethic: hard work and frugal living, a constant deferment of pleasure, a sublimation of desire, and a strong sense of duty. They lived for the future, not the present.

An Inflation of Values

FOR GENERATIONS OF STUDENTS, the real-world Professor Raats had been their teachers, their moral compass, and their tyrannical super-ego. They had been respected and hated in equal measure, as not only Heinrich Mann's novella but a whole host of other works attested. The hyperinflation of 1923 had changed all this. Initially an attempt by the German government to offset crippling reparations payments, inflation had been encouraged, but it had disastrously spiraled out of hand. Fortunes vanished overnight, formerly comfortable existences were destroyed, workers needed wheelbarrows to collect their pay and had to rush to the shops to spend everything before it lost even more of its value, diners in restaurants ate quickly to avoid having to pay double the price for their dinner, and children used bundles of worthless banknotes as building material for their playhouses.

But not only the economic structure of Germany had suffered. Suddenly the principles and virtues on which the German middle class was built seemed redundant. People who had worked hard, lived modestly, and saved all their lives had lost everything literally overnight and were reduced to penury. The virtues of work, self-denial, duty, and frugality they had preached and enforced as teachers, parliamentarians, judges, and journalists looked worse than useless. At a time when the defeated country needed nothing more than reconstruction and stability, the moral core and authority of the middle classes had been ripped out. It is arguable that Hitler's rise a decade later would be greatly facilitated by the catastrophic under-mining of humanist values and work ethic that resulted from the hyperinflation.

This moral catastrophe that befell the young Weimar Republic was of the greatest importance for the cultural and political development of Germany at a time of instability; the worst consequence, a dictatorship, had been only narrowly avoided. Several years later, economic performance and general confidence had slowly recovered, and it began to look as if the unloved German democracy had had a narrow escape and could now finally really take root. But then two blows struck Germany in quick succession.

The first was the death on October 3, 1929, of Gustav Strese-mann, the German foreign minister, whose farsighted policies had done much to begin a reconciliation with Germany's former enemies, with the aim of renegotiating the harsh conditions of the Versailles Treaty. The Germans desperately wanted to see their economy regain traction, which would give the fragile new democracy a chance.

They also wanted to secure foreign loans in order to keep up with the reparations payments and to maintain the social peace at home. Stresemann's death robbed Germany of its most seasoned and internationally respected negotiator, a crucial figure for postwar reconstruction. But even his negotiating talent could not have prevented the consequences of the Wall Street crash, after which new American loans dried up and lenders demanded immediate repayment of the existing loans. This was the second and fatal blow for a democracy that still had not been fully accepted by the people and for an economic system that was only just beginning to recover. The consequences in Germany were disastrous. Millions lost their jobs; by 1932 official unemployment had risen to 42 percent. And the achievements of the previous seven years were called into question once again.

Two economic crises in less than a decade had cost Weimar Germany its sense of purpose and its sense of hope. The present seemed chaotic beyond repair, the past bitterly contested, the future already overshadowed by rival totalitarian visions that were often too frightening to contemplate.

Within this climate of total uncertainty, with its absence of traditional identities and moral principles, a new culture could flourish. And it was this culture, more than the charms of a single girl, that proved the undoing of the Prussian professor in Heinrich Mann's novel and Sternberg's film. The representative of imperial nineteenth-century virtues is both overwhelmed and undermined by the dangerous new sexual culture of Weimar Germany, a culture that respected no precedent, and indeed nothing at all.

Berlin-Babylon

THE CAPITAL OF THIS NEW, anarchist culture of the 1930s in Germany and beyond was Berlin, a city whose history reads like an allegory of the country's fate. While other cities such as Cologne, Hamburg, Nuremberg, and Leipzig could look back on a proud and long history, Berlin had been a sleepy local town until Prussia's rapid ascent to power had propelled it to new prominence. As the Prussian kings became German emperors, their capital had been transformed into a large and representative center of power—a little too large, perhaps, a little too ostentatious, never quite sure of itself, and dangerously hybrid in its mix of populations.

Beyond the great avenues conceived for parades and marching bands lay the poor Berlin of industrial workers and recent immigrants—Poles and Russians, Jews from Galicia, emigrants, exiles, refugees, and fugitives—crowded into dank tenement buildings. And between the tenements and the court was an increasingly large, increasingly wealthy, and increasingly self-confident professional middle class.

The capital was particularly hard hit by the uncertainty of the era and its various crises. With four million inhabitants, it was by far the largest city in the country, a metropolis too complex, too fluid in its composition, and too teeming with life and with ambition to be properly controlled.

Now, as the hard shell of official morality was cracked wide open, this life asserted itself—not in the boulevards and squares, the elegant shopping streets and government buildings, but in the private apartments and anonymous hotel rooms, the half-shade of the street corners, the cafés and bars where people could meet without attracting too much attention, the discreet recesses of public parks at dusk and the banks of the lakes around the city. Here there were a hundred thousand faces and many more masks. Its reach extended from the witty double entendres of the lyrics sung in large concert halls by the Comedian Harmonists and on hundreds of thousands of records to a semiofficial demimonde and finally to a totally clandestine underworld of prostitution that catered to any predilection, any fantasy, any perversion.

One of the most famous and perhaps most frightening portraits by Otto Dix shows a woman in a red dress, her face little more than a chalk-white mask of cynical disdain with a small, cherry-colored mouth painted onto the pallor, large green eyes surrounded by charcoal-colored eye shadow, thin black arches for eyebrows, and a fringe of dull red hair. The woman portrayed here, the dancer Anita Berber, looks as if she had lived too much and seen too many things, despite the fact that she was only twenty-six years old. But by that time she was already famous, a living legend and a perfect embodiment of the reckless time. Like Marlene Dietrich a girl from a secure bourgeois family, Berber was a gifted dancer who started a solo career early on. Classical dance, however, did not interest her, and she specialized in custom-made expressionist performances of choreographies with titles such as "Cocaine," "Morphine," and "Opium Trance" (all of which she knew from firsthand experience, and washed down with at least one bottle of cognac a day). During her performances she wore very little, and sometimes nothing at all; audiences gasped with delight or outrage as her lascivious movements left nothing to the imagination.

The eighteen-year-old Klaus Mann, son of the writer Thomas Mann, met the dancer around the time her portrait was painted:

> Anita Berber was already a legend. . . . Post-war eroticism, cocaine, Salomé, the last word in perversion: words such as these made her fame radiant. . . . She had a cavalier with her and sekt was served. At 2 o'clock in the morning she took her cavalier and me to her hotel room. . . . When you're eighteen, you're shocked by such a painted face. Her face was a dark and wicked mask. . . . She spoke without interruption and lied terribly. It was clear that she had taken a lot of cocaine. She offered me some. . . . In a hoarse voice, she related the most incredible adventures; animals she had hypnotized; murderers she had skillfully escaped from.[1]

Berber was a trailblazer of the new and self-destructive way of living beyond convention. Her appearances in nightclubs or larger theaters were certain to scandalize her audiences and resulted in a stream of outraged letters to the police—and in ever-rising ticket sales. Naked, boyish, beautiful, and shamelessly exhibitionistic, she came, danced, and conquered. Photographs of her appeared in *Vanity Fair*; famous artists and prospective lovers queued up at her doorstep. But her drug consumption became overwhelming. Her character changed and she frequently became violent, hitting, scratching, and spitting her way through disagreements. Once, when a woman pointed her out on the street, Berber almost bit the woman's finger off. She got in trouble with the police and thought it was wiser to leave Berlin.

In Vienna, Berber performed at the prestigious Konzerthaus together with her husband. The evening was called "Dances of Vice, Horror, and Ecstasy" and predictably caused a public outcry. She traveled on, always one step ahead of the lawsuits, to the Middle East, where she performed until one day she collapsed onstage in Damascus. The doctors diagnosed a rapidly advancing case of tuberculosis, possibly exacerbated by an overconsumption of cocaine and alcohol, but the real diagnosis was simply total excess. She died in Berlin on November 10, 1928. She was twenty-nine years old.

Berlin Means Boys

MARLENE DIETRICH AS THE LASCIVIOUS LOLA in *The Blue Angel* famously sang that men were clustering around her like "moths around a flame," and in real-life Berlin there were countless places for moths of all descriptions. An estimated six hundred nightclubs in the city offered sexual services, from very explicit erotic revues to lap dancing and more.

Eighty-five of these clubs catered exclusively to lesbians, who could live openly due to a legal loophole. The infamous Paragraph 175 of the penal code criminalized only homosexual acts between men, very possibly because the nineteenth-century lawmakers had been unable to conceive of the female variety of homosexuality.

In addition to these official establishments, there were also hundreds of gay bars, saunas, massage parlors, and clubs. In 1928, the English poet Wystan Auden had come to the German capital from Paris, which bored him because he had found nothing but "bedroom mirrors and bidets, lingerie and adultery, the sniggers of schoolboys and grubby old men." Now he was almost ecstatic at the culture unfolding itself in front of his unbelieving eyes: "Berlin is a bugger's daydream. There are 170 male brothels under police control."[2]

Like other homosexual Englishmen traveling abroad to live as they could not at home, Auden became a regular at the Cozy Corner in the working-class Hallesches Tor district, which, according to another English visitor, was "filled with attractive boys of any age between sixteen and twenty-one . . . all dressed in extremely short lederhosen which showed off their smooth and sunburnt thighs to delectable advantage." At one point the visitor had to go to the toilet, where he "was followed in by several boys, who, as if by chance, ranged themselves on either side of me and pulled out their cocks rather to show them off than to relieve nature as I was doing."[3]

Auden enjoyed rough play and for a while he lived with a young man he described as "a cross between a rugger hearty and Josephine Baker," and who regularly left him badly bruised but happy.[4] Auden's school friend Christopher Isherwood, who joined him in the German capital, found an exquisitely beautiful young man who went by the nickname of Bubi. "By embracing Bubi," the writer later recalled, "Christopher could hold in his arms the entire mystery-magic of foreignness, Germanness. By means of Bubi, he could fall in love with and possess the entire nation."[5]

But the entire nation was not so easily possessed, or easily understood. Berlin boasted an erotic demimonde consisting of an estimated one hundred thousand women and thirty-five thousand men who regularly prostituted themselves. If its relative tolerance for sexual minorities made it a haven for refugees from bourgeois morality from the provinces and from abroad, it also became the world's premier tourist destination for sexual predilections of all kinds. Twenty years earlier, French men, including writer André Gide, had traveled to Algeria in search of young boys willing to indulge their sexual fantasies; Germans such as homosexual industrialist Alfred Krupp or photographer and aesthete Wilhelm von Gloeden preferred the equally poor and equally pliant south of Italy. But even at home, there was now no desire so outlandish that it could not be satisfied in the German capital.

Berlin had its guidebooks advising tourists which establishments catered to which particular proclivities and at which street corner or café they could pick up a woman or man of their choice. Different streets and areas of the city were frequented by different kinds of prostitutes: girls with high boots, freelance dominatrixes, secretaries and shopgirls looking for a bit of extra cash in hard times, registered professionals with official health certificates, underage girls, older women, pregnant women, women made up to look like boys, transvestites and transsexuals and rent boys and rough trade, children for sale at a steep price, sadists and masochists, flagellators, and coprophiles.

There was something machinelike about all this fornication, a mechanical escapism that seemed determined to deny the political reality. But it would not have been Germany if this bewildering variety of sexual behavior had not aroused the interest of science, and the infinite plurality of Berlin's nightlife and discreet daytime amusements was surveyed by the world's first dedicated sexologist, Magnus Hirschfeld, whose Institut für Sexualwissenschaft (Institute for Sexual Science) not only conducted statistical and psychological research but also maintained a museum of utensils and implements that made even Christopher Isherwood giggle nervously.

Hirschfeld was a remarkable man. A qualified physician from an assimilated Jewish family, he had begun to understand his own homosexuality not as a social curse, as it was widely considered at the time, but as a subject for research as well as a political mission. Together with fellow activists he began to lobby for the decriminalization of homosexuality while at the same time conducting extensive research about sexual attitudes and orientations among university students—the easiest constituency for this kind of study—and publishing his findings in journals and books.

According to Hirschfeld's findings, a fixed percentage of men and women in any population—around 2 percent, he believed—were bisexual, homosexual, or transsexual. In referring to the last group, he spoke of a "third sex," a hitherto unrecognized and alternative sexual identity. In November 1930 a Danish patient came to visit him.

Einar Wegener was a painter living in Paris, where he was married to another artist, Gerda Gottlieb, who had made a good career with her portrayals of elegant, delicate women.

There had been a minor scandal when it had become known that the model for these paintings had been her husband, who in addition to his masculine identity was living a parallel life as a woman, Lili Elbe. He came to Dr. Hirschfeld in order to take the last step and undergo sex reassignment surgery, the first such procedure ever to be carried out. Over the course of two years, Lili Elbe painfully came into being through a series of five operations. Initially the process appeared to be successful, but when the surgeon tried to complete the transformation by transplanting a uterus into his patient, Elbe died due to transplant rejection.

Murderers Among Us

BERLIN WAS A VIOLENT CITY, with physical danger always in the air. During the socialist May Day demonstrations of 1929, twenty-three people had been killed in street battles with fascist groups, with many more injured. The young Englishman Isherwood sensed a perilous possibility in the air: "Here was the seething brew of history in the making—a brew . . . seasoned with unemployment, malnutrition, stock market panic, hatred of the Versailles Treaty and other potent ingredients."[6]

Fritz Lang and his wife, Thea von Harbou, who had shown only a few years earlier that they were awake to the utopian longings of the day as well as to their inherent terror, were now working on a psychological portrait of Berlin, which was to be released the following year, in 1931. The film *M* was inspired by the real-life Düsseldorf serial killer Peter Kürten, whose trial and eventual execution had been followed closely by the press. For the film, the plot had been transplanted to an unnamed city very like the German capital. Even the story's main conceit was possible only in a society that had lost all faith in the state and in which upholding the law was a matter for vigilantes and criminals.

A sexual killer is on the prowl, preying on little girls and terrorizing the city. The level of public concern is so high that the increased police presence on the streets begins to interfere seriously with the activities of the underworld. Finally the boss of the city's largest criminal organization decides to mobilize his own men in order to eliminate the murderer and return to his normal, workable arrangement with the police. A huge manhunt commences, and eventually the murderer (played by the young Peter Lorre at the peak of his creative powers) is cornered and brought to trial by the criminal underworld, whose boss (played by Gustav Gründgens, looking demonic in a bowler hat and a long leather coat) will be judge and executioner.

The trial is the psychological climax of this oppressively dense atmospheric tableau, which is lightened only by occasional moments of comedy between the incompetent police and the criminals. Lorre gives an impassioned speech describing his mental state, with inner voices and overpowering urges forcing him to commit murder after murder, and the assembled thieves, burglars, pimps, and thugs want him to die. In a fragment cut from the eventual release, Lorre's character attributes his madness and depravity to his shattering experience as a soldier in the Great War, another in the long gallery of destroyed men coming out of the trenches and into fiction. It is a scene in which the violence and the nihilist sexuality of a rudderless society have become conflated and the only solution seems to be yet more violence. When the police finally raid the Piranesi-like catacombs in which the mock trial has taken place just in time to save the monstrous madman from certain death, their arrival is only a halfhearted gesture toward a restoration of order and authority.

Uncertainty and Possibility

OF COURSE, WEIMAR BERLIN was much more than the capital of decadence and a fertile breeding ground for political violence and thugs of all stripes. Away from this atmosphere of menace and dark desires was the modern, productive city, which was experiencing an unparalleled artistic and intellectual blossoming and attracted first-rate talents from everywhere. The lives of the demimonde were chronicled by artists such as Otto Dix and Georges Grosz, and by a younger generation including John Heartfield, Raoul Hausmann, and Hannah Höch. Dada and expressionism had almost run their course, but a new, starkly objective way of seeing things—Neue Sachlichkeit, or new objectivity—was all the rage, and the coolly factual perspective on a world in meltdown was mirrored by the aesthetic ideas of the Bauhaus movement, whose unadorned designs of architecture, furniture, and items of daily use were beginning to conquer not only the living rooms of the bourgeoisie but also the skylines of German cities.

Berlin attracted the best talents of the German-speaking world. At the Großes Schauspielerhaus on the Schiffbauerdamm, the Viennese theater director Max Reinhardt produced plays whose coherence

A new kind of woman:
August Sander's portrait of
a secretary at a radio station
in Cologne.

and depth of characterization would decisively influence an entire generation of directors and actors; Bertolt Brecht wrote and directed plays and revolutionized the conception of the drama. At the Philharmonie, the country's most prestigious concert hall, Wilhelm Furtwängler produced legendary performances as chief conductor of the Berlin Philharmonic Orchestra; he was the acknowledged master of a generation that also included Erich Kleiber, Otto Klemperer, and the young Bruno Walter. Albert Einstein continued to do his research here, as did the aging Max Planck. Writers such as Alfred Döblin and Erich Kästner translated the city's buzz into literature, and Kurt Tucholsky's articles, essays, and poems articulated the cynical, alert, and weary *Lebensgefühl*, the feeling of the time. Perhaps not only in spite of but partly also because of the volatility of the atmosphere, the German metropolis was abuzz with creativity.

This Berlin appeared to be full of future, pregnant with possibilities. A city that had never quite defined its identity now proved to be open for new identities. More than any other city in Europe, it looked modern and embraced the aesthetics and the promise of the future. The bright neon lights at the Potsdamer Platz rivaled the legendary glitter of New York's Times Square, and at the Haus Vaterland, the world's biggest entertainment palace and the flagship of the burgeoning Kempinski empire, eight thousand people could amuse themselves at any one time, thirty-five hundred meals could be served at once, and after a refurbishment in 1928 the establishment greeted its millionth visitor within a year. The Alexanderplatz was crawling with traffic day and night, and architectural iconoclasts were beginning to reshape the aspect of the city with daring new structures such as the Karstadt department store in Neukölln (1929) and with unrealized designs such as the astonishing steel-and-glass skyscraper designed by Ludwig Mies van der Rohe for the Friedrichstraße.

This Berlin was light-years away from the imperial capital with its uniforms, endless parades, and marching bands—or rather, this Berlin inhabited the same space as another city full of nostalgia, anger, and humiliation that had never gotten past the loss of its former greatness, exemplified by the mustachioed figure of Field Marshal Paul von Hindenburg, the aging president of the young republic.

Berlin was also a youthful city; a third of its inhabitants were under twenty. They had been small children during the war and now were eager to build a future for themselves. The shell shock that had gripped their parents and grandparents was nothing but a secondhand memory for them, represented by the sight of mutilated veterans begging in the streets, whispered conversations overheard at night, angry rhetoric from teachers and from drunks, penny-dreadful novels about heroism, and films.

But the memories persisted, and were also stirred up and questioned by a young generation of artists. The movie *All Quiet on the Western Front* reached the cinemas in 1930 after Erich Maria Remarque's eponymous 1929 novel had already caused a scandal. The story of a group of classmates who enthusiastically volunteer for service in 1914 only to find themselves trapped in the nightmarish reality of trench warfare powerfully communicated the message that the official values preached in schools and churches were nothing but a cynical lie and that heroism was impossible in the face of modern artillery producing death miles away. Toward the end of the novel only one of the protagonists survives, dulled by constant fear and indifferent to the living and the dead. When he, too, is killed just before the end of the war on a day without major military action, the official report for that day simply reads: "All quiet on the Western Front."

The Hollywood production that was released quickly to capitalize on the fame created by the novel had been severely cut for German release, and in a cowardly attempt not to enrage the anti-Semitic right, the names of Jewish actors starring in the film had been omitted from the credits. These changes were concessions to a hardening climate of public opinion in Germany, and especially the noisiest, most threatening presence in the streets: the rising National Socialist Party and its shrewd propaganda chief, Joseph Goebbels. Sensing an opportunity to seize the debate, he fulminated against the "treasonous" and "unpatriotic" work and directed members of the party's paramilitary wing, the Sturmabteiling or SA, to do everything possible to disrupt performances by tossing smoke bombs, releasing mice and other vermin in the cinemas, and beating up audience members. Exploiting this situation, Goebbels claimed in the press that the film not only damaged Germany's reputation and honor but also caused public disruption. By December the authorities had retracted their approval for the film, which meant it could no longer be shown publicly.

All Quiet on the Western Front assaulted and questioned the official memory of the war not only because it showed war as inhuman but also because there were no heroes. The protagonists were ordinary young men with ordinary desires and few principles left after their first experiences at the front. They were victims in a vast game, but instead of being stylized as paragons of lost innocence and nostalgic nationhood, they were shown as cynical, angry, and afraid. As characters, they repudiated everything the growing National Socialists sought to propagate and stood for everything the party and its followers hated.

Der blaue Engel (The Blue Angel), the film version of Heinrich Mann's novel *Professor Unrat*, had a similarly rocky ride with the press, even if cinema-goers immediately loved it. The right-wing press fulminated against the loose morals and lewd pictures; the left criticized director von Sternberg's decision to leave out Heinrich Mann's original social criticism. In his publication *Weltbühne* the well-known socialist journalist Carl von Ossietzky called it "a film against Heinrich Mann."[7] But everyone agreed about the delicate, naked thighs of the young star, Marlene Dietrich. Even those opposed to so much alluring flesh, such cinema, and the endangerment of impressionable minds nevertheless contributed to their fame, and the reader's galloping ideas, by devoting column inches to Dietrich's legs.

Opposing Forces

IN BERLIN, THE CITY OF CONTRADICTIONS and of underworlds, of shape-shifters and gender-benders, the androgynous diva Marlene Dietrich became a sexy symbol of the time's ambiguous identities. The seismic pull of opposing forces—of ideologies and necessities, of possibilities and lost certainties—seized the lamentable Professor Raat in *Der Blaue Engel*, revealing him as a bankrupt character, a former petty tyrant who finally becomes what he has secretly always been: a pathetic clown.

No longer held back by a morality that had been comprehensively discredited, no longer believing in anything more than the possibilities of getting laid and getting by, no longer really hoping for anything much, the amorphous sense of self in this postwar society was turned into an immense field for experimentation, and many strange flowers blossomed on this field. Some of them were among the finest German culture had produced; others—from erotic floor shows to paid quickies in public toilets—were signs of another kind of inflation, in which love had lost its currency and was replaced with a smaller, harder coin. Yet others, the commercial and ideological exploitation of human destructiveness, began to herald things to come.

In Berlin itself neither the burgeoning creativity nor the delicious decadence of the German capital could disguise the fact that the political climate was slowly but surely sliding into violence. Clashes between Nazis and Communists during demonstrations, in bars, and on the streets routinely bloodied the pavements and frequently left people dead, and when the interior minister forbade the wearing of brown shirts the Nazi militia simply switched to white shirts and continued to impose their political world with jackboots, truncheons, and knives.

In 1930, the movement gained an important martyr in Berlin, a hero whose name would adorn one of the most important National Socialist battle songs. Horst Wessel was an SA man who lived with his girlfriend, a prostitute, in the Friedrichshain neighborhood of Berlin. When he refused to pay his share of the rent, his woman asked a bruiser from Communist Red Front to make him see sense. Wessel was killed in the ensuing brawl, and Joseph Goebbels seized the opportunity to transform a brutal pimp into a noble fighter for the great cause who had been assassinated because he had been tirelessly working for a better Germany. A song written by him became the official battle hymn of the SA: "Oh, raise the flag and close your ranks up tight! / SA men march with bold determined tread. / Comrades felled by Reds and Ultras in fight / March at our side, in spirit never dead."[8] The heavy, plodding tune of the "Horst Wessel Lied," ideal for marching, was intoned during torchlit processions, Party meetings, and daytime rallies, usually with the tone-deaf anger of soccer hooligans, and it became the ire-filled hymn of the burgeoning National Socialist movement.

As social tensions escalated, a time of enjoyment was slowly becoming a time for marching and for political rallies. The streets were full of men with nothing better to do. The country's fragile recovery had been made possible to a large extent through investment and loans from the United States, which saw Germany, with its high interest rates, as an attractive opportunity. Thanks to Germany's strong exports and productivity the loans had mostly been repaid, but even before the crash, the US economy had begun to retract, and there was less money to invest. Now the existing loans were being called in and few new ones given.

Germany's industry and its political stability had depended on these loans, which had paid for the reparations, unemployment benefits, infrastructure, and industrial investments. As this lifeline was withdrawn, the country began floundering dangerously. Factories reduced production, workers were laid off, businesses closed. In 1928, 1.3 million Germans had been unemployed; three years later, the jobless totaled more than three million, and by 1932 the figure had reached almost six million, not counting the countless workers who had to make do with menial labor, reduced pay, or part-time jobs. Children could be seen playing "signing on" games in the courtyards of Berlin, Essen, and Hamburg, pretending to be unemployed workers at a labor exchange. Hungry, frustrated, and desperate, many grasped at the promises of political parties. Membership in the Communist Party surged from 117,000 to 360,000 within four years, and 80 percent of the new members were out of work. The rise of Hitler's National Socialist Party was even more spectacular: 109,000 strong in 1928, it topped one million members in 1932.

The atmosphere was hardening, and not just in Europe's largest and most central economy. Germany's industrial production slumped by 42 percent, while that of Great Britain fell by 11 percent. Unemployment in Britain was at 3.5 million, and a quarter of the population lived below subsistence level. In France production declined by almost a quarter, but there was less unemployment—the country had lost more than a million men in the war and many more were invalids, leaving more work for the others. Helped by German reparations, the country had even seen an economic upturn in the preceding years, and the crisis would take longer to bite here than elsewhere in Europe.

The immense energies transforming the lives of Europeans and Americans since the turn of the century were continuing to plow through the societies of the West. The war had brutally accelerated for millions the experience of living in a modern world, and the forces of the new had asserted themselves triumphantly in a postwar Europe shaken to its moral core. Their mainspring was in the factories, and they had announced themselves through smoking chimneys, mass production, and flourishing cities.

As the industrial base of this flood of change began to weaken, the social effects of the great transformation continued to make themselves felt. The currents of change turned inward, pitting classes, clans, and countries against one another. There was no going back, no viable alternative to life in the city for those who had cut off their ties with the countryside. There was no retreat from modernity, from its mass-produced goods, its cinemas, its opportunities.

Even if prophets and doom-mongers blamed the mechanistic and soulless nature of modernity for all the world's ills, hardly anyone was ready to live without it. Women enjoyed new freedoms, people who still had jobs lived better than before, and the dreams fostered by films and advertising, the horizons opened by education, and the desires awakened by shop windows were there to stay. The very fabric of life had changed since 1900, and there was no end in sight.

Now, trapped in a crisis in which there seemed to be no hope of escape and little prospect of improvement, this new, modern life began to look cold and threatening. As many retrenched into clannishness and united against common, often imaginary enemies, the postwar years began to pivot, beginning to feel again like prewar years. A decade earlier, in 1919, many observers, John Maynard Keynes and French president Paul Deschanel among them, had prophesied a second world war growing out of the deeply flawed peace. As the atmosphere hardened across Europe, the energies of modernization seemed to turn against those at the bottom of society, and millions sought refuge in ideologies that were viscerally hostile to one another, it seemed that another war (the same conflict renewed, perhaps) was only a question of time.

For the young Marlene Dietrich the 1930 premiere of *The Blue Angel* was only the beginning of her career, one that would take her out of Germany on the very night of the film's premiere. The great and the good had turned up for the first showing, expecting the famous Emil Jannings to be the star of the evening and finding to their surprise that the androgynous, amused-looking, and worldly beauty of an unknown starlet stole the show. But while Dietrich was celebrated and increasingly raucous toasts made to her and to the huge success of her appearance in Germany's second talkie, she carried in her pocket a contract with Paramount Pictures and soon would travel west to Hollywood.

She left behind a city seething with anticipation of things to come, as the British writer Stephen Spender noted: "Berlin was the tension, the poverty, the anger, the prostitution, the hope and despair thrown out on the streets. It was the blatant rich at the smart restaurants, the prostitutes in army top boots at corners, the grim, submerged-looking Communists in processions, and the violent youths who suddenly emerged from nowhere into the Wittenbergplatz and shouted: *'Deutschland, Erwache!'* (Germany, awaken!)."[9]

The Anatomy of Love in Italy

The feeling that the world is ending has given way to the sense of a new beginning. The ultimate goal now stands out unmistakably within the field of vision now opening up before us, and all faith in miracles is now harnessed to the active transformation of the present.

Julius Petersen, *Die Sehnsucht nach dem Dritten Reich in Deutscher Sage und Dichtung* (The Longing for the Third Reich), 1934

....

LITTLE IS KNOWN OF MICHELE "MICHAEL" SCHIRRU, THE ANARCHIST who traveled from his adopted home in America back to his native Italy with the plan to assassinate Il Duce. The only two known photos tell two stations of his story with startling immediacy. In one, his passport photo, a man of some thirty years stares intensely into the camera. He is wearing a dark jacket, white shirt, and tie. His hair is short at the sides and longer on top. In his eyes are challenge, anger, perhaps fear: the face of someone who does not want to tell too much about himself.

The second image is a police mug shot. In this pitiless portrait, his right ear appears to be missing, the hair around it shaven or torn off, the right eye deeply bloodshot. He is unshaven and wears an under-shirt and a prisoner's jacket. The photo was taken on or shortly after February 3, 1931, when he had shot two police officers and then had turned his gun against his right temple and pulled the trigger.

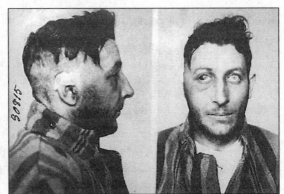

Michele Schirru, who failed in his bid to assassinate Mussolini, before and after his arrest.

According to his own testimony, Schirru was born in 1899 into the abject poverty of rural Sardinia, "a disheveled and savage young-ster."[1] Forced to leave school at the age of ten and apprenticed to a blacksmith, the boy grew to hate the powers that kept him and his kin poor and ignorant, and at fifteen he left his native island to find work and wider intellectual horizons in the dockyards of Turin. In 1917, he enlisted in the Italian army and fought on the gruesome Alpine front, only to find after his return that the soldiers' sacrifices were not honored and their hopes for their own country were dashed as the Fascists began to win the battle on the streets. The young man was involved in some of these battles and devoted his life to political agitation. Known to the police as a troublemaker, he finally had to return to his native Sardinia.

In 1920, Schirru decided to emigrate to the United States, as his father had done before him. He arrived in New York in November, immediately sought contact with other Italian anarchists and social-ists, and began writing for various magazines and newspapers. During the trial of Sacco and Vanzetti in 1926 he was one of those working to save them from the electric chair, in vain. But Italy was still on his mind, and the rise of the Fascists troubled him deeply. So in 1930 he decided to return and to act. After traveling through France, Belgium, and possibly Great Britain he arrived in Milan in January 1931 and then went to Rome, where he took a room at the Hotel Royal, close to the Trevi railway station. In his luggage were two bombs and a revolver.

Faced with Mussolini's inexorable rise and his iron grip on power, Schirru had decided that the only way to fight the dictatorship was to decapitate it. He was determined to kill the *duce* and was waiting for his chance. But his chance would not come. On February 3 he was arrested in his hotel room, probably betrayed by an informer. Among his possessions was a political testament he had written one month earlier and in which he announced:

> For fascism as well as for all dictatorships and tyrannies, I have always felt nothing but deep-rooted horror. Mussolini, delighting in cynical brutalities and atrocious persecutions . . . I have always considered a reptile most dangerous to humanity. In his Neronian attitudes, the role of hangman for the Italian people and their liberty, in which he prides, have always inspired hatred in me—hatred and revulsion, not so much for the man who is little over half a quintal of flaccid and damaged flesh, as for the despot, the murderer of my comrades, the betrayer of those poor workers who, up to a few years ago, had nourished him. Years of meditation have only accumulated and compressed this hatred into my heart: the day must come when it will explode.[2]

At his arrest, Schirru obviously knew what fate was awaiting him and was determined not to submit to it. Taken to the Trevi police post, he suddenly pulled out his revolver, shot at the officers around him, and then tried to kill himself, but only succeeded in wounding and disfiguring himself. For the next two months, while awaiting trial, he recovered from his injuries and frantically tried to establish contact with his family, but his letters were never answered and very possibly never delivered.

Schirru was tried by a special Fascist tribunal on May 28 under a new law. There was no jury and only the most perfunctory defense before the leader of the tribunal, a young Fascist activist, pronounced the sentence: the accused was to be shot in the back by a firing squad, which at Mussolini's insistence was to be composed of Sardinian volunteers. At two-thirty the next morning Schirru was awakened in his cell; he refused to see a priest before he was bundled off to the place of execution, where the sentence was carried out. He was thirty years old.

Hopes Disappointed

LIKE SO MANY OTHER IDEALISTS and poor migrants in search of a better life, Schirru had crossed an ocean only to find that there were deprivation and injustice in the New World as well as at home. In

Depression-era America this lesson was especially severe, and fraught with irony. If Schirru had access to newspapers in his prison cell, he may have read about the opening of the Empire State Building in New York, conceived as a visible testimony to the success of investor John Jakob Raskob, who had made most of his fortune from General Motors, a beneficiary of the automotive boom during the early decades of the century.

Four thousand workers had populated the building's construction site, including dozens of Mohawk Indians who were seemingly immune to feelings of vertigo as they negotiated scaffolding and beams hundreds of feet above the ground without anything to ensure their safety in the case of a fall. According to official statistics, five construction workers did fall to their deaths, one of whom had jumped after hearing that he had been fired.

Designed by William F. Lamb, the structure was to be the tallest in the world, overtaking the previous record holder, the Chrysler Building, which had held the title only for a matter of months. Towering above Manhattan, the new skyscraper was a steel-and-brick hymn to capitalism and the entrepreneurial spirit: 1,454 feet high, built of ten million bricks, and offering stunning views of New York from more than six thousand windows on 102 floors. However, when it opened on May 1, 1931 (International Labor Day), only a little over a year since construction had begun, the shining symbol had lost much of its luster, as dozens of floors of office space stood empty.

Down in the streets, in the mighty shadows of the Colossus, were the new emblems of America: bread lines. Despite the fact that President Hoover was still convinced that unemployment was "shamefully exaggerated" and that "many persons left their jobs for the more profitable one of selling apples," the situation was in fact so desperate that even Al Capone opened a soup kitchen in Chicago.[3] Of the country's ten million unemployed, only a quarter were getting financial assistance from the state, while the rest was simply left to their own devices. Together with their families, they amounted to thirty million people—a quarter of the working population, who were desperately struggling to subsist without an income. Hundreds of thousands of them took to the roads or rails, hitching rides in cars or on freight trains in search of work or at least something to eat, and bands of desperate youths were roaming the countryside. Half a million people abandoned the big cities and went to rural areas in search of work, and for the first time in American history there were more people leaving the country than were entering it.

As banks folded, businesses failed, industrial output slumped, and millions were scrounging for a little bread or a few potatoes, agricultural prices collapsed due to bumper harvests abroad. Imported grain was so cheap that in many areas harvesting the fields was more expensive than simply letting the crop rot on the plant: wheat, cotton, apples, and peaches were worth less than the meager hourly pay of the laborers usually hired to bring them in, and in Kansas farmers took to burning grain and corncobs to keep warm as a cheap alternative to coal, while ranchers killed thousands of heads of cattle because they could not afford to feed them. As the suicide rate went up and the birth rate went down, a hundred thousand people applied to work and live in the Soviet Union, and many were openly talking about revolution.

Prior to 1924, Italy had been one of the main sources for immigration into the United States. In particular, the south of the country was at times desperately poor, and millions of Italians were struggling to feed themselves from one day to the next. Extreme poverty combined with high numbers of children led to situations of Dickensian cruelty, none more so than the *carusi*, children working in sulfur mines in Sicily. In 1910, the African American activist Booker T. Washington had visited these mines, which he described as "the nearest thing to hell that I expect to see in this life," adding, "The cruelties to which the child slaves of Sicily have been subjected are as bad as anything reported of the cruelties of Negro slavery."[4]

Indeed, the work was slavery. To all intents and purposes the children were sold by their desperately poor parents to the owners of the mines, as Washington reported: "The father who turns his child over to a miner receives in return a sum of money in the form of a loan. The sum usually amounts to from eight to thirty dollars, according to the age of the boy, his strength and general usefulness. With the payment of this sum the child is turned over absolutely to his master. . . . [N]either the parents nor the child will ever have sufficient money to repay the original loan."[5]

Completely unmechanized, as they had been in antiquity, the mines were accessible only by steps hewn into the rock, as many as a thousand in the deepest mines, and the mineshafts themselves, unventilated and often hardly big enough for one man, were filled with sulfurous fumes. The temperatures were so stiflingly hot that the miners were completely naked. "Children of six and seven years of age were employed at these crushing and terrible tasks," Washington observed.

Little had changed after the war, and Sicily was only the poorest region in a generally poor country. Prior to the Depression, the work that earned $100 in Britain, $73 in Germany, and a remarkable $190 in the United States would currently bring a worker $39 in Italy as a whole, though much less again in the south of the country. Faced with a total lack of prospects, four million Italians had chosen to emigrate to the United States between 1880 and 1920. Like Michele Schirru, they had overwhelmingly gone to northern industrialized cities such as New York and Chicago, and they brought with them their social structures, their habits, and their food.

Many native-born Americans whose ancestors had come with earlier waves of emigration and who were mainly of Anglo-Saxon, German, or other northern European stock watched the arrival of large numbers of southern and eastern Europeans, many of them Jews, with great suspicion. The fight for Prohibition had partly been motivated by a culture war between rural communities of white Anglo-descended Protestants in the interior states and the growing urban populations with their very different attitudes toward alcohol and socializing. But the prohibitionists' victory against the German fondness for beer, the Italian love of wine, and the universal popularity of spirits was only part of a much larger campaign to keep America eugenically pure, white, and Anglo-Saxon.

The First World War had eased the flow of European emigration, as many young men who otherwise would have gone to the New World went to the battlefields instead and died there, creating a shortage of labor, and of young men, after 1918. But this temporary reduction was not enough for American activists, who sought a permanent solution to the problem. Their tireless campaign resulted in the 1924 Immigration Act, which established immigration quotas, capping the number of immigrants from any given country at 2 percent of the number of people from that national group in the United States in 1890—before the bulk of new immigrants from eastern and southern Europe had made the journey across the Atlantic. By implicitly declaring this ethnic mix normative for the United States, it determined quotas for immigrants from northwestern Europe that were far higher than the actual demand, while excluding most of those who sought to immigrate from eastern and southern Europe—mainly Italians, Russians, and Jews, disproportionately many of whom still lived in former tsarist and Habsburg territories.

The measure proved effective, and its intention was every bit as racist as it appears. In 1924, US senator Ellison DuRant Smith of South Carolina said: "I think we now have sufficient population in our country for us to shut the door and to breed up a pure, unadulterated American citizenship." The very idea of America had become dangerously diluted, the senator claimed: "If you were to go abroad and someone were to meet you and say, 'I met a typical American,' what would flash into your mind as a typical American, the typical representative of that new Nation? Would it be the son of an Italian immigrant, the son of a German immigrant, the son of any of the breeds from the Orient, the son of the denizens of Africa? . . . Thank God we have in America perhaps the largest percentage of any country in the world of the pure, unadulterated Anglo-Saxon stock."[6]

Even more than the Immigration Act, the Great Depression had slowed down the stream of Italian immigrants, and at times even reversed it. Michele Schirru was only one of tens of thousands of recent arrivals who found the situation in Depression-era America so hopeless and so hostile that they preferred to take their chances at home. It was not a good time for such a homecoming. After 1929, Italy's industrial output had fallen by a quarter, as had wages; the army of the unemployed had tripled; and many people had to battle daily to stave off starvation.

A New Greatness

BUT WHILE THE ECONOMIC SITUATION WAS DIRE, a larger, messianic narrative of hope and national greatness was unfolding. Mussolini and his Fascist Party looked at Italy as little more than the clay out of which a great future nation was to be formed. Their model was clear: like the futurist poet Filippo Marinetti, they wanted nothing less than to restore the grandeur of the Roman Empire, a proud, warlike, powerful country celebrating virility and violence. Contemporary Italians, Il Duce believed, were too soft, too craven, and too cowardly to be capable of creating a great civilization.

To build a new and greater Italy, Il Duce would have to build a new and greater Italian people first. Having come to power in 1922, Mussolini had attacked his great project with unflagging energy and relentless grandiloquence. The conservative German historian Oswald Spengler had called for a Caesar to stem the tide of European decadence and restore the greatness of the West. While he despised Hitler, whom he regarded as a proletarian upstart, Spengler believed the world had found such a man of destiny in Mussolini.

Spengler had described population growth as Italy's only weapon in the competition with other major powers, and the Fascists wholeheartedly agreed with him. Future wars would require future soldiers, and so the government passed a series of laws designed to encourage population growth: support for unwed mothers, taxes on bachelors,

Artists among themselves: Hitler and Mussolini at an exhibition of classical art, 1938.

special subsidies and medals for families with many children, and tight controls on the sale of contraceptives. A 1931 law made it a "crime against the integrity in the health of the race" to encourage or use birth control and made abortion punishable by lengthy prison sentences (and, later, even the death penalty).

Il Duce himself apparently made a solid contribution to the cause. An epic womanizer who thrived on casual encounters even while in office and who liked to brag that he would bed up to four playmates a day while discharging the affairs of state virtually as an afterthought, Mussolini had an almost carnal feel for politics and for the mood of the crowd. In his speeches he was both leader and lover, Il Duce and Don Juan, as one of his mistresses related: "The shouting becomes frenetic, the roar grows like an explosion, rising with the crash to a frenzy. . . . Hats in the air, handkerchiefs, radiant laughing faces. . . . They seem mad. It is a delirium, something indescribable, an inexplicable feeling of joy, the . . . torment of the soul overflowing into the cry of jubilation."[7]

Il Duce inspired intense devotion in his followers, as attested by the hundreds of letters arriving in his secretary's office every day. Some of these notes were simple statements of admiration and loyalty, but many showed a degree of devotion that had distinctly religious and also erotic connotations; some even veered into sexual fantasies. One housewife from Bologna wrote 848 letters to her "great Lord and beautiful Duce" between 1937 and 1943, and may have been one of the many women to have had a furtive adventure with him at some point. Another woman confessed to her diary: "The *duce* makes me tremble with excitement, because I only need to hear his words to be transported in heart and soul into a world of joy and greatness." A wounded veteran unburdened his soul, writing: "Attached to my bed is Your Effigy of when you were wounded and were on crutches, and I kiss Your Crutches—which I will soon have to use; I kissed them with passion, cause making myself equal to You in physical suffering, I will come to resemble You more in the ideal. For the blood given in Your name to the Fatherland; for the willing gift of my limb, Duce, I thank You!"[8]

Hoping to keep him safe for his historic mission, adoring men and women sent Mussolini amulets, holy pictures, and relics, and he was variously addressed as "the father of Italy," "the father of the poor," "the father of us all," "the one who does all and can do everything," "our God on earth," "the one who was loved as a father," and "the one who is venerated as the saints should be venerated." The distinctly religious overtones of these appellations are not surprising in Catholic Italy, and Mussolini was a master at exploiting the culture of everyday piety and ritual existing in the country. Spontaneous gestures of generosity were a particular favorite, and would often be reported, repeated, and embellished like stories from the lives of the saints. *Se lo sapesse il Duce* (if only Il Duce knew) was a popular expression at the time.

The revered leader proved himself a genius when it came to creating an image of his heroic and even saintly person in the public mind. Threshing wheat bare-chested for the cameras, "he looked to me like a Christ on earth," as one awestruck peasant remembered, and wherever he appeared, the local Party organization managed without difficulty to gather a large and adoring crowd. There were pilgrimages to Mussolini's birthplace organized by the National Association of Peasant Women, one of whose members reported in 1937: "Then, with religious emotion they visited the *duce*'s house, poor, rustic like their own, where mother has worked, loved, suffered, living a life like theirs, simple and loving, a life of sacrifice and happiness, teaching Her Great Son goodness, discipline and self-sacrifice."[9]

The strong messianic Christian overtones of these sentiments were crucial to the success of the Fascist regime. Ever since blustering, bullying, and murdering his way to power, he had masterfully exploited his country's collective psyche and preoccupations. In the fight against socialism, which during the 1920s had a very strong constituency among the working poor and the industrial laborers in the north of the country, his allies and financiers were landowners, factory owners, and urban middle-class people, concentrated in Milan and other manufacturing cities, where a socialist revolution appeared to be a real possibility. To gain a viable following, however, he needed to tap into a wider and more powerful kind of collective imagination.

Mussolini's gestures toward reviving the glory of the Roman Empire created strong images, as did his advocacy of a plan to modernize and industrialize a country that was still largely rural and in which many people lived and thought much as they had done a century before. But in order to capture hearts and minds, he needed more than a rhetoric that was ultimately derived from the futurists and from his former mentor Gabriele d'Annunzio. Il Duce found this elusive ingredient in the strong presence of the church and its rituals, statues, and symbols in all areas of personal and public life.

The relationship between heroes of Italian nationhood such as Garibaldi and the Catholic Church had never been easy and was sometimes marked by outright hostility, but among the many kinds of Catholicism in the peninsula—from the visceral, animist, and intensely superstitious faith of the peasants in the south to the bourgeois rituals in the northern industrial centers—the attachment of large parts of the population to Christian symbolism and rituals was beyond doubt. As a politician and a former journalist, Mussolini was tarred with the brush of the widely perceived failure of the institutions of liberal democracy; as an authoritarian and charismatic leader, he promised renewal; as a man of Providence especially blessed and protected by the Lord, he could represent eternity.

Rival Saviors

MICHELE SCHIRRU HAD NOT BEEN the first to try to slay Il Duce, but a series of failed assassination attempts only served to heighten and confirm Mussolini's godlike invulnerability. In November 1925, a former socialist deputy had plotted to shoot him during a speech on the balcony of Palazzo Chigi, but the conspiracy had been discovered in time. In April 1926 a mentally unstable Irishwoman had attempted to kill him, but her shot had only lightly grazed his nose. In October of the same year, two anarchists had hurled a bomb at his car but had merely succeeded in wounding eight bystanders.

The effect of these attacks on public opinion had been not only gratifying but also more profound than anything Mussolini could have achieved by normal propagandistic means. The Pope had publicly said that God himself had held his hand over Il Duce, church bells were rung throughout the country on Mussolini's behalf, and newspapers wrote stories about the great leader beloved by God. After the attack in October 1926, the cardinal of Venice ordered the bells of St. Mark's to be rung, and in Milan there was a huge demonstration on the Piazza del Duomo. Cinemas in the city suspended their performances to allow everyone to attend. Mussolini's brother wrote to him: "God protects you, the Italians worship you: two forces that render the criminality of assassins futile."[10]

Mussolini's personal pantheon had space for the veneration of Providence and of himself, but not for any personal God or for his humble representative on earth, the Pontifex Maximus in the Vatican, barely a mile away from Il Duce's desk. Mussolini had fought tenaciously to curtail the influence and power of Catholic organizations throughout Italy, and he was wary of the Pope's political agenda and privately had nothing but contempt for his beliefs, but he needed the sanction of the Catholic Church to burnish Fascism with this ultimate stamp of approval and to sink deep roots in the imagination of the faithful.

As it happened, Mussolini held a first-class bargaining chip. Ever since the proclamation of a secular Italian republic in 1861, a succession of popes had effectively refused to recognize the legitimacy of the government and of Rome as the capital of Italy, in which the church held no temporal power under the laws of the republic. Holed up in the Vatican, the furious princes of the church could only look on as their power was eroded. Under the Fascists, this situation had grown even worse, as the work of Catholic institutions and organizations was made more difficult or simply outlawed because they were effectively competing with the equivalent Fascist organizations.

Now Il Duce held out an olive branch: in return for formal recognition of the legitimacy and sovereignty of the Italian state as well as a guarantee that Catholic dignitaries would refrain from direct political involvement, Mussolini's government, officially acting for the king, was willing to recognize the Vatican as a sovereign state within its own borders. The 1929 Lateran Treaty was advantageous for both sides, as it offered the Holy See political legitimacy and the Fascist government a considerable moral bonus.

The treaty also proved that both sides had found a way of not only tolerating but instrumentalizing each other. On the surface, the Fascist emphasis on violence, war, and the revival of pagan rituals seemed inimical to the demands of the church and its message of brotherly love, forgiveness of sins, and purity of faith. But underneath this surface the two were as similar as fraternal twins. Though intermittently suspicious of each other, their common needs and enemies by far outweighed their disagreements. United in their hatred of communism, both were authoritarian and hierarchical, both despised democracy and liberal ideas, both believed in the supremacy of martyrdom and of faith over reason, and both allotted a subordinate role to women and to all people of other creeds (or, in the case of the Fascists, other ethnic backgrounds).

Speaking in Rome in 1927, Mussolini had outlined his vision of the world and of Italy's place in it in words that could almost have been chosen by the Pope himself: "This is the situation now: in a decadent Europe, weakened by vice, perverted by exotic habits, striving deliriously to attain the dreams of social democratic humanitarianism, the only vital principle is Fascist Italy. Europe no longer has any faith: it does not attach any real importance to religious values, but only to money, to the individual and collective instinct for survival, to the pursuit of enjoyment, and to a peaceful life. Fascist Italy—Catholic, disciplined, warlike—will be able to dominate Europe if it can defend its physical and moral health."[11]

While his union with the holy church might be dismissed as a political ruse on Mussolini's part, the Vatican very obviously had no problem whatsoever in dealing with and dignifying Fascist dictatorships. After the success of the Lateran Treaty, the Pope pursued further international agreements, largely in an attempt to bolster the political legitimacy of the newly created statelet as well as the social influence of Catholic organizations. In 1933 the newly elected Pope Pius XII celebrated two new concordats—with fascist Austria and Nazi Germany—to add to the existing ones.

A Shrine of Martyrs

HAVING MADE THE CHURCH HIS ALLY, Mussolini could make even more effective use of the potency of Catholic symbolism and ritual. In Padua, an eighteen-year-old girl by the name of Maria visited the Exhibition of the Fascist Revolution, housed in a building whose exterior had been transformed by looming, fifty-foot-high fasces jutting out in front of the elegant nineteenth-century façade. In the Shrine of Martyrs, she and other visitors were particularly impressed:

> It is very suggestive and moving. . . . There are a huge number of relics of the fascist martyrs, the Duce's handkerchief soaked in blood from his wound. With your soul thus prepared for religious feelings, you enter the Shrine of the Martyrs: a dark circular room with illuminated glass rectangles bearing the word "presente" [present] on the top three quarters of the walls. Below, in a purplish blue half-light, are lots of banners. You move silently around a platform with a tall cross rising out of it, while in the far, far distance you hear choirs singing patriotic hymns. You come out slightly dazed, partly also because there are no windows and the heat gets to your head.[12]

The holy blood from the sacred wound of the savior, the relics, the half-light, the silence, the choirs—the designers of this elaborate staging of the beginnings of a political movement hardly older than its eighteen-year-old admirer did not have far to go in search of an effective template that would resonate with Italians' collective imagination.

A New Hercules

MUSSOLINI AND HIS FASCIST PARTY were by no means alone in using religious feelings and symbolism to further their cause. After all, fascism as well as socialism and communism can be described as political religions: like religion, they responded to a longing for order, purpose, and meaning that was particularly acute in the atmosphere of fragmentation and nihilism during the 1920s and 1930s.

For obvious reasons Mussolini based his image on Catholic iconography, just as Stalin would increasingly appropriate not only the powers of the tsars but also the cultural and spiritual place they had occupied in Russian culture. The cult of "Little Father Stalin" eventually quite literally usurped the place the Orthodox saints had been allotted in Russian houses, the *iconostase*, an icon placed in a corner of the living room, illuminated with an eternally burning candle, and decorated with flowers. Now the *iconostase* showed not the Virgin Mary or Christ enthroned but the familiar mustachioed face of the first secretary smiling down on the home's inhabitants.

In Germany the propagandistic genius of Joseph Goebbels had already begun to sway millions of hearts and minds, and one reason the Weimar Republic never quite became more than tolerated by most Germans was that it failed to win the battle of the images. Perhaps the young democracy simply lacked sufficiently gifted communicators who might have been able to transform its poisoned legacy of disaster in war, the allegation that social democratic politicians had betrayed the victorious army by suing for peace, and the inheritance of an empire buried under the ruins of its own arrogance.

If Berlin was such a fascinating place to be, it was also because there was no single official version of its identity, and many possibilities could flourish in this vacuum. Next to the experimental and creative varieties, however, the rival political religions were imposing themselves on the imagination of a population torn between cynicism and a real hunger for legitimate hope. In the end, Hitler's messianic narrative succeeded where the difficult negotiations and hesitating attempts of democracy had failed.

The narratives of the totalitarian religions gave ordinary people a sense of transcendence, of touching something that was greater than they were, of essential truth. They offered a sense of the sacred and the immutable laws of Providence, which in the racist vocabulary of fascism invariably meant a sense of one's own superiority. There is, after all, no variety of racism which arrives at the conclusion that one's own group is anything but the finest and the most valuable while others are inferior or degenerate and deserve to be suppressed.

But the totalitarian religions, Mussolini's Fascism being a case in point, also did something else: they restored a sense of hope, a positive future. This future was invariably messianic and inflated in its vast expectations. But especially in times of crisis, in which so many people had so little to lose and so much to gain, they created a space people could inhabit in contrast to the present, which was difficult and even dangerous.

Il Duce was very much alive to the necessity of awakening and nourishing this messianic hope. While the Soviets had built Magnitogorsk and were dreaming up other gigantic programs, Fascist Italy did not lag behind. Mussolini's answer to Russia's city of steel was Carbonia in Sardinia, a coal mining town planned from scratch and inaugurated in 1937.

Carbonia was not the only city Il Duce founded; he cast himself as a second Alexander the Great. His largest project by far was the draining of the Pontine Marshes, south of Rome, a waterlogged region of three hundred square miles in which a mere sixteen hundred people were eking out a living. In the "battle of the swamps" Mussolini's government undertook to conquer the malaria-infested region by first building a network of canals and then transforming the marshland for agricultural use. More than 120,000 men worked on the project. It is unknown how many of them died of malaria. The result, however, was a great propagandistic success. "Once a fever-ridden swamp, now a prosperous colony," crowed a newsreel made by British Pathé in 1934 on the occasion of the first anniversary of the new town of Littoria, built in traditional style with a town plaza dominated by a square bell tower, surrounded by handsome country villas, and settled with reliable Fascist families from the north. In the short film, a cheering, almost exclusively male public salutes Il Duce on the balcony of the city hall.

By drying out the Pontine Marshes, Mussolini had achieved something his Roman predecessors had never managed, allowing him to portray himself not only as the legitimate heir of classical antiquity but also as its completion. He was obsessed with the idea of restoring Roman greatness wherever possible, and his plans for the Eternal City itself were truly astonishing. "In five years Rome must appear wonderful to the entire world, vast, orderly and potent, as she was in the days of the first empire of Augustus," he proclaimed in one of his many speeches.

Only few of the gigantic building programs he instituted were finished, but among them is another homage to antiquity, the Foro Mussolini (now Foro Italico), with the spectacular Stadio dei Marmi, in which sixty-four marble statues of athletes keep watch over the exploits of their real-life successors. But paying obeisance to the past was only part of the project to captivate the imagination of millions. In order to accomplish this, the future had to be enlisted as well.

Public building programs and new towns created work and effective images for newsreels. To go even further and embrace the aesthetics and technology of modernity, Mussolini only had to turn to one of his most enthusiastic supporters, the poet Filippo Marinetti, whose futurist movement consisted of an orgy of roaring engines, smoking factories, vertiginous speed, and sex. One of the greatest publicity triumphs of the regime was achieved when Fascism literally took to the skies. The futurists had always been infatuated with flying, and even the diminutive proto-fascist poet Gabriele d'Annunzio had proved his courage as a First World War flying ace. Now another Italian air force hero, Italo Balbo, who was minister of aviation from 1929 to 1933, gave Il Duce the international recognition he craved.

In 1931, Balbo succeeded in flying with a squadron of nine sea-planes from Italy across the South Atlantic, successfully advertising not only the heroism of the new Italy but also the power of collective action. In 1933 another and even more spectacular action took place when he guided twenty-four Savoia Marchetti machines across the North Atlantic, arriving in Chicago in front of a huge crowd and accompanied by forty-three American fighter planes spelling out the word "Italia" in the evening sky. Among the mountains of honors heaped on the Italian pilot was honorary membership in the Sioux tribe, and during the triumphal parade on Michigan Avenue the heroes were greeted by a million Americans, many of them with arms raised in a Fascist salute.

Reporting the incident for Italian radio was none other than Filippo Marinetti, who was unable to contain his excitement at the mystical marriage between technology and Fascist manliness:

> Listen to the music of the sky, with its mellowed tubes of pride, the buzzing drills of miners of the clouds, enthusiastic roars of gas, hammerings ever more intoxicated with speed and the applause of bright propellers. The rich music of Balbo and his transatlantic flyer hums, explodes and laughs among the blue flashes of the whole horizon. . . . The cruiser *Diaz* fires salvos. The crowd shouts with joy. The sound mirrors the Italian creative genius. . . . The delirious crowd yells: "here he is, here he is, here it is! Duce! Duce! Duce! Italy! Italy" the rumble, rumble, rumble of the motors that pass a few yards from my head.[13]

· 1932 ·

Holodomor

....

"I GREW UP IN A TYPICAL UKRAINIAN VILLAGE, IN THE COUNTY OF Cherkasy, some hundred miles south of Kiev," Miron Dolot remembered about his childhood.

> My village stood on the north bank of the Tiasmyn River, one of the many tributaries of the Dnipro (Dnieper) River, and it was beautiful. Green hills rose in the south behind the river, and the rich tar-black soil of the plains stretched to the north. The plains were divided into strips of fields. Every spring and summer these strips would disappear beneath miles of wheat. Waves of rich grain, green in spring and golden in summer, gently rolled in the summer breeze. After the harvest, the fields again bared their soil as if in mourning for the lost beauty. Near the end of the year, the new cycle of color—winters white— blended with the horizon of the plains into the grey-frosty sky.[1]

Much of history deals with the big cities and their inhabitants, the centers where the greatest changes take place. Urban areas are focal points of migration and culture and political power, fast-moving and cosmopolitan, centers of enterprise and fashion, of intellect and revolution. The denizens of the countryside often lived their lives away from these great developments. Their habits and their ways of thinking, their poverty and entertainments and work, changed at a different, much slower pace. Of course, tens of millions of country dwellers had moved to the cities and were still moving there, trying to escape the hunger and the harshness of life and hoping for a better deal, if not for themselves, then for their children. These mass migrations along with the declining power of the church and the introduction of farming machinery, synthetic fertilizers, radios, communism, and compulsory schooling had already transformed lives in the countryside in many Western European countries, as well as in a number of places within the USSR, but in other areas it almost seemed as if the catastrophes, transformations, and revolutions had passed by without leaving a trace.

Miron's village was like that. Four thousand people lived there in wooden houses clustering around the church, school, general store, government building, post office, and doctor's house. His memory of it was clear, if perhaps slightly idealizing:

> Most of the houses had only one room which was used for all purposes, including cooking and sleeping. Wooden floors were also rare; like the walls, the floors were made of clay. But no matter how plainly they were constructed, and how primitive our living conditions, the houses were clean and neat. Each home has its plot for flowers and a few fruit trees, and chickens, geese, and ducks were kept in the backyards. Barns housed a horse, one or two cows, and a few pigs. A dog would usually be lounging on the porch or at the gate.[2]

Having worked hard during the day, the young people in the village used the evening hours as their forefathers had done. They gathered "in neighborhoods at the crossroads and danced, sang, and played long into the night."[3]

The small farmers of Ukraine had reason to look into the future with optimism, though life had never been easy. Wedged between Poland, the Ottoman Empire, and the Russian Empire, the country had been invaded, carved up, and ruled by foreigners for much of its history. For centuries it was known simply as Little Russia, and its capital, Kiev, was an important spiritual and historic center of Russian culture.

With its rich, fertile soils it was also traditionally considered the bread-basket of the tsar's vast empire, which incorporated Ukraine in 1795.

During the nineteenth century, most of Ukraine was part of the Russian Empire, while the western part, Ruthenia, was ruled by the Habsburgs. The harsh tsarist policies of Russification, which all but outlawed the national language and repressed all stirrings of a distinctive culture, led to the displacement of many Ukrainian nationalist intellectuals and to an atmosphere of constant unrest. Possessing its own church, language, and history, Ukraine was almost like the Russian heartland of the so-called Golden Circle, but never quite.

Following the First World War and the Russian Revolution, the country was fought over, often savagely, by rival communist, White, and Ukrainian nationalist forces, and between February 1918 and June 1920 the capital, Kiev, changed hands no fewer than seven times. Finally, in March 1921, Ukraine became a Soviet Socialist Republic.

Initially the new rulers in Moscow were uncertain what to do with the troublesome republic. The Ukrainians were known to be intransigent, fiercely attached to their own ways, and unwilling to submit to Soviet rule. The Bolshevik leadership had responded with a policy of caution, reversing the harsh implementation of Russian language and culture and even allowing a national cultural movement to develop. The Ukrainian Orthodox Church had seceded from the Patriarch in Moscow, and in 1923 Stalin had given a thundering speech against Russian arrogance and in favor of a measure of cultural independence of the non-Russian Soviet republics. For the first time ever, a Ukrainian nation began to grow out of the destruction of war and revolution.

In spite of pressure to develop industrial cities such as Kharkov and Dnepropetrovsk and in spite of a continuing movement into the cities that saw the proportion of villagers and farmers decrease from 81 to 66 percent of the population within a decade, the country dwellers were no more resentful of the new regime than they had been of previous ones. Even if they remained wary of the representatives of Russian power and not many were interested in communism, they welcomed the fact that their new masters seemed to rule with a light touch.

A Massive Slaughter

THE TROUBLE HAD STARTED with the first Five-Year Plan, introduced by Stalin in 1928. To aid rapid industrialization, the plan demanded a large-scale collectivization of means of production, which included farming lands, tools, and farm animals, to increase production and free the suffering mass of poor peasants from hunger and oppression. In theory, this plan was as beautiful as it was necessary. To Soviet ideologues the *muzhiks*, backward peasants, were forever caught between subservience to their masters or to the church, on one hand, and the greedily oppressive *kulaks*, on the other. The kulaks were the main ideological enemies in this recasting of the rural economy. The word *kulak* can be translated as "grasping fist," and it was used to designate wealthy farmers who were said to exploit the peasants and who enriched themselves by holding back grain for their own profit while the poorest were starving.

The Bolshevik vision of *muzhiks* and rural misery was no mere propaganda, and Miron Dolot's account of idyllic village life certainly needs some redress. Even if Ukraine had the best soil in the Soviet empire, agricultural practices were indeed woefully inefficient, yields were lower than in western European countries with more advanced techniques, most people were poor, and literacy among the rural population, especially women, was low. Most peasant families occupied one dark and frequently dirty room, illuminated only by small windows and the flame of the candle burning in front of the *iconostase* in one corner. Alcoholism was endemic, brawls in the village square were frequent and usually brutal, domestic violence was rife and seen as part of life, and the women, like the children, lived practically in bondage to their men, who alone could decide all important questions. While there never was a fixed social category of kulaks, authority was frequently exercised by wealthier farmers over poorer ones, and many of them undoubtedly profited from lending money to indebted peasants unable to feed their hungry children.

The Bolsheviks had sworn to change all this. Instead of the backwardness, inefficiency, and injustice of traditional farming, scientific, socialist agricultural production would combine resources in huge collectives, transforming servile, ignorant country folk into proper agricultural proletarians and producing enough grain to feed the vast acceleration of industry the Soviet leadership had projected as part of its Five-Year Plan.

The first attempts to implement this policy were met with resistance, which embittered Moscow. Communism was blunted in the countryside, and Stalin and his close ally Lazar Kaganovich found the Bolshevik solution: they designated a guilty party and then set about eliminating it. The problem, it was thought, was the wealthy peasants, who resisted socialism in order to perpetuate their nefarious power. The Soviet leadership was therefore convinced that the only possible answer to this was to liquidate the kulaks as a class.

As collectivization was frustrated at every turn, the secret police and army units from other regions of the Soviet Union were sent in to enforce the plan. Miron Dolot remembers a meeting convened by Party officials shortly after a propaganda detachment had already visited the village and destroyed its church: "In the middle of the square was the raised platform. . . . Around the platform stood armed sentries. From the ruins of the church, the machine gun faced us. Heavily armed soldiers walked around the square. And in the middle of the square, the farmers stood, huddled together, silent but restless, for it was very cold."[4]

Any farmer who was thought to be a kulak (an ill-defined term, which in practice could mean nothing more than that someone had more than one cow, or used the labor of farm hands, or had a better roof on his house than others) was seized and deported. Some one hundred thousand families were transported to Siberia or to other regions during the early 1930s; some of them were on the trains of misery arriving in Magnitogorsk. Many more were arrested and simply executed. Denunciations by jealous neighbors were a daily occurrence. The Bread Procurement Commission began making its dreaded rounds, pressuring farmers to join the collective by impounding their grain for the state.

In Miron's village, the chairman of the commission was a known drunk and troublemaker from the village who had joined the Party in 1919 and was now master over life and death. In one incident, he came to the house of Miron's family at midnight and "on official business," dead drunk and accompanied by other members of the commission. When Miron's mother slapped him in the face after he had attempted to grope her, he tried to shoot her but hit the holy icon in the corner of the house instead. One of the brothers tried to wrestle the gun out of his hand as he took aim again. The lad was arrested for "assaulting a Party official" and later sentenced to hard labor. Two years later his remaining family would learn that he had died from exhaustion while being made to work on a canal project.

As the year 1932 turned to winter the repression against alleged "kulaks," "counterrevolutionaries," and "saboteurs" intensified. Several of Miron's uncles were arrested. One of them died in his own house from kicks to the head; another one was taken from his house and sent to Siberia without even a coat. Village elders, wealthier peasants, and anyone who had in the past aroused the displeasure of the chief of the commission were herded together in the village square, where a table with a bright red tablecloth had been set up in the snow. On the table stood a telephone, and behind the table the Party commissar sat in judgment. When the relatives of the families arrested began to move against the guards, a machine gun fired into the crowd, killing three. Then sleighs carried those who were convicted—all of the accused—to the railway station.

"As one sleigh moved to join a column, a young man sprang from it and raced toward another sleigh in which his helpless and weeping wife and children were riding," the young observer remembered. "The father obviously wanted to be with his family, but he did not reach them. Comrade Pashchenko, the chairman of the village soviet who was supervising the whole action, raised his revolver and calmly fired. The young father dropped dead into the snow, and the sleigh carrying his widow and orphans moved on."[5]

After the arrests, wrote Miron, "our lives became harsh and grim." While only a few farmers were living well enough even to be accused of being kulaks, all of them were subject to the new policy of collectivization and working on large *kolkhoz* farms. Peasants not wanting to give up their farms to the collective were summoned by the commission of the next village and then the next, each time entailing a forced march through the snow at night in order to arrive in time for the morning interrogation. The summonses continued to arrive until the exhausted and humiliated victims would finally resign themselves to their fate. After all her grain had been taken from her, and after many weeks of systematic harassment, Miron's mother also gave up and signed the application: "Whereas the collective farm has advantages over individual farming; and whereas it is the only way to secure a prosperous and happy life, I voluntarily request the collective farm's management to accept me as a member of your collective farm."[6]

But not all farmers submitted to the pressure of the commissars and the army soldiers billeted in their houses. Ordered to give up their tools and deliver their animals to the local *kolkhoz*, they initially refused, then hid or destroyed their plows rather than see them taken away, and slaughtered their animals, rendering the courtyards and meadows red with the blood of tens of millions of cows, horses, pigs, sheep, chickens, and geese. The animals handed over to the collective often fared little better. The farm workers were sloppy and forgot to feed them and otherwise look after them, the procurement of feed was unreliable, and diseases and malnutrition were rife among the livestock. In many collectives the horses were simply turned loose into the woods, as the *kolkhoz* leaderships confidently expected the imminent delivery of tractors.

On the collective farms, a life of fear and suspicion descended on the new recruits. "We were always suspected of treason. Even sadness

The tender dictator: Joseph Stalin with his daughter, Svetlana.

or happiness were causes for suspicion. Sadness was thought of as an indication of dissatisfaction with our life, while happiness, regardless of how sporadic, spontaneous, or fleeting, was considered to be a dangerous phenomenon that could destroy our devotion to the communist cause," Miron recounted.[7] At the same time, the resistance continued. Communist officials were beaten to death under cover of night and their bloodied corpses were found lying in the gutter in the morning, sometimes with defiant messages pinned to their chest. In response, more farmers would be arrested and sent to forced labor camps. Those attempting to resist or flee were shot immediately. In 1932, as Ukraine was threatening to sink into anarchy and the much-prized breadbasket of the nation was producing less grain, Stalin's response had been coolly punitive. In the troublesome province, where agriculture had already been severely compromised by the deportation and execution of part of the farming population and by the destruction of livestock and machinery, he upped the quota of grain to be delivered to the central government from 30 percent to 44 percent of the harvest, a number deliberately set far above anything achievable. "This was the memorable spring of 1932 when the famine broke out and the first deaths from hunger began to occur," recalled Miron.

"I remember the endless procession of beggars on roads and paths, going from house to house. They were in different stages of starvation, dirty and ragged. With outstretched hands, they begged for food, any food: a potato, a beet, or at least a kernel of corn."[8]

In order to fulfill the all-important quota, further impossible demands were heaped upon the farmers. One of the men in Miron's village received a demand for five hundred kilograms of wheat, which he fulfilled. Immediately the authorities demanded an additional one thousand kilograms from him, an order he could meet only by selling most of his possessions. The next demand was for two thousand kilograms, and this time he could no longer comply. Accused of being a kulak and a traitor, he was arrested and deported together with his family. The farm was confiscated and turned into the local soviet's headquarters. The farmer and his family were never heard from again.

The harvest quota was set according to unrealistically high estimates, and the demanded 44 percent of a hypothetical normal harvest exceeded the entire production of 1932, a year dogged not only by the disruption of harvesting practices but also by persistent bad weather. To expedite the campaign and fulfill the official quotas, some one hundred thousand young Bolshevik functionaries were sent to Ukraine to supervise the harvest work, but most of them were students and other city dwellers who had never even seen a plow. They had no idea when to harvest or how to organize the work, and their orders and punitive measures only made things worse. The harvested grain was kept in depots guarded by watchtowers. Anyone attempting to approach without authorization was shot.

Local Party officials were merciless in their execution of the orders from Moscow. Search parties armed with long pikes went from farm to farm, looking everywhere for grain. Once they had looked in the pantry and the storage rooms they would rip apart beds and cradles, break into locked chests, and hack into wooden walls and floors in their search for hiding places, leaving behind devastation and misery. Before long, the farmers had to take to foraging for food in the woods or already harvested fields: "Crowds of starving wretches could be seen scattered all over the potato fields. They were looking for potatoes left over from last year's harvest."[9]

When there was nothing left at all, those with sufficient strength would walk to the cities to find work there, but they only found the street army of the starving. At first they had something to sell—clothes and household items, heirlooms and embroidered linen—but when their possessions were used up they faced starvation once again. It was illegal to give work to anyone from the countryside, and so the emaciated frames of the desperate would haunt streets and squares, rummaging in the rubbish or begging from people with nothing left to give. In the end, people simply became used to their desperate begging.

The situation in the villages had become desperate, remembered Miron: "One could see strange funeral processions: children pulling homemade handwagons with the bodies of their dead parents in them or the parents carting the bodies of their children. There were no coffins; no burial ceremonies performed by priests."[10]

Execution by Hunger

THE CAMPAIGN TO BREAK the population of Ukraine by hunger was organized on a grand scale. Villagers had to obtain passports to leave their villages and the collective farms they were working on, but these documents were never issued. Streets throughout the countryside were guarded by military roadblocks, and the borders were practically closed. Grain continued to leave the republic, and the countryside was turned into "one vast Belsen," as Robert Conquest writes.

"Faced with starvation, the villagers tried everything possible to save themselves and their families," Miron recounted. "Some of them started eating dogs and cats. Others went hunting for birds: crows, magpies, swallows, sparrows, storks, and even nightingales. One could see starving villagers searching in the bushes along the river for birds' nests. . . . They even ate weeds, the leaves and bark of trees, insects, frogs, and snails."[11]

Stalin saw the plight of the villagers and reacted promptly. A new quota demanded that the skins of cats and dogs be delivered to the state, and young communist activists took it upon themselves to slaughter all remaining dogs and cats they could find, leaving the villagers only the surviving scrawny rats to eat. Once they were done, the enthusiastic volunteers went on to kill the nightingales and other birds.

As autumn turned into grainless winter, desperate villagers began to pillage graveyards and churches for gold and other valuables that could be used to buy food in city stores, in which every imaginable delicacy appeared to be available. People were even assaulted and killed for their gold teeth. The countryside was buried under a thick blanket of snow, and Miron noticed that there were no tracks in it, meaning that few animals were left in the wild. Foraging for food, he came to a neighboring village in which the hearths had fallen cold and the limbs of the starved protruded darkly from the all-covering

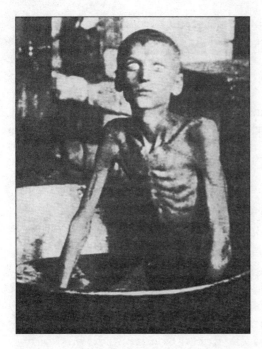

A victim of Stalin's artificial famine.

white. Most of the frozen bodies were found by the roadside, as they had obviously used their last strength trying to leave the village and reach the nearest city. Those who made it there were regularly rounded up by local militias, taken to a nearby field, and simply abandoned to the frost.

Trying to sell a gold amulet his mother had hidden until then, Miron went to the town of Torgsin, where many others were already assembled, suspended between a desperate hope of life and a resigned anticipation of death. "Emaciated and skeletonlike, or with swollen, puffed-up bodies, human beings stood around in the streets, leaned against the telephone poles and walls, or lay on the sidewalks and in the street gutters. They were patiently waiting for some merciful shoppers to share a pittance of their purchases with them. . . . Here and there among the crowds we could see the rigid bodies of the dead, but nobody paid any attention to them."[12]

With the proceeds from the amulet, eighteen rubles, Miron and his mother stood in line for an hour before it was their turn to enter one of the famed shops. "What a sight it was," he wrote. "I could not believe my eyes; it was like a dream. Here was everything we needed and more. There were things we had never even heard of or seen in our lives. There were even groceries known to me only from books I had read. All the items were tastefully arranged and exhibited in cases under glass. Looking at these splendid assortments of foods, I began to feel dizzy."[13]

Miron and his mother smuggled home the food they had been able to buy, a small reprieve from starvation. Others, who lacked these last resources or who were simply unlucky, were reduced to cannibalism. A man killed his wife with an axe to make soup out of her, small children were smothered and consumed, and the bodies of those who had recently died (and had often been preserved by frost) were frequently attacked with butcher knives to carve out some flesh. The practice became so widespread that a directive from Moscow demanded that the local Party print and distribute hundreds of posters with the slogan EATING DEAD CHILDREN IS BARBARISM. During the famine, more than twenty-five hundred Ukrainian peasants were convicted of cannibalism by Soviet courts. Faced with such horrors, even loyal Party members who had helped implement this policy with the best intentions were driven to suicide.

There Is No Bread

HOLODOMOR IS A UKRAINIAN WORD coined to describe the famine of 1932–1933; it derives from *holod*, "hunger," and *mor*, "death," "plague," or "mass dying," and it means "death by hunger." The campaign of systematic starvation waged by Stalin on the rural population of Ukraine reached its climax in the spring of 1933, when all food reserves, all foragable materials, and all wild animals were gone and the ripening fruits and vegetables were still far off. The Austrian-born British novelist Arthur Koestler spent three months in the city of Kharkiv during the famine and published his memories, in 1949, in *The God That Failed*, his account of his own communist dreams and their eventual betrayal. "I saw the ravages of the famine of 1932-1933 in the Ukraine," he testified, "hordes of families in rags begging at the railway stations, the women lifting up to the compartment window their starving brats, which, with drumstick limbs, big cadaverous heads and puffed bellies, looked like embryos out of alcohol bottles."[14]

The Welsh journalist Gareth Jones also managed to enter Ukraine to report on conditions there, one of only a handful of international visitors who succeeded in doing so. A graduate of Trinity College, Cambridge, and a former foreign policy advisor to prime minister David Lloyd George, Jones spoke fluent Russian and was in an ideal position to observe and evaluate. He managed to publish flaming indictments of the artificial famine in various international papers. In an interview with the *New York Evening Post* he said in April 1933:

> Millions are dying of hunger. . . . Everywhere was the cry, "There is no bread. We are dying." This cry came from every part of Russia, from the Volga, Siberia, White Russia, the North Caucasus, Central Asia. I tramped through the black earth region because that was once the richest farm land in Russia and because the correspondents have been forbidden to go there to see for themselves what is happening.
>
> In the train a Communist denied to me that there was a famine. I flung a crust of bread which I had been eating from my own supply into a spittoon. A peasant fellow-passenger fished it out and ravenously ate it.

Jones added that the most hated man in Ukraine was not Joseph Stalin but George Bernard Shaw, who after a recent carefully stage-managed trip to the region had let it be known that "there is no famine in the Ukraine," thoughtfully adding that he had partaken of one of the finest dinners of his life during his trip. But Shaw was not alone in denying that a monumental crime was taking place. Édouard Herriot was prime minister of France when he visited Ukraine in August 1933. On his return he describe the country as being "like a garden in full bloom."[15]

The most important voice, however, was that of Walter Duranty, the Moscow bureau chief of the *New York Times*, who won a Pulitzer Prize in 1932 for his reporting about the situation in Ukraine. Duranty had met Jones after his trip and had spoken to him extensively. After doing some asking around, he confidently announced with the weight of a great newspaper behind him that Jones was spreading a "big scare story."[16] Impeccably patronizing, he characterized his colleague as "a man of keen and active mind," noting that "he has taken the trouble to learn Russian, which he speaks with considerable fluency, but the writer thought Mr. Jones's judgment was somewhat hasty."

Admitting that the mismanagement of collective farming plus a "quite efficient conspiracy" by a Soviet official "have made a mess of Soviet food production," he argued: "You can't make an omelette without breaking eggs, and the Bolshevist leaders are just as indifferent to the casualties that may be involved in their drive toward socialization as any General during the World War who ordered a costly attack in order to show his superiors that he and his division possessed the proper soldierly spirit. . . . These conditions are bad, but there is no famine." The "present difficulties will be speedily forgotten," he prognosticated, and in this estimation he very largely proved correct.

It is difficult to estimate how many victims the *holodomor* claimed. Official Soviet statistics are largely false, dreamed up to suit their ideological purpose, and after the world war, the revolution, and the civil war in Russia, population estimates were not necessarily up to date or reliable. In addition to this, questions of definition arise. There were famines not only in Ukraine but also in neighboring Moldova, the Volga region, Kazakhstan, the Urals, northern Caucasus, and Western Siberia. Taking only the victims of the Ukrainian famine, there were deaths from starvation and shootings, but also from typhoid and other epidemics, as well as those who were sentenced to hard labor in Siberia or elsewhere and who never came back. The earliest serious and at the same time most conservative estimate comes from the Ukrainian émigré scholar Volodymyr Kubiyovych, who estimated the number of victims as being around 2.5 million. More recently, Timothy Snyder put the likely death toll at 3.5 million, while Robert Conquest estimates that some 5 million lives were lost. This number is increased significantly if the population shortfall is taken into account, including millions of "never-borns." Across the Soviet Union, the number of famine victims for the years 1932–1933 is likely to be between seven and eight million.[17]

An End to the Dying

THE WESTERN NATIONS and public figures had their own reasons to maintain silence about the information they received about the famine. One of the very rare protesting voices was Austria's Cardinal Innizer, who called for food aid for Ukraine and pointed to instances of cannibalism, only to be rebuffed by Soviet officials who scoffed that there were "neither cannibals nor cardinals" in the USSR. Many leftist intellectuals and politicians wanted the Soviet experiment to succeed and wanted to believe that any news pointing toward the establishment of a cruel dictatorship was simply capitalist propaganda. Those on the right often enough defended the harsh treatment of striking workers at home and of colonial mutinies and were therefore hardly in a position to criticize Stalin for his policies. Thus a veil of silence was draped over one of the greatest crimes of the twentieth century.

In early 1933 Stalin began to fear that the collapse of several Soviet republics might destabilize the entire USSR. Bandits roamed

the countryside, looting and killing. Thieves, even children, were frequently lynched, and village courts imposed cruel punishments in an
attempt to control the lawlessness. The Supreme Soviet took measures
to limit the crisis. Between January and July, 320,000 metric tons of
grain were sent to Ukraine to end the famine. The distribution was
organized strictly along "class principles." Members of the Red Army
were fed first, then workers on the *kolkhoz* farms, followed by industrial workers and the poorest peasants; last came "kulak, counterrevolutionary, parasitical, and enemy elements of all kinds that sought
to exploit the food problems for their own counter-revolutionary purposes, spreading rumors about the famine and various 'horrors,'
purposely leaving the dead unburied."[18]

To make up for the shortage of agricultural workers, Soviet authorities simply rounded up people in the cities and sent them into
the countryside, as an Italian diplomat reported: "The mobilization
of the urban forces has assumed enormous proportions. . . . This week,
at least 20,000 people were sent to the countryside. . . . The day before
yesterday, they surrounded the market, seized all able persons, men,
women, and adolescents, transported them to the station under GPU
guard, and shipped them to the fields."[19]

Miron Dolot, his last remaining brother, and their mother had
survived the great famine. "By the beginning of May," Dolot wrote,
"our village had become a desolate place, horror lurking in every
house and in every backyard. We felt forsaken by the entire world.
The main road which had been the artery of traffic and the center
of village life was empty and overgrown with weeds and grass.
Humans and animals were rarely seen on it. Many houses stood
dilapidated and empty, their windows and doorways gaping. The
owners were dead, deported to the north, or gone from the village in
search of food."[20]

They were facing a bleak future, but they were alive.

Pogrom of the Intellect

....

HE STOOD THERE, IN THE MIDDLE OF THE CROWD, AND WATCHED. He watched the faces in the flicker of the torches and the bonfire. The scene on the square on this tenth of May was part auto-da-fé, part political theater, and part witches' Sabbath, as one young man after another advanced to the burning embers and intoned fervently: "Against the soul-destroying overestimation of our impulses, for the nobility of the human soul! I consign to the flames the writings of Sigmund Freud"; "Against literary betrayal of the soldiers of the World War, for education of the people in the spirit of truth! I consign to the flames the writings of Erich Maria Remarque"; "Against impudence and arrogance, for respect and reverence towards the immortal German spirit of the Volk! Devour, flames, the writings of Tucholsky and Ossietzky!"

Earlier, another young man in the black uniform of Hitler's Sturmabteilung, a student perhaps, had been heard shouting: "Against

The Action Against the Un-German Spirit took place all over Germany.

decadence and moral decline! For breeding and morality in the family and the state! I consign to the flames the writings of Heinrich Mann, Ernst Glaeser and Erich Kästner."

Kästner himself, wedged in among the other onlookers, knew that it was dangerous for him to stand there and witness the symbolic destruction of his works. At any moment the gaping crowd might turn into an angry mob. Suddenly a woman's voice shouted, "But that's Kästner there!" It was time to get away, and quickly. He disappeared into the darkness, leaving the last stage of the Nazis' bonfire of German culture to continue without his grieving observation. "I saw our books flying into the roaring flames and heard the sentimental tirades of that slick little liar [Goebbels]. Funereal weather hung over the city. . . . It was revolting," the writer would recall after the war.[1]

Though Joseph Goebbels, now minister of propaganda in Hitler's new government, had indeed given a speech to mark the occasion of Germany's great book burning, the event had not been his idea, and initially he had even been hostile toward it. Only after the momentum for such an event had become too great to be ignored had he taken over its stage management. Goebbels distrusted grassroots initiatives, which had a tendency to make him feel out of touch and out of control; this particular initiative had landed on his desk already well advanced. It had surprised him, as he had not thought the Germans ready for such a spectacular event. What if the citizens of the self-proclaimed *Land der Dichter und Denker* (country of poets and thinkers), with their famous love for the classics and their exalted view of literature, simply failed to turn up?

He needn't have worried. The initiators of what was labeled the "Action Against the Un-German Spirit" were Nazi students, apparently as eager to impress their superiors as they were to change the world, and they left nothing to chance. Directly after Hitler's appointment as the Reich's chancellor on January 30, 1933, they set all the levers in swift motion.

Led by Hans Karl Leistritz, a student of law and the son of a school principal, the student organization set about planning a month-long campaign against the works of those writers, scientists, and teachers they deemed insufficiently "German" to contribute to the glorious future of the Third Reich. Leistritz himself wrote in a letter to local organizations: "The Jewish spirit, as it reveals itself in the worldwide campaign of hatred . . . and which has already had its effect on German literature, must be eliminated."[2] To publicize their position further, the students presented themselves as being inspired by the sixteenth-century Protestant reformer Martin Luther; they drew up a list of "theses against the un-German spirit," printed it in blood-red Gothic letters, and on April 12, 1933, plastered it to thousands of advertising spaces in cities and universities throughout the country. In arrogant, pseudo-philosophical prose, the young authors claimed:

> The German people are responsible for ensuring that its language and its writings are a pure and unadulterated expression of its peoplehood. . . . Jews can only think in a Jewish way. If a Jew says he is writing German, he is lying. A German who writes in German, but thinks in an un-German way, is a traitor. . . . Jewish works are to be published in Hebrew. . . . Gothic script is to be available only to Germans. The un-German spirit will be eliminated from all universities. . . . We demand from German students the will and the ability to overcome Jewish intellectualism and the related signs of decay now visible in German intellectual life.[3]

The declaration met with angry protests, often in the form of readers' letters to newspapers, from Jews and non-Jews alike. Parodies of it were printed, and refutations published. A British parliamentarian and medical doctor, Dr. M. C. Well, who happened to be in Berlin at the time, addressed an open letter to the Deutsche Studentenschaft, the German student union, pointing out that regarding their document, "whose [red] printers' ink had blushed with shame," he and his medical colleagues were uncertain which diagnosis would be appropriate for the authors, but that in any case all the illnesses they were considering necessitated immediate action: "Is it Lues cerebrospinalis [syphilis] ... ? I would recommend that the gentlemen concerned be examined in a mental asylum according to a blood test developed by a Jewish German by the name of Wasserman, though it is not published in Hebrew, and further that they be treated by means of the medicine Salvarsan, developed, though not in Hebrew, by the Jewish German Paul Ehrlich. Or is it a brain tumor? This would be the domain of the Jewish German Nobel Prize winner Warburg."[4]

But the harsh reactions appeared only to strengthen the determination of the student leaders. Taking as their base the Nationalsozialistischer Deutscher Studentenbund, the country's largest student organization, Leistritz and his helpers sent out circulars to all universities with a list of "forbidden" authors, which the students had drawn up themselves. They launched a full media campaign, including press releases, articles in newspapers, and radio programs. The response from other universities was more than encouraging.

On May 10, bonfires were prepared on the squares of some seventy cities, including all those with major universities. In Berlin, the city's fire brigade thoughtfully supplied gasoline. Tens of thousands of books had been collected from university and city libraries, as well as from private homes: the bonfire on Berlin's great avenue, Unter den Linden, was estimated to have been fueled by more than twenty thousand volumes. One newspaper in the university town of Göttingen had gone so far as to demand from its readers that they inspect and purge the libraries of their acquaintances, as well as their own. As darkness began to fall, members of the SA and uniformed young men of the student fraternities and other Nazi associations began to make their way to the designated places of burning in a torchlit procession, singing fraternity songs and assorted battle hymns as they marched to the execution by fire of everything they regarded as un-German.

This youthful vanguard was joined by thousands of onlookers; live reporting by the main radio stations meant that no "true German" need miss the spectacle. Newspapers accompanied the event with a flood of articles praising the resolution of German youth against the twin menaces of Judaism and communism, and encouraging the growth of a healthy, authentic art out of the deepest soul of the *Volk*.

At half past ten, the pyres were lit; flames licked the darkness of the night sky as uniformed students brought cartload after cartload of books and hurled them into the flames. In many cities, the event took on the character of a street party, complete with music and sausage sellers. Only in the ancient university town of Freiburg was the book burning canceled, on account of heavy rain.

Seven of Germany's ten bestselling authors were among those whose work went up in flames; they were consequently banned from publishing in Germany. Eventually, more than twelve thousand titles by some six hundred writers were to be banned. The authors included Thomas and Heinrich Mann, Sigmund Freud, the historian Emil Ludwig, the iconic theater critic Alfred Kerr, journalist Kurt Tucholsky, who was already in exile in Sweden, and Carl von Ossietzky, former publisher of the leftist magazine *Weltbühne* (World Stage), who was currently imprisoned in a concentration camp. Eventually, hardly an intellectual or artist of rank escaped this perverse distinction: communist playwright and poet Bertolt Brecht, playwright and Nobel Prize–winning pacifist Bertha von Suttner, and major Jewish writers including Alfred Döblin, Lion Feuchtwanger, Egon Erwin Kisch, Arthur Schnitzler, Franz Werfel, and Stefan Zweig all fell into disgrace as "un-German."

It was not only German-language authors whose names appeared on the list. The American adventure writer Jack London shared this honor with Russian Bolshevik Maxim Gorky and French pacifist Romain Rolland; Winston Churchill was listed together with John Dos Passos and Ernest Hemingway. Even the dead were represented: Karl Marx was one of the forbidden authors, as was the Jewish poet Heinrich Heine, who a hundred years earlier had prophetically declared, "A country that burns books will eventually also burn people."

The students' initiative had profound consequences for the listed authors. For many of them, it meant professional ruin. Unable to publish and so to earn an income from their work, most were forced to leave Germany, if indeed they had not done so already. Some would never recover from the blow. Kurt Tucholsky would die in exile the same year, 1933, from an overdose of sleeping pills. Novelist Heinrich Mann, unable to adapt to exile in California, fell victim to crippling depression; he would publish only a handful of new works. The Austrian Jewish Stefan Zweig, one of the most successful authors of his day, was equally unable to adapt to life in Brazil; he also chose to end his own life, and his young wife, Lotte, committed suicide soon afterward.

Some exiles thrived, particularly those already famous as literary stars, such as Thomas Mann, Brecht, Feuchtwanger, and Werfel. But for those starting out in their careers, a new country and, more especially, a new language meant many difficult years. One of the young hopefuls was twenty-six-year-old Hans Keilson, a medical student from northern Germany who had been earning money on the side as a jazz trumpeter; his first novel, *Das Leben Geht Weiter (Life Goes On)*, had recently been accepted by the prestigious S. Fischer publishing house. It was published in spring 1933, but the author had little opportunity to enjoy the fact. Persecuted as a Jew, as a "subversive" writer, and as a jazz musician, he was forced to leave Berlin on the urgent advice of his publisher, who told him simply, "*Machen Sie, dass Sie rauskommen*—get out of here." Keilson escaped to the Netherlands, where he lived under an assumed identity, eventually joining the Dutch resistance movement. After the war, Keilson would establish an outstanding reputation as a psychiatrist, treating Jewish children who had returned from the Nazi camps. He would receive no literary recognition, however, until decades later.

A Society in Lock Step

HUNDREDS OF CAREERS and private lives were broken or at least derailed in similar ways, and by no means only those of writers. In an ever-widening cultural campaign, the Nazis targeted prominent individuals in all arts and sciences and other socially influential fields, their goal nothing less than a total *Gleichschaltung* (compulsory coordination) of all German culture, high and low, including many aspects of ordinary daily life.

In Berlin, one institution had already felt the brunt of "healthy German feeling" four days before the book burning of May 10. Magnus Hirschfeld's Institute for Sexual Research was a trailblazer in sociology and in the investigation of sexual identities; it represented the scientific vanguard of the traditionally tolerant and permissive atmosphere in the capital city. Hirschfeld himself had taken the risk of openly declaring his homosexuality. He owned a library of some twenty thousand volumes on all aspects of sexuality, as well as a vast collection of photographs, forty thousand interviews and letters, and a large array of sexual ephemera, such as contraceptive devices, sex toys, and fetish objects. With forty full-time employees conducting research and offering advice, his institute had become a place of pilgrimage for medical and social scientists, and for homosexuals.

On May 6, 1933, some one hundred students of the Hochschule für Leibesübungen (Academy for Physical Education) assembled in military formation in front of the villa housing Hirschfeld's collections. Accompanied by appropriately martial music, they stormed the building. Breaking down doors and pushing aside everything and everyone in their path, they destroyed documents, smashed furniture, pictures, and other items in the collection, and stole whatever remained that they deemed "morally suspect."

Demanding to see Hirschfeld, the young Nazi activists were informed that he was abroad on a speaking tour, and suffering from malaria. They seemed almost pleased at the news, laughing that the illness might well kill him without help from them, so they would not have to trouble themselves with hanging him or beating him to death. In lieu of the original, they took a bronze bust of the founder and later used it to adorn the book burning on the public square in front of the opera house. Later on the same afternoon, SA men staged another raid, removing a further two truckloads of material from the institute. Hirschfeld himself recovered from the malaria, but he never returned to Germany. He tried to establish a new headquarters for the institute, first in Paris and then in Nice, where he died two years later of a heart attack.

Existential Choices

IN APRIL 1933 a new Law for the Reestablishment of the Status of Civil Servants facilitated the elimination of Jewish, leftist, and otherwise suspect state employees from ministries, city halls, courts of law, and university teaching and research posts. In the famous university of Göttingen, which housed one of the finest scientific faculties in the country, two-thirds of the physicists and mathematicians either were sacked or resigned, among them the Jewish physicists Max Born and James Franck, the latter a Nobel Prize winner who had laid the foundations for Göttingen's international reputation in his field. The two men went abroad, Born to Cambridge and his friend and colleague Franck to Baltimore and then Chicago, where he would later participate in the Manhattan Project to produce the first atomic bomb.

Though, like the prominent writers, eminent scientists such as Franck found help and new appointments with relative ease, junior colleagues faced greater difficulties. At Berlin University, biologist Wilhelm Feldberg was working in his laboratory at the Institute of Physiology when he was called into the office of the director, who gave him a copy of the new law to read, saying, "You're a Jew. You have to be out of here by midday." Feldberg, until then a valued faculty member, protested that he had only just begun a new series of experiments. "Well then," replied his superior, "you'll have to leave by midnight."[5] At thirty-two, Feldberg was at the beginning of his career; he began the difficult negotiations for legal emigration and the search for a job abroad.

From Britain, Feldberg and several thousands of other scientists were helped by Sir William Beveridge's Academic Assistance Council, founded by famous researchers such as physicist and chemist Sir Ernest Rutherford and physiologist J. S. Haldane as an answer to Hitler's "pogrom of the intellect." Among those the organization supplied with money, hope, and jobs were art historians Ernest Gombrich and Nikolaus Pevsner, chemist Max Perutz, and philosopher Karl Popper. In October 1933, Beveridge organized a support rally in London's vast Albert Hall, and the venue was sold out. More than five thousand people came to hear Albert Einstein and other eminent exiles speak in defense of academic liberty and intellectual and cultural freedom.

While the *Gleichschaltung* of all cultural and intellectual life disrupted the lives and careers of some of Germany's most talented writers and scientists, it also created opportunities for others. The students who had so enthusiastically organized and participated in the book burning were next in line to fill many of the newly created academic vacancies, thus turning the sciences as well as the humanities into a purely German concern. There were even attempts to lay the theoretical groundwork for an ideologically pure German physics and mathematics that could function without the contributions of Jewish scientists. From his exile in Britain, Albert Einstein remarked to the sculptor Jacob Epstein that a hundred German professors had recently condemned his general and special theories of relativity, adding, "Were I wrong, one professor would have been enough."

But not all who were threatened left Nazi Germany, nor did all of those who had the choice to leave. At seventy-four years of age, the great theoretical physicist Max Planck felt that he was simply too old to start life anew elsewhere; he stayed in Berlin, encouraging other scientists to do the same. Planck's loyalty was to the now superseded ideal of a Prussian polity, similar to that in which he had lived and worked for most of his career. Werner Heisenberg, preeminent among the younger generation of German theoretical physicists, also opted to continue his career under the Nazis. It is still a matter of debate whether Heisenberg later helped or hindered the government in Berlin in its desire to procure an atomic bomb, but his decision to remain caused a deep rift with many of his colleagues, most notably his former mentor, the Dane Niels Bohr.

Intellectuals and scientists who, like Heisenberg, opted to remain in Nazi Germany often went into what the writer Erich Kästner called "internal exile," a kind of Siberia of the soul. Kästner was no longer allowed to publish; his decision to stay owed much to the wishes of his mother, with whom the lifelong bachelor had a close connection. Kästner did manage to work under pseudonyms; several of his film scripts were to bring him into closer contact with the regime than he would later care to admit. But his literary reputation was never to recover from this period of almost total obscurity, and despite the fact that his greatest ambition, and his highest reputation, was for his adult fiction, he became known as the author of *Emil and the Detectives* and other books for children—books so popular that even the Nazis exempted them from their blacklists.

A more complex case is that of the great composer and conductor Richard Strauss. Sixty-nine years old when Hitler came to power, he almost immediately offered his services to the regime, making it known that he would be pleased to accept an appointment as president of the newly founded Reichsmusikkammer, the compulsory professional body to which all musicians were obliged to belong in the course of the general *Gleichschaltung* of cultural life. Strauss was certainly not a committed Nazi. He despised the brownshirts and their plebeian tastes in music; fin-de-siècle cosmopolitan that he was, he had no sympathy with Nazi ideology. Focused on his art, Strauss had little interest in politics and looked down on simplistic ideas of Aryan purity. His two favorite librettists, Hugo von Hofmannsthal and Stefan Zweig, were of Jewish or partly Jewish descent (Hofmannsthal had a Jewish grandfather), as were many of his friends and his daughter-in-law.

But for the Nazis, the appointment of Germany's most famous composer, with his glittering international reputation, was a great publicity coup. Classical music—traditionally one of the most effective assimilation vehicles for the rising Jewish bourgeoisie since the days of Felix Mendelssohn—had a particularly strong Jewish presence, and the exodus of orchestral musicians, teachers, and soloists, not to mention "decadent" atonal composers and jazz musicians, had left gaping holes in German musical life. This created career opportunities for ambitious young "Aryan" musicians such as the young conductor Herbert von Karajan, then still musical director at the municipal theater in Ulm. He wasted no time enlisting in the National

Socialist Party in 1933, a tactical move that quickly turned to his advantage: two years later, Karajan became the youngest musical director of a major orchestra in Germany.

The Nazi regime wanted stars to demonstrate to the world that German music was still thriving after the massive bloodletting it had sustained. It needed to show that it remained where it belonged, where Beethoven and Wagner had placed it: at the summit of civilization. The stars, however, refused to come. Some were Jewish, some were politically on the left, and some, such as conductor Fritz Busch, were simply disgusted with the system; all refused to perform in Hitler's Reich. German music could nonetheless boast the great Berlin Philharmonic orchestra, still under its legendary (and arguably politically naive) conductor, Wilhelm Furtwängler, and also the tacit support of the grand master of late Romanticism, composer Richard Strauss.

Why did Strauss agree to enter into a pact with a power he knew to be diabolical? It may be that he regarded it as necessary to secure the large audiences, frequent programming at the best theaters, and collaborations with the finest orchestras, singers, and conductors, and so on that his works had long enjoyed. The reason he himself lobbied for the position of president of the newly created Reichsmusikkammer was that he wanted to protect German music, and its musicians, many of them Jewish, against the worst of the barbarism. It is likely that these reasons were conflated and that Strauss was happy to accept the agreeable results for his own music that his public service brought in its train.

Strauss's political career in Nazi Germany was as short-lived as it was ill-conceived. In 1935, exasperated by the "Aryan" librettists foisted upon him by the Nazi authorities, he wrote an impassioned letter to Stefan Zweig, by then already in exile. Such was the composer's frustration that he expressed his feelings without any political or ideological subterfuge: "Do you seriously think that Mozart composed consciously 'Aryan' music?" he wrote. "For me there are only two categories of people; those who have talent and those who don't, and for me the *Volk* exists only from the moment when it becomes a public. Whether it consists of Chinese, Upper Bavarians, New Zealanders or Berliners is all the same to me, as long as they have paid the full price for their tickets." He was keeping his position "to do good and to prevent worse, simply out of an artistic sense of duty."[6]

The letter was intercepted by the Gestapo. Goebbels forced Strauss to resign as president of the Reichsmusikkammer almost immediately, "for health reasons." But instead of quietly retiring to his splendid Bavarian country house, Strauss appealed to Hitler himself: "Trusting in your high sense of justice, I most humbly request, my Führer, that you receive me for a personal word." Hitler did not think it necessary to reply.

If the old composer had donned a Nazi uniform in the service of art, the forty-nine-year-old philosopher Martin Heidegger was more genuinely engaged with National Socialist ideology. It is impossible to do justice to his notoriously complex and often obscure thought in a few sentences, but one important aspect of Heidegger's thought is the desire to shed the *Uneigentlichkeit* or inauthenticity of the modern world into which we are thrown without our choice, and to reach a realm of authentic being and selfhood.

Heidegger's most important philosophical inspirations were pre-Socratic philosophy, early Christianity, and the nineteenth-century poet Friedrich Hölderlin—nothing the theoreticians of National Socialism could have identified with. At the same time, the philosopher believed that fascism contained elements of an answer to one of his most pressing questions. His intellectual search for authenticity, often conducted in a secluded mountain hut, appeared to be mirrored in the Nazis' demand for a return to a genuine peoplehood, a *Volk* of blood and soil, not manipulated by the soulless mechanisms of modernity.

Unquestionably the philosopher's infatuation with the black-shirted men of action was intensified by the fact that his partisanship—he joined the Nazi Party in 1933—did no harm to his career. In that same year, he became chancellor of Freiburg University, where he already held a professorship. In his inaugural speech, he spoke of "the march that our people have started toward their future history" and "the power of the deepest conservation of the forces of soil and blood."[7]

One month later, in June 1933, Heidegger declared before a student organization that German research must not surrender to liberal cosmopolitanism. On the contrary: "We must fight against this in the spirit of National Socialism, which must not be suffocated by humanizing, Christian ideas." In the new university, studying would once again become "a daring act, no refuge for cowards. Those who do not prevail in the fight remain on the ground . . . because the fight . . . will be long. It will be fought with the forces of the new Reich, which Chancellor Hitler will bring into existence. A hard generation will fight this fight."[8]

Heidegger wanted nothing less than to reorganize the German university system as a series of training grounds for the future leaders

of a dominant people strictly obedient to its own great *Führer*. But
relations with the Party leadership soon soured. They had been looking for a figurehead, not a meddling reformist with too many ideas
and an infuriating tendency to express his thoughts in impenetrable
neologisms and endless subordinate clauses. Heidegger's enthusiasm
was philosophical, but he was no political zealot. Appointed university chancellor just two days before the nationwide book burning
of May 10, he forbade any event of this kind to take place at his
university. In this he was one of the few university leaders to do
so, but his decision was in any case without consequences, as on the
day in question it was raining heavily. Though opposed to book
burning, the philosopher-chancellor was content to support the regime
otherwise, blocking the appointment of scholars he deemed ideologically unreliable.

After only one year, Heidegger resigned and went back to his
mountain hut. He himself would later claim to be embarrassed by
the whole episode, that he had had a temporary lapse of judgment,
and that he would henceforth adopt a position of "intellectual resistance." But he was seen wearing a swastika lapel pin during a visit to
Italy, and was heard expounding on the deeper truth of National
Socialism even shortly before the outbreak of the war. In obtuse
philosophical language, he vacillated, making oracular statements
that could be interpreted as sympathetic to or critical of Germany's
new masters.

Heidegger's moral cowardice deeply disappointed one of his most
gifted students and a former lover, Hannah Arendt. Having corresponded with her erstwhile teacher even after their relationship had
ended, she broke contact with him completely in 1933, devoting herself to helping refugees who were Jewish like herself. Arendt was
arrested by the Gestapo and questioned for several days. It is not
certain whether Heidegger knew about her arrest; in any case he did
not intervene on her behalf at any point as she was preparing to
emigrate, first to Paris and then to Palestine.

Dr. Croce Goes Home

THE PHILOSOPHER HEIDEGGER was only one of scores of intellectuals
who initially felt that fascism might be an answer to the seemingly
intractable problems of a time that lacked strong political leadership,
had no credible values and perspectives, and was struggling economically. The erosion of values and the apparent lack of an alternative to the Manichaean struggle between communism and fascism

were preoccupations for a great many intellectuals at this time. Another philosopher living in a fascist country, who also was initially hopeful that a strong leader might change things for the better and chose not to emigrate even when the situation became desperate, the Italian Benedetto Croce, reached a very different conclusion from Heidegger.

Croce, who was sixty-seven in 1933, was a singular figure in several ways. As a seventeen-year-old he had lost his parents and only sister when an earthquake destroyed the family home; Croce himself had been trapped in the rubble for hours. Perhaps this severing of strong ties had created an early sense of autonomy, for he proceeded to cut other affiliations, most significantly with the Catholic Church. Independently wealthy, he did not seek a university career, preferring to pursue philosophical projects at his home in Naples.

Croce's strong sense of civic duty had compelled him to abandon his philosophical work temporarily to go into politics. As a senator in Rome, he had made himself unpopular with his opposition to Italy's participation in the First World War, and afterward, as minister for education from 1920 to 1921, he had attempted to reform the country's ramshackle and church-dominated education system. During the chaos of the postwar years, he had begun to regard Mussolini's Fascists as the only force capable of restoring a measure of order to the country, though Croce stated clearly at the outset that Fascism "cannot and must not be anything but a passing phase in the restoration of a strictly liberal system."[9]

The turning point for Croce's flirtation with Fascism had come in 1924, with the murder of the socialist deputy Giacomo Matteotti. After making several courageous speeches in the Chamber of Deputies protesting the rise of Fascist power, Matteotti had been abducted and stabbed multiple times with a carpenter's file. His assassins, five well-known Fascists, received light sentences and were soon pardoned by the pliant king, Vittorio Emanuele III. Croce, still a liberal senator, was disgusted; he turned his back on his former allies, including his close friend Giovanni Gentile, a philosopher with whom he had worked in the past and who had thrown in his lot with Mussolini. Croce returned to Naples, refusing any further involvement in politics.

When in 1925 Gentile published a "Manifesto of Fascist Intellectuals," which was signed by, among others, writer and politician Gabriele D'Annunzio, writer and diplomat Curzio Malaparte, futurist movement founder Filippo Tommaso Marinetti, and the great Sicilian dramatist Luigi Pirandello, Croce drafted a countermanifesto repudiating Fascism in the name of humanity: "We cannot sympathize with this chaotic and elusive 'religion' and abandon our old faith: the faith that for two centuries and a half has been the soul of Italy and which rose again from modern Italy; the faith that is made up out of a love of truth, a longing for justice, a generous human and civic sense, a zeal for intellectual and moral education and a commitment to freedom, the strength and guarantor of all progress."[10]

Croce, by now openly condemning Fascism as a "moral malady," was too famous to be assassinated, but the state had other means of silencing him. During the more than twenty years that Mussolini was in power, Croce's books were not published, nor was his name mentioned in academic or general publications. His Naples home, a meeting place for dissident intellectuals from all over the country, was "searched" by uniformed Fascists, who were careful to create a maximum of chaos and destruction in his library. But the philosopher refused to be intimidated. When Il Duce embarked on his ill-begotten and bloody invasion of Abyssinia, the senator-for-life at once returned his sign of office, the senatorial medal.

It is true, of course, that Italy was not Germany, where from the beginning the regime was highly organized and much more bloodthirsty. Opposition to the Nazi regime was much more tightly circumscribed; no public figure in Germany could have published a signed manifesto against Fascism and survived. Short of absolute heroism, a refusal to participate remained the only moral alternative for those who did not wish to emigrate. Croce's stance, however, did demonstrate that it was possible to maintain intellectual integrity.

Hitler and Hollywood

EVEN BEYOND GERMANY, the reach of Nazi cultural influence was unexpectedly wide. As historian Ben Urwand has documented in *The Collaboration* (2013), it extended into and even partly controlled the production of and also the scripts for many Hollywood movies.

The exile stories of great German-speaking film directors and actors such as Billy Wilder, Erich von Stroheim, Marlene Dietrich, Hedy Lamarr, Paul Henreid, Ernst Lubitsch, and Fritz Lang are well known, as is the Führer's famous fondness for light fare from across the Atlantic. Apparently he enjoyed nothing more than to relax from his superhuman historic task by spending an evening watching Laurel and Hardy, Mickey Mouse, or Greta Garbo—though he is known to have drawn the line at Tarzan, Hollywood's own version of a primitive superman.

The extent of the cooperation between the great studios and the government in Berlin before the Second World War, however, has long been underestimated. Unwilling to lose the lucrative German market, which had been opening up to Hollywood productions after the commercial disaster of Lang's *Metropolis*, the studio bosses decided to pay the Reich's vice consul in Los Angeles, Georg Gyssling, a particular courtesy. He was invited to preview their releases in private and to suggest cuts and alterations as he saw fit, effectively giving the Nazi government a veto over what emerged from Hollywood's burgeoning film industry.

Unsurprisingly, the Berlin propagandists were highly pleased with films such as *Gabriel over the White House* (1933), *Mutiny on the Bounty*, and *The Lives of a Bengal Lancer* (both 1935), all of which demonstrated the need for a strong leader, in a setting of swashbuckling and humor that only Hollywood could produce. Films critical of the Nazis, such as *The Mad Dog of Europe*, a 1933 project by Herman Mankiewicz, or *It Can't Happen Here*, a screenplay by Sidney Howard following a Sinclair Lewis novel, were quietly scuppered by Gyssling and the studio executives. In the latter case, it was Will Hays of the Hays office, Hollywood's own watchdog for decency and good taste, who notified Louis B. Mayer, boss of the MGM studio and himself Jewish, that the film might displease "certain foreign governments." Mayer took the hint. The film was not produced.

Two movies in particular framed the transatlantic collaboration, one of them even predating the Nazi ascent to power in Germany. *All Quiet on the Western Front* had been produced in Hollywood in 1930 and had experienced a tumultuous release in Germany. In response to this, the pioneering filmmaker Carl Laemmle Sr., a German émigré himself and also Jewish, agreed to make significant cuts in the work, in order to facilitate a potentially lucrative rerelease in his former home country.

In a blatant pandering to Nazi propaganda, in 1934 20th Century Fox made *The House of Rothschild*, depicting the head of the famous family as a money-grubbing, power-hungry caricature who might have stepped straight out of the classic anti-Semitic forgery *The Protocols of the Elders of Zion*. The production was so effective that the Nazis would use it as direct inspiration for their notorious propaganda movie *The Eternal Jew* (1940). But the original Hollywood film so alarmed officials of the American Jewish Anti-Defamation League that they persuaded studio executives to refrain in the future from including obviously Jewish characters in their films. The unintended result was that for the remainder of the 1930s, the persecution of Jews and their desperate plight in Europe were to remain almost completely absent from Hollywood films—not only those screened in Germany but also those seen all over the world, from Idaho to Shanghai.

Fatal Poetry

CULTURAL PROPAGANDA and cultural oppression were equally a feature of the other great totalitarian power of the time: the USSR. Following the great creative surge of the 1920s overseen by Anatoly Lunacharsky, the first Soviet people's commissar for enlightenment, Stalin's administration had put an end to almost all artistic experimentation and freedom, ruthlessly streamlining cultural production in a manner very similar to that of the Nazi *Gleichschaltung*. "The socialist proletariat must promote the principle of Party literature," Lenin had demanded as far back as 1905. With the energy of constructivism, supremacism, and other modernist artistic movements proving too great to control, in 1929 the Soviet hierarchy asserted its authority. Henceforth, creative freedom would follow the definition of novelist Mikhail Sholokhov, winner of the Stalin Prize and later Nobel laureate. "I write at the bidding of my heart," said Sholokhov, "and my heart belongs to the Party."[11]

Most writers who refused to toe the new Party line of socialist realism, rejecting its endless panegyrics of proletarian heroism and paeans to Comrade First Secretary Stalin, the Driver of the Locomotive of History, were very quickly silenced. The futurist poet and playwright Vladimir Mayakovsky, who was once the poster child of revolutionary art but who later despaired of the increasing censorship and ever more labyrinthine cultural bureaucracy, had shot himself in 1930. By the early 1930s, those resistant to the regime, such as the prose writer Isaac Babel and the poet Anna Akhmatova, found themselves effectively unable to publish; Babel would later be executed as a supposed spy.

The Kiev novelist and playwright Mikhail Bulgakov chose to work in secret on his great novel, *The Master and Margarita*, at the same time producing politically acceptable pieces for the stage. Boris Pasternak was forced to make radical changes to his poetry and to his prose style, in order to escape the perilous label of "bourgeois reactionary." Arrests, interrogations, and arbitrary sentences could strike anyone at any moment. Maxim Gorky alone possessed such iconic status as a writer and as a political figure that Stalin did not touch him—at least not openly. Always critical of the regime, and a frequent defender of other writers, Gorky died in unclear circumstances in 1936; it is thought he may have been murdered on Stalin's orders.

Mug shot: The poet Osip Mandelstam photographed by the NKVD.

One recklessly brave writer who did try to express his outrage in his art was to pay for his courage with his life. Toward the end of 1933, the forty-two-year-old poet Osip Mandelstam wrote a short work entitled, in a reference to Stalin's origins in the Caucasus Mountains of Georgia, "The Kremlin Highlander." In the poem, later to become famous as "The Stalin Epigram," Mandelstam describes his disgust for the great "Engineer of Human Souls":

Ten fat maggots his fingers,
his words drop like weights

his moustache is laughing with the antennae of cock-
roaches
the shaft of his boots glistens majestically

a thin-necked brood of bosses surrounds him
he toys with servile half-men

they whistle, meow and wail
he alone beats time with a hammer

Decrees are issued like horseshoes
one in the groin, one to the forehead, the eye—the grave

Executions taste like raspberries on his tongue
and his Ossetian chest swells with satisfaction.[12]

Mandelstam read this poem only to close and like-minded friends such as Boris Pasternak. But Pasternak, who immediately declared that he had heard nothing and that indeed Mandelstam had recited nothing, warned nonetheless that in Stalin's Russia even the tree branches had ears. Pasternak was right. Mandelstam was arrested on a warrant signed by the chief of the NKVD, Genrikh Yagoda, and interrogated. Pasternak tried to intervene on Mandelstam's behalf, appealing to Nikolai Bukharin, editor of the prestigious daily *Izvestia* and one of the few highly placed functionaries thought to be sympathetic to intellectual dissent.

Pasternak hoped that Bukharin might raise the issue at the highest level. A few days later, the telephone rang at his apartment and a voice informed him that "Comrade Stalin wants to talk to you." After a short pause, another voice began, and the poet realized that he was indeed speaking to Stalin, who went on to ask him what was being said about him and Mandelstam in literary circles. Beside himself with fear, Pasternak tried to distance himself from his friend and colleague, saying that as far as he was aware there were no longer any literary circles in Russia, that Mandelstam's views of poetry were very different from his, and that nobody was saying anything at all about the hostile poem. Stalin listened in complete silence. When Pasternak staggered to a halt Stalin said simply: "I see. You're not able to stick up for a comrade," and with that the dictator hung up.[13]

Despite Pasternak's anxious claim, there were some literary circles still left in the capital, and Mandelstam's arrest was followed by a swift crackdown on their members. The poet himself was exiled, together with his wife, to the provincial city of Cherdyn in the northern Urals; this fate was widely considered to be an extraordinary stroke of good luck, explicable only by leniency on Stalin's part. Others did not fare so well. His trusted friend Anna Akhmatova had also been present at the reading of "The Kremlin Highlander." Akhmatova's first husband had been executed by the Bolsheviks in 1921; now her common-law husband, the art historian Nikolay Punin, and her twenty-one-year-old son Lev were also arrested and accused of counterrevolutionary activities. They were both released eventually, only to be rearrested later; though Lev was to survive, Punin would die in the gulag.

To channel and steer the course of literature in the USSR, in 1932 the Soviet authorities had created their own equivalent of the Reichsschrifttumskammer (National Bureau of Literature), the Sojus Pissatelei SSSR, or Soviet Writers' Union. It was presided over by Maxim Gorky. In the swelteringly hot August of 1934, the organization hosted a writers' congress, to which it also invited foreign authors known for their communist sympathies, including the German expressionist poet Johannes Becher and French men of letters such as André Malraux, Paul Nizan, and Louis Aragon. Another invitee, Klaus Mann, wrote enthusiastically: "The writers' congress demonstrates one thing: the vital connection existing here between the literary producer and his clients, the readers, between writer and public, between literature and the people. . . . The great deed of a new social order . . . creates a mood of huge optimism among the Russian writers."[14]

In hindsight, Mann's naiveté appears grating, but others were similarly enthusiastic, and their attitude must also be contextualized by taking into account the German "pogrom of the intellect" one year earlier. The Soviet authorities were careful not to restrict the freedom of expression of their foreign guests, and many writers who had had to flee their homes and abandon their livelihoods believed they had found a literary paradise, as was apparent in the address given by the German socialist realist writer Willi Bredel, formerly president of the Akademie der Künste (Academy of Arts) in Berlin, who only months before had managed to escape from a German concentration camp and fled to Moscow: "I bring you warm, fraternal greetings from the anti-Fascists in the concentration camps and the prisons of Germany. . . . We will not rest until Fascism lies on the ground smashed, and Germany belongs to the working people; until the German worker, heir to classical philosophy and literature, makes Germany once again a great nation of science and the arts, a people of poets and thinkers."[15]

Thank You, Jeeves

*I was a shade perturbed. Nothing to signify, really, but still just a
spot concerned. As I sat in the old flat, idly touching the strings
of my banjolele, an instrument to which I had become greatly
addicted of late, you couldn't have said that the brow was actually
furrowed, and yet, on the other hand, you couldn't have stated
absolutely that it wasn't. Perhaps the word "pensive" about covers
it. It seemed to me that a situation fraught with embarrassing
potentialities had arisen.*

"Jeeves," I said, "do you know what?"

"No, sir."

P. G. Wodehouse, *Thank You, Jeeves*, 1934

....

BERTIE WOOSTER WAS, ONCE AGAIN, IN A SPOT OF BOTHER. THIS WAS
nothing particularly remarkable for an affable upper-class twit who
was liable to get himself in a bit of a squeeze, a natural consequence
of drinking too much and thinking too little. But fortunately for him
and the rest of humanity, there was Jeeves, his superhuman butler,
always at hand with a discreet bit of advice, a crucial piece of information, and a concoction guaranteed to kill hangovers.

P. G. Wodehouse's *Thank You, Jeeves*, the first full-length Bertie
Wooster novel, was published in March 1934. Fittingly, the author
himself called his novels "musical comedies without music." The fictional eccentrics populating his novels had made him wealthy, so
wealthy indeed that the creator of quintessentially British characters
such as Bertie, his frightful aunts, his uncle Lord Elmsworth, and his
pal Gussie Fink-Nottle was now living in France in order to escape

double taxation in his birthplace, Britain, and in the United States, his primary residence during his adult years.

Perhaps it was this prolonged absence from Britain that made Wodehouse's books such perfect time capsules, for despite the fact that he continued writing into the 1970s, the social and emotional world of his fictional characters was anchored firmly in the 1920s. Wodehouse had spent his childhood at a series of English boarding schools, where he had been deposited by his father, a judge working abroad in the colonial service.

The lightness of the Bertie Wooster universe was the secret to the popularity of the stories and novels, which poured from Wodehouse's typewriter at a prodigious rate. It was a time hungry for musical comedies, with or without music. In mid-1930s Britain, there was little else to laugh about. In the midst of the Great Depression, life had not been so grim for many Britons since Victorian times.

A Different Reality

BRITAIN HAD FINANCED THE WAR by liquidating foreign investments, increasing taxes, and borrowing, with the result that the national debt increased twelvefold, to £8 billion ($634 billion in today's money). This in turn had forced the Conservative government under prime minister Stanley Baldwin to raise taxes yet again in order to service the debt. In 1929, the electorate had reacted by voting in a Labour government under Ramsay MacDonald.

Traditionally strongly export-oriented, the British economy had suffered enormously from the interruption to world trade brought on by the Great War, as well as from the destruction of some 40 percent of its merchant navy by German submarines and from the generally weak world market after 1918. Its heavy industries, such as coal and steel, and also much of its manufacturing sector, especially for cotton products, which before the war had clothed half the world, were largely operating with outdated methods and machinery. Indeed, those industries were themselves old-fashioned. Even before the war, Germany and the United States had overtaken Britain in newer industries such as chemicals, electrical machinery, and precision tools.

In many ways, the war had accelerated a crisis that had already been looming before 1914, with Britain relying on the captive markets of its empire to support industries that were increasingly less competitive on the world stage. But its reach was wide, and its position had still been strong. With the sluggish demand that followed the war, however, the economy had gradually foundered. By 1930, textile

Strikebreakers in Rhondda, Wales.

production, which formerly had represented almost half of all exports, was down by two-thirds; shipbuilding, traditionally the economic engine of the Tyne and Clyde region, had collapsed to 7 percent of its prewar level; coal production was down by 20 percent. Even the prestigious Cunard shipping line was not faring well: on December 10, 1931, a notice had been nailed to the factory gates of John Brown's shipyard, where the latest Cunard liner was being built, that read simply: "The services of all employees . . . will terminate at noon today," putting three thousand men out of work and affecting a further ten thousand engaged in subsidiary labor. To many workers, the former workshop of the world was beginning to look like a poorhouse.

Coal-mining towns were hit particularly badly. In Wales and in the north of England, the mines and the businesses that supplied them were practically the only local employers, and together they had sustained a proud and very distinctive working-class culture. Coal exports, which had amounted to 287 million tons in 1913, had plummeted to 40 million, a decline of 86 percent. Whole towns fell eerily silent, their skies no longer filled with black smoke; houses and faces were washed clean of the black grime that had covered everything— uncommonly clean, but destitute. Hundreds of thousands of miners were forced to work only three or four days a week, and the meager pay that previously had only just sufficed to keep body and soul together had dropped below subsistence level. In many areas of Britain, dockyards, mines, and factories were quiet, the equipment rusting away in a graveyard-like silence.

A Journey Through Decline

NO WONDER, THEN, that those who could afford it sought distraction. But another book published in 1934 showed this desperate Britain, so very different from Wodehouse's charming diversions. Throughout the previous year, the journalist and essayist J. B. Priestley had traveled through the country by bus, recording his impressions in his soon-to-be-famous *English Journey*. His explorations extended from the prosperous south to the stricken north, painting a vivid picture of the huge disparities between those areas that were comfortably well off and those others that might as well have been in a different country.

Priestley's very first encounter, on the bus from London, went to the heart of the predicament that was to accompany him throughout his journey: the effects of the 1929 Wall Street crash. One of his fellow travelers was "a thinnish fellow, somewhere in his forties, and he had a sharp nose, a neat moustache, rimless eyeglasses, and one of those enormous foreheads, roomy enough for an Einstein, that so often do not seem to mean anything." This man had recently started his own business, and it had failed:

> "Tea rooms." And he pointed at one that we were passing. "I tried it once. The wife was keen. In Kent. Good position too, on a main road. We'd everything very nice, very nice indeed. We called it the Chaucer Pilgrims—you know, Chaucer. Old style—Tudor, you know—black beams and everything. Couldn't make it pay. I wouldn't have bothered, but the wife was keen. If you ask me what let us down, I'd say it was the slump in America. It was on the road to Canterbury, you see—Chaucer Pilgrims—but we weren't getting the American tourists. I wouldn't touch a tea room again, not if you gave it to me."[1]

Despite this particular unhappy venture, the south of England was still green and pleasant, the author noted. In Southampton he found the pavement "crowded with neat smiling people, mostly women, and the mile of shops seemed to be doing a brisk trade. . . . At first I felt like a man who had walked into a fairy-tale of commerce. The people who jostled me . . . all seemed well-fed, decently clothed, cheerful, almost gay. The sun beamed upon them, and so did I."[2] From here he moved to Bath, "like a beautiful dowager giving a reception," and Bristol, "a fine city. They are right to be proud of it."

Winding his way up through the Cotswolds and its picturesque villages with their manor houses and layered historic richness, he was able to call England a prosperous place, even for those on the lower rungs of the social ladder: "The men of the land are not well paid, but they can live on their wages. People looked comfortable here. The children were in noticeably good shape."[3] He visited factories on the way and jotted down impressions and conversations; he saw cars and buses and typewriters being built and chocolate marshmallows being made in a proud land of manufacturing and commerce.

From Birmingham, Priestley's tour went to the Black Country and the "metallic Midlands," and here things began to change. "I descended into the vast smoky hollow and watched it turn itself into so many workshops, grimy rows of houses, pubs and picture theatres, yards filled with rusted metal, and great patches of waste ground."[4]

In the industrial towns of the Midlands, Priestley began to notice more evidence of poverty, an almost Dickensian world. He went to a desultory fairground to see someone billed as the world's ugliest woman, and in Liverpool he visited "the queerest parish in England," run by a priest who had made it his mission in life to look after the children of prostitutes working in the harbor, many of whom had come from Britain's colonies, or, if they were English, had already plied their trade abroad. The children had mostly been abandoned by their mothers. "Faces that had shone for a season in brothels in Victoria's time now peered and mumbled at us. Port Said and Bombay, Zanzibar and Hong Kong had called here. The babies told the tale plainly enough. They were of all shades, and Asia and Africa came peeping out of their eyes."[5]

Arriving in Blackpool outside the vacation season, the traveler saw a ghost town: "Its bravery was very tawdry, after being neglected only a week or two in that Atlantic weather. They had all gone, the fiddlers, fortune-tellers, pierrots, cheap-jacks, waiters and sellers of peppermint and pineapple rock. Somebody was demonstrating with voice, piano and saxophone the 'Season's Hot Successes.'"[6]

In Blackburn, a different, darker reality announced itself. The once booming cotton trade had all but come to a complete standstill. "You can have a mill rent-free up there, if you are prepared to work it," he noted. "Nobody has any money to buy, rent or run mills anymore. The entire district has been sliding towards a complete bankruptcy for years."

The tales of men driven out of business were innumerable. "I heard of one former cotton king who was seen picking up cigarette ends in the street. Another was a bus conductor, another had a stall in the open market, another is a barman," Priestley wrote. One woman complained about the transformation of the landscape: "It's awful. . . . They've got no work at all. And I hardly recognized the place. It's all becoming clean. The smuts are wearing off because so few of the mills are working. The brick and stone are beginning to show through."[7]

This was a brutal Britain of industrial ruins and slums, of derelict factories and hungry children. A boxing match in Newcastle provided entertainment for men on the dole, as well as a desperately needed opportunity to earn a few shillings for those brave enough to enter the ring: "There was a lot of blood about, partly because most of the boxers were novices who hit out wildly and also bled easily. . . . The crowd did not seem to mind this: they were a blood-thirsty lot. . . . 'Oo, yer b——!' they cried in delight when one of the stained gloves got home with a nasty thud. . . . It was uncompromisingly ugly."[8]

When Priestley reached the town of Jarrow in the county of Durham, where 80 percent of the working population were unemployed, he acknowledged that he was staring into the social abyss: "There is no escape anywhere in Jarrow from its prevailing misery, for it is entirely a working-class town. One little street may be rather more wretched than another, but to the outsider they all look alike. One out of every two shops appeared to be permanently closed. Wherever we went there were men hanging about, not scores of them but hundreds and thousands of them. The whole town looked as if it had entered a perpetual penniless bleak Sabbath. The men wore the drawn masks of prisoners of war."[9]

The hulls of ships were "rusting away in rows," as investors had abandoned the shipyards or gone bankrupt. The mines in the surrounding villages were offering little work, and what there was paid less than a living wage; the men were so desperate that even the most rudimentary safety regulations were regularly ignored. "During the five years ending with 1931 more than 5,000 people were killed in the coal-mining industry, and more than 80,000 were injured," he wrote. "It was estimated that in 1932 nearly one in every five persons employed underground was injured. The women in a mining village live forever in the anxious atmosphere of the war years."[10]

Life on the dole was hard and unforgiving, and it did not just affect the vulnerable industries in the north. Max Cohen, an unemployed cabinetmaker, knew all about "the dull finality of having no money at all." Out of a job, he soon found that his days began to revolve around finding the next meal.

> Life . . . became divided into more or less rigid periods. . . . There was Friday . . . the day, when after feverish waiting at the Labour Exchange, I received the life-giving fourteen shillings. After paying six shillings and sixpence a week rent, I was able, with much care and discrimination, to exist in a more or less normal fashion during the first half of the week. Of course, I could spend nothing on replacing my clothes, or on minor luxuries of any kind, no matter how trifling. From Tuesday on came bankruptcy. . . . I had no money at all, and so, in a sense, nothing more to worry about. . . . I lived on whatever may have been left of those things I had bought at the beginning of the week—on dry bread and bits of tasteless cheese. All that was necessary was to pull my belt tighter, ignore the empty ache in my stomach and hang on till Friday and deliverance came round again.[11]

With a little luck, a skilled young man could hope to find a job again at some point. But for those locked in real poverty, there seemed no way out. There were still Dickensian slums in the East End of London, a part of the city one civil servant described as being "as unknown to us as the Trobriand Islands."[12] The housing shortage was so severe that in 1931 a third of the population of London had been living with more than three people to a room; only 37 percent of families had the luxury of a house or flat to themselves.

A Dandy Dreams of Dictatorship

FOR THE GOVERNMENT, the thirties were a time of perpetual crisis. With 2.5 million unemployed by 1930 there were real fears of revolution, and the hardship extended right into the government: Ramsay MacDonald, Labour prime minister in the coalition government and the illegitimate son of a maid on a Scottish farm, was obliged to eat in the official dining rooms at 10 Downing Street, since he could not afford the coal to heat his own apartment.

MacDonald tried to contain the emergency and assist those enduring the most hardship. When financiers in the City of London forced him to agree to a painful cut in unemployment benefits— effectively condemning millions of vulnerable people to going hungry—half of his cabinet refused to go along with the measure. The prime minister tendered his resignation, only to be instructed by King George V to remain at his post and "carry the country through."

MacDonald's chancellor of the exchequer, Philip Snowden, was a self-described socialist, but a firm believer nonetheless in the self-regulating mechanisms of the free market. He insisted on maintaining an economic policy of strict austerity. But by the end of 1931, both MacDonald and Snowden had admitted defeat: even with Liberal support, the massive difficulty of both repaying debt and supporting the millions unemployed had proved as great as that of fighting and financing the war.

MacDonald chose what he considered the lesser of two evils and invited the Conservatives into a government of national unity. Though this act led to his expulsion (and Snowden's) from the Labour Party, it was popular with the public: in a general election in November of that year, Labour crashed from 287 parliamentary seats to a mere 54, but MacDonald himself was returned to power with a resounding majority for his coalition. His new chancellor, the Conservative Neville Chamberlain, did manage to balance the budget by early 1934, though at huge cost to the poorest Britons. MacDonald had disagreed with his methods, but he remained dependent on Conservative support for his coalition.

With his own political weakness exacerbated by increasing health problems, MacDonald was not strong enough to overrule the powerful chancellor. Chamberlain had cut unemployment benefits by 20 percent, and others also had had to make major sacrifices. The result was serious social unrest. In 1932 and 1933, tens of thousands of unemployed workers from Scotland and the north of England converged on London for hunger marches. When sailors on the battleship HMS *Valiant* were informed that their pay was being cut by 25 percent while officers had to accept a cut of only 4 percent, the sailors mutinied.

There were other repercussions, too. MacDonald's first government had included the brilliant young baronet Sir Oswald Mosley, a committed Fabian and originally a Conservative, then an Independent, then a member of the Independent Labour Party. In early 1930, Mosley had put forward a proposal to rescue the flailing economy and beat back unemployment with a Keynesian plan of public works funded by deficit spending, supplemented by a program of high tariffs and the nationalization of heavy industries. In May 1930, his proposal rejected, he had resigned in protest and formed his own New Party. When they failed to gain any seats in the election of November 1931,

Moseley turned abroad for inspiration. On a visit to Rome he made an admiring study of Mussolini's Fascist government, and returned home determined to set up a similar movement.

The British Union of Fascists was established in 1932 and was soon boasting a membership of fifty thousand. Though this number was almost certainly exaggerated, the group did for a time enjoy the support of the *Daily Mirror*, a London tabloid with a circulation of some three million, owned by Lord Rothermere, an admirer and personal acquaintance of both Mussolini and Hitler. In January 1934 the paper ran an infamous editorial entitled "Hurrah for the Blackshirts" and lauding Mosley's "sound, commonsense, Conservative doctrine."

In 1938, Mosley and his Blackshirts would be satirized by P. G. Wodehouse in a Jeeves and Wooster novel as Roderick Spode and his Black Shorts, the dress code deriving from the fact that by the time Spode formed his movement "there were no shirts left." But even in the real world, the British Fascists failed to make much of an impact on interwar politics. Mosley himself was regarded as too narcissistic and too self-indulgent to be taken seriously as a political leader. He liked the high life, was a regular on the party circuit, and was seen at all the right clubs, dressed either with the flamboyant elegance his wealth allowed or in the austere black tunic of his party.

Lord chancellor Lord Birkenhead, Winston Churchill's closest friend, called Mosley a "perfumed popinjay of scented boudoirs."[13] (Birkenhead was famous for his witty rejoinders. A fellow judge is said to have sought his advice on sentencing in a sodomy case, asking, "What do you think one ought to give a man who allows himself to be buggered?" "Oh," replied Birkenhead, "thirty shillings or two pounds—whatever you happen to have on you."[14])

Mosley's views received at least qualified sympathy among the British upper class, many of whom, concerned at the increasing social unrest, feared a Bolshevik-style revolution. King George V himself acknowledged the virtues of authoritarian government. The flirtation of his eldest son, David, later—briefly—King Edward VIII, with not only fascism in general but Hitlerism in particular was to prove a running sore in British politics until the end of the Second World War and beyond. But there were warning voices, too. In his 1932 bestseller *The Coming Struggle for Power*, John Strachey, Mosley's former private secretary who had turned away from his employer and embraced socialism, warned of what would lie ahead for Britain if it went down a fascist route: "Direct, open terror against the workers, violent aggression against its rivals, can alone enable a modern empire to maintain itself. A name for such a policy has been found: it is fascism."[15]

As a popular movement, fascism failed to gain traction in Britain. After a violent incident between protesters and blackshirts at a party rally in 1934, it was entirely marginalized; in 1936, a Public Order Act outlawed military-style organizations and the wearing of political uniforms. But the now widespread sense of anxiety was mixed with a feeling of helplessness and even inevitability. In a later lament, the conservative Roman Catholic writer Evelyn Waugh wrote that the "seemingly-solid, patiently-built, gorgeously-ornamented structure of western life was to melt overnight like an ice-castle, leaving only a puddle of mud."[16] From the perspective of the left, things looked even more threatening. Beatrice Webb, blind to any possible Soviet threat, had noted shortly before the Nazis came to power:

> The U.S.A., with its cancerous growth of crime and un-counted but destitute unemployed; Germany hanging over the precipice of a nationalist dictatorship; Italy boasting of its military preparedness; France, in dread of a new combination of Italy, Germany and Austria against her; Spain on the brink of revolution; the Balkan states snarling at each other; the Far East in a state of anarchic ferment; the African continent uncertain whether its paramount interest and cultural power will be black or white; South American states forcibly replacing pseudo-democracies by military dictatorships; and finally—acutely hostile to the rest of the world, engulfed in a fabulous effort, the success of which would shake capitalist civilization to its very foundations— Soviet Russia.[17]

The climate of uncertainty was reflected in a plethora of publications that appeared during the early 1930s. Like Strachey's *The Coming Struggle for Power*, George Douglas Cole's *An Intelligent Man's Guide Through World Chaos* sold strongly (fifty thousand copies); bookshops offered it next to Fenner Brockway's *Hungry England*. In 1933, the literary success of the season was *Love on the Dole* by Walter Greenwood (forty-six thousand copies), a novel set in an industrial slum in Greenwood's hometown, Salford. The year 1934 saw the publication of a new journal, *Plan*, which in its first issue speculated that "economic breakdown and international anarchy threaten to destroy civilization."

Among the vice presidents of the Federation of Progressive Societies and Individuals responsible for publishing the journal were some of the most influential British intellectuals of their day, including feminist and pacifist Vera Brittain, Labour activist and publisher Leonard Woolf, *Brave New World* author Aldous Huxley and his biologist and philosopher brother Julian, mathematician and social critic Bertrand Russell, and science fiction writer H. G. Wells. The anonymously authored *Handbook of Marxism*, published by Gollancz in 1935, sold thirty-three thousand copies before the year was out. Other popular titles were Walter Brierley's novel *The Means-Test Man*, which narrated a week in the life of an unemployed miner in Derbyshire, and George Dangerfield's *The Strange Death of Liberal England*, a critical analysis of the Liberal Party's failure to respond to the new social and economic challenges of the twentieth century.

From his comfortable tax exile in France, the comic genius Wodehouse found his own way of reflecting the revolutionary rumblings at home. In *Thank You, Jeeves*, Bertie Wooster is once again in a "spot of bother": the irreplaceable butler has given notice, unable to abide his employer's cacophonous love affair with a banjolele, according to Bertie a fashionable cross between banjo and ukulele. Without Jeeves, he finds, he is the helpless victim of every daft idea that pops into his head. More disquieting, the butler he has hired as a replacement is not to be trusted: "A melancholy blighter, with a long, thin, pimple-studded face and deep, brooding eyes. . . . Outwardly he was all respectfulness, but inwardly you could see that he was a man who was musing on the coming Social Revolution and looked on Bertram as a tyrant and an oppressor. . . . He said nothing, merely looking at me as if he were measuring me for my lamp-post."[18]

The Blackpoolization of the World

AS J. B. PRIESTLEY HAD NOTED, not everyone was feeling the immediate effects of the economic slump. For the middle classes in southern England especially, the situation was actually improving, with the newer and more consumer-oriented sectors of the economy showing clear signs of growth. Over the decade of the 1930s, three million new houses were built in the suburbs of London and the Home Counties; the number of cars in private ownership doubled; telephones, radios, vacuum cleaners, and other household appliances were becoming a common sight; department stores and early supermarkets, such as Woolworths and Marks & Spencer, opened many new branches.

But despite this regional prosperity, the Wodehouse universe was vanishing, a victim of the fundamental change in social attitudes.

Despite the unemployment, even in the south, despite real deprivation and hardship, working people resisted entering domestic service. The potential Jeeveses of the 1930s preferred to eat kippers and dry bread washed down with tea rather than attend to the whims of those whom their parents' generation would have regarded as their "betters." Positions such as "gentleman's gentleman," footman, maid, or cook had employed millions in the past, making possible an easy domestic and social life for all who had enough to spare. A society without servants had seemed unthinkable.

There were still people in service in the 1930s, of course, but their numbers were falling steadily. A study found that in London in 1931, there were more women in domestic service than in any other industry, but numbers had dropped by a third since 1900, and wherever they could women were now choosing work that gave them more personal freedom; most of those asked, in fact, said that they would prefer almost anything else to being in service. The same was true in other, more deprived areas. A Ministry of Labour survey in the northwest of England found that of 380 unemployed single women under thirty, prime candidates for a life below stairs in some well-off household, only four were prepared to go into service. In the Lancashire town of Preston, of 1,248 women interviewed, only eleven would consider it.

Something in British society had changed—subtly, but irrevocably. At least in some parts of the country, an increasingly modernized, industrialized economy was offering other, better employment opportunities for working-class people. The life of a domestic servant was rigidly circumscribed. Bad pay, hard work, long hours, and little privacy were the rule; domestic staff were expected to be single, with maids having to put up with the iron rule of "no gentlemen callers." A factory job or a position as a sales assistant or clerk paid not much better, but the hours were regular and people were free to do as they pleased during their leisure hours. Increasingly, factory and clerical workers also received a week's unpaid holiday every year.

There was another change in attitude, too, one that the war itself had provoked. In a strongly class-bound society such as Britain's, those who had been in service had often felt a considerable degree of pride in serving and being associated with a great family or a prominent gentleman or lady. Here the experience of the war had caused a profound shift in emphasis. While the idea of a "lost generation" still haunted the imagination of the privileged, working-class attitudes had been profoundly changed by the perceived incompetence and remoteness of the upper-class officers. Whether or not it was a fair reflection of the strategies and decisions of Britain's High Command, the image of the working-class Tommy "lions" led by stupid and stubborn upper-class "donkeys" had persisted in the popular imagination. The democratization resulting from mass production methods and life in an industrial economy went hand in hand with, and also encouraged, a fading respect for those on top of the pile.

This is very much the attitude Jeeves harbors toward his master, Bertram Wooster, the quintessential upper-class twit. Jeeves is of course too professional ever to breathe even the slightest hint of this to his employer, but he knows that though Bertie holds the purse strings and the social connections, there is no question of who is really the superior man, or of who would be lost without whom. Wodehouse was using a convention as old as comedy itself, that of the clever servant and his numbskull master, seen in plays from Aristophanes to Molière, but this time, in the real world, the game really appeared to be up. Jeeves might remain in his position for reasons of his own, but there could be no doubt that a man of his abilities would have other opportunities in the future.

On his journey through England, J. B. Priestly described this same change by sketching the three "countries" he had encountered:

> There was, at first, Old England, the country of the cathedrals and minsters and manor houses and inns, of parson and squire. . . . It has long ceased to earn its own living. . . . Then, I decided, there is the nineteenth-century England, the industrial England of coal, iron, steel, cotton, wool, railways; of thousands of rows of little houses all alike. . . . To the more fortunate people it was not a bad England at all, very solid and comfortable.

And on top of these two, or next to them, was another country entirely:

> The third England belonged far more to the age itself than to this particular island. America, I supposed, was its real birthplace. This is the England of arterial and bypass roads, of filling stations and factories that look like exhibition buildings, of giant cinemas and dance-halls and cafes, bungalows with tiny garages, cocktail bars. . . . It is a large-scale, mass-production job. You could almost accept Woolworths as its symbol. Its cheapness is both its strength and its weakness. It is its strength because being cheap it is accessible. . . . In

this England, for the first time in history, Jack and Jill are nearly as good as their masters and mistresses. . . . Jack, like his master, is rapidly transported to some place of rather mechanical amusement. Jill beautifies herself exactly as her mistress does. It is an England, at last, without privilege. Years and years ago the democratic and enterprising Black-pool, by declaring that you were all as good as one another so long as you had the necessary sixpence, began all this. Modern England is rapidly Blackpooling itself.[19]

The seaside town of Blackpool was a popular tourist resort for the working-class people of northern England and Scotland; their sixpences bought them entertainment, cheap goods, and a new kind of identity free from deference to "the toffs." Though these factory workers and shop girls could hardly be said to be forming a new elite, they were carving out spaces where social hierarchy was determined by the number of sixpences in your pocket—in other words, by how much money you had. Birth and breeding, the great protectors and promoters of "sound" but dim chaps like Bertie Wooster, had begun their final decline into irrelevance. As Priestley had seen, the Americanization of the ancient English hierarchies was under way.

Elsewhere, too, new elites were taking over from the old, more swiftly and in some cases more violently. In the Soviet Union and Italy, and to a lesser extent in other dictatorial states such as Hungary, societies were being forcibly remade in a new mode, not necessarily more egalitarian, but certainly not based on ancestry or upbringing. The Russian aristocracy had long since fled, swelling the ranks of impoverished journalists in Paris and taxi drivers in New York. Now the bourgeoisie, always small, was in retreat, with coveted positions reserved for those of impeccable working-class descent. In Germany, the Nazis were the new arbiters of social standing; the grand old *Bildungsbürgertum* or upper bourgeoisie, which had driven the country's rise all through the nineteenth century and into the twentieth, had now been pushed aside, and in the universities, in business, in the arts, and in other positions of public prominence, party loyalty was the only thing that counted.

The new situation brought opportunities to many who would once have been excluded from any possibility of advancement, and they naturally took advantage of it, too often ignoring—or even enjoying—the concomitant loss of status for others less politically compliant or less favored by race or birth. Ironically, in America,

"Americanization" was hardly progressing at all. So severe was the Depression in the United States that the old elites, albeit of money rather than birth, not only maintained but even solidified their positions of power. They were white, of course, and few yet thought to question this. The Depression was driving America's black people ever further down the economic (and thence social) scale. For the most part, they were less likely than ever to be able to accumulate the necessary sixpences.

· 1935 ·

Route 66

Our recent transition from rain-soaked eastern Kansas with its green pastures, luxuriant foliage, abundance of flowers, and promise of a generous harvest, to the dust-covered desolation of No Man's Land was a difficult change to crowd into one short day's travel. . . . Wearing our shade hats, with handkerchiefs tied over our faces and Vaseline in our nostrils, we have been trying to rescue our home from the accumulations of wind-blown dust which penetrates wherever air can go. It is an almost hopeless task, for there is rarely a day when at some time the dust clouds do not roll over.

Caroline Henderson in a letter to a friend, June 30, 1935

....

ON SUNDAY, APRIL 14, PEOPLE IN AMERICA'S CORN BELT DREW A SIGH of relief. There had been dust storms recently, terrible, choking, malicious blows that covered everything in sight with a gritty residue, but this morning was clear and bright and it was a relief to see the sun once more. Then, as the morning wore on, the breeze died down and the light changed to a glowering bleak glare. Birds began to twitter nervously.

The cloud appeared on the horizon, like a black band as far as the eye could see. It grew quickly, preceded by thousands of screaming birds. The storm that now descended upon the farming villages and towns was like nothing anyone had ever seen or felt before. When it finally swooped down on houses and their inhabitants, it was a raven-hued wall: furious, a hundred feet high, total, roaring, blinding blackness. Black Sunday, as this catastrophic storm came to be called, rained three hundred tons of dust in one afternoon and left the formerly fertile prairies looking like a baked desert of sand dunes and certain death.

It was the hardest day in a succession of natural catastrophes, a final blow to the hopes of hundreds of thousands of farmers who had toiled for decades to build better lives in what had once been described as a paradise, with soil as thick and rich as chocolate dropping from the blades of the plows. Farmers had been encouraged to come here and to make the land their own, and hundreds of thousands had wagered their futures on the Great Plains. In 1916, as the United States had become involved in the war, there was an army to feed, and the stock market was fueling speculation in grain.

Farmers in the fertile lands of Kansas, Texas, Colorado, and New Mexico responded by working harder and producing more to feed the hungry market. As affordable tractors and combine harvesters appeared, farmers invested heavily in the new miracle machines, taking out loans to finance the equipment's purchase price, which was far higher than their annual profits. But it was worth it. With a team of horses, a farmer could plow three acres a day. With a tractor, he could return home much less tired and satisfied, having done a daily average of fifty acres. A combine harvester could bring in the wheat from five hundred acres within a fortnight, delivering neat sacks of grain in a row next to the huge swaths it cut into the field. But the farmers soon found that there were unexpected costs attached. Whereas earlier the expense for harvesting one acre had been nothing but the labor and the horses' feed, it stood now at four dollars for gasoline and supplies. As long as grain prices remained high, farmers could make a living. After the war, however, after several good harvests had filled the grain silos of the speculators, prices followed the laws of the market and began to decline. The farmers responded by breaking new soil to increase production. In parts of Kansas, the surface in agricultural use jumped from two million acres in 1925 to three million acres five years later; in other regions the fields doubled in size. The virgin soil was rich. More good harvests followed.

Most farmers worked around the clock in shifts, and while the machines cast a metallic glint in the brilliant sun by day, at night tractors and combines crept across the plains like giant glowworms. The earth would be made to produce ever bigger yields. The weather was kind. Abundant rain and sunshine translated into record harvests, and every day thousands more acres were brought under cultivation.

Then, in 1931, the rains stopped coming. It was nothing out of the ordinary at first, then puzzling, then concerning. A poor harvest

Like a black wall: A dust storm approaches a settlement.

was followed by another, smaller one. The sun withered the crops in the fields, turning them whitish gray and rustling in the wind long before they were ripe. The unforgiving heat parched and cracked the soil, and as field after field of wheat and corn turned arid, the topsoil began to dance in the air in the circular dust storms that had always visited these plains.

The wind drew unusual amounts of dust into the air this time, though, and farmers soon understood that this was a result of their land cultivation. Not only were millions of acres under cultivation, but the pull of demand and the development of new agricultural machines also meant they had been cultivated in a different way. Traditional horse-drawn plows had dug deep into the earth, turning large, heavy sods in their entirety, like a blanket on a bed. The modern "sodbusters" were faster and considerably more efficient. Each tractor could pull several rows of disks that cut into the soil superficially, breaking the top layer into finer crumbs. There was less resistance that way and a huge gain in speed, and the depth of the broken earth was still sufficient for sowing. Now, as the crops were failing, the chopped-up topsoil offered no resistance to the uplift of the winds.

As temperatures rose higher with every passing year, another kind of storm arrived. Black blizzards carried huge clouds of dust over hundreds of miles. In 1933 thirty-eight such storms were recorded, the next year fewer. Then they returned in force. By 1936 there would be five dust storms per month, carrying with them the precious fertile soil. A storm in May 1934 lifted up 350 million tons of dust from the fields of Montana and Wyoming and pressed them east, into the Dakotas. By the evening, six thousand tons of dust were showering down on Chicago, supported by winds of 110 miles an hour. The storms moved on to Boston, New York, Washington, and Atlanta, even covering ships almost three hundred miles out from the East Coast.

The storms devoured everything in their path, and they were dangerous. Children wandering out into the blast and car drivers who had lost the road in clouds of dust so thick they could not see their hands in front of their face were found days later, suffocated. Cattle left outside would suffer the same fate. Cows would grind their teeth to the gums in order to extract some blades of grass from the desert before dropping dead. "In a rising sandstorm cattle quickly become blinded," wrote photographer Margaret Bourke-White, one of a growing number of press people sent to cover the catastrophe. "They run around in circles until they fall and breathe so much dust that they die. Autopsies show their lungs caked with the dust and mud."[1]

Wild animals were also affected. Fish choked to death in the remaining puddles of water under a layer of acrid dust; dead birds, field mice, and rabbits were strewn over the plains, the survivors so disoriented that they could simply be picked up without resistance. In 1934, the government began to destroy thousands of head of cattle, giving grim labor and a few dollars to destitute farmers as they set about butchering their investments in the future.

Evangelists and self-appointed prophets proclaimed the end of the world and the second coming. At home and in church, people began to debate whether this was the end of days, as prophesied. With grave faces they quoted Deuteronomy 28:24: "The Lord shall make the rain of thy land powder and dust: from heaven shall it come down upon thee, until thou be destroyed." Ada Watkins, a Kansas farmer, had drawn a hopeful conclusion: "I guess the good Lord is going to lead us out into the promised Land again," she said.[2]

By 1935, few were so hopeful. For the farmers, the storms were now dictating every aspect of their lives. They windproofed their houses as well as they could, but after every blow they had to shovel the dust out by the bucketload. Their food was saturated with dust, and their water left grit between their teeth. Most were reduced to beans and cornbread for lunch, for dinner, and for the next breakfast. At night, farmer Avis Carlson settled into a dreary routine: "A trip for water to rinse the grit from the lips. And then back to bed with washcloths over our noses. We try to lie still, because every turn stirs the dust on the blankets. After a while, if we are good sleepers, we forget."[3]

Buried hopes: After a dust storm in South Dakota, 1936.

Nature did not allow them to forget for long. Growing anything became almost impossible. As nothing but withered stalks was left where there once had been fields of shoulder-high wheat, even irrigated vegetables did not escape the deadly hand of the weather. Huge buildups of static electricity from the storms devastated these crops, turning watermelons black and wheat brown within hours.

As the landscape turned into a scorching inferno, hundreds of thousands of jackrabbits descended from the open plains into the fields and razed the little that was left of the stunted harvest. They came in droves so vast that it seemed as if the baked earth itself was migrating in the dizzy heat. On Sundays, after church, farmers would congregate for rabbit drives and kill hundreds or thousands of animals, first with shot, and then, when that proved too costly and too dangerous for other hunters, with clubs.

After the jackrabbits came the clouds of grasshoppers, tiny eating machines that could not be clubbed to death. After the grasshoppers came hopelessness. Already the fields had lost up to five inches of precious topsoil, transformed into dust drifts dotting the landscape like a ghostly Gobi Desert. In the Texas panhandle, residents found a crow's nest built out of rusty barbed wire, the only building material the birds had been able to find on the arid plains. One hundred million acres had become a wasteland.

Sometimes the skies were so dark that it seemed to be night for twenty-four hours, while high winds could blow five days in a row. People were living with cloth masks in front of their faces, and a new form of pneumonia was sweeping the countryside. Undernourished and weakened from the constant threat, children fell sick and began to die. Reporting for the *New York Times*, George Greenfield wrote from Kansas: "Today I have seen the cold hand of death on what was one of the great bread baskets of the nation . . . a lost people living on a lost land."[4]

The poet Archibald MacLeish was horrified by what he saw. He understood that the catastrophe had been caused not just by a freak of nature but also by a destructive interpretation of the American dream, an exploitative, aggressive hunt for profits that had exposed the earth to the elements and the farmers to misery. The great ideas of the founding fathers, he implied, had been perverted.

> We wonder whether the dream of American liberty
> Was two hundred years of pine and hardwood
> And three generations of the grass
> And the generations are up: the years over . . .
> We wonder whether the great American dream
> Was the singing of locusts out of the grass to
> the West and the
> West is behind us now . . .
> We wonder if the liberty is done:
> The dreaming is finished.[5]

Leaving Home

WITH NO SUBSTANTIAL RAINFALL in four years and no change in sight, families began to give up, packing up what little they had left and leaving. By the second half of the 1930s, the trek had swollen to fifty thousand people every month beating a path west. They did not shut their doors behind them, but just drove away, their remaining possessions piled on their pickup trucks: a few sticks of furniture, pots and pans, beans and corn flour, bundles of ragged clothes, and spare water, gasoline, and tires. In a contemporary documentary, a family's two children are shown simply sitting on the back of the truck, looking back, their bare feet dangling over the hot dust. Those who had no trucks braved the barren heat and the hundreds of miles of road ahead of them on bicycles.

Almost half a million men, women, and children took to the road westward, hoping for a new beginning. The main artery for this great migration was the newly completed Route 66, running from Chicago to Santa Monica Pier in California. A desolate caravan of "Okies" (originally short for "Oklahomans") trudged westward along its long straight stretches and winding hills. After spending days on the road making their way through arid wastelands, the distressed travelers would spot the first green again—the first trees, fertile fields, and flowers they had seen in years. They were going to a landscape of gardens with pleasant weather and two harvests a year. They would find work in the orchards, or even buy a little land and start over.

They were not welcome. The United States was in the midst of the Depression, and bread lines in the big cities stretched for several blocks, while men who had run their own businesses were now begging in the streets and sleeping rough. Andrew Mellon, the multimillionaire secretary of the treasury, had what he saw as a patent medicine against economic crises, and he saw to it that it was implemented. "Liquidate labor, liquidate stocks, liquidate the farmers, liquidate real estate. It will purge the rottenness of the system. . . . People will work harder, live a more moral life. Values will be adjusted and enterprising people will pick up the wrecks from less competent people."[6] But the bread lines grew longer. They would not begin to decrease until Roosevelt's New Deal instituted a series of public works programs that began to revive the economy in the mid-1930s. Even then, the climate would remain tough for those who had left their homes to look for work.

Having been celebrated as pioneering heroes in advertising and public speeches only a generation earlier, the Okies suddenly found themselves abused on the streets, chased away when they pitched their tents or built their huts, and paid less than a living wage, if they found work at all. In the gigantic California orchards, there were four immigrants applying for every job, and even the lucky would earn too little to make ends meet. When they rebelled, they were cruelly treated. Trade unionists and "troublesome" men were sacked without protection, and strikes were beaten down, with the strike leaders frequently jailed or even shot.

In the best case, the Okies were portrayed as primitive, Bible-thumping hillbillies. Vice President Henry Wallace gleefully told of an encounter with a recent arrival in California, whom he would imitate: "Well, Mister, I was farmin' back ther in Oklyhomy and it jist kep a gittin' droughthier and droughthier, and droughthier so . . . Here I be."[7]

On many occasions, however, the abuse was far worse. A businessman in the San Joaquin Valley called the newcomers "ignorant filthy people" and opined that they should never "think they're as good as the next man," a sentiment that was echoed by many Californians, who labeled the newcomers as "shiftless trash who live like hogs." A doctor in Kern County was baffled by them, calling them "a strange people—they don't seem to know anything. They can't read at all. . . . There is such a thing as a breed of people. These people have lived separate for too long, and they are like a different race." The celebrity journalist H. L. Mencken, notorious for loudly disagreeing with almost everyone, for once concurred, and recommended that all Okies be sterilized.[8]

The prejudice about simple-minded, indolent Okies of inferior stock was in part a revival of well-established attitudes toward blacks, and even well-meaning people helped to perpetuate them. A schoolteacher believed herself a shrewd judge of character when she remarked: "I can spot a migrant on the street every time by watching him walk. He shuffles. He doesn't hold up his shoulders and face the world. His glance is often timid and wandering. I say these things, not harshly, but with sorrow. Generations of living as the underdog has made him like a scared bush rabbit."[9]

Edward Everett Davis, a professor of agriculture in Texas, gave this idea more implicitly racist implications when he drew an apocalyptic picture of the rural South: "Below us lies a cotton field, the great open air slum of the south, a perennial Hades of poverty, ignorance, and social depravity. . . . Too much of America's worthless human silt has filtered into the cotton belt. . . . The most serious rural problem in the South is . . . that of the biologically impoverished tribes of marginal humanity—black, white and Mexican—subsisting on cotton. . . . The human creature of weak body and moronic mentality who would perish without reproducing his hideous kind amid the blizzards and wheat fields of the Dakotas can survive successfully and populate half a schoolroom in the mild cotton regions of Texas."[10]

The new migrants were humiliated, and also surprised. They were, after all, white, of Anglo-Saxon stock, and strictly Protestant. They had anticipated that the going might be rough in their new home, but they had never expected to be treated as second-class human beings. In John Steinbeck's great novel *The Grapes of Wrath* an old man reflects: "Well, Okie use'ta to mean you was from Oklahoma. Now it means you're a dirty son-of-a-bitch. Okie means you're scum. Don't mean nothing itself, it's the way they say it."[11]

And perhaps the Okies were despised for another reason. They were the ragged, living embodiment of a great dream failing due to shortsighted greed, reckless exploitation of resources, and priorities dictated by profits. They were proof that the American dream could collapse not only due to bad luck or lack of ability or determination but also through a flaw in the vision itself, through the lure of the quick buck and the siren voice of untold fortunes just around the corner.

Building Empathy

HELP DID COME FROM THE GOVERNMENT, but it was cruelly little. In the end, the tide of public opinion was turned by artists. The sympathetic portrayal of the sharecroppers in Erskine Caldwell's 1932 novel *Tobacco Road* gained the book huge popularity; a Broadway play based on it opened in the following year, playing to full houses for eight straight years. Even its great success was eclipsed in 1938 with the publication of John Steinbeck's *Grapes of Wrath*, a searing indictment of the hopelessness and humiliation of the rural migrants who had lost everything, only to be abandoned by a greed-filled society.

Steinbeck blamed the Dust Bowl catastrophe on a system blinded by profits and estranged from nature. "The man who is more than his chemistry, walking on the earth, turning his plow point for a stone, dropping his handles to slide over an outcropping, kneeling in the earth to eat his lunch; that man who is more than his element knows the land that is more than its analysis. But the machine man, driving a dead tractor on land he does not know and love, understands only chemistry; and he is contemptuous of the land and of himself. When the corrugated iron doors are shut, he goes home, and his home is not the land."[12]

By the end of the decade, Steinbeck's migrant tragedy would sell 430,000 copies and still be on the bestseller list. It owed its status in part to its charged political tone. Whereas many readers felt compassion for the characters and their plight, others were convinced that the author's engagement with the dregs of humanity was nothing short of socialist and smacked of revolution. The Associated Farmers of California were particularly outraged about the treatment of their colleagues in the novel, hotly denouncing it as "communist propaganda." Copies of the book were publicly burned. Other reviewers expressed a more balanced opinion. The critic for the *New York Times* reflected: "All this is true enough but the real truth is that Steinbeck

*Madonna of the Dust Bowl:
Dorothea Lange's portrait of
a refugee with two of her
children, 1936.*

has written a novel from the depths of his heart with a sincerity
seldom equaled. It may be an exaggeration, but it is the exaggeration
of an honest and splendid writer."[13]

But the task of creating the most complete and most iconic record
of the hopeless misery of the Okies fell to the photographers. In 1935,
the Farm Security Administration was set up under the terms of the
New Deal to alleviate rural poverty. Roy Striker, one of its civil servants, had begun to employ a loose group of young photojournal-
ists—among others Walker Evans, Dorothea Lange, Marion Post
Wolcott, and Arthur Rothstein—to document the destruction of
agricultural assets and of human lives that was taking place. Striker
wanted to move the hearts of his fellow citizens and to record the
success of relief efforts, and he ended up doing this and much more.

In the film documentary *The Plow That Broke the Plains*, Striker
explained to the American public how intensive farming was partly
to blame for the unfolding ecological disaster. Using the photographs
of gifted observers such as Rothstein and Lange, he presented the
human side of the economic and ecological catastrophe. It was
Dorothea Lange who captured the single most famous image of the
Dust Bowl refugees, a portrait of a mother and her two children taken
in an improvised California camp. Perhaps more than anything else,
this modern Madonna helped to build a broad consensus to mobilize

more government funds to aid the stricken region, to which the rain would return only in autumn 1939.

Safe Havens

THE OKIES WERE NOT THE ONLY MIGRANTS let down by Depression-era America, and while they were looked down on, they were still US citizens. For all those wanting to come from the outside, things were harder still. Once the world's premier goal for immigration, the United States had become progressively closed to new arrivals. After the crash, as life grew ever harder for many of those just off the boats, America had for the first time in its history become a country of emigration. In 1921, net migration (immigration minus emigration) had stood at 557,000; in 1925, the year after the Immigration Act, the figure was 201,000. But in 1931, with the country bludgeoned by the Depression, 68,000 people more left the United States than entered it, admitting defeat and returning home. Among them was the Italian Michele Schirru, anarchist and would-be assassin of Mussolini.

In Europe, another gigantic, choking cloud had risen up from what once was good, fertile soil, darkening the skies and threatening to bury all that was in its shadow: Hitler's Nazi Germany. It also triggered a wave of migration. Jews and those of liberal or leftist views in Germany and Austria, which at the time had its own fascist regime, were increasingly despairing at the possibility of a future in their home country and planning to move abroad. Visa restrictions to most countries were such that victims of persecution soon resolved to go anywhere they could, if only they were let in. The situation in Germany had been becoming increasingly alarming for Jews, and the 1935 Race Laws, which forbade everything from cinema attendance by Jews to intermarriage and Jewish ownership of property, had given the final push. More than ever, potential emigrants besieged embassies, desperate for the elusive visas.

Recent history, however, had resulted in tight visa regulations almost everywhere. Initially, interwar Europe had seen an intense period of internal migration. The crumbling of four empires (German, Austro-Hungarian, Russian, and Ottoman) after the First World War had resulted in nationalist campaigns and the vicious settling of old scores. In eastern Turkey, more than one million Armenians had been butchered in a vast campaign of what would decades later be termed "ethnic cleansing" shot through with centuries of ethnic hatred, especially on the side of Kurdish militants, whose infamous Hamidiye

Brigade was responsible for a large proportion of the often savage mass killings.

The Turkish and Greek populations in disputed areas of the eastern Mediterranean had been engaged in mutual skirmishing and increasing bloodshed, which culminated in the 1922 Smyrna Massacre of the Greek population. White Russians had fled the revolution in their own country, and minorities of Germans, Hungarians, Tyrolians, Slovenes, Irish, Finns, Jews, Muslims, Orthodox Christians, and Catholics had fled local oppression, while millions of economic migrants were continuing to seek better lives for themselves in the big cities or in the industrial areas of other countries. Europe had been in a state of tremendous and often murderous upheaval of entire populations.

Only the last waves of this flood of displacement and misery washed into western European countries, where life was precarious but less uprooted. For Jewish Germans (and soon afterward for Jewish Austrians), this feeling of relative security had ended abruptly after Hitler's rise to power in 1933 and the implementation of the Race Laws two years later. Some Jews went from Berlin to Vienna or, more frequently, the other way, in the hope of finding a more tolerant climate and some professional opportunities. Others went further afield. Believing they could ride out the time of Hitler's dictatorship, which many still thought of as a brief moment of madness in Germany's history, many Jewish Germans and Austrians, along with many non-Jewish but committed anti-Nazi citizens of those countries, moved to Paris, London, Amsterdam, Prague, Budapest, or even Moscow in an attempt to evade persecution.

In Paris, the languid and glamorous "lost generation" of American writers was replaced by another, less fashionable, more anxious group. A "Little Germany," consisting of bookshops and delicatessens, arose there during the 1930s. In the first months after Hitler's appointment as Reich chancellor in 1933, some 26,000 Germans, most of them Jewish, had left Germany for Paris. By 1940 some 150,000 Jews, communists and socialists, painters and poets, journalists, musicians, and businessmen had come to France. Some awaited a visa to their final destination; others sought passage to any safe country. Many went on their way as soon as they could, but others stayed, waiting for some ray of hope, or simply for the storm clouds to pass.

In the grip of the Depression and enduring often bloody warfare between the radical factions of the right and left, France was not a welcoming land for immigrants. The public mood was hostile to newcomers. Jewish arrivals were often regarded with special suspicion by the citizens of a society that had been rent by the anti-Semitic extravagances of the Dreyfus affair at the end of the nineteenth century. In 1934, the scandal surrounding the Polish-born Jewish financier Alexandre Stavisky, whose embezzlement of millions of francs had led to his apparent murder by the police, had further stoked public anti-Semitism, to the extent that extreme right-wing organizations such as the Croix-de-Feu were openly calling for France to adopt the same attitude toward Jews and left-wing radicals as Nazi Germany had done.

As always, refugees found it hard to obtain legal papers. Those who had entered the country without personal documents could find themselves in an impossible position if they were formally expelled or ordered to leave France within twenty-four hours, as many were: without passports, they could not legally return across the border, and their enforced stay was frequently interpreted as defiance of the law. The unfortunates who found themselves in this legal vacuum were often imprisoned for the "crime" of refusing to obey a legal order, only to be expelled again after they had served their term—a vicious circle from which only an intercession by influential friends or a charitable organization could rescue them. Everyone, however, was at the mercy of the *préfecture de police* and its officers, who might be persuaded to be lenient if moved by their conscience—or possibly a discreetly passed envelope. The situation was temporarily eased in 1936 under the leftist Popular Front government of prime minister Léon Blum, a man sensitive to the plight of those who had lost their homes.

Emigration made people frighteningly vulnerable. Many of those coming to Paris were intellectuals who found themselves terribly reduced in their new home by the loss of their native language, their central professional asset as well as their most important social one. Many were consequently forced to live off charity. By 1941, organizations such as the Comité d'Assistance aux Refugiés would be paying out 2.5 million francs (some $24 million in today's money) every month to the increasingly desperate emigrants. Jewish charities with various ideological orientations from Zionist to Orthodox also did much to help.

Professionals such as doctors, engineers, and lawyers could not practice their professions without having passed the relevant French examinations; other skilled and unskilled workers were forced into the shadow economy, if they could find work at all. The nostalgic evocations of emigrant cafés filled with cultivated men and women who had nothing to do all day other than read the papers and debate politics contained some truth, but many of those reading and debating were in fact enduring the enforced idleness of unemployment

Some of those who had lost their country and their livelihood were determined not to let their culture slip away, and those of the German diaspora in particular sprang into action to create intellectual hubs and cultural centers, and to provide a degree of sanity in the often desperate situations in which they found themselves as emigrants. In 1933, there were four German-language theaters and cabarets in Paris, as well as an émigré symphony orchestra and a choral society. The Freie Deutsche Universität (Free German University) offered courses taught by distinguished professors without charge; lecture series were organized, and when in 1934 the International Anti-Fascist Archive announced the foundation of a library that was to comprise all books burned by the Nazis the previous year, it received donations of more than twenty thousand volumes within only a few weeks.

Professional writers had often lost their income together with their German publishers, a situation that was critical especially for those novelists, poets, and journalists who were not already famous and wealthy. Exile publishers tried to step into the breach, and did manage to publish a series of important works, while emigrants' newspapers offered paltry fees in line with their authors' usually desperate financial situation. Some four hundred different German-language newspapers and magazines were published regularly (though not always for long) during the 1930s in Paris alone; the *Pariser Tagblatt* sold fourteen thousand copies a day. Its editor in chief was Georg Bernhard, a social democratic journalist and politician who had been a Reichstag (parliamentary) deputy and, before that, the editor of Berlin's prestigious *Vossische Zeitung*. In 1933, having opposed Hitler in parliament and knowing that his arrest was imminent, Bernhard had fled. Having worked all his life for democracy in Germany, he was embittered by his exile. When he met the globetrotting Count Harry Kessler he vehemently told him that he would never again set foot in "that country," and that he no longer regarded himself as a German. Bernhard was as good as his word and died ten years later in New York.

Amsterdam was another important destination for emigrants. Some ten thousand German Jews came there after 1933, hoping to survive in a safer and more tolerant culture with a face not too different from what home had been like. Among them was the Frank family from Frankfurt, whose little daughter Anne would reach a sad, posthumous fame through the diary she wrote while in hiding. With thirty-five thousand refugees arriving in the Netherlands and most of them heading for Amsterdam, the local bookseller and publisher Emanuel Querido established a branch of his firm to publish works written in German by exiles from the Nazis; he also founded *Die Sammlung* (The Collection), a journal for a wider group of literary exiles. Both from a humanitarian perspective and from a financial one, the latter proved a winning proposition.

Among Querido's contributors were stars such as Albert Einstein, Ernest Hemingway, André Gide, Lion Feuchtwanger, Aldous Huxley, and Jean Cocteau, as well as authors whose names had previously been known mainly in the German-speaking world, such as the poet Stefan Heym and the novelists Jakob Wasserman, Max Brod, and Joseph Roth, the last of whom demonstrated in a letter to fellow writer Stefan Zweig, also in exile, that he saw the situation with desperate lucidity: "By now you will have realized that we are drifting toward great catastrophes. Disregarding the private ones—our literary and material existence is destroyed—the situation will lead to another war. I would no longer give a penny for our lives. It has been brought to pass that barbarism rules. Do not deceive yourself. Hell reigns."[14] Querido, himself Jewish, still managed to help many exiled writers. He would eventually die at the hands of the Nazis in the Polish concentration camp Sobibór in 1943.

Quotas of Survival

MOST OF THE JEWISH AND OTHER REFUGEES who stopped in Paris, Amsterdam, Copenhagen, Prague, and other continental European destinations felt that their journey was not yet at an end, and many wanted to reach the United States. The US immigration authorities, however, had domestic politics in mind and were determined to deter and if necessary deport all immigrants who did not bring sufficient economic assets with them. Moreover, there was a clearly anti-Semitic set of priorities at work in the approval process for potential new citizens.

The Immigration Act of 1924 had already done much to effectively limit Jewish immigration by setting low quotas for central and eastern Europe, the regions in which most Jews in Europe were living, while privileging "northerners" from Germany and Scandinavia. By 1933, however, most German immigrants were Jewish, and the US authorities became noticeably more reluctant to grant visas to German nationals. In the period 1933–1940, during which 211,000 German Jews could have been issued immigration visas under the quota fixed in the 1924 act, only 100,987 were actually issued documents. When two compassionate US politicians, the Democratic senator Robert F. Wagner and the Republican representative Edith Rodgers, sponsored a bipartisan bill making it possible to admit fifteen thousand Jewish refugee children on a visa waiver, their initiative was opposed by colleagues who scoffed that the "cute Jewish kids" would eventually become "ugly Jewish adults." The bill did not survive the committee stage. Presumably, many of the children concerned did not survive, either.[15]

Among those fortunate enough to get the desperately sought visas were the Freudenheims of Berlin, a thoroughly assimilated German Jewish family. Hans Freudenheim was a cultured and wealthy man, a manufacturer of exotic wooden veneers to be used for upmarket furniture and keyboard instruments; the renowned concert piano firm Bechstein was one of his best customers. Proudly Prussian in his work ethic, Freudenheim had served on the Western Front, where he had been awarded the Iron Cross, a distinction that led him in the early 1930s to believe that he and his family would remain safe from Nazi persecution. He was, in fact, the very model of a middle-class German: a successful businessman, conscientious citizen, determined democrat, and highly educated man, with a small library of his own and an annual subscription to the Berlin Philharmonic Orchestra. The family's Jewish identity consisted of little more than family ties to Orthodox relatives in Bohemia. After the passing of the Race Laws in 1935, however, Freudenheim understood the seriousness of the situation and decided to flee with his family. In 1937, they finally got American visas through the personal intervention of Admiral Claude Bloch, a distant cousin.

Bloch's was an unusual Jewish success story. Born in Kentucky to first-generation immigrant parents, he had chosen a military career and had advanced to the rank of four-star admiral; he was the highest-ranking Jewish officer in the American armed forces and, after 1938, commander in chief of the US fleet. His guarantee that his relatives, whom he had never met, would not become charges of the state made it possible for them to obtain emigration papers.

The Freudenheim family packed their bags on the same evening they received the papers and left Berlin in the morning for Paris, from where they planned to travel on to the United States. But when they arrived in the French capital, they quickly found themselves part of the intense cultural life of the emigrant community, which reminded them of Berlin, the home city they were already missing. It seemed possible that they could make a life in Paris. Hans's son Herbert, then seventeen years old, would later recall days spent sauntering down the Champs-Élysées, admiring the local girls and the elegant shop windows, all the while dreaming of becoming a proper Frenchman.

This hopeful situation was suddenly ended when Herbert's father realized that Jews in France might soon be no more protected from the Nazis than they had been in Germany itself. He had thought himself safe behind the Maginot Line, the huge series of bulwarks and concrete forts with multistory subterranean installations constructed after the First World War as a defense against future German attacks. He soon recognized, however, that this protective wall stopped at the Belgian border, leaving France itself vulnerable to exactly the route of attack the German army had chosen in 1914. Only a dividing line of water could keep his family safe from Hitler, he decided. Freudenheim and his family moved to London, taking with them nothing more than what they could carry. When they arrived in the British capital, the total family funds amounted to £6.

The Freudenheims established themselves in northwest London, the new home of many German Jewish refugees. As in Paris, there were German cafés, restaurants, bookshops, and grocers, as well as clubs and newspapers. Destitute but not despairing, the Berlin businessman set about providing for his family, first by buying white cabbage, salt, and old wine barrels to make sauerkraut, a German delicacy then unavailable in London, and later, with that trade developing briskly, purchasing surplus wines from the cellars of great country houses and becoming a wine dealer, an occupation for which his previous wealthy existence and the many dinners he had enjoyed in fine restaurants stood him in good stead.

For his younger son, Herbert, the adjustment to yet another big city was at first not so successful. Though he spoke French, he had no English; London seemed gray and depressing to him, and he resented his father's unbroken German patriotism and inflexible Prussian manner. When he found his father's Iron Cross, he felt so angry that he went to flush it down the toilet. Freudenheim saw what his son was about to do, and he fished the medal out, then slapped the defiant young perpetrator—the only time that he had done so. "The Emperor was an officer and a gentleman!" he cried.[16]

Of All the Gin Joints in All the Towns in All the World

FOR SOME GERMAN REFUGEES, the only help came through family connections, such as that of the Freudenheims to their distant American uncle. For others, it helped to be famous. Albert Einstein, Thomas Mann, and the now almost forgotten bestselling novelist

Lion Feuchtwanger had no problem being accepted and finding their feet abroad. Many of these either had jobs waiting or needed none, being independently wealthy.

For actors, composers, directors, and others in the film industry, the only way of ensuring an American visa was an invitation from Hollywood, a document guaranteed to convince the immigration authorities. This was not easy to procure, but it did provide a way out for a great number of artists, sometimes on spurious contracts. Their careers, though, more often than not suffered serious interruptions, from which some never recovered. For actors, the new language often proved an insuperable barrier, and some artists who had been revered at home were reduced to playing bit parts or small character roles.

One Austrian actor who chose to emigrate rather than being forced out was Paul Georg Julius, Freiherr von Hernried, Ritter von Wassel-Waldingau. As long-winded aristocratic names were little help in the theater, the actor was known professionally simply as Paul von Hernried. He had been doing well, making a good career as an actor with legendary stage director Max Reinhardt, and working in film as well. After the 1934 civil war in Vienna, with the Austrian fascists taking power, Hernried emigrated in 1935 to England.

Working in a different language onstage and in films proved difficult, and he was reduced to playing small roles, mostly—ironically—as Nazi officers. His great chance came only after his move to Hollywood in the early 1940s. There he was offered the role of the heroic resistance fighter Victor Laszlo in a new movie set in North Africa among desperate emigrants, unscrupulous criminals, and corrupt local officials. For easier pronunciation among English-speaking audiences, the studio changed his name from Paul von Hernried to simply Paul Henreid; the 1942 movie was entitled *Casablanca*.

The cast of this legendary evocation of high passion and the desperate scramble for visas among very different people, all rendered equal in their exile, illustrates the impact that the flight from Nazi Germany had on Hollywood during the 1930s. The American leading actor, Humphrey Bogart, and his love interest, the Swedish Ingrid Bergman, were exceptions, as were director Michael Curtiz—born Manó Kertész-Kaminer in Budapest, he emigrated to Los Angeles in the 1920s—and the composer of the score, Vienna-born Max Steiner, another early arrival in Hollywood. Apart from these willing exiles, the emigrant community in Rick's Café was real enough. The cast had been selected with authenticity in mind, particularly regarding the patrons' appearance and accents. In this respect, the casting agents uncovered an embarrassment of riches, finding actors whose personal stories often matched those of the characters they played. Paul Henreid proved perfect as Laszlo, Bogart's rival in love.

The kind, chubby waiter was S. Z. Sakal, born Gerö Jekö in Hungary to a Jewish family, who had fled in 1940. In a poignant irony, the dastardly Major Strasser was played by Conrad Veidt, who, as a fierce opponent of the Nazis, had turned his back on his German homeland in 1933. Curt Bois, the pickpocket, had left Berlin in 1934; the croupier, Marcel Dalio, born Israel Moshe Blauschild, had been forced out of his native Paris; another Austrian was Helmut Dantine, who had briefly been imprisoned in a concentration camp before being able to travel to the United States, and who was more than credible as the desperate young lover whom Rick (Bogart) allows to win some money.

And there were others, all of them refugees themselves, getting by on small Hollywood parts: Louis V. Arco (from Vienna), Trude Berliner (from Berlin), Ilka Grüning (from Vienna), Richard Ryen (born Richard Révy, from Hungary), Ludwig Stössel (from Austria), and, as the desperate and sinister Signor Ugate, the famous Peter Lorre, born László Löwenstein. Lorre had risen to the summit of his profession in Germany in the 1920s, particularly after his role as a murderer in Fritz Lang's celebrated *M*, only to be forced to flee; in his adopted country, he found himself locked into the half-sinister, half-comic character role of the bug-eyed villain.

As the situation in Europe grew ever more dangerous, desperate would-be emigrants, unable to obtain visas for preferred destinations such as the United States, proved willing to go almost anywhere that seemed safe. Another branch of the Freudenheim family set out on an odyssey involving seven countries, finally arriving in the Uruguayan capital, Montevideo. Eleven-year-old Fritz Freudenheim drew a map of the whole journey, chirpily entitled "From the Old Homeland to the New!"

South America became an important emigrant destination. People whose lives and careers in Berlin, Munich, or Hamburg had done little to prepare them for thriving in their new homelands nevertheless often proved well able to adapt. Others sought refuge elsewhere. In 1935 the Marburg philologist Erich Auerbach emigrated to Istanbul, where he would write, much of it from memory, his timeless masterwork of literary criticism, *Mimesis*. The Viennese philosopher Karl Popper fled as far as it was possible to flee, becoming a lecturer at the then Canterbury University College in Christchurch, New Zealand.

Here he was to pen his most influential work, *The Open Society and Its Enemies.*

Perhaps the most extraordinary, because furthest removed culturally, of all places of exile was Shanghai, the legendary city of commerce, vice, and urban sophistication. At that time, the city had no visa provisions at all. "The last place in the world we could go was Shanghai," remembers one émigré. Until late 1938 and the Germany-wide pogrom of Kristallnacht, so called because of the thousands of windows of Jewish businesses and homes that were smashed during the night of November 9–10, only about fifteen hundred Jews had made the long journey to Shanghai. Afterward, their number would increase tenfold. The newcomers were lucky to find that some members of the resident Sephardic community, whose ancestors had arrived with Russian traders in the nineteenth century, were not only wealthy but also prepared to help. Still, life was uncertain, and living standards remained basic for thousands of refugees, who were frequently too hard up to afford a strudel at one of the delicatessens of Shanghai's "Little Vienna," or even a coffee at one of the immigrants' *Kaffeehäuser.*

Berlin in the Levant

AMONG ALL THOSE WHO SOUGHT REFUGE from Nazi Germany, one option was open only to Jews. Ever since the Balfour Declaration of 1917, in which the British foreign secretary had stated that "His Majesty's government view with favour the establishment in Palestine of a national home for the Jewish people," the Zionist cause in Europe and beyond had been gaining in momentum.[17] After 1918, through years of increasing nationalism, anti-Semitism, and strife, Palestine had come to be seen by many Jews as a viable option, or even as an absolute historical necessity; others rejected it with equal vehemence.

Especially for younger Jews in Europe, involvement in Zionist youth organizations and sports clubs had been an effective way of countering their progressive exclusion in societies increasingly preoccupied by their own respective national myths. There were many different and often contradictory currents within Zionism, from a determinedly secular variant, whose aim was to eliminate anti-Semitism by making the Jews a "normal" people among other "normal" peoples, to Orthodox communities longing to return to the Promised Land in order to prepare themselves for the coming of the Messiah. There were pragmatic Socialists seeking to realize dreams of ideal communities in harmony with the local Arab population, and far-right nationalists determined to remove or eliminate anyone standing in the way of the establishment of a Jewish land. These last were a minority, however; most newcomers arrived with peaceful ideas.

The goal of Zionism was not only to establish a Jewish state in Palestine (indeed, there was a major, ongoing debate about both the necessity of a state and its possible location) but also to create a new kind of Jew. The pale, emaciated *yeshive bokher* (yeshiva student) was rejected as an archetypal victim image in a world of growing emphasis on militarism and masculinity—to the extent, in some places, of caricaturing the Nietzschean *Übermensch*. The old, effeminate image was to be supplanted by that of a new, muscular, tanned, proud, and self-reliant Jew, able to till the soil and to fight, a pioneer and a hero capable of meeting any physical challenge.

In practice, the experience of life in 1930s Palestine was less epic than imagined, though still fraught with practical challenges. Gaining a visa to the British Mandate area was not easy, but even for those who did arrive, life in an essentially Arab country required an enormous mental adjustment for men and women more used to the cafés and lecture halls of Lemberg, Vienna, London, Berlin, or Paris than to pioneer life in the Levant. The real pioneers, the settlers in the kibbutzim throughout the country, encountered among the local Arabs people tolerant of the apparently crazy Europeans keen to break their backs working the desert ground, but also many who were hostile to the intrusion, greeting the new arrivals with resentment or even violence.

In the cities, life was less conflicted, though no less strange. Jerusalem, still a picturesque place of legendary if mutually contradictory promises and squalid daily reality, carried too much historical baggage and too many expectations to be an attractive place to live. Apart from the Holy City and the port town of Haifa, German Jews preferred a newly founded settlement outside the old Arab town of Jaffa, a place with a more European character, including Bauhaus villas and large public buildings, poetically named Tel Aviv, which means "spring hill."

Among those who had emigrated to build a future for themselves and for their people were many Jews from the former Habsburg lands of central Europe, and also many from the shattered Russian Empire. After centuries of oppression, they were determined to make a fresh start. Emblematic of this was their wish to communicate with one another not in one of their old languages and certainly not in Yiddish, the idiom of their humiliating ghetto lives. To achieve this, to carry them into the future, they revived and reconstructed the ancient

Hebrew language and made it a living idiom, with new words invented to match realities unknown to Bible scribes. The philosopher Martin Buber, together with younger intellectuals such as the scholar Gershom Scholem from Berlin and the historian Hugo Bergmann from Prague, tried to fill the shell of the old Jewish cultural tradition with new values and even mystical meanings for an essentially secular context.

Other refugees who had arrived in Palestine out of sheer necessity, rather than any Zionist conviction, tried to ignore the fact that they were now walking down Sheinkin or King David Street rather than Unter den Linden. They continued to wear their three-piece suits even in the worst summer heat, reading German newspapers in cafés that did everything in their power to make their patrons forget that camels were still the preferred means of transportation on local streets. The bookshops of these people, and their shelves at home, were stacked with the works of Goethe and Schiller, Heinrich Heine and Thomas Mann. Not for them the dream of the new Jew—they simply mourned their old lives, trying to navigate the hot, deprived, provincial present as best they could.

According to emigrant legend, one German Jewish academic kept a portrait of Hitler on the desk of his Tel Aviv study. When a fellow émigré came to visit him and saw it, he was scandalized and began to remonstrate with his friend, asking him how he could have in his own home a picture of such a monster. "I need it," the academic replied. "It reminds me not to feel homesick."

Beautiful Bodies

....

IT WAS A SUDDEN TURN OF EVENTS THAT CAUSED WOLFGANG FÜRSTNER
to take his own life. A captain in the German army, his career had
symbolized the virtues of the newly strengthened fatherland of which
he had been so proud. His father a battleship commander, his mother
a member of the aristocratic von Reventlow family, Fürstner had
been personally connected with many of Germany's most distinguished individuals—and one or two of the most bohemian. An officer and a fervent patriot, he had adored the former and looked down
at the latter.

Having served with gallantry in the war, Fürstner had then embarked on a course of uncompromising right-wing activism. A portrait
photo shows him looking straight into the camera, erect and proud,
hair close-cropped, an Iron Cross from the Great War adorning his
left breast pocket, the eagle and swastika of Hitler's army on the right

An officer from top to toe:
Wolfgang Fürstner chose to
commit suicide after having
attended an official dinner.

side of his chest. In the chaotic years leading up to 1921, he had commanded a section of the Freikorps, a fascist paramilitary unit, fighting communists in the streets of Berlin. Organizing and disciplining large crowds was his passion. While still a serving officer he had run the sports program of the Deutsche Offiziersbund, the German Officers' Association. An early member of the Nazis' NSDAP, he had risen to a high position in the German sports world, eventually being elected to the organizing committee of the 1936 Olympic Games.

The games had been awarded to Germany in 1931 as a gesture of postwar reconciliation, effectively readmitting Germany to the family of nations. For Hitler's government, the event was challenge and opportunity in equal measure. Finally the country would be able to show to the world that the new Germany under its great leader was as peaceful as it was powerful. Preparations on a gigantic scale were undertaken; no plan was too great, no detail too small to be considered. Joseph Goebbels, Hitler's minister of propaganda, regarded the Games as a massive public relations exercise for the Nazi regime. In early 1934, as part of his ambitious scheme, he named Fürstner, a decorated soldier and trusted ally, as commander of the Olympic Village. The well-being of all the athletes, as well as a great number of the impressions they would take home with them, were to be his responsibility.

Fürstner threw himself into the task of converting a former military barracks into an Olympic village, with 160 individual houses as well as meeting halls, common spaces, doctors' offices, and more. The newly appointed commander took into account the needs and habits of athletes from different disciplines and nations. Weightlifters were fed on beefsteak tartare and chopped raw liver. Indian athletes were provided with a vegetarian diet. The British delegation found Horlick's malted milk and cooked vegetables. The regulations stipulated that athletes from the United States received steak for lunch and "no kippered herrings." The Chileans were noted for their fondness of "large quantities of jam," just as the Finns could feast on blueberries. While Fürstner left nothing to chance as far as the athletes' accommodation was concerned, police officers took to "beautifying" the streets of Berlin by arresting hundreds of vagrants and "Gypsies" and imprisoning them in an internment camp on the outskirts of the city, far from the gaze of potential tourists.

As the preparations for the Games reached their final phase, Fürstner was commended for his good work. His village was now looking like a picture postcard and functioning like clockwork, dentist and barbers and international newspapers included. He knew how much was depending on his skill in providing a perfect Olympic Village, as Germany wanted to gain the goodwill of all visiting nations. But the buildup to the event had been marred by controversy. The International Olympic Committee (IOC) had insisted that there must be no discrimination against Jewish athletes during the Games, and that Jewish athletes must be allowed to compete on the German teams themselves.

Several Jewish organizations had demanded a general boycott of the event, left-wing organizations had organized a rival Workers' Olympiad to be held in Barcelona, and for several months it had been unclear whether the Games would take place at all. From his exile in Paris, the German writer Heinrich Mann had declared, "A regime that is founded on forced labour and mass slavery, a regime that is preparing for war and only exists due to mendacious propaganda, how could such a regime respect peaceful sports and peace-loving athletes? Believe me, the international athletes who will go to Berlin will be nothing else there than gladiators, prisoners and court jesters of a dictator who already thinks of himself as master of the world."[1]

Only a compromise had secured the Games for Berlin. There would be Jewish athletes, the Reich had assured the IOC, and there would be no discrimination against Jews during the game. Quietly the Party leadership also gave the order to remove anti-Jewish street signs and public messages for the duration.

Germany was consequently obliged to produce at least one Jewish athlete for the national team. The choice fell on the half-Jewish Helene Mayer, a blond, blue-eyed fencer who had already fled discrimination at home and was by now living in Los Angeles. Mayer was an exceptional athlete and a strong hope for Olympic gold. In 1924, at age thirteen, she had won the German national championships, and four years later a gold medal at the Amsterdam Olympics. None of this, however, had protected her from being expelled from her fencing club in 1933, and she had fled to the United States. Now the Nazi authorities contacted her, inviting her to participate and giving her to understand not only that her participation would be welcome but also that her refusal would certainly not make things easier for her remaining family in Germany.

Believing herself in a good bargaining position, Mayer had demanded her German citizenship back, but had finally had to resign herself to returning home without any guarantee of this. Newspapers were instructed not to write about her arrival, and under no circumstances to mention her Jewish ancestry. In the event, she received only a silver medal; on the rostrum she gave a Nazi salute, not out of pride in her homeland but to protect her family.

Very public gestures as a disguise for private fear were commonplace during the Olympics, particularly for Jews, who lived through a bizarre "holiday" from daily abuse while Germany stood in the international spotlight. The linguist Victor Klemperer, who had lost his university post, kept a sad diary about the developments in his country. A deeply cultured man in the old German tradition, he regarded all Olympics—not just those now under way—as an undignified feast of hysterical nationalism in which a nation's culture was equated not with high intellectual or artistic achievements, nor less with its humane treatment of its citizens, but simply with how fast an individual could run. The present Olympics, however, were "a political enterprise through and through," he wrote. "Natives and foreigners are constantly having it drummed into them that what they are seeing is the upswing, blossoming, new spirit, unity, solidity and splendor, naturally also the peaceful and lovingly world-embracing spirit of the Third Reich."[2]

In May, five months before the official opening of the Games, Wolfgang Fürstner was suddenly and summarily dismissed from his position as commander of the Olympic Village. The official reason was that during an open day at the village some careless local visitors had caused damage to the structures, but the real reason soon emerged. Eight months previously, at their annual rally in Nuremberg, the Nazis had announced the introduction of new Race Laws, under which, among other things, Jews were to be deprived of their German citizenship and forbidden to marry or have sexual relations with Gentiles. Thorough as ever, the Reich's genealogists determined that Fürstner had a Jewish grandfather and was therefore classed as a "quarter-Jew." The officer, who may not have known about this detail of his ancestry, was dumbstruck. He was demoted to vice commander and supplanted by a junior, "Aryan" officer, who was now to reap the rewards of Fürstner's painstaking preparations.

Facing not only demotion but also dismissal from the army, Fürstner appeared stoic. He saw the Games through, and even attended the dinner given on August 19, in honor of his successor. During the meal he excused himself. He went home to the army barracks, took his pistol from its leather holster, aimed it at his head, and pulled the trigger. He was forty years old.

The German press was instructed to report the death as a tragic car accident. Fürstner was buried with military honors at the Berlin Invalidenfriedhof, a military cemetery where national heroes such as the flying ace Manfred von Richthofen, "the Red Baron," were buried. The reputation of the Reich was thus protected, and Fürstner took his secret and his despair with him to the grave.

The Color of Gold

ONLY A FEW PEOPLE in the barracks heard the shot fired by Captain Fürstner. A fortnight earlier, on August 3, 1936, the sound of a different shot had reverberated around the world. It was the short, dry report of the starting pistol for the men's 100-meter sprint, perhaps the most prestigious event of the entire Games. Hitler himself was present when the sprinters went to their positions at the starting line. Germany's great white hope was Erich Borchmeyer, already a veteran at thirty-one. Close by him stood a student from the United States, who was ten years Borchmeyer's junior. "I looked down that field to the finish 109 yards and 2 feet away and then began to think in terms of what it had taken for me to get there," the younger man later reflected. "And as I looked down at the uniform of the country that I represented and realized that after all I was just a man like any other man, I felt suddenly as if my legs could not carry even the weight of my body."[3]

Jesse Owens sprang out of the starting blocks and into sporting history, posting a time of 10.3 seconds. Footage from the event shows a stony-faced Hitler, an animated spectator during most other events, turning around in disgust. Owens was African American, as was the winner of the silver medal, Ralph Metcalfe. Though scheduled to congratulate the victor in person, Hitler left the stadium before the awards ceremony could take place.

The Führer's snub meant little to Owens, though newspapers in the United States were full of disgusted comments about the insult. But the media outrage at home revolted him. The same people who were now clamoring for the fair treatment of an American athlete in Germany had always treated him as a second-class citizen at home. The youngest of nine children, he had been born into poverty to a sharecropper in Alabama. As a boy, Jesse had often hidden from the local girls, because he did not have enough clothes to cover himself decently. During the First World War, the Owens family had moved to Cleveland, Ohio, one of hundreds of thousands of southern black families to seek a better life in the states further north.

At school, the boy's prowess as a runner had soon attracted attention, and he was entered into competitions from which he reliably emerged the winner. In 1932, at sixteen, he was selected for the US Olympic team. The following year, he matched the world record of 9.4 seconds over 100 yards. Despite the fact that he had never learned to read fluently, he was awarded a place at the predominantly white Ohio State University, where he could concentrate on his running.

Even as a student with a special scholarship as a gifted athlete, Owens was not allowed to sleep in one of the men's dormitories at the university. Local restaurants refused to serve him, and he had to use the back entrance to stadiums in order to get in to run in many of the events he eventually won. His financial situation was precarious: while training, he earned a living as an elevator operator and as a janitor at the university cafeteria. After taking part in a competition in a different city, he and his fellow black athletes would frequently have to eat in their car and sleep at the local flophouse, the only place open to them. Once, in Kokomo, Indiana, they narrowly escaped being lynched.

Owens went on to win three further gold medals at the 1936 Olympics, a historic achievement in itself. But when he returned to the United States, America's most outstanding athlete did not receive so much as a telegram of congratulations from President Franklin D. Roosevelt. Elections were imminent, and the president could not afford to be seen cozying up to blacks. Owens was later to say that this snub stung him far more than Hitler's petty irritation at his victory.

Creating the New Man

DESPITE THE FACT that Germany had fielded the largest Olympic team and harvested the greatest number of medals (89 out of a total of 388), the Nazi hierarchy had every reason to be dismayed about the strong performance of blacks and Asians, as well as Jews, during the Games. It had been the intention of the regime not only to show the world the generosity and openness of the German people and their new government but also, and equally important, to display "Aryan" Germany's superiority of mind and body over all other nations, especially those of "inferior" racial stock. Jesse Owens had punctured these Nazi pretensions, and though Hitler was overheard by his architect, Albert Speer, to mutter something along the lines of blacks being "closer to animals" than whites and therefore presumably able to run faster than men, the propaganda of the master race had been shown up for what it was.

For Nazi ideologues, this was a vital point. Physical fitness was not just a means of asserting racial superiority; it was at the very heart of National Socialism, as it was in other political movements of the time, including Soviet communism and Zionism. The ultimate aim was not just to produce a stronger people but to transform human nature, creating, in effect, a New Man.

Like every powerful ideological element, this hope of human transformation had strong mythological antecedents. The New Man was an important motif in Christian apocalyptic theology, and it had also been taken up with enthusiasm by Renaissance thinkers wanting to be reborn in the image of classical antiquity. In Geneva, Jean-Jacques Rousseau had dreamed of spiritual rebirth in his 1762 treatise *The Social Contract*, and his words were to have a profound impact on twentieth-century totalitarian thought. "He who dares to undertake the founding of a people should feel that he is capable of changing human nature," he wrote, "of transforming each individual . . . into a part of a larger whole from which this individual receives, in a sense, his life and his being; of altering man's constitution in order to strengthen it; of substituting a partial and moral existence for the physical and independent existence we have all received from nature. So that . . . each citizen is nothing, and can do nothing, without the others."[4]

Early in the nineteenth century, the philosopher Friedrich Wilhelm Hegel had set out his vision of Germany's eventual apotheosis through an inexorable process of human progress into a time and place beyond history. A quasi-messianic fantasy that identified the summit of history

Statues of athletes at the entrance to the sports complex in Dresden, 1936.

with north German Protestantism, and specifically with Prussia, Hegel's idealism was nonetheless to prove immensely influential within Europe and beyond. One hundred years later, Friedrich Nietzsche spat out a contemptuous reply to Hegel's vision of a supposedly inevitable progress, and, in a profound response to the alienation and quasi-enslavement attendant on incipient modernism, sketched out his own vision of the transcendence not of peoples but of free individuals.

Nietzsche's concept of the superman, expounded in his *Thus Spake Zarathustra* of 1883–1885, was more poetic, more complex, and more subtle than most of his readers were able to see; carried away by his metaphorical, strangely exalted prose, they constructed a variety of vulgarized ideas of the *Übermensch*, mostly concentrating not on his surprisingly Buddhist or Epicurean idea of self-transcendence but on fantasies of hulking, half-naked heroes bestriding a fearful imaginary landscape.

Through the central decades of the nineteenth century, the idea of the transcendence of the here and now, of a teleological goal of history and a world populated by New Men and New Women, had also provided the kernel for another German's utopian worldview. Individuals would only truly flourish, wrote Karl Marx, once a political revolution had defined the appropriate conditions by ending oppression and creating social justice. The demise of capitalism and the servitude of the masses would make possible the spiritual as well as physical regeneration of individuals.

Marx and Nietzsche were the prophets of a new age of many diverse paths, one of them leading to "scientific racism" and thence to Nazism. Two further theories with no intrinsic link to racism contributed to the same fearful political and social ideology. Darwin's unveiling of evolutionary processes was quickly integrated into a conservative teleology in which human beings were held to be evolving toward an innate potential, with biological competition gradually removing all imperfections from the genetically most favored group. The pithy term "survival of the fittest" came to mean not the survival of those best adapted to their environment but rather the inevitable dominance of the strongest, not just in a state of nature but also, ominously, in advanced human societies.

The pseudo-scientific, teleological vision of an evolutionary paradise of perfect beings in some distant future was nothing but a tattered lab coat pulled on over an old, essentially religious idea—the idea of humanity's eventual transcendence and the advent of the New Man. Nonetheless, "survival of the fittest" soon became both apology and rallying cry for laissez-faire capitalism, and also for eugenicist demands to give evolution a helping hand by preventing "inferior" people from breeding.

By the end of the nineteenth century, against this harmonious choir of supermen of various timbres, one voice was sounding a decidedly dissonant note of skepticism. To the pioneering psychoanalyst Sigmund Freud, the dream of transcendence was a mere social fiction imposed on individuals in order to check their natural, unruly impulses. Visions of transformation into a superior being and a life of eternal bliss, he held, were mere mirages in the emotional desert of Viennese bourgeois life—and, by extension, of human life. They might be necessary to the survival of hope, but they remained illusions nonetheless.

Dreams Becoming Nightmares

IN HIS 1921 DYSTOPIAN NOVEL *We*, precursor to Aldous Huxley's *Brave New World*, published in 1932, the Russian author Evgeny Zamyatin had satirized the Bolshevik vision of society as a vast machine, along with its love of mechanization, hyperefficiency, and the "scientific management" system of Taylorism. In the technologized future of the novel, individuality is all but eliminated:

> I watched the men below, how they would bend over, straighten up, turn around, all in accordance with Taylor, smoothly and quickly, keeping in time, like the levers of a single immense machine. Pipes glistened in their hands. . . . They were the same, all one: humanized, perfected men. It was the sublimest, the most moving beauty, harmony, music. . . . I wanted to go down there at once, to them, to be with them. And there I'd be: shoulder to shoulder with them, welded to them, caught up in the steel rhythm, the measured movements, the firm round ruddy cheeks, the mirror-smooth brows, unclouded by the insanity of thought.[5]

The nightmare imagined by Zamyatin seemed to be threateningly close, and the possibilities of reacting to it seemed limited. More than ever after Stalin's rise to power and the institution of the Five-Year Plan, the Soviet answer to the problem of technology was an ardent embrace, declaring human beings valuable if and only if they were able to perform their allotted roles as cogs in a big machine. The Soviet New Man would hatch in a fully automatic incubator.

Some politically engaged avant-garde artists, such as designer and architect El Lissitzky and poet Vladimir Mayakovsky, had adopted a constructivist approach to the human form, presenting the image of the body as machine in a glorious Soviet future. Their daring vision, however, had proved uncongenial to the authorities and also uncontrollable by them; it was quickly marginalized. Still, the emergent dominance of socialist realism, declared official artistic policy in 1931, remained firmly attached to the idea of a new *Homo sovieticus*, muscled and proud, endowed with superhuman gifts through Soviet education—and depicted in simple representational form acceptable to both the masses and the authorities.

The New Man transcended not only human limitations but also political boundaries. Glorious young men in marble, concrete, and bronze were also a potent symbol of the self-appointed "master race" to the west. Though socialist examples often included glorious New Women, too, where fascist examples were more focused on masculinity, observers were soon remarking on how hard it was to distinguish the heroic leftist visions from those of their rightist enemies.

Fascist ideologues and their sympathizers from Italy, France, and Germany had all arrived at this point via different paths. In contrast

Toward a better future?
Vera Ignatjevna Mukhina's
Worker and Kolkhos Woman.

to the Bolsheviks, who wanted to mold individuals into spare parts for machines, fascists sought to liberate themselves from the yoke of an anonymous modern existence, and from the crisis of meaning that appeared to be part of it, by retreating into the political projection of a mythical past in which human bodies had supposedly been expressions of heroic archetypes, strong, beautiful, and in perfect harmony with nature. Nature, in this sense, was the very antithesis of modernity, with its essentially urban emphases on liberalism, cosmopolitanism, and reason. The fascists regarded nature as the inner voice of man, which spoke different idioms to different people, or different races.

The fascists called on the New Man to rise up and to wrest history—and of course political power—back from those who, they held, had been actively working against them. In this the German Nazis went much further than other fascists, calling for an apocalyptic clash of ideologies in which the battle lines would be drawn along racial distinctions. Capitalism, the Nazi theorists claimed, was alien to the Germanic soul, a Jewish conspiracy designed to suppress the greater spiritual strength slumbering in all Aryans and their greater intrinsic worth as human beings. In his film *Metropolis*, Fritz Lang had imagined the huge factory machines as the extended arms of the capitalist bosses, controlling and coercing a people noble by nature. In the Nazis' belief, which they disseminated widely, the German people had been robbed of their deserved victory in the First World War, "stabbed in the back" by the cowardly politicians at Versailles; they would now redress the balance and achieve a position befitting their natural supremacy. To do so, they would have to transform themselves, developing the innate gifts of their race until they appeared as supermen to the rest of the world.

The Nazi cult of fitness was thus tied to an apocalyptic goal of racial warfare, but it could draw on a broad existing culture of physical awareness, health, natural living, and nudism that had been prevalent since the nineteenth century, not only in Germany but also in Britain and other, particularly northern European, countries. The interwar culture of the body was by no means fascist per se.

Frequently, though not necessarily, the rediscovery of the human body as a part of nature rather than of society went hand in hand with a degree of social nonconformism. Founded in 1896 and hugely popular during the interwar years, the *Wandervogel* (bird of passage) movement had encouraged young people to get out of the cities and away from the social constraints of their families to roam the countryside on foot or on a bicycle, sing folk songs by a campfire, commune with nature, and admire the starry skies—and to meet one another in ways that would probably have been impossible closer to home.

In the ferment of Weimar Germany, however, the young ramblers who had so scandalized their parents before 1914 looked markedly unadventurous. By the early 1920s, there were communities of socialist nudists and even sun-worshiping alternative schools where no clothes were worn. Thousands of gymnastics and sports clubs had sprung up, dedicated to creating stronger and more beautiful bodies; holiday camps for workers included hours of clothes-free gymnastics; beaches set aside large areas for the movement dedicated to "air- and light-bathing." Throughout the 1920s, tens if not hundreds of thousands of Germans had participated in these *Freikörperkultur* (FKK) or Free Body Culture movements, which became a synonym for a new life without bourgeois restrictions, free of embarrassment, and free of clothes. On the eve of the Nazi seizure of power in 1933, Germany's FKK associations had around one hundred thousand registered members and many more sympathizers.

For the National Socialists, the preoccupation with physical culture was highly significant. Their entire rhetoric was suffused with body imagery, emphasizing health, fitness, and strength. When Hitler gave a speech in 1935 in front of fifty thousand members of the Hitlerjugend (Hitler Youth), he urged them to become "hard as Krupp steel, quick as whippets and tough as leather." References to the collective "body of the people" (*Volkskörper*) and to physical strength and life in harmony with nature suffused Nazi speeches, articles, and propaganda. Beautiful bodies were important.

In order to transform their utopian ideas into concrete politics, the Nazis had had to appropriate these practices themselves, as well as the organizations and individuals representing them, and this they had done with great alacrity. Just as cultural life, university education, public administration, and trade unionism had been ideologically streamlined within a matter of months after the 1933 takeover, body culture, too, was swiftly taken into the grip of the new strongmen.

Under the new government, even the previously peaceful and universalist FKK clubs had felt compelled to expel all their Jewish members; sports associations had become temples of "Aryan" bodies, with journals such as *Gesetz und Freiheit* (Law and Freedom) and *Deutsche Leibeszucht* (German Body Culture) satisfying a steady, partly voyeuristic demand for chaste, naked bodies. In 1936, the best-selling 1925 book *Mensch und Sonne—arisch-olympischer Geist (Man and Sun, the Aryan-Olympian Spirit)* was republished, just in time for the Olympic Games. Whatever anarchic potential there might have been in earlier clubs and publications was now ironed out with truly utopian prudishness, as the Nazi press produced torrents of suggestive yet prim photos of nude bodies: these living sculptures, oiled biological machines cast in the mold of antiquity, extolling life and nature, were still obliged to cloak their nakedness in shadows created in the darkroom.

Keeping sex firmly in the shadows was also an expression of a fundamental concern that the National Socialists shared not just with Mussolini's Fascists and with French and other right-wing sympathizers but with the Bolsheviks as well. It was one thing to liberate the body from the alienation of a capitalist environment and from Christian morality's imprint of shame, but quite another to create a generation of libertines. As Europe's totalitarian movements set about building their various utopian futures, and their democratic counterparts were engaged in the more modest task of clearing slums and fighting the diseases of poverty in the big cities, hygiene and cleanliness became key words, both physically and morally. Cleanliness was preached as a way of life, and it soon supplanted the ancient fear of sin with a set of new horror visions. Masturbation, homosexuality, promiscuity, and the lack of impulse control were portrayed not as wicked, as they might once have been, but as dirty, diseased, and potentially deadly to the individual as well as to society and, of course, to the race.

Perhaps the most curious as well as the most eloquent object documenting the Western obsession with cleanliness during the interwar period is still standing in Dresden, where it was installed in 1930. The German Hygiene Museum had been built in 1911 but was rehoused in a new, proudly rational, and Bauhaus-influenced structure three years before Hitler came to power. The museum was devoted to explaining not only the functioning of the human body but also basic facts about healthy nutrition and living. Pride of place was given to the "glass man," a model of a human body with raised arms and transparent skin, revealing the bones, organs, and major veins and arteries. Graceful and poised, the glass man (which was actually made not of glass but of Cellon, an early plastic) seemed the ideal embodiment of modernity: transparent, functional, and thoroughly rational.

Other initiatives to bring health and hygiene to the people were more obviously belligerent in their intent. Founded in 1933, the organization *Kraft durch Freude* (Strength Through Joy) provided strictly regulated cheap entertainment and vacation camps for German workers, including plenty of exercise for children and adults. Even cruise ships for the people were part of the program. The organizers had carefully developed a range of exercises and activities designed to weld together unruly individuals into a single, obedient body, preparing them, whether they realized it or not, for the societal and other battles of the future. There was now no berth on a cruise ship without mass gymnastics on deck, no escape to the Baltic coast or the Black Forest without morning reveille and collective military-style activities producing a sea of bodies moving in unison. By 1945, seven million journeys to vacation camps and 690,000 sea voyages would be sold at cost, as a "gift from the Führer."

In Germany as elsewhere, breeding the New Man also had another, more literal connotation. Eugenics movements were by now also popular among intellectuals in Britain, the United States, France, Belgium, the Netherlands, Switzerland, Czechoslovakia, Argentina, Russia, Italy, and Scandinavia. In several countries, the forcible sterilization of "mental defectives" and other undesirables became both policy and practice (and in some cases, such as in the United States and Sweden, lasted into the 1970s). The Nazi regime, however, pushed eugenicist ideas even further. Beginning in 1933, in German hospitals and clinics, some four hundred thousand people would be sterilized, mostly involuntarily. After 1939, a murderous wave of "euthanasia" of "useless eaters"—people deemed "unfit to live"—would follow.

Eugenics was by no means a prerogative of the political right or of hard-nosed scientists such as Francis Galton. In fact, the idea produced a remarkable consensus among people of otherwise different views, though it is true that most of them hailed from notably privileged backgrounds. In Britain, for instance, John Maynard Keynes supported eugenicist ideas, as did Winston Churchill, Virginia Woolf, George Bernard Shaw, and Bertrand Russell. Woolf herself had a seriously mentally disabled brother with whom she had been forced to share her meals during her childhood. When as an adult she encountered a "long line of imbeciles" during a country outing, she noted in her diary: "It was perfectly horrible. They should certainly be killed."[6] All felt that some form of "scientific" management could improve the national breeding stock.

The poet William Butler Yeats was convinced that a physical regeneration would hasten not only the political regeneration of his beloved Ireland but also its spiritual rebirth. At the same time, however, he observed: "Since about 1900 the better stocks have not been replacing their numbers, while the stupider and less healthy have been more than replacing theirs. . . . If some financial reorganization . . . [can] enable everybody without effort to procure all necessities of life and so remove the last check upon the multiplication of the uneducated masses, it will become the duty of the educated classes to seize and control one or more of those necessities. The drilled and docile masses may submit, but a prolonged civil war seems more likely, with the victory of the skillful, riding their machines as did the feudal knights their armoured horses."[7]

And there were more direct ways of creating a supposed genetic utopia. In Germany, the state-administered Lebensborn (Spring of Life) organization, founded in 1935, set about producing the new Aryans of Hitler's dreams by selecting men and women who met the approved racial criteria for a future Germanic people to produce babies for Führer and Volk. Prospective mothers with the requisite blond hair were brought together in an institutional setting with handsome young men of apparently Aryan stock; the children they bore were then integrated into a strict system of National Socialist education. In 1936 this scheme was only in its infancy, but by the end of the war some fifteen thousand children, the toddling exponents of the new master race, would have been born and schooled in what German critics called "Hitler's chicken farms."

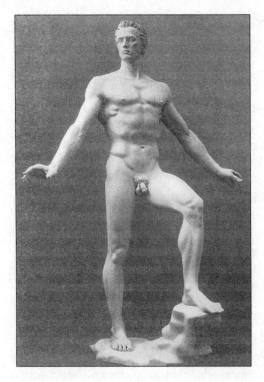

The Victor *by the German*
sculptor Arnold Breker,
a perfect example of the
Nazi idea of the New Man.

The official image of the new race lay in the willing hands of Arno
Breker, a talented sculptor who had begun his career in Paris, where
he had been friendly with important artists including Pierre-Auguste
Renoir, Pablo Picasso, Jean Cocteau, and Aristide Maillol. Breker had
returned to Germany in 1934, limiting his gifts to the production of
images of heroic nudity. Breker's uninspired expanses of fleshy pom-
posity were soon adorning public buildings, and Hitler showed himself highly pleased with the tight muscles, high foreheads, firm loins,
and visionary poses of the sculpted Aryan giants. What little grace
they possessed, however, was owing not to the racial superiority of
their models but to Breker's thorough knowledge of the sculpture
of antiquity, which he continued to copy, and unwittingly satirize,
throughout his career.

Breker was by no means alone in taking his inspiration from
Greek and Roman art. After the Great War, the once vigorous cubist
movement had abruptly faltered, as if the artists had lost both nerve
and appetite for presenting splintered bodies and disintegrated selves.
Picasso, both reflector and initiator of artistic currents, had begun to
paint in a neoclassical manner as early as 1918, and others were
soon to follow. In Russia, the young Sergey Prokofiev premiered his

Classical Symphony in the same year; in Paris, Jean Cocteau was using a similarly simplified neoclassical idiom for his drawings and stage designs; and Igor Stravinsky turned from the extravagant modernity of his *Sacre du Printemps* to tame variations on eighteenth-century Italian musical forms. A pall had fallen over the seemingly boundless experimentation of the art world, and many artists joined the great Western project of making humans whole again, rescuing the New Man from the shell-shocked ruins of the old.

There were countercurrents, of course. German expressionists such as George Grosz and Otto Dix had sought to portray precisely the grotesque ugliness of a sick civilization—but their distorted faces and obscene tableaux were themselves indictments of the society producing such aberrations, the flipside of hope. The surrealists in Paris had produced an anti-art that claimed to be not interested in beauty, but as André Breton's later political engagement showed, this was also intended to attack the society that had produced the war and its crushed victims. A vision of a New Man lurked behind these movements, too.

Nobody was a more ardent, even idolatrous admirer of the resurrected classical body than the director of the official film of the Berlin Olympics, Leni Riefenstahl, who had already produced a dramatic and highly propagandistic account of the 1934 Nazi Party rally in Nuremberg. In both films, Riefenstahl's introduction gives the clearest indication of the intention behind the images. Her documentary *Triumph des Willens* (*Triumph of the Will*) started with shots of the plane taking the "greatest leader of all time" to a huge rally and showed the Führer descending on Germany from the clouds, like a latter-day god, albeit in a Junkers plane. Riefenstahl's Olympic film begins in ancient Greece, with the camera almost caressing the sculptures. Then, as if by magic, the marble figure of a discus thrower comes to life, hurling the discus into an unknown future. More athletes appear, their heroic exercises culminating in the harmonious movements of a series of runners carrying the blazing Olympic torch directly from Athens to Berlin, with the last man in the long relay running straight into the stadium and lighting the torch in honor of the Games.

Gum-Chewing Supermen

THE CULT OF THE NEW MAN was not only a strong voice calling for the future but also a voice rejecting the recent past. It was a headlong flight into an imaginary, timeless, perfect realm in which all dirt, sickness, disorder, and degeneration would be overcome and replaced by hygiene, health, and wholeness. Depending on its author's imagination, it was to be decorated either with sturdy oaks and classical ruins or with a blaze of electric light, glistening machines, and a vast ballet of mechanical perfection. In its emphasis on bodies that were to be both beautiful and strong, it was also a response to the shuddering wrecks of shell-shocked men fresh from the trenches, and to the pitiful sight of amputated veterans, to the ruins of once proud men now seen, in Germany as throughout Europe, workless and begging in the streets.

Even before 1914 there had been warning voices announcing that human bodies could no longer compete with machines, and the experience of industrial warfare had rammed this insight home. Humanity, it seemed, was no match for the technology it had created, and like the sorcerer's apprentice, it would lose control over the world. The dream of the New Man, a superman transcending all limitations, was the answer to a cultural fear that was deeply rooted in all industrialized nations.

In 1936, as Germany celebrated health, physical beauty, and sporting prowess amid the insignia and fanfares of fascism, the development appeared to have come full circle. Not everyone, however, was ready to bow before Nietzschean heroes or utopian demigods. Sailing to Europe in the same year, the American diplomat George Kennan found that he was sharing the passage from New York with the supposed flower of American youth. Unimpressed by the Olympians and their small-town ways, he commented amusedly: "The ship was carrying the American Olympic team to Germany for the games that were to take place there that summer. For a week we dodged the motions of gum-chewing supermen with crew cuts, and a variety of hefty amazons, as they practiced their particular skills on deck."[8]

War Within a War

*Everybody saw Spain as the epitome of the particular conflict
with which they were concerned. It was for this reason that the
writers of the Western world became so emotionally involved in
the Spanish conflict. For myself, and a great number of people
like me, it became the great symbol of the struggle between
Democracy and Fascism everywhere.*

Jason Gurney, *Crusade in Spain*, 1974

*We are faced with a conspiracy, with a group of people who
intended to mount a coup against the state . . . a fairly complex
conspiracy linking the conspirator with foreign, fascist powers.
How can one ask for formal proof under such circumstances?*

Andrey Vyshinsky, chief prosecutor
of the Moscow show trials, 1937

....

WITH ITS DOMED TOWER ON THE ROOF, THE TELEPHONE EXCHANGE
commands the elegant expanse of the Plaza de Cataluña, one of the
main squares of Barcelona. In early May 1937, with the country in
the grip of civil war, the capital of the newly autonomous region of
Catalonia was in the hands of Republican troops loyal to the elected
government. Not far from the city, Republican troops were locked in
vicious fighting with the rebel Nationalist troops. The front line was
at Zaragoza, far enough away not to threaten the lives of those inside
the city. Nevertheless, the atmosphere was so tense that the regional
government, the Generalitat, had forbidden the traditional communist
parade on May 1, fearing that a procession of thousands of armed
men in the streets might ignite the already volatile situation. For
within Barcelona itself, communists, Marxists, and anarchists were
all struggling against one another for power and influence. "The storm

Street battles between communists and anarchists in Barcelona, 1936.

clouds are hanging, more and more threateningly, over Barcelona," declared *Solidaridad Obrera*, a locally printed anarchist paper that at the time boasted the largest newspaper circulation in Spain.[1]

On May 3, three trucks pulled up in front of the telephone exchange. Under orders from Eusebi Rodriguez Salas, the commissioner for public order, armed militiamen dismounted and began to surround the building. When they called for the anarchist staff inside to surrender, they were greeted by a hail of bullets. They took cover, but the city's fragile peace was now shattered.

George Orwell, in Barcelona as a member of the International Brigades on leave from the front, witnessed the fighting: "That afternoon, between three and four, I was half-way down the Ramblas when I heard several rifle-shots behind me. I turned round and saw some youths, with rifles in their hands and the red and black handkerchiefs of the Anarchists round their throats, edging up a side-street that ran off the Ramblas northward. They were evidently exchanging shots with someone in a tall octagonal tower—a church, I think— that commanded the side-street. I thought instantly: 'It's started!'"[2]

As word about the attack on the telephone exchange spread through the city, barricades made of ripped-out paving stones, sandbags, and large pieces of furniture were thrown up in the streets. In the course of the following week, with snipers on the roofs, house-to-house shootouts, and running battles, some four hundred people were killed. The Republican side of the civil war was beginning to consume itself.

A Country Falls Apart

COMPARED TO OTHER EVENTS of this terrible war—famous battles, obscure massacres, and routine executions—this week in May seemed not much more than a skirmish. In the cruelty and hopeless drudgery of a war in which victims were usually counted in the thousands, four hundred lives was an almost insignificant loss.

The war had begun in 1936 when a group of generals, led by Francisco Franco, staged a military coup against the elected government of Republican prime minister Manuel Azaña. Though seriously destabilizing the government, the generals had failed to assume power directly, and a brutal civil war was unleashed. The roots of the ensuing bitter conflict reached back centuries into Spanish history. The country was internally divided into different regions, each with its own traditions and dialect or even language, and all united only by the overwhelming presence of the Catholic Church. The Enlightenment appeared to have passed by Spain, which was cut off physically by the Pyrenees and mentally by the church itself from the winds of change sweeping down from northern Europe.

No other European country was marked by such wide cultural divides. The sophisticated cities housed seminal intellectuals and artists such as the cultural philosopher José Ortega y Gasset, the novelist and philosopher Miguel Unamuno, the poet and dramatist Federico García Lorca and his close friend, painter Salvador Dalí, and architect Antoni Gaudí. But away from the cities, as Piers Brendon describes, "men used Stone Age harrows, sickles which had not changed since the Bronze Age, threshing-boards like those described in the Old Testament, ploughs such as were depicted on ancient Greek vases. Peasants might wear black corduroy suits but they had an essentially medieval mentality: some feared witchcraft, others thought that Protestants had tails."[3] It did not help that the priests in some villages actively prevented children from learning to read, fearing that they might become infected by the habit of independent thinking.

Even in 1930, the population of Spain was still largely rural; a landmass more than twice the size of Britain counted substantially fewer railways and overland streets. Millions still lived in "sleepy *pueblos* whose sordid, zigzag streets were flanked by grey adobe houses, most of them flea-ridden hovels where the floors were beaten earth, the windows were black holes and the rooms reeked of smoke and dung."[4] Within the cities, however, there was a culture of fierce opposition to the deep and obscurantist conservatism of the church, to the landowners, and to the aristocracy. In the industrial slums and the poor suburbs of Madrid and Barcelona, anarchists were preaching their radical gospel against all authority. In spite of their hatred of the priests, they were in their way no less Catholic, believing in an austere creed of abstinence from drinking, smoking, sexual indulgence, and bullfighting.

Warding off the perceived dangers of anarchism and communism, the Spanish army understood itself not as a force protecting the country from enemies beyond its borders but as an occupying force within the country itself. Its priority of defending the ancient social hierarchy and the unquestioned domination of the church was reflected in its organization. Eight hundred generals commanded a force that possessed no tanks, no fighter planes, and just one bomber; the common soldiers, equipped with long-outdated weapons, frequently deserted. The ammunition in the country's armories would have been exhausted after twenty-four hours of warfare.

Preferring the apparent safety of dictatorship to the vagaries of parliamentary democracy, King Alfonso XIII had supported a military coup led by General Miguel Primo de Rivera in 1923. Under the slogan "Country, religion, monarchy," Primo de Rivera had so badly mismanaged the government that Republican parties carried the election of 1931 in a landslide, prompting the king to flee without even bothering to abdicate. The new government instituted a hugely ambitious program of reform, including the introduction of secular schools, the scaling back of the army and officer corps, an expropriation of church property, and comprehensive land reform. The country's new constitution granted freedom of speech and association to all Spaniards, and introduced female suffrage.

This sweeping transformation was fiercely opposed by those who lost influence and power because of it, and by those who believed that the secular government was robbing Spain of its very soul. At the center of this opposition was the former director of the military academy of Zaragoza, Francisco Franco Bahamonde. When in 1931 his academy was closed down by the minister of war (later prime minister), the bookish Manuel Azaña, Franco had found himself faced with the prospect of demotion to the rank of colonel.

El Caudillo

SMALLISH, POTBELLIED, and prematurely balding, General Franco was hardly of heroic appearance, but his puritanical devotion to his work and his utter fearlessness in battle had earned him the respect of his comrades in arms. He had risen to the rank of general in 1926, the youngest man of that rank in Europe since Napoleon Bonaparte. In 1934, Franco had given the country a foretaste of what was to come. Elections in 1933 had returned a right-wing government, who suspended the social reforms of the previous Azaña administration. In response, the coal miners of Asturias, in the north of the country, initiated a major strike, which resulted in the occupation of the regional capital, Oviedo, by an army of some thirty thousand workers. They vented their fury by attacking priests and nuns and by burning down churches and the university.

Franco was ordered to put down the revolt. Unwilling to risk the inexperienced and potentially disloyal Spanish regular forces, he called instead on Spain's hardened colonial troops. Using Moroccan units and the Spanish Foreign Legion, he unleashed an orgy of bloodshed. In response to the killing of thirty-three priests and some three hundred soldiers, the Moroccans and legionnaires were given leave to rape, pillage, and loot for days; they killed some two thousand people and imprisoned an estimated twenty thousand to forty thousand. In the ferocity of their reprisals, they destroyed much of the city of Oviedo.

By February 1936, a corruption scandal had brought the right-wing government down, and Azaña was back in power, if very insecurely, as president of the republic. Franco was dispatched to the Canary Islands to serve as military commander there, a posting he regarded as tantamount to banishment. Right-wing forces, led by Emilio Mola, once director-general of security and now also "banished" to the post of military governor of monarchist Pamplona, had determined to mount a coup against the left-wing government; though privately making fun of Franco's "feminine voice [and] clammy handshake," they were keen for the experienced general to join them.[5] The coup was planned for July 18; on July 12, the leader of the right-wing opposition, José Calvo Sotelo, was murdered by government Assault Guards. This finally persuaded Franco to join the conspiracy, and at the same time it allowed the rebels to present their military coup as an act of disinterested patriotism.

Expecting a swift return to authoritarian rule, the conspirators were surprised by the stiff resistance put up by anarchists, socialists, communists, and others. While cities in the deeply Catholic and monarchist south and west of the country quickly declared for the rebels, Madrid, the autonomous region of Catalonia, the Basque country, and the regions along the Mediterranean coast held firm to left-wing Republican ideals. One communist member of parliament, the fiery Dolores Ibárruri, known as "La Pasionaria," provided them

all with a common battle cry echoing that of the French general
Robert Nivelle at the Battle of Verdun in 1916: "No pasarán!—They
shall not pass!" she declared.

Failing to take the government by force, the rebels, or Nationalists, as they now called themselves, had to capture the country city by
city and village by village. Spain was descending into civil war. The
following weeks and months saw escalating bloodshed around
the country as the victors of battles on both sides settled scores.
Republican-held Madrid was invaded by rebel forces. Amid the confusing jigsaw of barricades and pitched battles, the Popular Front
administration issued fifty thousand rifles to trade unionist fighters,
only to find that a mere five thousand were equipped with the bolts
necessary for firing them: the remaining bolts were still in storage in
the city's vast Montaña Barracks, now captured by the rebels. In a
massive assault, regular troops loyal to the government, together with
left-wing fighting units, stormed the barracks and massacred almost
all defenders. On August 22, Republican fighters put down a riot by
Falangist (right-wing) prisoners in the city's Model Prison, executing
thirty inmates, among them former rightist government ministers.

Some thirty-eight thousand people, mostly civilians, were slaughtered by Republican forces during the first months of the civil war—
8,815 in Madrid alone, and a similar number in Catalonia. Catholic
clergy bore the brunt of the anger directed at the forces of the old
order. Some 4,200 priests, 2,400 members of lower orders, and
283 nuns were killed, often with great cruelty. Some of them were
burned alive in their churches, while others were shot, often after having had to dig their own graves; some, it appears, were castrated or
disemboweled. One favored method of executing anyone suspected
of being a political opponent was abduction in a car—as the slang
phrase went, "being taken for a ride." The actress Maria Casares,
daughter of a former prime minister, who was working in a hospital
in Madrid during the war, found blood one morning on the backseat
of her car. Her young driver apologized with a shame-faced grin and
a shrug, explaining, "We took a guy for a ride at dawn, and I'm sorry,
I haven't had time to clean up the car."[6]

Though widespread and often cruel, the violence inflicted by leftists was, on the whole, unplanned; it was carried out by mobs or by
small groups acting on their own authority. On the Nationalist side,
by contrast, the violence was part of a campaign of systematic terror,
ordered from above. Vowing to "purge" Spain of all its internal
enemies, Nationalist forces executed politicians, left-wing members
of parliament, teachers, Freemasons, doctors, trade unionists, and

sometimes people whose only crime was to be wearing glasses and thus to look like intellectuals. Though not a member of any political party, the celebrated poet Federico García Lorca was deemed to be liberal enough in his general sympathies to deserve death. One of his executioners, a Falangist landowner, would later casually remark: "We killed [him]. I gave him two shots in the arse as a homosexual."[7]

In towns and villages throughout Nationalist-held areas, committees composed of officers, Falangists, landowners, and priests condemned prisoners to death within minutes in parodic trials without witnesses or legal representation. Firing squads sometimes worked all day to dispatch the many condemned. Stood against the wall of the local cemetery, many gave a last, desperate exhortation: "¡Viva la libertad!" One village peasant in the Rioja region heard, and recorded in his notebook, 1,005 executions. Not all of those executed would be buried, and the corpses of known leftists were often displayed for days, rotting in the heat in village squares and at crossroads.

Seville, one of the first cities to fall to the Nationalists, was "cleansed" with particular ferocity. With the prisons already overflowing with city officials, workers from the local olive oil factory, and other Republican sympathizers, those marked for death were held in local cinemas and theaters.[8] Some eight thousand people were executed in Seville in the latter half of 1936 alone. In Córdoba, taken with little resistance, clergymen and landowners drew up the initial lists of those who were to die; the lists proved not long enough for Major Bruno Ibáñez, the local military commander, who "could have shot the whole city," according to a Falangist lawyer. "They sent him to Córdoba with carte blanche."[9] Every day, the cellars of his headquarters were filled to the bursting point with prisoners, only to be empty by the evening. Some ten thousand people were victims of these summary executions, 10 percent of the entire population of the city.

A Republican atrocity in the town of Badajozin in Estremadura province, close to the Portuguese border, called down one of the most terrible reprisals of the war. On an August night in 1936, leftists locked priests and other Nationalist sympathizers inside churches and set the buildings alight. Twelve people died, eight of them burned alive. Other murders carried out by leftists may have totaled as many as 243. But when Nationalist forces under the command of Lieutenant Colonel Juan Yagüe captured the town, they indiscriminately put men, women, and children to the knife. They then began arresting anyone they suspected of Republican sympathies and herding their prisoners into the local bullring.

Checking who had fought for the city's defense by ripping open the shirts of all men they encountered to see whether their shoulders bore the telltale bruises of a recoiling rifle, the Nationalists gathered fighters and suspected sympathizers by the thousands. The American journalist Jay Allen, a correspondent for the *Chicago Tribune*, described what happened next. "At four o'clock in the morning they are turned out into the ring through the gate by which the initial parade of the bullfight enters. There machine guns await them. After the first night the blood was supposed to be palm deep on the far side of the lane. I don't doubt it. Eighteen hundred men—there were women, too—were mowed down there in some twelve hours. There is more blood than you would think in 1800 bodies."[10] Altogether, the Nationalist forces massacred some four thousand people, mostly local farmers and workmen, in this way. Yagüe, later Franco's minister of aviation, earned for this the epithet "Butcher of Badajoz," with the Republican death toll in the Estremadura province as a whole estimated to have been between six thousand and ten thousand.

Many towns suffered doubly as they changed hands between Nationalists and Republicans. In the southern city of Málaga, a British diplomat recorded that the Republicans had killed more than a thousand people, with or without trial, between July 1936 and February 1937. When the Nationalists took the city, 3,500 people were killed during the first week alone; by the end of the war, a further 16,952 individuals would be sentenced to death and executed. There are no exact figures of those put to death on the Nationalist side; historian Antony Beevor estimates that some two hundred thousand Spanish civilians were summarily executed or massacred by Franco's troops, in what Beevor calls "the White terror." The number of women and girls raped and then killed by Franco's notorious Moroccan units is unknown.

While great parts of Spain were in a state of war, the inhabitants of Barcelona had been looking forward to a festive day on July 19, 1936. It was the day of their Popular Olympiad, designed to be a leftist answer to Hitler's fascist Olympic Games in Berlin. But with the outbreak of rebellion on July 18, barricades were hastily erected in the city, and sporadic firing could already be heard. The athletes remained stranded in their hotels, the Olympiad forgotten.

Barcelona lay in the hinterland of the murderous conflict, along a front line stretching from the north of Catalonia to the besieged capital, Madrid, and from there south to Granada. The Nationalist rebels had planned to take the city with twelve thousand troops already stationed there, but when these units attempted to occupy strategic buildings and streets, they met with strong resistance from organized workers. Though the president of the Catalan Generalitat, Lluis Comanys, refused to arm Republican workers, fearing worse bloodshed if more weapons were in circulation, the CNT, the anarcho-syndicalist trade union, quickly improvised a fighting force. Weapons were seized from watchmen in the port, gun shops were raided, and armories were emptied at gunpoint, while metalworkers transformed small trucks into armored cars by attaching steel plates—some so heavy that the truck's engines could not cope with the weight of them, and failed to move at all.

There was no quick victory for the Nationalists in Barcelona. As they left their barracks in the small hours of the morning of July 18, factory sirens throughout the city sounded the alarm; they were soon engaged, first in skirmishes and then, as the day wore on, in more determined fighting. One infantry regiment was attacked so fiercely that they had to retreat to their barracks, while other units contended with homemade bombs being tossed from rooftops and sniper fire from windows and dark alleyways.

Some Nationalist fighters managed to take the Hotel Colón, the Ritz, and the telephone exchange, but as dawn gave way to day, the situation remained confused, with rebel strongholds besieged by detachments of armed workers. Inside, the Nationalists waited for reinforcements from the 1st Mountain Artillery Regiment, but these reinforcements never arrived: on their way to the city center, the entire regiment had been convinced by Republican workers that it would be a crime to shoot at their brothers, and they had joined the ranks of the Republicans. When artillery captured from the rebels was turned on their own men barricaded in the buildings they had taken, the Nationalist commander, General Goded, capitulated. The attempt to take Barcelona had failed.

With the Nationalist threat within the city defeated, the mood turned from anxiety to chaotic celebration, and also to bloody vengeance. Churches were torched, hundreds of clergy were murdered, priests had their ears cut off, and the corpses of buried nuns in various stages of decomposition were dug up and exhibited in suggestive poses and macabre displays. The night of July 19 was bright and starlit, but in the sky the silhouettes of burning church belfries stood out against the orange sky, like martyrs burned in one huge auto-da-fé. The purges of "subversives" were brutal, with hundreds taken for a last and fatal "ride." Thousands died in what finished, in the words of historian Piers Brendon, as "the frenzy of visionaries and criminals."[11]

Once the bloodshed had stopped, the victors began to celebrate. Young and often drunk fighters armed with guns careened dangerously through the streets in requisitioned cars. Loudspeakers on public squares blared out revolutionary music and news of Republican victories. Trade unionists, anarchists, and Communists were exhilarated by the sudden possibility of not only defeating the generals but also bringing about the revolution they had dreamed of for so long. People in the streets addressed strangers with the familiar *tú* and gave the antifascist clenched-fist salute; many felt certain that Europe's democracies would soon come to their aid.

As the leftist revolutionaries appeared to have triumphed, wealthy bourgeois stayed in their apartments or disguised themselves with shabby clothes before going out. It was the hour of revolutionary fervor, of retribution and experimentation. Workers' councils were established everywhere, heatedly debating every aspect of the city's present defense against fascism and of its future. The elegant boulevard Las Ramblas was taken over by working people from the suburbs; the Ritz became a public canteen, named Hotel Gastronomic No. 1. Even the brothels were collectivized, though not for long.

Operation Fiery Magic

BY MAY 1937 the first, chaotic period of Barcelona's war had passed. There were tensions between anarchists and Communists, but everybody knew that their first priority was to keep a united front against Franco, whose army had made substantial territorial gains throughout Spain. Yet in spite of this realization, in that same month the Communists chose to attack the anarchist-held telephone exchange, plunging the leftist-held city into a suicidal internal war. The reason for this disastrous move, which damaged the Republican cause profoundly, lay not in Barcelona, however, but in Moscow.

The Spanish Civil War had long since become an international conflict, and foreign powers had found ways to intervene, directly or indirectly. Franco's successes on the battlefield were primarily owing not to his feared colonial troops, and certainly not to the regular army, but to support from abroad, which he had solicited as soon as the unsuccessful military coup had transformed into a war.

The involvement of foreign powers had begun right at the start of the war. Seeking to gain a decisive edge against the ill-equipped but determined Republicans, Franco had sent an emissary to Germany on July 22, 1936, just four days after the initial uprising. Hitler had received Franco's men personally, on his return from a performance of Wagner's opera *Siegfried*, conducted by Wilhelm Furtwängler. The Führer apparently frowned at the Spaniards' seemingly amateurish way of fighting a war without equipment, funds, a properly trained army, or logistical support. Then, however, he had discovered common ground with Franco: the threat of Bolshevism. After treating his guests to a lengthy tirade about the evil looming in Russia and the need to keep it from developing elsewhere, he resolved to send help.

Unternehmen Feuerzauber (Operation Fiery Magic) seems to have borne the imprint of the opera the Führer had just heard, in which the fiery magic accompanying Siegfried's heroic progress is set to stirring music. Less poetically, but more usefully for the Spanish rebels, Hitler agreed to send them transport planes, bombers, funds, pilots, soldiers, and more. The airlift of troops from Morocco to Seville that enabled Franco to pursue his campaign of conquest throughout Spain was made possible by German planes.

Franco wasted no time drumming up support. Days after Hitler had received the Spanish emissaries, the Italian foreign minister, Count Ciano, Mussolini's son-in-law, was visited by a delegation of prominent Spanish fascists and royalists. Initially, despite a stream of begging telegrams from Franco's headquarters in Tangiers, Il Duce had shown little inclination to get involved in the Spanish rebellion. But when it began to look more likely that the rebellion might succeed and that Mussolini might secure lasting influence over a brother Fascist state in the Mediterranean, a squadron of Italian Savoia-Marchetti bombers and Fiat fighters was dispatched to Morocco. Three of the twelve planes promptly crashed, setting a pattern for the bravery combined with ineptitude that was so often to characterize Mussolini's troops, fairly or unfairly, in the popular imagination.

As the fighting wore on, German and Italian involvement deepened and expanded, turning a military coup that might have fizzled out for lack of equipment and manpower into a prolonged and bloody civil war. Hitler sent volunteer pilots with twenty Junkers bombers, Heinkel fighter planes, and Stuka attack planes capable of giving air cover to Nationalist advances and terrorizing the lightly armed forces on the Republican side. To bolster Franco's forces, Mussolini would eventually send more than one hundred thousand soldiers throughout the course of the war. Ammunition and equipment, including tanks and artillery, followed in a regular stream.

On the Republican side, things looked very different. While Franco could rely on his fascist allies as well as colonial troops and the Spanish Foreign Legion, both accustomed to fighting ruthlessly and only too happy to follow the order to terrorize the local population, the Republican forces consisted of loyal army units without battle experience and without modern weapons, alongside volunteer forces made up of socialists, communists, anarchists, and trade unionists who fought with deadly resolve and great courage but were not only badly equipped but also entirely untrained. To have a chance against a growing and increasingly well-equipped enemy, they desperately needed weapons, ammunition, supplies, training, and support.

The government turned to France, Britain, and the United States. The Republicans were in control of the country's gold reserves, an outstanding collateral to secure any purchases. Franco, after all, had nothing but the promise of victory. On July 19, as soon as the initial coup had taken place, Prime Minister José Giral had sent a telegram to his socialist French counterpart, Léon Blum, asking him fraternally for arms and planes.

Moved by the appeal and wanting to help, Blum hesitated nevertheless. He understood the moral imperative to help the beleaguered Spanish Republican government and he was alive to the threat of being surrounded by fascist states on three sides, but the internal situation in France was still highly volatile. Despite the fact that government had won the 1936 elections by a landslide, Paris had already witnessed violent riots, and right-wing and fascist forces at home were only waiting for an excuse to carry their anger into the streets again. Hostile newspapers savagely attacked the prime minister, and in Le Figaro the prominent Catholic writer François Mauriac wrote menacingly: "Take care! We will never forgive you for such a crime."[12] Blum had every reason to fear that open support for socialist and anarchist forces in neighboring Spain might be enough to spark serious unrest at home, or even to risk war with Italy and Germany.

Faced with these high stakes, Blum sounded out the position of the British government on a visit to London and received a stern warning against intervention. Her Majesty's ministers, and indeed the greater part of the country's social elite, were less afraid of a fascist Spain than of a communist state. Indeed, social agitation, hunger marches, and miners' strikes had sharpened British suspicion of a communist takeover, and the British consul in Barcelona, Norman King, called the Spanish "a bloodthirsty race" and advised his government that its best bet was to throw its weight behind the Nationalist rebels. If they were defeated, he wrote, "Spain will be plunged into the chaos of some form of bolshevism and acts of savage brutality can be expected."[13]

The strong establishment preference for Franco and his generals had another reason. As demonstrated by the brief career of Oswald Mosley and his Blackshirts, there was considerable sympathy for fascist ideas inside the British elite. There were also significant British investments in Spanish olive oil, fruit, and wine. Boys from the Spanish upper classes had been sent to British boarding schools for generations, and a sense of class solidarity led politicians such as the foreign secretary, Sir Anthony Eden, to favor a policy of strict non-intervention. If Prime Minister Blum was willing to supply arms to the Republicans, he would be on his own, and would be answerable for the consequences.

Nonintervention, of course, was anything but neutral. As the Nationalist army grew in strength and could bring to bear its bombers, fighter planes, tanks, and heavy guns, Republicans had to count every bullet in their antiquated rifles. Starved of support, they were practically condemned to lose the war. Heartbroken and unsure what to do, Blum sent some airplanes, but not enough to make a decisive impact on the war. He then set about securing a coalition of neutrality, effectively an arms embargo, that brought together the major democratic states, including the increasingly isolationist United States. Led by the pro-Franco Hearst press and the Catholic lobby in Washington, popular opinion there was also behind the Nationalist cause, despite the concerns voiced by Protestants and individual diplomats. The president of the Texaco Oil Company, Torkild Rieber, even openly supported the Nationalists with donations totaling some $6 million.

While democratic countries wavered or stalled, Franco's fascist allies were keen to use the war for their own ends. In July 1936 the German Luftwaffe had begun to send selected young men on a vacation in the sun organized by the Kraft Durch Freude organization, responsible for the vacations of millions of Germans. Disguised as harmless sun seekers, these hand-picked travelers were actually members of the newly formed Legion Condor, a covert German fighting unit operating in Spain and dressed in uniforms bearing no indication of belonging to the Third Reich. Some ten thousand German soldiers were part of the legion. Initially most of them belonged to airborne units, but after January 1937 they were joined by tanks complete with crews.

The goal of the Legion Condor was not just to help Franco. German military planners were especially interested in assessing the effectiveness of new weaponry and strategies. They abandoned the traditional V formation of their fighter planes in favor of paired hunting

The result of two decades? Pablo Picasso's Guernica, *1937.*

groups, which would become important in the Battle of Britain; they tried new methods of combined artillery and fighter plane attacks on enemy positions, experimented with tank assaults, and tested the accuracy and destructive force of new bombs such as thousand-pound explosive charges and phosphorus incendiary devices.

One such training run happened on April 26, 1937, when the Legion, supported by planes of the Italian Aviazione Legionaria, attacked the small Basque town of Guernica, ten miles behind the front lines. The town itself, with its ten thousand inhabitants, was of little strategic significance. It was expected that it could be used as a fallback position by retreating Republican units, and the town had a small factory for military equipment as well as an important bridge, but the planes appearing in the sky on this market day did not drop their loads on the factory or the bridge. Instead, they annihilated the town center in wave after wave of attacks.

Commanded by Wolfram von Richthofen, a cousin of the famous World War I flying ace Manfred von Richthofen, the Legion Condor used the raid as a valuable opportunity to try out carpet bombing, a tactic designed to wreak a maximum of havoc and terrorize the civilian population. The exact circumstances and intention of the attack are still being debated, and the evidence is inconclusive. Some historians argue that it is likely that Guernica was chosen simply for its transport links, but in this case it is impossible to understand why the bridge and roads were not bombed. Equally, Guernica's status as a town symbolic of Basque independence was unlikely to have influenced the decision to bomb it, as von Richthofen apparently learned of its importance only after the bombing. Whatever the precise intentions, the town was annihilated, first by some forty tons of bombs that smashed the buildings, and then by incendiary ordnance that turned the rubble into a sea of flames. After two hours of bombing, Guernica was reduced to bloody, blackened rubble. It is not known how many people died in the attack, with plausible estimates ranging from three hundred to three thousand.

Help from the East

ABANDONED BY THEIR NEIGHBORS—callously in the case of Britain and against his own moral judgment by Blum—the Republican government made a last bid for survival by turning to the Soviet Union, only to find that Moscow, too, was ambivalent about helping its socialist brothers. Stalin knew all too well that the USSR was not ready for war. He was unwilling to risk antagonizing Germany and Italy, and he preferred to wait. Only when the Italian fighter planes crashed in Morocco did he begin to modify his stance. Dangerous as it was to provoke the Third Reich, another fascist state in Europe would undermine Soviet ambitions even more, and ultimately the great mother country of the revolution could not be seen to stand by while proletarian brothers perished in their revolutionary struggle. In September, after carefully orchestrated demonstrations by 150,000 people on Red Square, the first food deliveries were made to the Republican side.

In the end a different consideration pushed Stalin to act in favor of the beleaguered republic. Soviet nonintervention created a power vacuum within the Communist International that could be filled by others, notably by his former archrival Leon Trotsky, who was already living in exile in Mexico and who might use Republican Spain as a personal power base. To maintain the ideological leadership within the communist movement, it was imperative for Stalin to be seen to act in Spain, and to prevent any competing ideological positions from gaining ground. Though he had at first declared that the USSR would not send weapons to Spain, while at the same time infiltrating spies and military personnel into the country, these considerations finally prevailed. The first ship carrying heavy arms, the *Komsomol*, reached the harbor of Cartagena on October 15, 1936. The rebellion of the generals had finally become a war beginning to affect the entire continent.

Moscow's slow route to involvement on the Iberian Peninsula had another momentous consequence: the founding of the International Brigades. Recruitment centers run by the Comintern (the Moscow-led Communist International) and other organizations began to enlist volunteers, an initiative that met with considerable enthusiasm from antifascists of all ideological stripes who felt outraged about the lack of an international response and wanted to stop Franco and by extension Hitler and Mussolini.

In Barcelona a first nucleus of an international fighting force had already come into existence, as athletes sympathetic to left-wing ideals who had assembled for the abortive Popular Olympiad joined the Republican fighters in a brigade named after the imprisoned German communist Ernst Thälmann. As recruitment centers in Paris, London, and the Netherlands began to smuggle volunteers into Spain by the truckload, their numbers quickly grew, and by the end of the war some thirty-five thousand foreigners from fifty-three countries had been enlisted for the Republicans.

The International Brigades attracted mainly idealistic young men (women were allowed only as nurses or in other non-combat-related capacities). Most of them were workers from Wales or the north of England, the industrial areas of Germany and France, Italy, and the United States. Many but by no means all were communists, and some were intellectuals seeking to marry their strong convictions with the authentic experience of battle. Among them were George Orwell, who fought close to Barcelona and was wounded in the neck; the German communist and former Reichstag member Hans Beimler; and the Croatian communist Josip Broz, who was later to become famous as Marshal Tito. Another fighter on the Republican side was one Fritz Leissner, who after the Second World War would become head of the Stasi under his real name, Erich Mielke.

For fighters and civilians on the Republican side, the International Brigades provided not only much-needed military support but also a huge morale boost. There were spontaneous celebrations on the streets of Barcelona when the first columns of volunteers entered the city. In Madrid, the practically untrained and woefully underequipped young idealists were greeted like heroes, as a British journalist reported:

> The few people who were about lined the roadway, shouting almost hysterically, "¡Salud! ¡Salud!," holding up their fists in salute, or clapping vigorously. An old woman with tears streaming down her face, returning from a long wait in a queue, held up a baby girl, who saluted with her tiny fist. . . . The crowd took them for Russians. The barman turned to me saying "the Rusos have come, the Rusos have come." But when I heard a clipped Prussian voice shout an order in German, followed by other shouts in French and

Italian, I knew they were not Russians. The International
Column of Anti-Fascists had arrived in Madrid. The boost
to the morale of the *Madrileños* was incalculable.[14]

Writing About the War

A TASTE FOR ADVENTURE and the chance of a great story also brought
journalists to Spain, most of whom had never before worked as war
correspondents and who were attracted by the human drama of the conflict. Ernest Hemingway made a name for himself as a daredevil reporter
not averse to picking up a gun himself. The German socialist Herbert
Frahm covered the conflict for the newspaper in his place of exile, Nor-
way, where he was already working under his operational name Willy
Brandt, under which he would become German chancellor in 1969.

The English poet Stephen Spender was in Spain to observe and
report on the war, as was the American writer and activist Langston
Hughes, who wrote for the *Baltimore Afro-American*. The Austro-
Hungarian novelist Arthur Koestler even used his journalistic assignment from the London *News Chronicle* as cover for a mission to spy
on Franco's headquarters. He managed to escape after being recognized, but he would soon return to Spain, only to be captured by
Nationalist soldiers and condemned to death. Only an exchange for
a high-profile hostage saved his life after his cellmates had already
been executed.

As with the Dust Bowl catastrophe in the United States, images
proved a crucial factor in influencing public opinion. In 1937, the
photographer Robert Capa published the image of a Republican soldier at the very moment of his death, falling to the ground as he was
hit by a bullet. The photograph went around the world and became
an emblem of Republican and pacifist sympathies. As was discovered
later, after decades of controversy, the history of this iconic picture
was more complicated than it appeared, and it now seems certain
that nothing was quite as it seemed. Painstaking research has identified the spot at which the photo was made and proven conclusively
that the soldier depicted was nowhere near the front when it was
taken and was not dying, but probably simply lost his footing while
running down a hill during a training exercise.

The truth behind Capa's famous image, however, was even more
convoluted. It was taken not by Capa himself but by his partner
Gerda Taro, who was in Spain with him on an assignment for French
newsmagazines. Even "Robert Capa" was an invention that had first
seen the light of day in Paris, when the two young people had decided

that their actual names, Endre Ernö Friedmann and Gerda Pohorylle, were hindering their professional progress and had invented the "famous American photographer" Robert Capa, under whose name they both sold images to magazines. Their imaginative marketing had paid off, as magazine editors were immensely more willing to buy images from a US star they had never heard of than from a Hungarian Jew or his German Jewish girlfriend. In the end, Friedmann appropriated the alias for himself and Gerda adopted the surname Taro. She would never witness the fame of the photo she had taken, however. On July 25, 1937, she was crushed by a reversing tank and died of her wounds. Capa would later sell the photo under his own name. It became the most famous of his career.

The International Brigades, a conflation of extraordinary talents and immense courage, were powerless to save the fragile Spanish republic, which was now slowly but surely being crushed between the iron jaws of fascism and Soviet communism. Stalin's commissars and secret agents were hard at work not only to defeat Franco but also to purge the Republican forces of all dissent. The communist Hans Beimler, the commander of the famous Thälmann brigade, criticized the Soviet line in Spain and was shot in December 1936, probably by a comrade who was also a Soviet agent. Many others suffered a similar fate.

The internecine warfare in Barcelona in May 1937 in which communists and Marxists fought against anarchists and Trotskyists was part of this cleansing operation, which was directed by Stalin's most important operative in Spain, Alexander Mikhailovich Orlov, a professional agent, guerrilla fighter, and killer who had lived in many European countries under several assumed names. It was Orlov who organized the payment for the Soviet deliveries of weapons and supplies by transferring Spain's entire gold reserves, all 510 tons of it, to Moscow in a major organizational coup, using trucks in a convoy during four successive nights bound for the port of Cartagena and thence to Russia.

Orlov was also entrusted with purging the Spanish left of communist heretics. His main target was the POUM, the Workers' Party of Marxist Unification, a dominant force in the Republican camp and a communist alternative to the Moscow-controlled Comintern. "In Barcelona," wrote George Orwell,

> there was a particular evil feeling in the air—an atmosphere of suspicion, fear, uncertainty, and veiled hatred. The May fighting had left ineradicable after-effects behind it. With the

fall of the Caballero Government the Communists had come definitely into power, the charge of internal order had been handed over to Communist ministers, and no one doubted that they would smash their political rivals as soon as they got a quarter of a chance. Nothing was happening as yet, I myself had not even any mental picture of what was going to happen; and yet there was a perpetual vague sense of danger, a consciousness of some evil thing that was impending. However little you were actually conspiring, the atmosphere forced you to feel like a conspirator. You seemed to spend all your time holding whispered conversations in corners of cafes and wondering whether that person at the next table was a police spy.[15]

After the May events, the POUM was outlawed and marginalized by the Republican leadership, which was unwilling to risk Soviet support of the war. Its leader, Andreu Nin i Pérez, was arrested on Orlov's orders and most likely flayed alive in a jail controlled by Soviet sympathizers before being murdered on June 20. "We sent our young unexperienced secret agents as well as our trained inspectors with years of experience into the theatre of war. Spain proved a good training ground for future secret service operations. The Spanish Revolution suffered defeat. Stalin's men and women, however, were victorious," wrote the NKVD agent Pavel Souplanov about his participation in the Spanish Civil War.[16]

Yezovshchina

THE POLITICAL MURDERS and brutal purges of communists and other leftists in Spain who were deemed not totally and unquestionably loyal to the Stalinist party line were only a small mosaic stone in Stalin's vast panorama of terror in his own country. In a paranoid bid to secure total power he began a season of persecution, torture, and death from which literally nobody was safe.

There had always been waves of political executions in Russia, settling scores between political opponents or simply terrorizing the population for terror's sake. After the 1922 Kronstadt rebellion, for example, Anna Akhmatova's husband had been one of the unfortunates who had been rounded up and shot. Whenever anything was seen to go wrong, guilt had to be assigned. Scientific communism and the paradise of workers and peasants had no place for chance, coincidence, and bad luck. Everything that went wrong was bound to be somebody's responsibility, somebody's act of sabotage, counter-revolution, and bourgeois wickedness. The enemy within was lurking everywhere—a crucial precept of a revolution that was threatening to solidify into a new order. Only the continued presence of enemies could keep the urgency of revolution alive.

The purges had begun in 1934, after the murder of Sergei Kirov, a protégé of Stalin's who had begun to stray from the total obedience expected of him. A popular party official in Leningrad and a member of the Politburo, he had dared to challenge Stalin's decision to arrest all dissenters within the party. What happened next was never fully explained. A mentally disturbed man, Leonid Nikolaev, had been picked up by police close to Kirov's office. In Nikolaev's briefcase officers had found a loaded pistol, but they had let the suspect go and even returned his weapon to him. Soon afterward, Kirov's bodyguards were assigned to other tasks.

Nikolaev was a social misfit who had been expelled from the party. Resentful of the hierarchy, he sought revenge. On December 1, he entered the Smolny Institute, in which Kirov had his office, went up to the third floor without being challenged, and fatally shot Stalin's old friend and potential rival. He was then immediately apprehended and arrested together with several other men. One of these men, who had helped to subdue the assassin, died several days later, allegedly by accident, having fallen from an NKVD truck.

Stalin personally took it upon himself to interrogate Nikolaev. After the questioning, the mentally disturbed murderer was portrayed as part of a vast conspiracy involving dozens of others as well as foreign diplomats. On December 29 he was tried together with 115 other alleged conspirators. They were all sentenced to death and shot an hour after the trial. Three months later, Nikolaev's wife was executed as well, and it appears that his mother and other members of his family suffered the same fate.

Kirov's death was the signal for what was to become known as the Great Purge. During the following four years, and especially in 1936 and 1937, about a million people were arrested and shot by the NKVD. Initially the campaign concentrated on people who had been close to Lenin or supporters of Trotsky, but soon the arrests became random and the accusations absurd. Nothing, not loyalty and lifelong devotion, not hard work or blind faith in the revolution, could save those who stood accused, and accusations grew out of nothing: a foreign-sounding name, a jealous neighbor, a quota for arrests yet to be fulfilled, a rumor, a job done too conspicuously well, an accident at work that could be made to look like sabotage, a name mentioned in a letter, the whim of a Party official, or simply being in the wrong place at the wrong time.

As in Nikolaev's case, the murder of political opponents and arbitrary victims was used to spread fear, but also to serve propaganda purposes. The accused men and women had to be shown to have been plotting and acting against the revolution. This particularly applied to some of the better-known victims of the purges. In 1936 Stalin had used the witch hunt following the Kirov murder to eliminate two of his main political rivals, Grigory Zinoviev and Lev Kamenev, with whom he had ruled the Soviet Union in a triumvirate after Lenin's death in 1923. He had already sidelined and humiliated his two rivals, but now he totally destroyed them. In 1934, they were condemned to long prison terms for "moral complicity" in Kirov's death. Then, after months in secret prisons and countless interrogations, Zinoviev and Kamenev had agreed to admit to the false charges of conspiracy leveled against them in return for avoiding the death penalty.

Stalin's most useful lieutenant in the secret interrogations of political prisoners was Nikolai Yezhov, the people's commissioner for internal affairs and director of the notorious secret police, the NKVD. He was a slight man known by ladies as a charmer, by friends as a party animal with a fine baritone voice, by casual acquaintances as a man of impeccable manners, and by prisoners as a cruelly efficient torturer. Yezhov's first task as chief of the NKVD had been to question and break Genrikh Yagoda, his predecessor in this position, who was suspected by Stalin of harboring sympathies for his revolutionary comrades in arms and of slowing down the investigation of their cases. Yezhov proved an ideal tool in Stalin's hands. Ruthless, imaginative, and sadistic, he extracted the appropriate confessions from his prisoners, among them Yagoda, who would be tried for spying and corruption in 1938.

During the trial Yagoda had apparently believed that Stalin himself would pardon him, as Alexander Solzhenitsyn would later recall. Even though Stalin was nowhere to be seen in the courtroom, Yagoda addressed his former ally and patron directly, shouting: "'I appeal to you! For you I built two great canals!' And a witness reports that at just that moment a match flared in the shadows behind a window on the second floor of the hall, apparently behind a muslin curtain, and, while it lasted, the outline of a pipe could be seen."[17] Stalin's jurists did their work thoroughly. Yagoda and some three thousand NKVD men seen as loyal to him were found guilty and sent to their deaths in the cellars of Moscow's notorious Lubyanka prison. Before Yagoda was shot, Yezhov ordered him to be stripped naked and severely beaten by the guards.

Yezhov's efficiency earned him a place in the Russian language, as the term *yezhovchina* was coined for the paranoid and bloody climax of the purges, during which secret police units are believed to have executed some one thousand men and women every day, the overwhelming majority an hour after their farcical secret trial on trumped-up charges. Other victims were sent to a slower but almost certain death of overwork, malnourishment, and cold in a gulag, a Soviet labor camp.

While most trials were held in secret, Stalin loved to turn the destruction of his most prominent victims into vast and carefully orchestrated public spectacles during which the accused had to repeat prepared confessions of often absurd and outlandish crimes before being sentenced. There were no acquittals. Even though they had been guaranteed prison sentences instead of death, Zinoviev and Kamenev (who had confessed only after having been threatened with the arrest and execution of his son) were condemned to death and executed in 1936.

The greatest of the show trials opened on January 23, 1937, in the House of the Unions, a graceful classicist building close to Red Square. Within a week, the sixteen high-profile accused had been sentenced in a trial carefully crafted as a media event to send a message to communists at home and abroad. After the trials, the prosecutors and judges were also arrested and executed. Nikolay Yezhov, the gifted torturer at the head of the NKVD, was to suffer the same fate two years later.

Having asserted his annihilating power over the Party and the secret police, Stalin turned his attention to the army, the other great source of danger to his absolute authority, in a campaign that would send ripples as far as the Spanish Civil War. His last remaining potential challenger was Marshal Mikhail Tukhachevsky, who commanded almost universal respect for his courage and competence, and who had overseen a comprehensive reform of the army in a bid to turn it into a thoroughly modern and efficient fighting machine able to survive the threatening confrontation with fascism.

Tukhachevsky was arrested on May 27, 1937, and once again it was Yezhov who oversaw his interrogation and eventual confession, spurred on by Stalin's personal encouragement to see to it that the prisoner would be "forced to tell everything." The written confession signed by the army's former leading mind is sprayed with brownish dots of blood. When confronted with the indictment, Tukhachevsky was overheard to say, "I think I must be dreaming."[18] On June 11 he and other high-ranking officials were sentenced. They were shot shortly before midnight.

The elimination of powerful and prominent members of the hierarchy had effects reaching far beyond their immediate trial. Everyone associated with them in any way—family, friends, colleagues, chance acquaintances—became tarnished and was in danger of suffering the same fate. This is what befell the composer Dimitri Shostakovich, who had enjoyed a measure of protection through the patronage extended to him by the cultured Tukhachevsky. While this meant that Shostakovich had been able to work relatively undisturbed as long as Tukhachevsky was in power, the situation was reversed dramatically after his fall.

Even before Tukhachevsky's arrest, Stalin had withdrawn his favor from the composer, partly in an effort to undermine his rival. Shostakovich was attacked in the press for producing bourgeois music, and in particular, his opera *Lady Macbeth of Mzhensk* was singled out for damning criticism. Increasingly isolated, deprived of commissions, and at times suicidal with fear for himself and for his family, Shostakovich saw himself forced to abandon large-scale works. He turned to writing "useful" film music and, in a bid to satisfy his own artistic thirst for expression, to chamber music, which could be performed in private by friends or vanish in the drawers of his desk for years or decades. He was wise to be cautious, as several people belonging to his immediate circle fell victim to the terror. Vsevolod Frederiks, his brother-in-law, was arrested, his friends Nikolai Zhilyayev, Boris Kornilov, and Adrian Piotrovsky executed, and his mother-in-law, Sofiya Varzar, and others close to him swallowed by the gulag system.

Tukhachevsky's demise also had an immediate consequence for the Russian involvement in Spain. Here, too, the terror was spreading fear and paranoia among the cadres involved in the war, and one of the consequences of this climate of dread was that nobody dared to be seen to implement the tactics devised by the brilliant marshal, who had written books about the theory of warfare and had especially revolutionized the use of tanks in battle. As his ideas were suddenly associated with treason and any approval could be turned into a deadly threat, the Soviet tanks in Spain were used in a desultory and improvised fashion, giving the fascist forces a considerable advantage.

Stalin's man in Spain, the murderous Alexander Orlov, knew how to read the signs that he had so often used himself. When he was ordered in 1938 to meet a Soviet ship in Antwerp, he took his wife and daughter to Canada. Before leaving he made certain that the Soviet hierarchy knew that he had made arrangements to reveal the entire Soviet spy network if anything happened to him or to his family.

The terror received its fitting emblem during the Universal Exhibition held in Paris in June 1937. While the Soviet pavilion featured colossal statues of the muscled heroes of the revolution such as Vera Mukhina's *Worker and Kolkhos Woman* and showed how the state had advanced the interests of workers and peasants, the Spanish exhibit, organized by the Republican government, was centered on an equally monumental work of art, created by an exiled artist. Pablo Picasso's huge painting *Guernica* was an homage to the victims of the German bombing of the Basque market town, and a tribute to the victims of war and persecution everywhere.

· 1938 ·

Epilogue: Abide by Me

....

On Sunday, January 16, 1938, some two thousand people congregated to celebrate a bourgeois ritual. The temple to which they strode, puffing into the air clouds of white breath and dressed under their thick coats as elegantly as circumstances allowed, was not a church but the Vienna Musikverein, the city's most famous concert hall. Here they would hear the Vienna Philharmonic under its director, Bruno Walter, in the way the parents and grandparents of many audience members had for generations. To attend concerts at the Musikverein or, better still, to be a subscriber to their Sunday concert series was a precious moment of unbroken tradition among the nightmarish upheaval of recent years.

In the hall with its gilt female figures adorning the columns and exposing their incongruously geometric neoclassical breasts, amid the riot of ornaments dominated by the great organ and contained by a

lavish gold ceiling with painted medallion insets, the crowd settled
into their seats. Many simply kept on their coats. Even an institution
such as this one had little money for heating on a cool winter's day.
The musicians behind the stage were ready to come on and trying to
keep their fingers warm. Strung across the stage were looming black
microphones. The central work on the program was Gustav Mahler's
Ninth Symphony, which had never yet been recorded. Sound engineers
from EMI in London had come over for the occasion to document
this performance for posterity.

Among the listeners was Hans Fantel, a young boy from a bourgeois Jewish family, who came here in the company of his father to
be initiated into the mysteries of Mahler, a composer whose works
were hardly ever performed. "Mahler performances were rare in
Vienna in those days," Fantel remembered. "Mahler's city had already
been contaminated by the acolytes of Adolf Hitler. By their reckoning,
Mahler's music was loathsome—a product of 'Jewish decadence.'
To put Mahler's music on the program was therefore a political act.
It was to protest and deny the hateful faith that blazed across the
border from Germany. That much I understood quite clearly, even
as a boy."[1]

Led by Bruno Walter, who had been Mahler's assistant as a young
man, the symphony commenced, a strange universe consisting of
tentative beginnings, torn intermezzi, intemperate outbursts, savage
irony, and sadness. The audience knew of the symbolic power of the
moment, and for some among them the Sunday ritual became a kind
of communion with something much greater and more important.
When at the beginning of the last movement the strings launched with
one huge heaving musical sigh into their passionately ruminative
chorale theme, some members of the audience recognized the hymn
Mahler had used: "Abide by Me."

As the audience dispersed into the city after this concert, some
crossed the Ring to go into the center and perhaps have coffee at their
favorite coffeehouse, while some went toward the graceful width of
the Karlsplatz, overlooked by a large baroque church, the Karlskirche,
an impressive symbol of tolerance and the Enlightenment with its
towers resembling minarets, its cupola formed like that of a temple,
its façade Greek, and its claim to stand for the one great Truth
of mankind.

The members of the audience went their separate ways knowing
that they had partaken in something extraordinary. They could not
possibly know that with this concert they had been present at the end
of an era, that the people composing the audience would never again

come together quite like this, that many of them would soon be dispersed around the world, or dead. "We could not know on that winter Sunday that this would turn out to be the last performance of the Vienna Philharmonic before Hitler crushed his homeland to make it part of the German Reich," remembered Fantel.

Bruno Walter had indeed scheduled the concert of his teacher's music, which he would continue to champion, in open defiance of the new cultural climate, which was poisoning all culture and every moment of every day. Five years earlier, after the Nazi rise to power in January 1933, Walter had been forced to withdraw from a concert in Leipzig when the new masters made it clear that there would be violence in the hall if he, a Jewish conductor, dared to raise his baton in a German hall. To Walter's disgust, Richard Strauss had agreed to conduct in his stead.

In March 1938 Walter's busy concert schedule took him to Amsterdam, where he was to conduct the Concertgebouw orchestra. It was here, huddled before a radio in their hotel room, that he and his wife followed the demise of their country: "The end had come. From early afternoon until late into the night we sat at the radio, listening from afar to Austria's agony . . . to the following confusion of the pathetic Austrian announcements, and to the Nazis' triumphant proclamations. And all this took place to the accompaniment of music, as if no historical tragedy were being enacted, the suffering and death of human beings were not involved, nor the victory of evil, but as if we were witnessing the insipid melodrama of a theatrical pen-pusher itching for a sensation."[2]

A musician first and foremost, Walter particularly noticed the change in the style of the pieces played between the announcements. "After Schuschnigg's farewell words 'God protect Austria!' the country we had loved had passed away to the solemn strains of Haydn's national anthem played by a string quartet," he wrote, adding that "every pause was filled by Viennese waltzes, only to be interrupted again by announcements of new disasters. Suddenly that mad mixture of death groans and dance music stopped. A new sound came to our ears. The announcements over the Vienna radio were made by a harsh Prussian voice. The listeners were told in terse brief sentences of the progress of Austria's conquest. Blaring Prussian military marches took the place of the waltzes, a musical symbol of what had happened."

Things went from bad to worse for the conductor when his manager informed him during the intermission of one of his Amsterdam concerts that his daughter had been arrested in Vienna. Walter still had some influence, and after a few days of hectic telephone calls and impassioned pleas he managed to secure her release. During the following months he even managed to find safe havens for other members of his family.

Walter himself moved to the United States and would not return to Vienna until after the Second World War, which was now beginning to seem not so much a distant threat as a concrete and imminent catastrophe. Among the other refugees who had been present at the historic Musikverein concert was Hans Fantel, who had been able to secure a visa for the United States, ironically through his love of classical music, which was shared by an American diplomat. He would later become a columnist on stereo equipment and musical recordings for the *New York Times*.

Fantel's father, who had awakened this passion for music and who had been a producer of sound equipment himself, did not make the journey with him and was murdered by the Nazis. As the son would later write, it was this that made Walter's 1938 recording precious to him: "This disk held fast an event I had shared with my father: 71 minutes out of the 16 years we had together."

One moment of recorded time among so much that slipped away; two stories—one famous and one not—taken out of the millions the following years would have.

Throughout this book, I have tried to excavate aspects of how people experienced the aftermath of the war and the years that followed, and how the unfolding story of modernity played out in their lives. The great forces of modernity that had begun to dominate the lives of urbanites in Europe and the United States around 1900 were intensified and accelerated by the war and continued to assert themselves in the years after 1918. In the first chapter, a victim of shell shock stood for a traumatized European continent and the experience of a modern war. The effects of this experience became legible in the succeeding chapters: the conservative revolutionaries exposed the anatomy of discontent; the story of Prohibition illuminated the culture wars within the United States; the Kronstadt rebellion showed the final perversion of the idea of the Russian Revolution; the Harlem Renaissance showcased the energies for innovation and social change that were so prominent and which veered between the hopes invested in the Soviet Union and the search for different ways.

Among other things, these first five chapters investigated ideologies and visions of culture. In 1923, other, polarizing changes occurred. Scientific theories made the physical world as unpredictable and alien as society appeared to many people at the time. The surrealists heightened this tension in 1924 with their onslaught against yesterday's discredited morality, and the traditional world confronted the modern intellectual vision in the Scopes trial. The 1926 film *Metropolis* offered more visions of the cultural contradictions between man and machine, the fear of robots, and the idea that somehow technology had begun to threaten humanity. In 1927, the burning of the Vienna Palace of Justice served as a concrete example of social, cultural, and political tensions—in this case between the right and the left. The answer many younger people sought to this, the following chapter suggests, was escapism amid signs of slow economic recovery.

That was the point when this rudderless period began to tilt from optimism to pessimism, and from a postwar time into a prewar time. The chapter on 1929 began in Magnitogorsk, but the specter of the Wall Street crash, the very antipode and seemingly also the confirmation of all Soviet hopes, was never far away. The economic and cultural dissolution in the wake of this disaster revealed itself in Berlin and its anything-goes nightlife. The only antidote to this kind of moral dissolution was faith, and this faith suffused Fascist Italy, ready to cross the Alps. At the same time the last remnants of faith in the Russian experiment were shaken by the secret genocide of the Ukrainian artificial famine and the hesitant response of Western intellectuals. The book burnings in Germany were a defiant gesture against the intellect and in favor of blind belief.

As all signs began to point in the direction of another war, the book moved to Britain, taking a look at the often desperate lives of ordinary people during the crisis. This survey continued with a look at Dust Bowl refugees within the United States and at refugees from Germany, whose plight was becoming increasingly dire. The 1936 Berlin Olympics brought an apparent answer to the cultural and economic forces tearing at the fabric of society in the shape of the beautiful athletes' bodies, carefully celebrated by Leni Riefenstahl, and the dream of the beautiful, strong Nietzschean *Übermensch* capable of transcending his own time and of providing an answer to the shattered, compromised bodies that were a traumatic cultural presence after the war. In 1937, finally, the dreams and nightmares of these years become solidified in a single, dirty war, a ready projection screen for millions of people around the world. Both sides were played by dictators following their own agenda, in both cases with murderous results.

At the beginning of the book I argued that not rupture but continuity is the key to an understanding of the interwar years—that the experience of technological modernity was intensified by the war, while the values underpinning Western societies were deeply damaged.

This book has chronicled different aftereffects of this tremendous shock, from trauma and new beginnings to first confrontations and sheer hedonism, from political faith and its limits to an aesthetic realization in art. It has explored the increasingly cataclysmic manifestations, from street battles to streams of refugees and mass shootings, in a game of ideologies that had already degenerated into the dirtiest of politics. Nineteen eighteen was ushered in by a world at war, and there was a widespread sense at year's end that the conflict had not been resolved, that the Treaty of Versailles had merely bought time. Not only the German revanchists on the right but also the opinions of such eminent observers as John Maynard Keynes, the French marshal Ferdinand Foch, and French president Paul Deschanel testified to this.

It was not over. Instead, it would turn into what historians have called Europe's "second Thirty Years' War," from 1914 to 1945. The so-called interwar years, then, were not so much years of peace as, to paraphrase Clausewitz, a continuation of war by other means. The new fronts ran between classes, between town and country, between ideologies, between rich and poor, and between ethnic groups. Perhaps these conflicts came closer to a manner of resolution during the late 1920s as economies stabilized and attitudes softened, but the global economic slump following the Wall Street crash hardened minds and conflicts once again as poverty and the fear of destitution exposed the fault lines anew.

....

IN JUNE 1940 Adolf Hitler tried to vanquish not only Europe but history itself. On a survey of his troops in Belgium, he visited the military cemetery at Langenmarck, near Ypres. The name Langenmarck had a mythical ring to Germans. It was here, on November 10, 1914, that young German soldiers had shown real patriotic spirit as they charged the enemy with the national anthem, "Deutschland, Deutschland über Alles," on their lips as they gallantly faced the enemy, as the official reports from the front had noted and as newspapers had embellished the event in subsequent weeks. Most of these brave young soldiers had been students of Germany's top universities, and most of them had given their lives that day on the field of honor. Adolf Hitler himself, then stationed twelve kilometers away, later wrote about the event in *Mein Kampf*, claiming to have heard the soldiers singing as they went to their deaths and remembering how the anthem had spread to all German trenches until the enemy was faced with a singing front line, breathing and fighting in unison.

It was a myth, of course, a mixture of wartime propaganda and fervent wishful thinking. The attack had taken place "to the west of Langenmarck," as the official reports shrewdly put it. The accurate place name, Bikschote, was not fit for a German myth. The name of the next village had a more heroic ring to it; it brought to mind Bismarck. In the course of a fight that would become known as the Battle of Ypres, there was a German attack made by a regiment consisting of mainly young, almost untrained troops. Some of them were students, though probably not even one in twenty. One or two of these might have been studying at one of the old universities.

There was also singing on this day and one of the songs appears to have been the national anthem, as several reports suggest, but that was behind the front. In any case, experienced soldiers said, run full out through the mud of a Belgian turnip field after an exhausting march, clods of thick soil sticking to your boots, and then try to sing anything at all, never mind a melody as ponderous as "Deutschland, Deutschland über Alles," the theme of the slow movement of a Haydn string quartet. Singing or not, two thousand young men from one regiment were killed in a single day as they stumbled toward the enemy trenches and were mown down by machine guns, most before they could even make it to the trench.

But the Langenmarck myth had grown. Germany needed tales of heroism in this increasingly squalid and hopeless war. Langenmarck associations had been formed, a memorial was commissioned, poems were written, and speeches were made extolling noble sacrifice and true heroism. The notion that these young people knew how to die for their country was a paradoxical refrain recurring in solemn lead articles and sermons. Hitler set foot on sacred ground when he visited the cemetery in which the soldiers who had senselessly perished that day had been buried. It was Germany's very emblem of the war, an already sublimated memory of the death of its sons and of its empire. The "Greatest Führer of All Times," as he liked to be styled, always had an eye for symbolic gestures. At Langenmarck in 1940 he declared Germany's First World War finally to be over. Providence had spoken. His historic act came five years early.

....

IT IS THE TRAGEDY of the interwar period that it did not have an open future. The vertigo years, 1900 to 1914, are often wrongly thought of mainly as a prewar time necessarily culminating in war. But even in the early summer of 1914 nobody knew that there would be war, and certainly nobody could envisage the kind of war and the intensity of devastation it would wreak on human lives, economies, and fundamental certainties. It was a time coming to grips with its own modernity, and endowed with an open future. The Great War was anything but inevitable, and it is only the terror of this cataclysm and its seeming senselessness that have left later generations looking at the years before and endlessly trying to piece together clues, often neglecting the fact that great events frequently do not have strong and logical causes, that disaster can stem from even diffuse networks of attitudes and oversights, incompetence and misunderstandings.

The feeling of mystification and helplessness is a legacy of the interwar years, of course, and it was dealt with in two ways. On the one hand, there were the strong explainers, usually those who were ideologically committed. Depending on their ideological family, they blamed the war on the capitalists, the Jews, the military, decadence and modernity *tout court*, or a mixture of these.

The second reaction sought not so much an explanation as a refuge. In the decade after 1918, artists and writers had already begun to cast a new, nostalgic light on the period before 1914, which they had all lived through. In operettas, novels, poems, memoirs, and historical accounts, the prewar era was being bathed in the kind, golden rays of nostalgia, producing the notion of a time of stability and order. This was quite different from how the period had actually been experienced at the time, and it added to the impossibility of explaining the industrial slaughter that erupted out of it. As the early postwar years lurched from crisis to civil war, blame and nostalgia were equally out of place but equally powerful. One aggressive and the other sentimental, they were two sides of the same coin.

The forces unleashed into the societies of the West during the period between 1918 and 1938 exacted a terrible toll. Most of the millions who were killed perished in the Soviet Union, but every Western country had victims of political violence to mourn. The peace was fragile at best; the next war, a continuation of the first, was waiting in the wings. Societies that would have had to learn to deal with the memory and the legacies of the war had no time to heal. Plunged into a war again after Hitler's rise to power, they suffered a second catastrophe.

The long-range consequences of this dynamic can still be felt today, even after the fall of the Soviet Union and the reunification of Germany. It is present in the composition of our populations: African Americans in urban centers in the United States, Jews and other emigrants across the world. It is present in Germany's continuing aversion to inflation, in the specter of the Holocaust in Western memory, in the existence of the United Nations and the state of Israel and the situation in the Middle East, in America's cultural hegemony over the Western world, in the change from German to English as the main language of science and the global spread of English, in the speedy decline of the colonial empires and its aftermath, in Islamic fundamentalism as an answer to godless Western politics, and in the sound of our popular music and its goddesses, whose lives are a far cry from that of early jazz diva Mamie Smith, but who are still fulfilling the same promise: to bring the street into their music.

The street has stayed in our music. When jazz exploded into a torn and confused world, it changed the way we hear. The culture associated with it did not only permeate our lives in the shape of dirty notes and driving rhythms; its proud vindication of rebellion and marginal identities would also give us rock, hip-hop, and rap. The street has stayed in fashion, too, and in the notion of black cool. It is a culture of revolt that has become our culture, and it had its first stirrings as a mass phenomenon in the interwar period, before being hit hard by the war that followed and the conservative climate in the years afterward. It would rise again as a revolt of the children in the 1960s, and its anthems carried the echoes of the clubs, the concert halls, and the spirit of the Harlem Renaissance.

The entry of the street into the cultural mainstream and into high culture is exemplary of wider changes. Many of them had already begun before 1914, but the immensely democratizing disillusionment of the postwar years meant that some people simply refused to take any notice of the values and borders that had existed before the war, while others went on the attack against anything they perceived as bourgeois, middle-class, safe, restrictive, and constructed out of lies. The millions of Americans who frequented speakeasies every day during Prohibition had simply voted with their feet. Their morality was different from that of the lawmakers—many of whom were sitting at the bar themselves.

The experience of the war acted as a catalyst for modernity. By subjecting millions to the absolute authority of planning, training, mass production, standardization, and logistics, it hastened the arrival of the new. Its effect was later intensified and distorted by political mistakes with devastating economic and cultural consequences. On a global scale, the Wall Street crash hardened the economic and political climate and led to new eruptions of violence and hostility. In Germany, the hyperinflation of 1923 caused a further erosion of optimism and socially cohesive attitudes. Together these two developments and their aftereffects broke the recovery of the 1920s and facilitated the rise of fascism.

To Europeans, and in a more mediated form also to Americans, the war framed the experience of the decade following it and informed the events of the 1930s. From our more distant perspective it is possible to see it in a different light. Neither of the world wars was the defining event of the twentieth century; both are almost side effects of the same vast revolution, the revolution of modernity, of technology, and of the Enlightenment.

Historians of mentality such as Michel Foucault have drawn a straight line from Immanuel Kant's cult of absolute reason in the eighteenth century to the concentration camps and the gulags of the twentieth, and they were right to do so—at least in part (in *A Wicked Company* I have written about this idea of the Enlightenment and its marginalized alternatives). The Kantian and Enlightenment conception of reason released a cascade of developments, innovations, and revolutions. It could, however, also be twisted into a cold rationality that did not hesitate to crush human lives in the quest for progress or even utopia.

Around 1900, as modernity took hold of the great cities with their ever-increasing number of inhabitants, the revolution profoundly changed the ways in which people thought about the world, and about themselves. It also accelerated with enormous might, taking less than a generation to undermine, batter, and eventually crush social structures, moral norms, and traditional ideas that had existed for centuries. History began to outpace humanity, identities became fragile and questionable, and technology developed faster than it could be understood.

This development is still continuing, and the wars, mass murders, ethnic cleansing, and oppression that began in the twentieth century and have continued into the twenty-first are part of this large story, just as the innovation, the liberation, and the deepening of scientific understanding are. Modernity, it turns out, stubbornly remains morally neutral as it continues to unfold and to change our identities with every passing day. Despite this constantly rising tide of change, the social and cultural effects of the interwar period have remained pervasive. Having invited the street into our intimate space, we are all living on the street now. Our lives are more public, with more diversity, a wider tolerance for different social norms, and flatter hierarchies—even if they frequently hide a discrepancy in income that exceeds anything seen in the early years of the twentieth century.

It is immensely tempting to draw parallels between our present and the world between 1918 and 1938, but while such comparisons are seductive, they can also prove to be misleading. Like the Great Depression of 1929, the subprime mortgage crisis of 2008 created high unemployment and broke countless lives, especially of people who were hoping for the first time to partake of the amenities and privileges of a middle-class existence. Politicians and economists alike used this parallel to warn of a second global depression with devastating economic and political circumstances, but I believe that what is most interesting is not the similarity between the events but the difference.

Despite a stock market panic comparable to that of 1929, the economic crisis of 2008 did not turn into an economic meltdown with 25 percent unemployment, as in the United States in the 1930s, or more than 40 percent, as in Germany. We avoided this fate because lessons had been learned and institutions created. World markets were more strongly intertwined and governments were more ready to intervene, even if the chosen form of intervention—the bailout of the very banks that had caused the problem—was highly controversial. Indeed, 2008 was replete with resonances of the troubled interwar years: during the euro crisis Germany stood firmly against any policy that might risk high inflation, an attitude profoundly shaped by memories of 1923 and the tide of extremism and totalitarianism that followed.

Perhaps the similarities between the interwar years and our present are to be found on a different plane. Both the interwar years and the first decades of the twenty-first century have been marked by a pervasive sense of insecurity, and in both periods the reasons and possible remedies for this insecurity have been the subject of intensive debates. But while the situation can be analyzed from different ideological perspectives, there can be no doubt that compared with the decades immediately after the Second World War, our lives have become more precarious—not because of a war but because of political choices made by us and on our behalf by politicians elected by us. We are all living closer to personal economic catastrophe than our parents did; even in the protected meadows of academia, job security is largely gone. For decades, this rapid erosion of social rights and protections was covered by the political idea that this was the flexibility demanded by the free market, and that the reward of such risk taking was a chance of immense gains.

The ideological justification of this increasing and willed precariousness even in wealthy countries was carried by a growing distrust of the state, of democracy, and of politicians, who were regarded either as unwilling and unable to make the changes necessary or as not entitled to interfere with individual liberty. The fathers of this neo-liberal school of economics, Friedrich von Hayek and Ludwig von Mises, were Europeans who had passed their formative years in the chaotic interwar years and whose conclusion was that state intervention and planned economies were hallmarks of dictatorship and could only lead to economic disaster and totalitarianism. They believed that it was healthier to take ideology out of politics and base the workings of society on the objective, nonideological laws of the free market.

This change of emphasis meant that citizens were no longer regarded as organs of a collective body working in unison, as in fascism, or as cogs in a gigantic machine, as in Bolshevism. Rather, they were seen as independent agents making choices in a free market, governed by principles offering opportunity and freedom without taking sides. The Enlightenment cult of reason and of the common good was replaced by the concepts of rationalization and the maximization of profits, which were applied to a reevaluation of social institutions—infrastructure, schools, universities, prisons, health care, and so on—according to business-driven criteria of profitability and cost-effectiveness. Especially in the United States but also increasingly in Europe, we began to run our societies as businesses. Beginning in the late 1970s and gaining speed in the 1980s, this gospel changed and polarized our societies—but it also provided an umbrella of meaning and necessity under which we could hide from challenges from without as well as doubts from within. For many in the West, the idea of the market became their ideological home. Living in accordance with its guiding providence and iron laws created a sense of stability, of virtue even. But 2008 shattered this collective piety and made millions understand that they had been lied to, that their precarious position was not counterbalanced by a real possibility of getting ahead, getting a better job, or paying for the kids' college education. As country after country was rocked by the economic consequences of irresponsibility and greed in the American housing market and cynical lending practices by large banks, anger turned to bitter disillusionment and millions of citizens retreated from the political process, losing any hope of and even any aspiration to ever being more than a consumer whose value to society is measured by the size of his or her credit line. Politically there is nothing in it, they appear to understand; no real change is to be hoped for, and perhaps politics have ceased to matter. Today, a real revolution would have to turn not against the seat of government but against the headquarters of the corporations whose political, social, and cultural influence has so vastly increased that presidents and prime ministers seem to be little more than decorated puppets placed at center stage for cosmetic purposes.

The consequences of this collective disillusionment, which is in many ways comparable to that suffered by Europeans after 1918, did not express itself through political action. Despite movements such as Occupy, the Tea Party, or European populist right-wing parties, most citizens in the West have remained essentially passive, retreating more deeply into the private sphere, partly because their own precarious situation and the obligations created by private debt are powerful disincentives against rocking the boat. After 1918, and once again after 1929, people were faced with the question "How can I live in a world with values and ideas that have suddenly become discredited?" After 2008 this question has returned. The idea of the infallible market has become a travesty, and the gospel of growth and the myth of meritocracy have collapsed in the minds of many of our contemporaries. But in a world after the demise of the great ideologies there seems to be little or nothing to replace these things, and so they fester on.

The irony at the base of this situation is that the gospel of the free market is just as ideological as those of communism and fascism. The belief in the seemingly unideological power of the market has helped only a small minority, creating for the rest a world in which hundreds of millions of people live less well and more precariously than their parents. Large areas of our societies, such as health care and education, are becoming increasingly segregated between an underfunded public sector struggling to keep up standards and a private alternative run for profit. Those who can afford to opt in to the private system have to pay vastly more than people did one generation ago. Those who cannot are increasingly excluded.

And yet the very people who have to be more afraid for their livelihoods, whose standard of living is more threatened, and who have to pay more for basic needs frequently defend the system, perhaps because it offers something even more fundamental than security: hope, orientation, a kind of transcendence. We treat the market as the fundamental reality of society. It gives us something to believe in. We have chosen to adhere to a political gospel, much like the communists and fascists of the 1930s.

The belief in a perfect market has been fundamentally ideological from the very beginning. Its theory rests on unproven and unprovable assertions such as the idea that markets will regulate themselves, break up monopolies, and eliminate inefficient and antiquated structures, that it represents a level playing field on which all participants operate with a similar degree of knowledge and choice, and that the decisions of these economic actors are fundamentally rational. But experience in the real world shows that more and more powerful monopolies are being created, economic exchanges are rarely ever symmetrical and involve little real choice, and rational criteria are rarely at their base. Undoubtedly the economically most momentous decision many people take in their lives is to have children, even if this is, in the West, likely to make them poorer, more vulnerable, less able to choose. We are not rational agents, nor should we be.

In spite of this gaping abyss between economic theory and human practice, the gospel of the market has taken a deep hold on our thinking. It has its own rituals, its own priests and prophets, who parade across our screens and preach in our newspapers. The markets are described in anthropomorphic terms: they are worried, they are depressed. We must bring them sacrifices, and like in ancient Greece, the priests keep the best pieces of sacrificial meat for themselves. The interwar years brought the street into our culture; the millennium has abolished any idea of culture. The culture of the interwar years celebrated newfound freedoms; we have retreated from freedom into the realm of an imaginary perfect market in which our survival strategy is based on being more compatible with the system, more competitive, and more conformist. During the interwar years many people dreamed of a better future; today we are trying to prevent this future from materializing because we have lost all hope that change may be for the good, that we can transform our societies in the image of a common good. Our future has essentially become a threat, and all we want is to live in a present that never ends.

During the interwar years political ideologies were the answer to the sense of a moral and political vacuum following the war. They provided a framework, a family, a great explanation, and a reason to hope. They gave a positive answer to the question of how to live with values borrowed from another time by readily replacing them with new ones. Hope came with a membership number.

The alternative to this essentially religious approach to the moral void was equally limited both in its scope and in its possibilities, and it is strongly reminiscent of our own projected consumer paradise. The feckless hedonism of the flappers, the Bright Young Things, the Berlin bars, the shoppers, and party-goers everywhere offered an escape from worry about the future and from endless ideological debates, but no road toward a safer future. It was the response of a young generation not willing to live by the values of their parents and not bothering to define their own as long as there was fun to be had here and now. For tomorrow, they knew, was a long way off, and was probably not much to contemplate. Tomorrow you may die. "No future" started in the trenches.

Rigid ideology and hedonistic consumer oblivion were understandable but deeply destructive responses to a communal loss of faith. Both led to a withering of reasoned political debate. Communists and fascists exchanged bullets instead of arguments; for the flappers and their friends, another cocktail was always more pressing than musings about the future of civilization. As debate and political dialogue dried up, another war was rapidly becoming predictable and imminent.

To those who believe that we can learn from history, this parallel is certainly not reassuring. After the First World War had crushed mighty empires and the moral universe sustaining their outlook on life, millions took refuge from the challenging void and fled into ideologies or simply danced and shopped until they dropped—or, if they were too poor to participate, at least they dreamed of shopping and the high life.

The great political faiths were accompanied by a refusal to engage with the challenges of the time. There is a comparison to be made here, and we can only hope that the verdict spoken about us by the generation of our grandchildren will have cause to be kinder than the judgment we deliver about our grandparents, who lent their lives and hopes and abilities to murderous illusions.

Acknowledgments

Having finished the work of several years, it is a particular pleasure to remember all those whose suggestions, assistance, and generosity have made this project possible. As it is impossible to do justice to all contributions, the names appear in roughly chronological and alphabetic order.

At the inception of this book, the enthusiasm and support of my agents and publishers were crucial in encouraging me to undertake a project of such magnitude, dealing with a period that was so vast and so diverse. Victoria Hobbs and Sebastian Ritscher saw my ideas through their first stages. Then Lara Heimert at Basic Books in New York, Ravi Mirchandani and Margaret Stead of Atlantic Books in London, Tobias Heil and Michael Krüger at Hanser in Munich, and Leonoor Broeder of the Bezige Bij in Amsterdam helped to make it possible. I have sorely tried their patience when other projects forced me to delay the delivery date of the manuscript, but their support was unflagging and immensely valuable.

Among the events intervening during the writing of this book was a great gift. Thomas Gaethgens, director of the Getty Research Institute in Los Angeles, invited me to continue my research at the institute, and my one-year stay left wonderful memories and friendships, as well as a first draft of this book. In a beautiful office overlooking the Pacific I could read, research, and write about the interwar years, and conversations with and kind suggestions by my fellow scholars and the academic staff of the institute were instrumental in the creation of this book. My thanks go out to the entire wonderful staff of the Getty Center, and especially to Thomas Gaethgens and his wife, Barbara, Alexa Sekyra and Peter Schnitzler, Angie Donougher, Amy Lind, Louis Marchesano, Sabine Schlosser, Rebecca Zamora, and my wonderful research assistant Raquel Zamora. Among the scholars, William Bainbridge Stefano Cracolici, Lothar von Falkenhausen, Thomas Hines, Gordon Hughes, Ann-Sophie Lehmann, Marina Pugliese, Salvatore Setis, Alla Vronskaya, and Miao Zhe allowed me to refine and expand my ideas. The hospitality and hard work of Amy Meyers made my time in Los Angeles an unforgettable pleasure.

Many other discussions helped to shape and focus my ideas and to develop an understanding of the anatomy of the interwar period. Thomas Angerer, Rainer Rosenberg, Barbara Coudenhove-Calergi, Franz Koessler, Cornelius Obonya, Timothy Snyder, Jürgen Osterhammel, Karl Schlögel, Ulrich Sieg, Ana Jornet, Herbert Freudenheim, Robert Neumüller, Jasper Sharp, Christian Witt-Döring, and Elisabeth Stein all listened carefully to my ideas or allowed me to develop my understanding by building on theirs. Carl Bodenstein kindly helped me with bibliographical research.

A particular debt of gratitude is owed to Veronica Buckley, my wife, who not only supported me in every way possible during the writing of this book but was there to encourage me when I was daunted by my task and without whose constant love, searching questions, insightful observations, editorial queries, and surprising perspectives this book would never have been completed. Thank you, my darling. You made all the difference; you always do.

Credits

Photographs

Page 20: Nameless horror. Bildrecht. Otto Dix, Der Krieg. "Verwundeter." Aus dem Radierzyklus: Der Krieg von Otto Dix. 1924/© Bildrecht, Wien, 2014

Page 42: Gabriele d'Annunzio. Public Domain

Page 50: Harlem Hellfighters. Public Domain

Page 53: Ku Klux Klan. AKG Images

Page 74: Berlin. Bildrecht. Ludwig Mies van der Rohe, The force of the new: design for an office building in central Berlin, 1921/© Bildrecht, Wien, 2014

Page 76: German war veteran. Bundesarchiv, Koblenz

Page 87: Anna Akhmatova. Hulton Archive

Page 99: Street scene in Harlem. Getty Images

Page 101: W. E. B. Du Bois. Public Domain

Page 111: Josephine Baker. Public Domain

Page 129: Franz Kafka. AKG Images

Page 141: Ballet, mécanique. © Bildrecht, Wien, 2014

Page 154: Clarence Darrow and William Jennings Bryan. Public Domain

Page 166: The "average American male." Public Domain

Page 176: Still from *Metropolis*. AKG Images

Page 183: Fritz Kahn's workings of the human body. Thilo von Debschitz

Page 185: Charlie Chaplin in *Modern Times*. Modern Times © Roy Export S.A.S. Scan Courtesy Cineteca di Bologna

Page 189: Tsiga Vertov's vision of *Homo sovieticus*. Public Domain

Page 193: Le Corbusier's vision of Paris. Bildrecht. Le Corbusier, plan Voisin (für HC) Paris, Plan Voisin, 1925/© Bildrecht, Wien, 2014

Page 196: The burning Palace of Justice in Vienna. Getty Images

Page 200: Karl-Marx-Hof in Vienna. AKG Images

Page 216: Betty Boop. AKG Images

Page 238: Steel ovens in Magnitogorsk. Bundesarchiv, Koblenzk

Page 251: Marlene Dietrich in *Der blaue Engel*. AKG Images

Page 260: August Sander's portrait of a secretary in Cologne. Bildrecht. August Sander, Sekretärin beim Westdeutschen Rundfunk in Köln, 1931/© Photographische Sammlung/SK Stiftung Kultur-August Sander Archiv, Köln/Bildrecht, Wien, 2014

Page 268: Michele Schirru. Public Domain

Page 274: Hitler and Mussolini. AKG Images

Page 289: Joseph Stalin with his daughter, Svetlana. AKG Images

Page 292: A victim of Stalin's artificial famine. Getty Images

Page 298: Action Against the Un-German Spirit. Getty Images

Page 313: Osip Mandelstam photographed by the NKVD. Getty Images

Page 319: Strikebreakers in Rhondda, Wales. AKG Images

Page 335. A dust storm approaches a settlement. Public Domain

Page 337: After a dust storm in South Dakota, 1936. Public Domain

Page 342: Portrait of a Dust Bowl refugee with her children. AKG Images

Page 356: Wolfgang Fürstner. Bundesarchiv, Koblenz

Page 362: Statues of athletes at a sports complex in Dresden, 1936. Getty Images

Page 365: Mukhina's *Worker and Kolkhos Woman*. AKG Images

Page 370: *The Victor* by the German sculptor Arno Breker. Bildrecht. Arnold Breker, Der Sieger/© Bildrecht, Wien, 2014

Page 374: Street battles in Barcelona, 1936. Getty Images

Page 386: Pablo Picasso's *Guernica*, 1937. Bildrecht. Pablo Picasso, *Guernica*, 1937/ © Succession Picasso/Bildrecht, Wien, 2014

Poetry

Pages 54, 107: Claude McKay. Public domain.

Page 136: Tristan Tsara. Excerpt from *Chanson Dada*. Translation c. 1987, 2005 by Lee Harwood. Black Widow Press, Boston, MA. www.blackwidowpress.com.

Page 137: André Breton. Reprinted from *The Lost Steps* by André Breton by permission of the University of Nebraska Press. Copyright 1924, 1969 by Editions Gallimard. English translation copyright 1996 by Mark Polizzotti.

Page 173: Mina Loy. Selection reprinted with permission of Dalkey Archive Press.

Page 224: John Betjeman. Excerpt from "For Patrick, aetat: LXX" from *Collected Poems by John Betjeman*. Copyright © 2006 by The Estate of John Betjeman. Reprinted by permission of Farrar, Strauss and Giroux, LLC.

Page 338: Archibald MacLeish. Excerpt from *Land of the Free* by Archibald MacLeish. Copyright © 1938 and renewed 1966 by Archibald MacLeish. Reprinted by permission of Houghton Mifflin Harcourt Publishing Company. All rights reserved.

Bibliography

Adams, Samuel Hopkins, Isabel Leighton, et al. *The Aspirin Age, 1919–1941*. New York: Simon and Schuster, 1976.

Alexander, Robert J. *The Anarchists in the Spanish Civil War*. London: Janus, 1999.

Allen, Amy Ruth. *Growing Up in the Great Depression, 1929 to 1941*. Minneapolis, MN: Lerner Publications, 2014.

Allen, Roy F. *Literary Life in German Expressionism and the Berlin Circles*. Ann Arbor, MI: UMI Research Press, 1983.

Amersfoort, Herman, and Wim Klinkert. *Small Powers in the Age of Total War, 1900–1940*. Amsterdam: Brill, 2011.

Annan, Noel. *Our Age: English Intellectuals Between the World Wars—A Group Portrait*. New York: Random House, 1990.

Andrews, Clarence A. *Chicago in Story: A Literary History*. Iowa City, IA: Midwest Heritage, 1982.

Andrews, James T. *Science for the Masses: The Bolshevik State, Public Science, and the Popular Imagination in Soviet Russia, 1917–1934*. College Station: Texas A&M Press, 2003.

Antonowa, Irina, and Jörn Merkert, eds. *Berlin Moskau, 1900–1950* = *Moskva Berlin, 1900–1950*. Munich: Prestel, 1995.

Archer Straw, Petrine. *Negrophilia: Avant-Garde Paris and Black Culture in the 1920s*. London: Thames & Hudson, 2000.

Armstrong, Tim. *Modernism, Technology and the Body: A Cultural Study*. Cambridge: Cambridge University Press, 1998.

Arnold, Sabine, et al. *Politische Inszenierung Im 20. Jahrhundert: Zur Sinnlichkeit Der Macht*. Vienna: Böhlau, 1998.

Arwas, Victor. *Art Deco*. New York: Abrams, 1980.

Aschheim, Steven E. *The Nietzsche Legacy in Germany, 1880–1990*. Berkeley: University of California Press, 1992.

Augé, Marc. *Paris années 30: Roger-Viollet*. Paris: Hazan, 1996.

Avrich, Paul. *Kronstadt, 1921*. Princeton, NJ: Princeton University Press, 1970.

Baczko, Bronislaw. *Wege in die Gewalt: die modernen politischen Religionen*. Frankfurt am Main: Fischer-Taschenbuch-Verl., 2000.

Badger, Anthony J. *The New Deal: The Depression Years, 1933–1940*. New York: Farrar, Straus and Giroux, 1989.

Baeumler, Alfred. *Männerbund und Wissenschaft*. Berlin: Junker und Dünnhaupt, 1934.

Bahr, Ehrhard. *Weimar on the Pacific: German Exile Culture in Los Angeles and the Crisis of Modernism (Weimar and Now: German Cultural Criticism)*. Berkeley: University of California Press, 2007.

Bajac, Quentin, and Clément Chéroux. *La subversion des images: surréalisme, photographie, film: exposition présentée au Centre Pompidou, Paris, Galerie 2, du 23 septembre 2009 au 11 janvier 2010, au Fotomuseum Winterthur, du 26 février au 23 mai 2010, à l'Institute de Cultura-Fundación Mapfre, Madrid, du 16 juin au 12 septembre 2010*. Paris: Centre Pompidou, 2009.

Balakian, Peter. *The Burning Tigris: The Armenian Genocide and America's Response*. New York: 2003.

Ball, Alan M. *And Now My Soul Is Hardened: Abandoned Children in Soviet Russia, 1918–1930*. Berkeley: University of California Press, 1996.

Banner-Haley, Charles Pete T. *From Du Bois to Obama: African American Intellectuals in the Public Forum*. Carbondale: Southern Illinois University Press, 2010.

Baritz, Loren. *The Culture of the Twenties*. Indianapolis: Bobbs-Merrill, 1970.

Barron, Stephanie, ed. *"Degenerate Art": The Fate of the Avant-Garde in Nazi Germany*. Los Angeles: Los Angeles County Museum of Art, 1991.

Barron, Stephanie, Sabine Eckmann, Matthew Affron, Los Angeles County Museum of Art, Montreal Museum of Fine Arts, and Neue Nationalgalerie (Germany). *Exiles + Emigrés: The Flight of European Artists from Hitler*. New York: Abrams, 1997.

Bartov, Omer. *Mirrors of Destruction: War, Genocide, and Modern Identity*. New York: Oxford University Press, 2000.

Bartusiak, Marcia. *The Day We Found the Universe*. New York: Pantheon, 2009.

Bataille, Georges. *Oeuvres complètes*. Paris: Gallimard, 1970–1988.

Baxter, Archibald. *We Will Not Cease*. New York: Penguin, 1987.

Becker, Jean-Jacques. *1917 en Europe: l'année impossible*. Bruxelles: Complexe, 1997.

Beckman, Wendy Hart. *Artists and Writers of the Harlem Renaissance*. Berkeley Heights, NJ: Enslow, 2002.

Beddoe, Deirdre. *Back to Home and Duty: Women Between the Wars, 1918–1933*. San Francisco: Pandora, 1989.

Beetham, David. *Marxists in Face of Fascism: Writings by Marxists on Fascism from the Inter-war Period*. Manchester: Manchester University Press, 1983.

Behrenbeck, Sabine. *Der Kult um die toten Helden: Nationalsozialistische Mythen, Riten und Symbole 1923 bis 1945*. Vierow: SH-Verlag, 1996.

Bell, Julian, and Quentin Bell. *Essays, Poems and Letters*. London: Hogarth Press, 1938.

Benadusi, Lorenzo. *The Enemy of the New Man: Homosexuality in Fascist Italy*. Madison: University of Wisconsin Press, 2012.

Benda, Julien. *The Treason of the Intellectuals*. New Brunswick, NJ: Transaction Publishers, 2007.

Bendavid-Val, Leah. *Propaganda and Dreams: Photographing the 1930s in the USSR and the US*. Zürich: Edition Stemmle, 1999.

Benson, Timothy. *Expressionist Utopias: Paradise, Metropolis, Architectural Fantasy*. Los Angeles: Los Angeles County Museum of Art, 1993.

Bergan, Ronald. *Jean Renoir: Projections of Paradise*. Woodstock, NY: Overlook Press, 1994.

Berlin, Isaiah. *The Soviet Mind: Russian Culture Under Communism*. Washington, DC: Brookings Institution Press, 2004.

Berman, Sheri. *The Social Democratic Moment: Ideas and Politics in the Making of Interwar Europe*. Cambridge, MA: Harvard University Press, 2009.

Bernanke, Ben. *Essays on the Great Depression*. Princeton, NJ: Princeton University Press, 2000.

Besier, Gerhard, Francesca Piombo and Katarzyna Stoklosa. *Fascism, Communism and the Consolidation of Democracy: A Comparison of European Dictatorships*. Berlin: Lit, 2006.

Bessel, Richard. *Germany After the First World War*. New York: Oxford University Press, 1993.

Best, Gary Dean. *The Dollar Decade: Mammon and the Machine in 1920s America*. Westport, CT: Praeger, 2003.

Birnbaum, Paula. *Women Artists in Interwar France: Framing Femininities*. Farnham, Surrey: Ashgate, 2011.

Black, Edwin. *War Against the Weak: Eugenics and America's Campaign to Create a Master Race*. New York: Four Walls Eight Windows, 2003.

Blackman, Cally. *The 20s and 30s: Flappers and Vamps*. Milwaukee: Gareth Stevens, 2000.

Blake, Jody. *Le Tumulte Noir: Modernist Art and Popular Entertainment in Jazz-Age Paris, 1900–1930*. University Park: Pennsylvania State University Press, 1999.

Blamires, Cyprian, and Paul Jackson. *World Fascism: A Historical Encyclopedia*. Santa Barbara, CA: ABC-CLIO, 2006.

Bloch, Marc Léopold Benjamin. *Memoirs of War, 1914–1915*. Translated by Carole Fink. Ithaca, NY: Cornell University Press, 1980.

Blocker, Jack S. *American Temperance Movements: Cycles of Reform*. Boston: Twayne, 1989.

Blom, Philipp. *The Vertigo Years: Change and Culture in the West, 1900–1914*. New York: Basic Books, 2008.

Bloom, Harold, ed. *The Harlem Renaissance*. Philadelphia: Chelsea House, 2004.

Bollauf, Traude. *Dienstmädchen-Emigration: die Flucht jüdischer Frauen aus Österreich und Deutschland nach England 1938/39*. Vienna: Lit-Verl, 2010.

Bolloten, Burnett. *The Spanish Civil War: Revolution and Counterrevolution*. Chapel Hill: University of North Carolina Press, 1991.

Borsodi, Ralph. *This Ugly Civilization*. New York: Simon and Schuster, 1929.

Bourke, Joanna. *Dismembering the Male: Men's Bodies, Britain and the Great War*. Chicago: University of Chicago Press, 1996.

Bouvet, Vincent, and Gerard Durozoi. *Paris Between the Wars, 1919–1939: Art, Life and Culture*. New York: Vendome Press, 2010.

Bowler, Peter J. *Reconciling Science and Religion: The Debate in Early-Twentieth-Century Britain*. Chicago: University of Chicago Press, 2013.

Bradford, Perry. *Born with the Blues: The True Story of the Pioneering Blues Singers and Musicians in the Early Days of Jazz*. New York: Oak Publications, 1965.

Braun, Emily, ed. *Italian Art in the 20th Century: Painting and Sculpture, 1900–1988*. New York: Neues, 1989.

Breicha, Otto. *Fritz Wotruba: Werkverzeichnis Skulpturen, Reliefs, Bühnen- und Architekturmodelle*. St. Gallen: Erker-Verlag, 2002.

Brendon, Piers. *The Dark Valley: A Panorama of the 1930s*. New York: Knopf, 2000.

Brenner, Michael, and Gideon Reuveni. *Emancipation Through Muscles: Jews and Sports in Europe*. Lincoln: University of Nebraska Press, 2006.

Bréon, Emmanuel. *L'art des années trente*. Paris: Somogy, 1996.

Breton, André. *Oeuvres complètes*. Paris: Gallimard, 1988–2008.

———. *Surrealism*. Edited by Herbert Read. London: Faber and Faber, 1936.

Brittain, Vera, and Alan Bishop. *Chronicle of Friendship: Diary of the Thirties, 1932–1939*. London: V. Gollancz, 1986.

Broer, Lawrence R., and John D. Walther, eds. *Dancing Fools and Weary Blues: The Great Escape of the Twenties*. Bowling Green, OH: Bowling Green State University Press, 1990.

Brokoff, Jürgen. "Die Apokalypse in der Weimarer Republik." *Arbitrium: Zeitschrift für Rezensionen zur germanistischen Literaturwissenschaft* 21, no. 3 (2003).

Brown, Frederick. *An Impersonation of Angels: A Biography of Jean Cocteau*. Harlow: Longmans, 1969.

Brown, Nicholas. *Utopian Generations: The Political Horizon of Twentieth-Century Literature*. Princeton, NJ: Princeton University Press, 2005.

Bucur, Maria. *Eugenics and Modernization in Interwar Romania*. Pittsburgh: University of Pittsburgh Press, 2010.

Busche, Jürgen. *Heldenprüfung: Das verweigerte Erbe des Ersten Weltkriegs*. Munich: Verl.-Anst., 2004.

Cable, Mary. *Top Drawer: American High Society from the Gilded Age to the Roaring Twenties*. New York: Atheneum, 1984.

Calo, Mary Ann. *Distinction and Denial: Race, Nation, and the Critical Construction of the African American Artist*. Ann Arbor: University of Michigan Press, 2007.

Camfield, William A. *Max Ernst, Dada and the Dawn of Surrealism*. Munich: Prestel, 1993.

Canetti, Elias. *Die Fackel im Ohr: Lebensgeschichte 1921–1931*. Munich: C. Hanser, 1993.

———. *Masse und Macht*. Munich: C. Hanser, 1960.

———. *The Torch in My Ear*. New York: Farrar, Straus and Giroux, 1982.

Cannon, Poppy. *The Presidents' Cookbook: Practical Recipes from George Washington to the Present*. New York: Funk & Wagnalls, 1968.

Carbone, Teresa A. *Youth and Beauty: Art of the American Twenties*. New York: Skira Rizzoli, 2011.

Caron, Vicki. *Uneasy Asylum: France and the Jewish Refugee Crisis, 1933–1942*. Stanford, CA: Stanford University Press, 1999.

Carr, Edward Hallett, and Michael Cox. *The Twenty Years' Crisis, 1919–1939: An Introduction to the Study of International Relations*. Basingstoke: Palgrave Macmillan, 2010.

Carroll, Anne Elizabeth. *Word, Image, and the New Negro: Representation and Identity in the Harlem Renaissance*. Bloomington: Indiana University Press, 2005.

Carson, Cathryn. *Heisenberg in the Atomic Age: Science and the Public Sphere*. Cambridge: Cambridge University Press, 2010.

Cassata, Francesco. *Building the New Man: Eugenics, Racial Science and Genetics in Twentieth-Century Italy*. Budapest: Central European University Press, 2011.

Cassidy, David C. *Uncertainty: The Life and Science of Werner Heisenberg*. New York: W. H. Freeman, 1992.

Cather, Willa. *Not Under Forty*. New York: A. A. Knopf, 1936.

Caws, Mary Ann. *Bloomsbury and France: Art and Friends*. Oxford: Oxford University Press, 2000.

Cecil, Hugh, and Peter Liddle. *Facing Armageddon: The First World War Experienced*. London: Cooper, 1996.

Chambers, Clarke A. *The New Deal at Home and Abroad, 1929–1945*. New York: Free Press, 1965.

Chaney, Otto Preston. *Zhukov*. Norman: University of Oklahoma Press, 1996.

Chanlaine, Pierre. *Les Horizons de la Science: Entretiens avec les Notabilités du Monde Politique, Religieux et Scientifique*. Paris: E. Flammarion, 1928.

Chase, Stuart. *Men and Machines*. New York: Macmillan, 1929.

Cheng, John. *Astounding Wonder: Imagining Science and Science Fiction in Interwar America*. Philadelphia: University of Pennsylvania Press, 2012.

Cheng, Yinghong. *Creating the New Man: From Enlightenment Ideals to Socialist Realities*. Honolulu: University of Hawaii Press, 2009.

Childs, Donald J. *Modernism and Eugenics: Woolf, Eliot, Yeats, and the Culture of Degeneration*. Cambridge: Cambridge University Press, 2001.

Christianson, Gale E. *Edwin Hubble: Mariner of the Nebulae*. New York: Farrar, Straus and Giroux, 1995.

Clair, Jean. *The 1920s: Age of Metropolis*. Montreal: Montreal Museum of Fine Arts, 1991.

———. *The 1930s: The Making of the New Man*. Ottawa: National Gallery of Canada, 2008.

———. *Vienne, 1880–1938: l'apocalypse joyeuse*. Paris: Editions du Centre Georges Pompidou, 1986.

Clark, Christopher M. *The Sleepwalkers: How Europe Went to War in 1914*. New York: Harper, 2013.

Clark, Jon. *Culture and Crisis in Britain in the Thirties*. London: Lawrence and Wishart, 1979.

Clark, Katerina. *Moscow, the Fourth Rome: Stalinism, Cosmopolitanism, and the Evolution of Soviet Culture, 1931–1941*. Cambridge, MA: Harvard University Press, 2011.

———. *Petersburg: Crucible of Cultural Revolution*. Cambridge, MA: Harvard University Press, 1996.

Clark, Katerina, and Evgeniĭ Aleksandrovich Dobrenko. *Soviet Culture and Power: A History in Documents, 1917–1953*. New Haven, CT: Yale University Press, 2007.

Clout, Hugh D. *After the Ruins: Restoring the Countryside of Northern France After the Great War*. Exeter: University of Exeter Press, 1996.

Cocteau, Jean. *Cocteau: catalogue de l'exposition "Jean Cocteau sur le fil du siècle."* Paris: Centre Pompidou, 2003.

Cohen, Deborah. *The War Come Home: Disabled Veterans in Britain and Germany, 1914–39.* Berkeley: University of California Press, 2001.

Cohen, Lizabeth. *Making a New Deal: Industrial Workers in Chicago, 1919–1939.* Cambridge: Cambridge University Press, 2008.

Cohn, A. A. *The Jazz Singer.* Edited by Robert L. Carringer. Madison: University of Wisconsin Press, 1979.

Collier, Christopher. *Progressivism, the Great Depression, and the New Deal, 1901 to 1941.* New York: Benchmark Books, 2001.

Conkin, Paul. *When All the Gods Trembled: Darwinism, Scopes, and American Intellectuals.* Lanham, MD: Rowman & Littlefield, 1998.

Conquest, Robert. *The Great Terror: A Reassessment.* New York: Oxford University Press, 1990.

———. *The Great Terror: Stalin's Purges of the Thirties.* New York: Macmillan, 1968.

———. *Stalin and the Kirov Murder.* New York: Oxford University Press, 1989.

Cooper, Wayne F. *Claude McKay: Rebel Sojourner in the Harlem Renaissance, a Biography.* Baton Rouge: Louisiana State University Press, 1987.

Costello, John. *Deadly Illusions.* New York: Crown, 1993.

Coudenhove-Kalergi, Barbara. *Zuhause ist überall: Erinnerungen.* Vienna: Zsolnay, 2013.

Cowan, Michael, and Kai Marcel Sicks. *Leibhaftige Moderne: Körper in Kunst und Massenmedien 1918 bis 1933.* Bielefeld: Transcript Verlag, 2005.

Cruz, Rafael. *Pasionaria: Dolores Ibárruri, Historia y Símbolo.* Colección "Perfiles del Poder" 1. Madrid: Biblioteca Nueva, 1999.

Cuomo, Franco. *I Dieci: Chi Erano gli Scienzati Italiani che Firmarono il Manifesto della Razza.* Milan: Baldini Castoldi Dalai, 2005.

Currell, Susan, and Christina Cogdell, eds. *Popular Eugenics: National Efficiency and American Mass Culture in the 1930s.* Athens: Ohio University Press, 2006.

Curtis, Michael. *Three Against the Third Republic.* Princeton, NJ: Princeton University Press, 1959.

Dabrowski, Magdalena. *Aleksandr Rodchenko.* New York: Museum of Modern Art, 1998.

Daniels, Roger. *Coming to America: A History of Immigration and Ethnicity in American Life.* New York: HarperCollins, 1990.

David-Fox, Michael. *Showcasing the Great Experiment: Cultural Diplomacy and Western Visitors to Soviet Union, 1921—1941.* New York: Oxford University Press, 2012.

Davidson, Roger. *Dangerous Liaisons: A Social History of Venereal Disease in Twentieth-Century Scotland.* Amsterdam: Rodopi, 2000.

Davies, Sarah, and James Harris. *Stalin: A New History.* Cambridge: Cambridge University Press, 2005.

De Camp, L. Sprague. *The Great Monkey Trial.* Garden City, NY: Doubleday, 1968.

de Grazia, Victoria. *How Fascism Ruled Women: Italy, 1922–1945.* Berkeley: University of California Press, 1992.

Dean, Carol. *The Frail Social Body: Pornography, Homosexuality, and Other Fantasies in Interwar France*. Berkeley: University of California Press, 2000.

Demaris, Ovid. *America the Violent*. New York: Cowles Books, 1970.

Dewey, John. *Individualism: Old and New*. New York: Minton, Balch, 1930.

———. *The Public and Its Problems*. New York: Henry Holt, 1927.

Diehl, Paula. *Körper im Nationalsozialismus: Bilder und Praxen*. Paderborn: Schöningh, 2006.

Dinter, Artur. *Die Sünde wider das Blut: ein Zeitroman*. Leipzig: Verlag Matthes und Thost, 1921.

Dix, Otto. *Dix: Galerie der Stadt Stuttgart, Nationalgalerie, Staatliche Museen Preussischer Kulturbesitz Berlin*. Stuttgart: G. Hatje, 1991.

Dmitrieva, Marina, and Heidemarie Petersen. *Jüdische Kultur(en) im Neuen Europa: Wilna 1918–1939*. Wiesbaden: Otto Harrassowitz Verlag, 2004.

Dolot, Miron. *Execution by Hunger: The Hidden Holocaust*. New York: W. W. Norton, 1985.

Dreiser, Theodore. *An American Tragedy*. Cleveland, OH: World, 1948.

Drowne, Kathleen Moran, and Patrick Huber. *The 1920s*. Westport, CT: Greenwood Press, 2004.

Düffer, Jost, and Gerd Krumeich, eds. *Der verlorene Frieden: Politik und Kriegskultur nach 1918*. Essen: Klartext, 2002.

Duggan, Christopher. *Fascist Voices: An Intimate History of Mussolini's Italy*. London: Bodley Head, 2012.

Dumenil, Lynn. *The Modern Temper: American Culture and Society in the 1920s*. New York: Farrar, Straus and Giroux, 1995.

Duppler, Jörg, and Gerhard Paul Gross. *Kriegsende 1918: Ereignis, Wirkung, Nachwirkung*. Munich: Oldenbourg, 1999.

Durst, David. *Weimar Modernism: Philosophy, Politics, and Culture in Germany, 1918–1933*. Lanham, MD: Lexington Books, 2004.

Eatwell, Roger. *Fascism: A History*. New York: Random House, 2011.

Eby, Cecil D. *Comrades and Commissars: The Lincoln Battalion in the Spanish Civil War*. University Park: Pennsylvania State University Press, 2013.

Edmondson, Jacqueline. *Jesse Owens: A Biography*. Westport, CT: Greenwood, 2007.

Edwards, Brent Hayes. *The Practice of Diaspora: Literature, Translation, and the Rise of Black Internationalism*. Cambridge, MA: Harvard University Press, 2003.

Egan, Timothy. *The Worst Hard Time*. Boston: Houghton Mifflin, 2006.

Ekstein, Modris. *Rites of Spring: The Great War and the Birth of the Modern Age*. Boston: Houghton Mifflin, 1989.

Eichengreen, Barry J., and T. J. Hatton. *Interwar Unemployment in International Perspective*. Dordrecht: Springer, 1988.

Emmerich, Alexander. *Olympia 1936: trügerischer Glanz eines mörderischen Systems*. Cologne: Fackelträger-Verlag, 2011.

Erben, Tino. *Traum und Wirklichkeit Wien, 1870–1930*. Vienna: Museen der Stadt Wien, 1985.

Evans, Richard J. *The Coming of the Third Reich*. New York: Penguin, 2004.

Exner, Gudrun. *Bevölkerungswissenschaft in Österreich in der Zwischenkriegszeit (1918–1938): Personen, Institutionen, Diskurse*. Vienna: Böhlau Verlag, 2004.

Ezra, Elizabeth. *The Colonial Unconscious: Race and Culture in Inter-war France.* Ithaca, NY: Cornell University Press, 2000.

Fair-Schulz, Axel, and Mario Kessler. *German Scholars in Exile: New Studies in Intellectual History.* Lanham, MD: Lexington Books, 2011.

Fass, Paula. *The Damned and the Beautiful: American Youth in the 1920s.* New York: Oxford University Press, 1977.

Feingold, Henry L. *A Time for Searching: Entering the Mainstream, 1920–1945.* Baltimore: Johns Hopkins University Press, 1992.

Feinstein, Elaine. *Anna of All the Russias: The Life of Anna Akhmatova.* New York: Knopf, 2007.

Ferguson, Niall. *The Pity of War: Explaining World War I.* New York: Basic Books, 2000.

Feuchtwanger, E. J. *From Weimar to Hitler: Germany, 1918–33.* New York: St. Martin's Press, 1993.

Fiedler, Jeannine. *Social Utopias of the Twenties: Bauhaus, Kibbutz and the Dream of the New Man.* Wuppertal: Müller + Bussman, 1995.

Figes, Orlando. *A People's Tragedy: The Russian Revolution, 1891–1924.* London: Jonathan Cape, 1996.

———. *The Whisperers: Private Life in Stalin's Russia.* New York: Metropolitan Books, 2007.

Fishburn, Matthew. *Burning Books.* Basingstoke, Hampshire: Palgrave Macmillan, 2008.

Fisher, Peter S. *Fantasy and Politics: Visions of the Future in the Weimar Republic.* Madison: University of Wisconsin Press, 1991.

Fitch, Noel Riley. *Sylvia Beach and the Lost Generation: A History of Literary Paris in the Twenties and Thirties.* New York: Norton, 1983.

Fitzgerald, F. Scott. *Novels and Stories, 1920–1922: This Side of Paradise; Flappers and Philosophers; The Beautiful and the Damned; Tales of the Jazz Age.* New York: Penguin Books, 2000.

Fitzpatrick, Sheila. *The Cultural Front: Power and Culture in Revolutionary Russia.* Ithaca, NY: Cornell University Press, 1992.

———. *Everyday Stalinism, Ordinary Life in Extraordinary Times: Soviet Russia in the 1930s.* Oxford: Oxford University Press, 1999.

———. *The Russian Revolution.* Oxford: Oxford University Press, 2007.

———. *Stalin's Peasants: Resistance and Survival in the Russian Village after Collectivization.* Oxford: Oxford University Press, 1994.

Fitzpatrick, Sheila, and Michael Geyer, eds. *Beyond Totalitarianism: Stalinism and Nazism Compared.* New York: Cambridge University Press, 2009.

Fitzpatrick, Sheila, and Yuri Slezkine, eds. *In the Shadow of Revolution: Life Stories of Russian Women from 1917 to the Second World War.* Princeton, NJ: Princeton University Press, 2000.

Flanner, Janet. *Paris Was Yesterday, 1925–1939.* New York: Viking Press, 1972.

Fleming, Donald, and Bernard Bailyn, eds. *The Intellectual Migration: Europe and America, 1930–1960.* Cambridge: Belknap Press, 1969.

Föllmer, Moritz, and Rüdiger Graf. *Die "Krise" der Weimarer Republik: zur Kritik eines Deutungsmusters.* New York: Campus Books, 2005.

Forman, Paul. "Weimar Culture, Causality, and Quantum Theory, 1918–1927: Adaptation by German Physicists and Mathematicians to a Hostile Intellectual Environment." *Historical Studies in the Physical Sciences* 3 (January 1971): 1–115.

Forman, Paul, Cathryn Carson, et al. *Weimar Culture and Quantam Mechanics: Selected Papers by Paul Forman and Contemporary Perspectives on the Forman Thesis*. London: Imperial College Press, 2011.

Franck, Dan. *The Bohemians: The Birth of Modern Art: Paris 1900–1930*. Translated by Cynthia Hope Liebow. London: Weidenfeld and Nicolson, 2001.

Franke, Julia. *Paris, eine neue Heimat? Jüdische Emigranten aus Deutschland 1933–1939*. Berlin: Duncker & Humblot, 2000.

Friedrich, Thomas. *Berlin Between the Wars*. New York: Vendome Press, 1991.

Frost, Laura Catherine. *Sex Drives: Fantasies of Fascism in Literary Modernism*. Ithaca, NY: Cornell University Press, 2002.

Froula, Christine. *Virginia Woolf and the Bloomsbury Avant-Garde: War, Civilization, Modernity*. New York: Columbia University Press, 2013.

Furet, François, and Ernst Nolte. *Fascism and Communism*. Lincoln: University of Nebraska Press, 2001.

Fussell, Paul. *The Great War and Modern Memory*. Oxford: Oxford University Press, 1975.

Gabriel, Heinz Eberhard, and Wolfgang Neugebauer. *Vorreiter der Vernichtung? Eugenik, Rassenhygiene und Euthanasie in der österreichischen Diskussion vor 1938*. Vienna: Böhlau Verlag, 2005.

Galbraith, John Kenneth. *The Great Crash, 1929*. Boston: Houghton Mifflin Harcourt, 1997.

Garrard, John Gordon, and Carol Garrard. *Inside the Soviet Writers' Union*. London: I. B. Tauris, 1990.

Gatewood, Willard B. *Controversy in the Twenties: Fundamentalism, Modernism and Evolution*. Nashville, TN: Vanderbilt University Press, 1969.

Gay, Peter. *Weimar Culture: The Outsider as Insider*. New York: Harper & Row, 1968.

Gentile, Emilio. *The Sacralization of Politics in Fascist Italy*. Translated by Keith Botsford. Cambridge, MA: Harvard University Press, 1996.

Gerstle, Gary. *American Crucible: Race and Nation in the Twentieth Century*. Princeton, NJ: Princeton University Press, 2001.

Getzler, Israel. *Kronstadt: 1917–1921*. Cambridge, MA: Cambridge University Press, 2002.

Gilbert, Martin. *The First World War: A Complete History*. New York: Henry Holt, 1994.

Ginzburg, Yevgenia Solomonovna. *Journey into the Whirlwind*. San Diego: Harcourt, Brace, 1995.

Glassman, Bruce. *The Crash of '29 and the New Deal*. Morristown, NJ: Silver Burdett, 1986.

Goebbels, Joseph. *Goebbels Reden Bd. 1*. Munich: Heyne, 1971.

Golan, Romy. *Modernity and Nostalgia: Art and Politics in France Between the Wars*. New Haven, CT: Yale University Press, 1995.

Goldberg, David Joseph. *Discontented America: The United States in the 1920s*. Baltimore, MD: Johns Hopkins University Press, 1999.

Goldman, Wendy Z. *Inventing the Enemy: Denunciation and Terror in Stalin's Russia*. New York: Cambridge University Press, 2011.

Goodliffe, Gabriel. *The Resurgence of the Radical Right in France: From Boulangisme to the Front National*. New York: Cambridge University Press, 2011.

Gordon, Mel. *Voluptuous Panic: The Erotic World of Weimar Berlin*. Los Angeles: Feral House, 2006.

Gorsuch, Anne E. *Youth in Revolutionary Russia: Enthusiasts, Bohemians, Delinquents*. Bloomington: Indiana University Press, 2000.

Gossman, Lionel. *The Passion of Max von Oppenheim: Archaeology and Intrigue in the Middle East from Wilhelm II to Hitler*. Cambridge: Open Book Publishers, 2013.

Gourley, Catherine. *Flappers and the New American Woman: Perceptions of Women from 1918 Through the 1920s*. Minneapolis, MN: Twenty-first Century Books, 2008.

Graham, Loren R. *Between Science and Values*. New York: Columbia University Press, 1981.

Graves, Robert. *The Long Weekend: A Social History of Great Britain, 1918–1939*. Middlesex: Penguin Books, 1971.

Green, Martin. *Children of the Sun: A Narrative of "Decadence" in England After 1918*. New York: Basic Books, 1976.

Gregory, James N. *American Exodus: The Dust Bowl Migration and Okie Culture in California*. New York: Oxford University Press, 1991.

Griffin, Roger. *Modernism and Fascism: The Sense of a Beginning under Mussolini and Hitler*. Basingstoke: Palgrave Macmillan, 2007.

Grimshaw, Allen D. *A Social History of Racial Violence*. New Brunswick, NJ: Transaction Publishers, 2009.

Grolier Educational. *Depression America*. Danbury, CT: Grolier Educational, 2001.

Grosskurth, Phyllis. *Havelock Ellis: A Biography*. New York: New York University Press, 1985.

Grossman, Manuel L. *Dada: Paradox, Mystification, and Ambiguity in European Literature*. New York: Pegasus, 1971.

Grosz, George. *Briefe 1913–1959*. Reinbek bei Hamburg: Rowohlt, 1979.

———. *George Grosz, an Autobiography*. Translated by Nora Hodges. New York: Macmillan, 1983.

Gruber, Helmut, and Pamela M. Graves. *Women and Socialism, Socialism and Women: Europe Between the Two World Wars*. New York: Berghahn Books, 1998.

Gumbrecht, Hans Ulrich. *In 1926: Living at the Edge of Time*. Cambridge, MA: Harvard University Press, 1997.

Gunning, Tom. *The Films of Fritz Lang: Allegories of Vision and Modernity*. London: British Film Institute, 2000.

Hacohen, Malachi Haim. *Karl Popper: The Formative Years, 1902–1945: Politics and Philosophy in Interwar Vienna*. Cambridge: Cambridge University Press, 2002.

Haldane, J. B. S. *Daedalus or Science and the Future*. London: Dutton, 1925.

Haldane, R. B. *The Reign of Relativity.* London: J. Murray, 1921.

Halfeld, Adolf. *Amerika und der Amerikanismus: Kritische Betrachtungen eines Deutschen und Europäers.* Jena: E. Diederichs, 1927.

Hallwas, John E. *The Bootlegger: A Story of Small-Town America.* Urbana: University of Illinois Press, 1998.

Hamilton, Neil A. *Rebels and Renegades: A Chronology of Social and Political Dissent in the United States.* New York: Routledge, 2002.

Hardtwig, Wolfgang. *Ordnungen in der Krise: Zur politischen Kulturgeschichte Deutschlands 1900–1933.* Munich: Oldenbourg, 2007.

Harrington, Anne. *Reenchanted Science: Holism in German Culture from Wilhelm II to Hitler.* Princeton, NJ: Princeton University Press, 1996.

Hart, Peter. *The Great War: A Combat History of the First World War.* New York: Oxford University Press, 2013.

Hatfield, H. Stafford. *Automation; Or, the Future of the Mechanical Man.* New York: E. P. Dutton, 1928.

Hattersley, Roy. *Borrowed Time: The Story of Britain Between the Wars.* Boston: Little, Brown, 2007.

Hehn, Paul N. *A Low Dishonest Decade: The Great Powers, Eastern Europe, and the Economic Origins of World War II, 1930–1941.* New York: Continuum, 2002.

Heiting, Manfred, and Roland Jaeger, eds. *Autopsie: deutschsprachige Fotobücher 1918 bis 1945.* Göttingen: Verlag Steidl, 2012.

Henderson, Caroline. *Letters from the Dust Bowl.* Norman: University of Oklahoma Press, 2012.

Hentschel, Klaus, and Ann Hentschel. *Physics and National Socialism: An Anthology of Primary Sources.* Boston: Birkhäuser Verlag, 1996.

Heppner, Ernest G. *Shanghai Refuge: A Memoir of the World War II Jewish Ghetto.* Lincoln: University of Nebraska Press, 1993.

Herf, Jeffrey. *Reactionary Modernism: Technology, Culture and Politics in Weimar and the Third Reich.* New York: Cambridge University Press, 1984.

Herzfelde, Wieland. *Zur Sache: geschrieben und gesprochen zwischen 18 und 80.* Berlin: Aufbau-Verlag, 1976.

Heynickx, Rajesh, and Tom Avermaete. *Making a New World: Architecture and Communities in Interwar Europe.* Leuven: Leuven University Press, 2012.

Hillstrom, Kevin. *The Harlem Renaissance.* Detroit: Omnigraphics, 2008.

Hilton, Christopher. *Hitler's Olympics: The 1936 Berlin Olympic Games.* Stroud: Sutton, 2006.

Hipp, Daniel. *The Poetry of Shell Shock: Wartime Trauma and Healing in Wilfred Owen, Ivor Gurney and Siegfried Sassoon.* Jefferson, NC: McFarland, 2005.

Hitchcock, Hugh Wiley. *Music in the United States: A Historical Introduction.* Englewood Cliffs, NJ: Prentice-Hall, 1974.

Hochschild, Adam. *To End All Wars: A Story of Loyalty and Rebellion, 1914–1918.* Boston: Houghton Mifflin, 2011.

Höchtl, Daniela. *Buenos Aires—eine neue Heimat? Die Integration der deutschen Juden in der argentinischen Hauptstadt 1933–1939.* Munich: GRIN Verlag, 2008.

Hofer, Hans Georg. *Nervenschwäche und Krieg—Modernitätskritik und Krisenbewältigung der österreichischen Psychiatrie, 1880–1920.* Vienna: Böhlau, 2004.

Hoffmann, David L. *Cultivating the Masses: Modern State Practices and Soviet Socialism, 1914–1939.* Ithaca, NY: Cornell University Press, 2011.

———. *Stalinist Values: The Cultural Norms of Soviet Modernity, 1917–1941.* Ithaca, NY: Cornell University Press, 2003.

Holden, Wendy. *Shell Shock: The Psychological Impact of War.* London: Channel 4, 1998.

Holmes, Richard. *Tommy: The British Soldier on the Western Front.* London: Harper Collins, 2011.

Holmes, Deborah, and Lisa Silverman. *Interwar Vienna: Culture Between Tradition and Modernity.* Rochester, NY: Camden House, 2009.

Holub, Robert C. "Nietzsche: Socialist, Anarchist, Feminist." In *German Culture in Nineteenth Century America: Reception, Adaptation, Transformation,* edited by Lynne Tatlock and Matt Erlin. Rochester, NY: Camden House, 2005.

Howe, Irving, and Kenneth Libo. *World of Our Fathers: The Journey of the East European Jews to America and the Life They Found and Made.* New York: Book-of-the-Month Club, 1993.

Hughes, Robert. *American Visions: The Epic History of Art in America.* New York: Alfred A. Knopf, 1997.

Hughes-Hallett, Lucy. *The Pike: Gabriele d'Annunzio: Poet, Seducer and Preacher of War.* London: Fourth Estate, 2013.

Hyman, Paula. *From Dreyfus to Vichy: The Remaking of French Jewry, 1906–1939.* New York: Columbia University Press, 1979.

Internationale Arbeitstagung Politische Religionen: Forschungskonzepte, Ergebnisse. *"Totalitarismus" und "Politische Religionen."* Volume 2. Paderborn: Schöningh, 1997.

Isenberg, Noah William. *Weimar Cinema: An Essential Guide to Classic Films of the Era.* New York: Columbia University Press, 2009.

Jacobs, Jack Lester. *Bundist Counterculture in Interwar Poland.* Syracuse, NY: Syracuse University Press, 2009.

Jang, Gyoung Sun. "The Sexual Politics of the Interwar Era Global Governance: Historicizing the Women's Transnational Movements With(in) the League of Nations, 1919–1940." Ph.D. dissertation, Clark University, 2009.

Jefferies, Matthew, and Mike Tyldesley. *Rolf Gardiner: Folk, Nature and Culture in Interwar Britain.* Farnham, Surrey: Ashgate, 2013.

Jeismann, Michael, and Reinhard Koselleck, eds. *Der politische Totenkult: Kriegerdenkmäler in der Moderne.* Munich: Fink, 1994.

Jenkins, Alan. *The Thirties.* New York: Stein and Day, 1976.

———. *The Twenties.* New York: Universe Books, 1974.

Jones, Sharon L. *Rereading the Harlem Renaissance: Race, Class, and Gender in the Fiction of Jessie Fauset, Zora Neale Hurston, and Dorothy West.* Westport, CT: Greenwood Press, 2002.

Judt, Tony. *The Burden of Responsibility: Blum, Camus, Aron, and the French Twentieth Century.* Chicago: University of Chicago Press, 1998.

Jullian, Philippe. *D'Annunzio.* London: Pall Mall Press, 1972.

Jünger, Ernst. *In Stahlgewittern*. Stuttgart: E. Klett, 1961.

———. *Sämtliche Werke*. Stuttgart: Klett-Cotta, 1978–2003.

———. *Storm of Steel*. New York: Penguin Books, 2004.

Kaes, Anton, ed. *Weimarer Republik: Manifeste und Dokumente zur deutschen Literatur 1918–1933*. Stuttgart: J. B. Metzler, 1983.

———. *The Weimar Republic Sourcebook*. Berkeley: University of California Press, 1994.

Kalman, Samuel. *The Extreme Right in Interwar France: The Faisceau and the Croix de Feu*. Farnham, Surrey: Ashgate, 2008.

Kasson, John F. *Houdini, Tarzan and the Perfect Man: The White Male Body and the Challenge of Modernity in America*. New York: Hill and Wang, 2001.

Kaufmann, Walter. *Nietzsche: Philosopher, Psychologist, Antichrist*. Princeton, NJ: Princeton University Press, 1974.

Keegan, John. *The First World War*. New York: Vintage, 2000.

Kemp, Wolfgang. *Foreign Affairs: die Abenteuer einiger Engläner in Deutschland 1900–1947*. Munich: Hanser, 2010.

Kennan, George F. *Memoirs, 1925–1950*. Boston: Little, Brown, 1967.

Kennedy, David M. *Freedom from Fear: The American People in Depression and War, 1929–1945*. New York: Oxford University Press, 1999.

Kessler, Harry. *The Diaries of a Cosmopolitan: Count Harry Kessler, 1918–1937*. Translated by Charles Kessler. London: Weidenfeld and Nicolson, 1971.

Keynes, John Maynard. *The Economic Consequences of the Peace*. New York: Harcourt, Brace and Howe, 1920.

Kienitz, Sabine. *Beschädigte Helden: Kriegsinvalidität und Körperbilder, 1914–1923*. Paderborn: Schöningh, 2008.

King, David C. *Al Capone and the Roaring Twenties*. Woodbridge, CT: Blackbirch Press, 1999.

Kinnear, Mary. *Margaret McWilliams: An Interwar Feminist*. Montreal: McGill-Queen's University Press, 1991.

Kirk, D. *Europe's Population in Interwar Years*. London: Taylor & Francis, 1969.

Kirschke, Amy Helene. *Aaron Douglas: Art, Race, and the Harlem Renaissance*. Jackson: University Press of Mississippi, 1995.

Kirschl, Wilfried. *Albin Egger Lienz, 1868–1926: das Gesamtwerk*. Vienna: Brandstätter, 1996.

Kitchen, Martin. *Europe Between the Wars: A Political History*. New York: Longman, 2000.

Kiyem, Sigrid. *Der Wiener Justizpalastbrand am 15. Juli 1927. Darstellung in Quellen und Medien*. Vienna, 2001.

Klein, Holger Michael, ed. *The First World War in Fiction: A Collection of Critical Essays*. New York: Barnes and Noble, 1977.

Klein, Maury. *Rainbow's End: The Crash of 1929*. New York: Oxford University Press, 2001.

Klüver, Billy. *Kiki's Paris: Artists and Lovers 1900–1930*. New York: Abrams, 1989.

Kniesche, Thomas W., and Stephen Brockmann, eds. *Dancing on the Volcano: Essays on the Culture of the Weimar Republic*. Columbia, SC: Camden House, 1994.

Kobler, John. *Ardent Spirits: The Rise and Fall of Prohibition.* New York: Da Capo Press, 1993.

Köhler, Thomas, and Christian Mertens. *Justizpalast in Flammen: ein brennender Dornbusch, das Werk von Manes Sperber, Heimito von Doderer und Elias Canetti angesichts des 15. Juli 1927.* Vienna: Verlag für Geschichte und Politik, 2006.

Kojevnikov, Alexei, Cathryn Carson, and Helmuth Trischler. *Weimar Culture and Quantum Mechanics: Selected Papers by Paul Forman and Contemporary Perspectives on the Forman Thesis.* Singapore: World Scientific, 2011.

König, Mareike. *Deutsche Handwerker, Arbeiter und Dienstmädchen in Paris: eine vergessene Migration im 19. Jahrhundert.* Munich: Oldenbourg Verlag, 2003.

Kooy, G. A. *Het Echec van een "volkse" beweging: nazificatie en denazificatie in Nederland 1931–1945.* Utrecht: HES, 1982.

Korte, Barbara, Sylvia Paletschek, and Wolfgang Hochbruch, eds. *Der Erste Weltkrieg in der populären Erinnerungskultur.* Essen: Klartext, 2008.

Kos, Wolfgang, ed. *Kampf um die Stadt: Politik, Kunst und Alltag um 1930.* Vienna: Wien Museum, 2010.

Kossmann, E. H. *De lage landen 1780–1980: twee eeuwen Nederland en België.* Amsterdam: Elsevier, 1986.

Kosta, Barbara. *Willing Seduction: The Blue Angel, Marlene Dietrich, and Mass Culture.* New York: Berghahn Books, 2012.

Kotkin, Stephen. *The Cultural Gradient: The Transmission of Ideas in Europe, 1789–1991.* Lanham, MD: Rowman & Littlefield, 2003.

———. *Magnetic Mountain: Stalinism as Civilization.* Berkeley: University of California Press, 1995.

Kozhevnikov, A. B. *Stalin's Great Science: The Times and Adventures of Soviet Physicists.* Singapore: World Scientific, 2004.

Kramer, Alan. *Dynamic of Destruction: Culture and Mass Killing in the First World War.* Oxford: Oxford University Press, 2007.

Krasner, David. *A Beautiful Pageant: African American Theatre, Drama, and Performance in the Harlem Renaissance, 1910–1927.* New York: Palgrave Macmillan, 2002.

Krementsov, Nikolai. *Stalinist Science.* Princeton, NJ: Princeton University Press, 1997.

Kufeld, Maria. *Jüdische Emigration aus Deutschland in die USA und nach Brasilien in den Jahren 1933–1945.* Munich: GRIN Verlag, 2004.

Kühl, Stefan. *Die Internationale der Rassisten: Aufstieg und Niedergang der internationalen Bewegung für Eugenik und Rassenhygiene im 20. Jahrhundert.* Frankfurt am Main: Campus-Verlag, 1997.

Kyvig, David E. *Daily Life in the United States, 1920–1940: How Americans Lived Through the "Roaring Twenties" and the Great Depression.* Chicago: Ivan R. Dee, 2004.

———. *Unintended Consequences of Constitutional Amendment.* Athens: University of Georgia Press, 2000.

Lackerstein, Debbie. *National Regeneration in Vichy France: Ideas and Policies, 1930–1944.* Farnham, Sussex: Ashgate, 2012.

Lagendijk, Vincent. *Electrifying Europe: The Power of Europe in the Construction of Electricity Networks.* Amsterdam: Amsterdam University Press, 2008.

Langhamer, Claire. *The English in Love: The Intimate Story of an Emotional Revolution*. Oxford: Oxford University Press, 2013.

Langsam, Walter Consuelo. *The World Since 1919*. New York: Macmillan, 1971.

Larson, Edward. *Summer of the Gods: The Scopes Trial and America's Continuing Debate over Science and Religion*. New York: Basic Books, 1997.

Lawrence, Christopher, and Anna-K. Mayer. *Regenerating England: Science, Medicine and Culture in Inter-war Britain*. Amsterdam: Rodopi, 2000.

Leacock, Stephen. *The Iron Man and the Tin Woman, with Other Such Futurities: A Book of Little Sketches of To-Day and To-Morrow*. New York: Dodd, Mead, 1929.

Le Bon, Gustave. *Psychologie der massen*. Leipzig: A. Kröner, 1938.

Le Corbusier. *Quand les cathédrales étaient blanches: voyage au pays des timides*. Paris: Plon, 1937.

Leese, Peter. *Shell Shock: Traumatic Neurosis and the British Soldiers of the First World War*. New York: Palgrave, 2002.

Leinwand, Gerald. *1927: High Tide of the Twenties*. New York: Four Walls Eight Windows, 2001.

LeMahieu, Dan. *A Culture for Democracy: Mass Communications and the Cultural Mind in Britain Between the Wars*. New York: Oxford University Press, 1988.

Lenoe, Matthew E. *Closer to the Masses: Stalinist Culture, Social Revolution, and Soviet Newspapers*. Cambridge, MA: Harvard University Press, 2004.

Lerner, Paul. *Hysterical Men: War, Psychiatry and the Politics of Trauma in Germany, 1890–1930*. Ithaca, NY: Cornell University Press, 2002.

Leser, Norbert, and Paul Sailer-Wlasits. *1927, als die Republik brannte: von Schattendorf bis Wien*. Wien-Klosterneuberg: Edition Va Bene, 2001.

Lesy, Michael. *Murder City: The Bloody History of Chicago in the Twenties*. New York: Norton, 2007.

Lettevall, Rebecca, Geert Somsen, and Sven Widmalm, eds. *Neutrality in Twentieth-Century Europe: Intersections of Science, Culture, and Politics After the First World War*. New York: Routledge, 2012.

Levie, Sophie. *Reviews, Zeitschriften, Revues: Die Fackel, Die Weltbuhne, Musikblätter des Anbruch, Le disque vert, Mécano, Versty*. Amsterdam: Rodopi, 1994.

Levin, Harry. "Two Romanisten in America: Spitzer and Auerbach." In *The Intellectual Migration: Europe and America, 1930–1960*, edited by Donald Fleming and Bernard Bailyn. Cambridge, MA: Belknap Press, 1968.

Levy, Silvano. *Surrealism: Surrealist Visuality*. Edinburgh: Edinburgh University Press, 1997.

Lévy, Sophie, ed. *A Transatlantic Avant-Garde: American Artists in Paris, 1918–1939*. Berkeley: University of California Press, 2003.

Lewis, David L. *W. E. B. Du Bois*. 2 volumes. New York: Henry Holt, 1993–2000.

Lewis, Helena. *The Politics of Surrealism*. New York: Paragon House, 1988.

Lewis, Sinclair. *Main Street and Babbitt*. New York: Library of America, 1992.

Lewis, Wyndham. *Time and Western Man*. London: Chatto and Windus, 1927.

Lienesch, Michael. *In the Beginning: Fundamentalism, the Scopes Trial, and the Making of the Antievolution Movement*. Chapel Hill: University of North Carolina Press, 2007.

Lifton, Robert Jay. *The Nazi Doctors: Medical Killing and the Psychology of Geno-cide*. New York: Basic Books, 1986.

Light, Alison. *Forever England: Feminicity, Literature, and Conservation Between the Wars*. New York: Routledge, 1991.

Lilla, Mark. *The Reckless Mind: Intellectuals in Politics*. New York: New York Review of Books, 2001.

Lippmann, Walter. *A Preface to Morals*. New York: Macmillan, 1929.

Locke, Alain. *The Negro and His Music*. Washington, DC: Associates in Negro Folk Education, 1936.

Longley, Marjorie. *America's Taste, 1851–1959: The Cultural Events of a Century Reported by Contemporary Observers in the Pages of the New York Times*. New York: Simon and Schuster, 1960.

Loughran, Tracey Louise. "Shell-Shock in First World War Britain: An Intellectual and Medical History, c. 1860–c. 1920." Ph.D. dissertation, University of London, 2006.

Lovell, Mary S. *The Sisters: The Saga of the Mitford Family*. New York: Norton, 2002.

Loving, Jerome. *The Last Titan: A Life of Theodore Dreiser*. Berkeley: University of California Press, 2005.

Low, Ann Marie. *Dust Bowl Diary*. Lincoln: University of Nebraska Press, 1984.

Low, Archibald Montgomery. *Our Wonderful World of Tomorrow: A Scientific Fore-cast of the Men, Women, and the World of the Future*. London: Ward, Lock, 1984.

Low, Robert. *La Pasionaria*. London: Hutchinson, 1992.

Lowe, Peter. *English Journeys: National and Cultural Identity in 1930s and 1940s England*. Amherst, NY: Cambria Press, 2012.

Lucie-Smith, Edward. *Art of the 1930s: The Age of Anxiety*. New York: Rizzoli, 1985.

Ludington, Townsend. *A Modern Mosaic: Art and Modernism in the United States*. Chapel Hill: University of North Carolina Press, 2000.

Lyttelton, Adrian. *The Seizure of Power: Fascism in Italy, 1919–1929*. Princeton, NJ: Princeton University Press, 1988.

Malino, Frances, and Bernard Wasserstein. *The Jews in Modern France*. Hanover, NH: University Press of New England, 1985.

Mallac, Guy de. *Boris Pasternak, His Life and Art*. Norman: University of Oklahoma Press, 1981.

Mandell, Richard D. *The Nazi Olympics*. Urbana: University of Illinois Press, 1971.

Mandelstam, Nadeshda, and Max Hayward. *Hope Against Hope: A Memoir*. New York: Modern Library, 1999.

Mann, Carol. *Paris: Artistic Life in the Twenties and Thirties*. London: Laurence King, 1996.

Marable, Manning. *W. E. B. Du Bois, Black Radical Democrat*. Boston: Twayne, 1986.

Martel, Gordon, ed. *A Companion to Europe 1900–1945*. Malden, MA: Blackwell, 2006.

Martin, Benjamin F. *Years of Plenty, Years of Want: France and the Legacy of the Great War*. DeKalb: Northern Illinois University Press, 2013.

Masterman, Charles F. G. *England After War: A Study.* New York: Harcourt Brace Jovanovich, 1923.

Matthews, J. H. *The Surrealist Mind.* Selinsgrove, PA: Susquehanna University Press, 1991.

Mawdsley, Evan. *The Stalin Years: The Soviet Union, 1929–53.* Second edition. Manchester: Manchester University Press, 2003.

McConnachie, Kathleen. "Science and Ideology: The Mental Hygiene and Eugenics Movements in the Interwar Years, 1919–1939." Ph.D. dissertation, University of Toronto, 1987.

McElvaine, Robert S. *The Great Depression: America, 1929–1941.* New York: Times Books, 1984.

McLaren, Angus. *Reproduction by Design: Sex, Robots, Trees, and Test-Tube Babies in Interwar Britain.* Chicago: University of Chicago Press, 2012.

McWhirter, Cameron. *Red Summer: The Summer of 1919 and the Awakening of Black America.* New York: Henry Holt, 2011.

Medawar, J. S., and David Pyke. *Hitler's Gift: The True Story of the Scientists Expelled by the Nazi Regime.* New York: Arcade, 2001.

Mencken, H. L. *Heathen Days, 1890–1936.* New York: Knopf, 1943.

Mencken, H. L., and Charles Fecher. *The Diary of H. L. Mencken.* New York: Random House, 1989.

Meskimmon, Marsha, and Shearer West, eds. *Visions of the "Neue Frau": Women and the Visual Arts in Weimar Germany.* Brookfield, VT: Ashgate, 1995.

Metzger, Rainer. *Berlin: The Twenties.* New York: Abrams, 2007.

Meyer, Jessica. *Men of War: Masculinity and the First World War in Britain.* Basingstoke: Palgrave Macmillan, 2008.

Micale, Mark. *Hysterical Men: The Hidden History of Male Nervous Illness.* Cambridge, MA: Harvard University Press, 2007.

Miles, Peter, and Malcolm Smith. *Cinema, Literature and Society: Elite and Mass Culture in Interwar Britain.* London: Croom Helm, 1987.

Miller, Tyrus. *Late Modernism: Politics, Fiction, and the Arts Between the World Wars.* Berkeley: University of California Press, 1999.

Miller, Zane L. *The Urbanization of Modern America: A Brief History.* San Diego: Harcourt Brace Jovanovich, 1987.

Millward, Robert, and John Singleton. *The Political Economy of Nationalisation in Britain, 1920–1950.* Cambridge: Cambridge University Press, 2002.

Mogulof, Milly. *Foiled: Hitler's Jewish Olympian: The Helene Mayer Story.* Oakland, CA: RDR Books, 2002.

Möhring, Maren. *Marmorleiber: Körperbildung in der deutschen Nacktkultur (1890–1930).* Cologne: Böhlau, 2004.

Mommsen, Wolfgang J. *Der Erste Weltkrieg: Anfang vom Ende des bürgerlichen Zeitalters.* Frankfurt: Fischer Taschenbuch Verlag, 2004.

Monaco, Paul. *Cinema and Society: France and Germany During the Twenties.* New York: Elsevier, 1976.

Moore, Lucy. *Anything Goes: A Bibliography of the Roaring Twenties.* New York: Overlook Press, 2010.

Mosier, John. *The Myth of the Great War: A New Military History of World War I.* New York: Perennial, 2002.

Mosse, George L. *The Crisis of German Ideology: Intellectual Origins of the Third Reich.* New York: Grosset & Dunlap, 1964.

———. *Fallen Soldiers: Reshaping the Memory of the World Wars.* New York: Oxford University Press, 1991.

———. *Germans and Jews: The Right, the Left, and the Search for a "Third Force" in Pre-Nazi Germany.* New York: Grosset & Dunlap, 1971.

———. *The Image of Man: The Creation of Modern Masculinity.* New York: Oxford University Press, 1996.

———. *Masses and Man: Nationalist and Fascist Perceptions of Reality.* New York: H. Fertig, 1980.

———. *Nationalism and Sexuality: Respectability and Abnormal Sexuality in Modern Europe.* New York: H. Fertig, 1997.

———. *Nazi Culture: Intellectual, Cultural and Social Life in the Third Reich.* Madison: University of Wisconsin Press, 2003.

Mott, Frederick Walter. *War Neuroses and Shell Shock.* Oxford: Oxford University Press, 1919.

Mowat, Charles Loch. *Britain Between the Wars, 1918–1940.* Chicago: University of Chicago Press, 1955.

Mowry, George E. *The Twenties: Fords, Flappers, and Fanatics.* Englewood Cliffs, NJ: Prentice-Hall, 1963.

Müller, Hans-Harald. *Der Krieg und die Schriftsteller: der Kriegsroman der Weimarer Republik.* Stuttgart: J. B. Metzler, 1986.

Myers, Bernard Samuel. *Expressionism, a Generation in Revolt.* London: Thames and Hudson, 1963.

Myers, Charles Samuel. *Shell Shock in France, 1914–1918.* Cambridge: Cambridge University Press, 1940.

Naumann, Hans. *Kampf wider den undeutschen Geist Reden, geh. bei d. von d. Bonner Studentenschaft veranst. Kundgebg wider d. undeutschen Geist auf d. Marktplatz zu Bonn am 10. Mai 1933.* Bonn: Bonner Univ. Buchdr., 1933.

Nell, Liza, and Jan Rath. *Ethnic Amsterdam: Immigrants and Urban Change in the Twentieth Century.* Amsterdam: Amsterdam University Press, 2009.

Nelson, Cary. *Madrid 1937: Letters of the Abraham Lincoln Brigade from the Spanish Civil War.* New York: Routledge, 1996.

Néret, Gilles. *The Art of the Twenties.* New York: Rizzoli, 1986.

Neuman, Andrés. *El Viajero del Siglo.* Madrid: Alfaguara, 2009.

Nicolson, Juliet. *The Great Silence: Britain from the Shadow of the First World War to the Dawn of the Jazz Age.* New York: Grove Press, 2009.

Nin, Anaïs. *The Diary of Anaïs Nin.* New York: Swallow Press, 1966.

Nussbaumer, Harry. *Discovering the Expanding Universe.* Cambridge: Cambridge University Press, 2009.

Nye, Mary Jo, ed. *The Cambridge History of Science,* volume 5, *The Modern Physical and Mathematical Sciences.* New York: Cambridge University Press, 2008.

Ogren, Kathy J. *The Jazz Revolution: Twenties America and the Meaning of Jazz.* New York: Oxford University Press, 1989.

Okrent, Daniel. *Last Call: The Rise and Fall of Prohibition*. New York: Scribner, 2010.

Orlov, Aleksandr. *The Secret History of Stalin's Crimes*. London: Jarrolds, 1954.

Ortega y Gasset, José. *Rebelión de las masas [Der Aufstand der Massen]*. Translated by Helene Weyl. Stuttgart: Deutsche Verlags-Anstalt.

Osborne, Peter. *The Politics of Time: Modernity and Avant-Garde*. London: Verso, 1995.

Overy, R. J. *The Inter-war Crisis, 1919–1939*. New York: Longman, 2010.

———. *The Morbid Age: Britain Between the Wars*. London: Allen Lane, 2009.

———. *The Twilight Years: The Paradox of Britain Between the Wars*. New York: Viking, 2009.

Pacé, Suzanne. *Années 30 en Europe: Le temps menaçant, 1929–1939*. Paris: Flammarion, 1997.

Payne, Stanley G., David J. Sorkin, and John S. Tortorice. *What History Tells: George L. Mosse and the Culture of Modern Europe*. Madison: University of Wisconsin Press, 2004.

Peale, Norman Vincent. *The True Joy of Positive Living: An Autobiography*. New York: Morrow, 1984.

Pells, Richard. *Modernist America: Art, Music, Movies, and the Globalization of American Culture*. New Haven, CT: Yale University Press, 2012.

Perret, Geoffrey. *America in the Twenties: A History*. New York: Simon and Schuster, 1982.

Phelan, Tony. *The Weimar Dilemma: Intellectuals in the Weimar Republic*. Manchester: Manchester University Press, 1985.

Pinto, Louis. *Les Neveux de Zarathoustra: la réception de Nietzsche en France*. Paris: Editions du Seuil, 1995.

Pipes, Richard. *Russia Under the Bolshevik Regime, 1919–1924*. London: Harville, 1994.

———. *The Russian Revolution*. New York: Vintage Books, 1991.

Polizotti, Mark. *Revolution of the Mind: The Life of André Breton*. New York: Farrar, Straus and Giroux, 1995.

Pollard, Sidney. *Wealth and Poverty: An Economic History of the Twentieth Century*. New York: Oxford University Press, 1990.

Pound, Reginald. *The Lost Generation of 1914*. New York: Coward-McCann, 1965.

Prelinger, Elizabeth. *Käthe Kollwitz*. Washington, DC: National Gallery of Art, 1992.

Preston, Paul. *The Spanish Civil War: Reaction, Revolution and Revenge*. New York: W. W. Norton, 2007.

———. *The Spanish Holocaust: Inquisition and Extermination in Twentieth-Century Spain*. New York: W. W. Norton, 2012.

Prévost, Jean-Guy. *A Total Science: Statistics in Liberal and Fascist Italy*. Montreal: McGill-Queen's University Press, 2009.

Priestley, John Boynton. *English Journey: Being a Rambling but Truthful Account of What One Man Saw and Heard and Felt and Thought During a Journey Through England During the Autumn of the Year 1933*. New York: Harper & Brothers, 1934.

Pronger, Brian. *Body Fascism: Salvation in the Technology of Physical Fitness.* Toronto: University of Toronto Press, 2002.

Rampersad, Arnold. *The Life of Langston Hughes.* 2 volumes. New York: Oxford University Press, 1986–88.

Ratner-Rosenhagen, Jennifer. *American Nietzsche: A History of an Icon and His Ideas.* Chicago: University of Chicago Press, 2012.

Rawls, Walton H. *Wake Up, America! World War I and the American Poster.* New York: Abbeville Press, 1988.

Rayfield, Donald. *Stalin and His Hangmen: The Tyrant and Those Who Killed for Him.* New York: Random House, 2004.

Reeder, Roberta. *Anna Akhmatova: Poet and Prophet.* New York: St. Martin's Press, 1994.

Reich, Wilhelm. *Die Massenpsychologie des Faschismus.* Cologne: Kiepenheuer & Witsch, 1971.

Reid, Fiona. *Broken Men: Shell Shock, Treatment and Recovery in Britain, 1914–1930.* London: Continuum, 2010.

Reilly, Philip. *The Surgical Solution: A History of Involuntary Sterilization in the United States.* Baltimore: Johns Hopkins University Press, 1991.

Renneberg, Monika, and Mark Walker. *Science, Technology and National Socialism.* New York: Cambridge University Press, 1984.

Renouvin, Pierre. *War and Aftermath: 1914–1929.* New York: Harper & Row, 1968.

Rewald, Sabine. *Glitter and Doom: German Portraits from the 1920s.* New York: Metropolitan Museum of Art, 2006.

Rife, Patricia. *Lise Meitner and the Dawn of the Nuclear Age.* Boston: Birkhäuser, 1999.

Rigg, Bryan Mark. *Hitler's Jewish Soldiers: The Untold Story of Nazi Racial Laws and Men of Jewish Descent in the German Military.* Lawrence: University Press of Kansas, 2004.

Ringer, Fritz. *The Decline of the German Mandarins: The German Academic Community, 1890–1933.* Cambridge, MA: Harvard University Press, 1969.

Rodgers, Daniel T. *Atlantic Crossings: Social Politics in a Progressive Age.* Cambridge, MA: Belknap Press, 1998.

Rohkrämer, Thomas. *Eine andere Moderne? Zivilisationskritik, Natur und Technik in Deutschland, 1880–1933.* Paderborn: Schöningh, 1999.

Romein-Verschoor, Annie, and Jan Marius Romein. *De lage landen bij de zee: geïllustreerde geschiedenis van het nederlandse volk.* Zeist: W. de Haan, 1961.

Romsics, Gergely. *The Memory of the Habsburg Empire in German, Austrian and Hungarian Right-Wing Historiography and Political Thinking, 1918–1941.* Boulder, CO: Social Sciences Monographs, 2010.

Romsics, Gergely, Thomas J. DeKornfeld, Helen D. DeKornfeld, and Habsburg Történeti Intézet. *Myth and Remembrance: The Dissolution of the Habsburg Empire in the Memoir Literature of the Austro-Hungarian Political Elite.* Wayne, NJ: Center for Hungarian Studies and Publications, 2006.

Roper, Michael. *The Secret Battle: Emotional Survival in the Great War.* Manchester: Manchester University Press, 2008.

Rosenthal, Bernice Glatzer. *Nietzsche and Soviet Culture: Ally and Adversary.* Cambridge: Cambridge University Press, 1994.

Roth, Benjamin. *The Great Depression: A Diary*. New York: Public Affairs, 2009.

Saehrend, Christian. *Der Stellungskrieg der Denkmäler: Kriegsdenkmäler im Berlin der Zwischenkriegszeit (1919–1939)*. Bonn: Verl. Neue Ges., 2004.

Sanders, David. "Ernest Hemingway's Spanish Civil War Experience." *American Quarterly* 12, no. 2 (1960): 133. doi:10.2307/2710752.

Sauder, Gerhard. *Die Bücherverbrennung: zum 10. Mai 1933*. Munich: Hanser, 1983.

Schiffhauer, Nils. *Stichtag der Barbarei: Anmerkungen zur Bücherverbrennung 1933*. Hannover: Postskriptum, 1983.

Schivelbusch, Wolfgang. *The Culture of Defeat: On National Trauma, Mourning, and Recovery*. Translated by Jefferson Chase. New York: Metropolitan Books, 2003.

Schlesinger, Arthur Meier. *The Coming of the New Deal, 1933–1935*. Boston: Houghton Mifflin, 2003.

Schlögel, Karl. *Moscow, 1937*. Malden, MA: Polity, 2012.

———. *Russische Emigration in Deutschland 1918 bis 1941: Leben im europäischen Bürgerkrieg*. Berlin: Akademie Verlag, 1995.

Schnorbus, Philipp. *Die Emigration der Juden aus dem Deutschen Reich von 1933 bis 1941: Analyse der Faktoren für Nichtauswanderung*. Munich: GRIN Verlag, 2008.

Schnurbein, Stefanie V., and Justus H. Ulbricht. *Völkische Religion und Krisen der Moderne: Entwürfe "arteigener" Glaubenssysteme seit der Jahrhundertwende*. Würzburg: Königshausen & Neumann, 2001.

Schoenbaum, David. *Hitler's Social Revolution: Class and Status in Nazi Germany, 1933–1939*. Garden City, NY: Doubleday, 1966.

Schrader, Bärbel. *The "Golden" Twenties: Art and Literature in the Weimar Republic*. New Haven, CT: Yale University Press, 1988.

Schulze, Hagen. *Weimar: Deutschland 1917–1933*. Berlin: Siedler, 1994.

Schumacher, Julie A., ed. *The Harlem Renaissance*. Logan, IA: Perfection Learning, 2001.

Schwitters, Kurt. *Anna Blume und ich; die gesammelten "Anna Blume"—Texte*. Zürich: Im Verlag der Arche, 1965.

Scopes, John Thomas, and James Presley. *Center of the Storm: Memoirs of John T. Scopes*. New York: Holt, Rinehart and Winston, 1967.

Scott, John. *Behind the Urals: An American Worker in Russia's City of Steel*. Bloomington: Indiana University Press, 1989.

Sebag Montefiore, Simon. *Stalin: The Court of the Red Tsar*. New York: Knopf, 2004.

Sembach, Klaus-Jürgen. *Style 1930: Elegance and Sophistication in Architecture, Design, Fashion, Graphics, and Photography*. New York: Universe Books, 1971.

Severn, Bill. *The End of the Roaring Twenties: Prohibition and Repeal*. New York: J. Messner, 1969.

Shack, William A. *Harlem in Montmartre: A Paris Jazz Story Between the Great Wars*. Berkeley: University of California Press, 2001.

Shogun, Robert. *The Battle of Blair Mountain: The Story of America's Largest Labor Uprising*. Boulder, CO: Westview Press, 2004.

Shorten, Richard. *Modernism and Totalitarianism: Rethinking the Intellectual Sources of Nazism and Stalinism, 1945 to the Present*. Hampshire, UK: Palgrave Macmillan, 2012.

Sieg, Ulrich. *Geist und Gewalt: deutsche Philosophen zwischen Kaiserreich und Nationalsozialismus*. Munich: Hanser, 2013.

———. "Jüdische Intellektuelle im Ersten Weltkrieg: Kriegserfahrungen, weltanschauliche Debatten und kulturelle Neuentwürfe." Ph.D. dissertation, University of Marburg, 1999.

Siegel, Jerrold E. *Bohemian Paris: Culture, Politics, and the Boundaries of Bourgeois Life, 1830–1930*. New York: Viking, 1986.

Silver, Kenneth. *Chaos and Classicism: Art in France, Italy, and Germany, 1918–1936*. New York: Guggenheim Museum, 2010.

———. *Esprit de Corps: The Art of the Parisian Avant-Garde and the First World War, 1914–1925*. Princeton, NJ: Princeton University Press, 1989.

Sime, Ruth Lewin. *Lise Meitner: A Life in Physics*. Berkeley: University of California Press, 1996.

Sinclair, Andrew. *Prohibition, the Era of Excess*. Boston: Little, Brown, 1962.

Sivulka, Juliann. *Soap, Sex, and Cigarettes: A Cultural History of American Advertising*. Belmont, CA: Wadsworth Publishing Co., 1998.

Smith, Douglas. *Transvaluations: Nietzsche in France, 1872–1972*. New York: Oxford University Press, 1996.

Smith, Elton Edward. *The Angry Young Men of the Thirties*. Carbondale: Southern Illinois University Press, 1975.

Smith, Shawn Michelle. *Photography on the Color Line: W. E. B. Du Bois, Race, and Visual Culture*. Durham, NC: Duke University Press, 2004.

Smith, Willie. *Music on My Mind: The Memoirs of an American Pianist*. London: MacGibbon & Kee, 1964.

Snyder, Timothy. *Bloodlands: Europe Between Hitler and Stalin*. New York: Basic Books, 2010.

Solomon R. Guggenheim Museum and Museo Guggenheim Bilbao. *Chaos and Classicism: Art in France, Italy, and Germany, 1918–1936*. New York: Guggenheim Museum, 2010.

Sonn, Richard David. *Sex, Violence, and the Avant-Garde: Anarchism in Interwar France*. University Park: Pennsylvania State University Press, 2010.

Southard, Elmer Ernest. *Shell Shock and Other Neuropsychiatric Problems Presented in Five Hundred and Ninety Case Histories from the War Literature, 1914–1918*. New York: Arno, 1973.

Spengler, Oswald. *Jahre der entscheidung. Erster Teil: Deutschland und die weltgeschichtliche entwicklung*. Munich: Beck, 1933.

———. *Untergang des Abendlandes: Umrisse einer Morphologie des Weltgeschichte*. Munchen: C. H. Becksche Verlagsbuchhandlung, 1923.

Spies, Werner, ed. *Paris–Berlin, 1900–1933: Ubereinstimmungen und Gegensätze Frankreich, Deutschland: Kunst, Architektur, Graphik, Literatur, Industriedesign, Film, Theater, Musik*. Munich: Prestel, 1979.

Spinney, Robert G. *City of Big Shoulders: A History of Chicago*. DeKalb: Northern Illinois University Press, 2000.

Stackelberg, Roderick. *Hitler's Germany: Origins, Interpretations, Legacies*. London: Routledge, 1999.

Stanley, Adam. *Modernizing Tradition: Gender and Consumerism in Interwar France and Germany*. Baton Rouge: Louisiana State University Press, 2008.

Stanley, Jerry. *Children of the Dust Bowl: The True Story of the School at Weedpatch Camp*. New York: Crown, 1993.

Stark, Johannes. *Nationalsozialismus und Wissenschaft*. Munich: Zentralverlag der NSDAP, F. Eher Nachf., 1934.

Steegmuller, Francis. *Cocteau, a Biography*. Boston: Little, Brown, 1970.

Steele, Valerie. *Fashion and Eroticism: Ideals of Feminine Beauty from the Victorian Era to the Jazz Age*. New York: Oxford University Press, 1985.

Stehr, Nico. *Society and Knowledge*. New Brunswick, NJ: Transaction Publishers, 2005.

Steininger, Rolf, Günter Bischof, and Michael Gehler. *Austria in the Twentieth Century*. New Brunswick, NJ: Transaction Publishers, 2008.

Stern, Ludmilla. *Western Intellectuals and the Soviet Union: 1920–1940*. New York: Routledge, 2007.

Sternhell, Zeev. *Neither Right nor Left: Fascist Ideology in France*. Translated by David Maisel. Princeton, NJ: Princeton University Press, 1995.

Stevenson, David. *Cataclysm: The First World War as Political Tragedy*. New York: Basic Books, 2005.

Stieg, Gerald. *Frucht des Feuers: Canetti, Doderer, Kraus und der Justizpalastbrand*. Vienna: Edition Falter im ÖBV, 1990.

Stites, Richard. *Revolutionary Dreams: Utopian Vision and Experimental Life in the Russian Revolution*. New York: Oxford University Press, 1989.

Stone, Dan. *Breeding Superman: Nietzsche, Race and Eugenics in Edwardian and Interwar Britain*. Liverpool: Liverpool University Press, 2002.

Streissguth, Thomas. *The Roaring Twenties: An Eyewitness History*. New York: Facts on File, 2001.

Sudhalter, Richard M. *Stardust Melody: The Life and Music of Hoagy Carmichael*. New York: Oxford University Press, 2002.

Szalay, Michael. *New Deal Modernism: American Literature and the Invention of the Welfare State*. Durham, NC: Duke University Press, 2000.

Szöllösi-Janze, Margit. *Science in the Third Reich*. New York: Berg, 2001.

Szreter, Simon, and Kate Fisher. *Sex Before the Sexual Revolution: Intimate Life in England 1918–1963*. Cambridge: Cambridge University Press, 2010.

Taylor, D. J. *Bright Young People: The Lost Generation of London's Jazz Age*. New York: Farrar, Straus and Giroux, 2009.

Taylor, Paul. *Jews and the Olympic Games: The Clash Between Sport and Politics: With a Complete Review of Jewish Olympic Medallists*. Brighton: Sussex Academic Press, 2004.

Taylor, Richard, ed. *The Film Factory: Russian and Soviet Cinema in Documents*. Cambridge, MA: Harvard University Press, 1988.

Taylor, S. J. *Stalin's Apologist: Walter Duranty, the* New York Times*'s Man in Moscow*. New York: Oxford University Press, 1990.

Terkel, Studs. *Hard Times*. New York: New Press, 2012.

Theweleit, Klaus. *Männerphantasien*. Frankfurt am Main: Verlag Roter Stern, 1977–1978.

Tillery, Tyrone. *Claude McKay: A Black Poet's Struggle for Identity*. Amherst: University of Massachusetts Press, 1994.

Tillich, Paul. *The Courage to Be*. New Haven, CT: Yale University Press, 1952.

Timms, Edward. *Visions and Blueprints: Avant-Garde Culture and Radical Politics in Early Twentieth Century Europe*. Manchester: Manchester University Press, 1988.

Tismaneanu, Vladimir. *The Devil in History: Communism, Fascism, and Some Lessons of the Twentieth Century*. Berkeley: University of California Press, 2012.

Todman, Daniel. *The Great War: Myth and Memory*. London: Hambledon, 2005.

Toepfer, Karl Eric. *Empire of Ecstasy: Nudity and Movement in Germany Body Culture, 1910–1935*. Berkeley: University of California Press, 1997.

Travers, Martin. *Critics of Modernity: The Literature of the Conservative Revolution in Germany, 1890–1933*. New York: P. Lang, 2001.

Tress, Werner. *Wider den undeutschen Geist: Bücherverbrennung 1933*. Berlin: Parthas, 2003.

Tumblety, Joan. *Remaking the Male Body: Masculinity and the Uses of Physical Culture in Interwar and Vichy France*. Oxford: Oxford University Press, 2012.

Turda, Marius, and Paul Weindling. *"Blood and Homeland": Eugenics and Racial Nationalism in Central and Southeast Europe, 1900–1940*. Budapest: Central European University Press, 2007.

Vaihinger, Hans. *Die philosophie des als ob. System der theoretischen, praktischen und religiösen fiktionen der menschheit auf grund eines idealistischen positivismus*. Berlin: Verlag von Reuther & Reichard, 1911.

van Es, Joneike, and Jan E. Schierbeek. *Art et résistance: les peintres allemands de l'entre-deux-guerres*. La Haye: Museum Paleis Lange Voorhout, 1995.

Vermilye, Jerry. *The Films of the Thirties*. Secaucus, NJ: Citadel Press, 1982.

Verrips, Jojada. *En boven de polder de hemel: een antropologische studie van een Nederlands dorp 1850–1971*. Groningen: Wolters-Noordhoff, 1978.

Von Ankum, Katarina, ed. *Women in the Metropolis: Gender and Modernity in Weimar Culture*. Berkeley: University of California Press, 1997.

Vondung, Klaus, ed. *The Apocalypse in Germany*. Translated by Stephen D. Ricks. Columbia: University of Missouri Press, 2000.

Wakounig, Marija, Wolfgang Mueller, and Michael Portmann. *Nation, Nationalitäten und Nationalismus im östlichen Europa: Festschrift für Arnold Suppan zum 65. Geburtstag*. Vienna: LIT Verlag, 2010.

Walker, Ian. *City Gorged with Dreams: Surrealism and Documentary Photography in Interwar Paris*. Manchester: Manchester University Press, 2002.

Walker, Mark, ed. *Nazi Science: Myth, Truth, and the German Atomic Bomb*. New York: Plenum Press, 1995.

———. *Science and Ideology: A Comparative History*. New York: Routledge, 2003.

Wallace, Max. *The American Axis: Henry Ford, Charles Lindbergh, and the Rise of the Third Reich*. New York: St. Martin's Press, 2004.

Watkins, Raymond J. "The Modern Savage: Figures of the Fascist 'Primitive' in Interwar Europe." Ph.D. dissertation, University of Iowa, 2006.

Watkins, T. H. *The Hungry Years: A Narrative History of the Great Depression in America*. New York: Henry Holt, 2000.

Weber, Eugen Joseph. *Action Française: Royalism and Reaction in Twentieth Century France*. Stanford, CA: Stanford University Press, 1962.

———. *The Hollow Years: France in the 1930s*. London: Sinclair-Stevenson, 1995.

Weber, Stefan. *Ein kommunistischer Putsch? Märzaktion 1921 in Mitteldeutschland*. Berlin: Karl-Dietz-Verlag, 1991.

Wedemeyer-Kolwe, Bernd. *"Der neue Mensch": Körperkultur im Kaiserreich und in der Weimarer Republik*. Würzburg: Königshausen & Neumann, 2004.

Weingart, Peter, Jürgen Kroll, and Kurt Bayertz. *Rasse, Blut und Gene: Geschichte der Eugenik und Rassenhygiene in Deutschland*. Frankfurt am Main: Suhrkamp-Taschenbuch Verlag, 1992.

Weinzierl, Erika. *Der Februar 1934 und die Folgen für Österreich*. Vienna: Picus Verlag, 1995.

Weitz, Eric D. *Weimar Germany: Promise and Tragedy*. Princeton, NJ: Princeton University Press, 2009.

Wende, Peter, ed. *Politische Reden*. Frankfurt am Main: Deutscher Klassiker Verlag, 1990–1999.

Whalen, Robert Weldon. *Bitter Wounds: German Victims of the Great War, 1914–1939*. Ithaca, NY: Cornell University Press, 1984.

Whitney, Susan B. *Mobilizing Youth: Communists and Catholics in Interwar France*. Durham, NC: Duke University Press, 2009.

Widdig, Bernd. *Culture and Inflation in Weimar Germany*. Berkeley: University of California Press, 2001.

Wildmann, Daniel. *Begehrte Körper: Konstruktion und Inszenierung des "arischen Männerkörpers" im "Dritten Reich."* Würzburg: Königshausen & Neumann, 1998.

Wilk, Christopher, ed. *Modernism: Designing a New World, 1914–1939*. London: Victoria & Albert Publications, 2006.

Wilson, Edmund. *The Thirties: From Notebooks and Diaries of the Period*. New York: Farrar, Straus and Giroux, 1980.

———. *The Twenties: From Notebooks and Diaries of the Period*. New York: Farrar, Straus and Giroux, 1975.

Wingler, Hans Maria. *Das Bauhaus, 1919–1933: Weimar, Dessau, Berlin*. Cologne: M. DuMont Schauberg, 1962.

Winkler, Heinrich August. *Weimar 1918–1933: Die Geschichte der ersten deutschen Demokratie*. Munich: Beck, 1993.

Winter, Jay. *The Experience of World War I*. Oxford: Oxford University Press, 1989.

———. *Remembering War: The Great War Between Memory and History in the Twentieth Century*. New Haven, CT: Yale University Press, 2006.

———. *Sites of Memory, Sites of Mourning: The Great War in European Cultural History*. Cambridge: Cambridge University Press, 1995.

Winter, Jay, and Antoine Prost, eds. *The Great War in History Debates and Controversies, 1914 to the Present*. Cambridge: Cambridge University Press, 2005.

Winter, Jay, and Blaine Gagget. *1914–18: The Great War and the Shaping of the 20th Century*. London: BBC Books, 1996.

Winter, Jay, and Jean-Louis Robert, eds. *Capital Cities at War: Paris, London, Berlin, 1914–1919*. Cambridge: Cambridge University Press, 1997.

Wiskemann, Elizabeth. *Europe of the Dictators, 1919–1945*. New York: Harper and Row, 1966.

Wohl, Robert. *The Generation of 1914*. Cambridge, MA: Harvard University Press, 1979.

Wolin, Richard. *The Seduction of Unreason: The Intellectual Romance with Fascism, from Nietzsche to Postmodernism*. Princeton, NJ: Princeton University Press, 2004.

Woods, Roger. *The Conservative Revolution in the Weimar Republic*. Houndmills, Basingstoke: Macmillan, 1996.

Woolf, Virginia. *The Diary of Virginia Woolf*, volume 5, *1936–1941*. New York: Harcourt Brace Jovanovich, 1985.

Worster, Donald. *Dust Bowl: The Southern Plains in the 1930s*. Oxford University Press, 2004.

Zanden, Jan Luiten van. *Een klein land in de 20e eeuw: Economische geschiedenis van Nederland 1914–1995*. Utrecht: Het Spectrum, 1997.

Zeitz, Joshua. *Flapper: A Madcap Story of Sex, Style, Celebrity and the Women Who Made America Modern*. New York: Crown, 2006.

Zeldin, Theordore. *A History of French Passions 1848–1945*. Oxford: Clarendon Press, 1993.

Zhadova, Larisa. *Malevich: Suprematism and Revolution in Russian Art 1910–1930*. New York: Thames and Hudson, 1982.

Notes

Introduction: 1,567 Days

1. Perry Bradford, *Born with the Blues: The True Story of the Pioneering Blues Singers and Musicians in the Early Days of Jazz* (New York: Oak Publications, 1965), 114. Bradford's claim to have participated in the recording was disputed by Willie "the Lion" Smith, who later also claimed to have been the session pianist.
2. Hugo Ball, "Kandinsky: Vortrag gehalten in der Galerie Dada (Zürich, 7. April 1917)," in *Der Künstler und die Zeitkrankheit: Ausgewählte Schriften,* ed. Hans Burkhard Schlichting (Frankfurt am Main: Suhrkamp, 1984), 41.
3. Ibid.
4. Ernst Jünger, *Feuer und Blut* (Magdeburg: Stahlhelm-Verlag, 1925), 466.
5. John Dewey, *The Public and Its Problems* (New York: Henry Holt, 1927), 8.

1918: Shell Shock

1. *Times* (London), April 24, 1915.
2. Some six hundred French and eighteen German soldiers were also executed for "desertion." In 2006, with the admission that it was not possible to establish which of the "deserters" had been suffering from shell shock, all British and Commonwealth soldiers executed during the First World War were posthumously pardoned.
3. Paul Nash, quoted in Robert Wohl, *The Generation of 1914* (Cambridge, MA: Harvard University Press, 1979), 97.
4. *Labour Leader,* May 6, 1915.
5. Wilfred Owen, letter to his mother, January 16, 1917, in *Letters,* 427–428, quoted in Daniel Hipp, *The Poetry of Shell Shock: Wartime Trauma and Healing in Wilfred Owen, Ivor Gurney, and Siegfried Sassoon* (Jefferson, NC: McFarland, 2005), 47.
6. Siegfried Sassoon, quoted in Max Egremont, *Siegfried Sassoon: A Life* (London, Macmillan, 2005), 144.
7. Reginald Pound, *The Lost Generation of 1914,* quoted in Wohl, *Generation of 1914,* 122.
8. Vera Brittain, *Testament of Youth* (London: Gollancz, 1933), 475.
9. Rosa Mayreder, *Zur Kritik der Weiblichkeit* (Jena: E. Diederichs, 1905), 118.

10. The British Dominion of Newfoundland did not formally become part of Canada until 1949.

11. John Milne, *Footprints of the 1/4 Leicestershire Regiment* (London: Naval and Military Press, 2009), 58.

12. Fernand Léger, *Fernand Léger: une correspondance de guerre à Louis Poughon* (Paris: Bibliothèque publique d'information du Centre Pompidou, 1997), 72; translation by author, with special thanks to Gordon Hughes.

13. Elmer Ernest Southard, *Shell-Shock and Other Neuropsychiatric Problems, Presented in Five Hundred and Eighty-Nine Case Histories* (Boston: Leonard, 1919).

14. F. W. Mott, "Lettsomian Lecture on the Effects of High Explosives upon the Central Nervous System" (part 3), *Lancet,* March 11, 1916, 553.

15. Marcel Arland, 1926, quoted in Wohl, *Generation of 1914,* 26.

16. Jean Prévost, "Dix-huitième année," quoted and trans. in Wohl, *Generation of 1914,* 32.

17. Wohl, *Generation of 1914,* 31.

1919: A Poet's Coup

1. Gabriele d'Annunzio, quoted in Philippe Jullian, *D'Annunzio* (London: Pall Mall Press, 1972), 285.

2. D'Annunzio, quoted in Jullian, *D'Annunzio,* 257.

3. Osbert Sitwell, *Noble Essences,* quoted in Jullian, *D'Annunzio,* 287.

4. Lucy Hughes-Hallett, *The Pike: Gabriele d'Annunzio, Poet, Seducer and Preacher of War* (London: Fourth Estate, 2013), Kindle locations 7203–7205.

5. Oswald Spengler, *The Decline of the West: Form and Actuality,* trans. Charles Francis (New York: Atkinson, 1926), 105.

6. Ibid., 377.

7. Ibid., 137.

8 Ibid., 460.

9. Ibid., 464, 463.

10. Ibid., 464.

11. Cameron McWhirter, *Red Summer: The Summer of 1919 and the Awakening of Black America* (New York: Macmillan, 2011), 56.

12. Ibid.

13. From *Negroes in America,* quoted in Wayne F. Cooper, *Claude McKay: Rebel Sojourner in the Harlem Renaissance, a Biography* (Baton Rouge: Louisiana State University Press, 1987), 187. McKay made this point forcefully in an address to the Fourth Congress of the Third International in Moscow in 1922.

14. Claude McKay, "If We Must Die," 1919, in *Harlem Shadows: The Poems of Claude McKay* (New York: Harcourt Brace, 1922), 22.

15. Lothrop Stoddard, *The Rising Tide of Color Against White World Supremacy* (New York: Charles Scribner's Sons, 1921), 5.

16. Ibid., 179.

17. Ibid., 90.

18. Ibid., 23.

19. Ibid., 123.

20. Ibid., 253.

21. Francis Ludwig Carsten, *The Rise of Fascism* (Berkeley: University of California Press, 1982), 62.

1920: Moonshine Nation

1. Quoted in William Vance Trollinger, *God's Empire: William Bell Riley and Midwestern Fundamentalism* (Madison: University of Wisconsin Press, 1990), 179.
2. Quoted in Daniel Okrent, *Last Call: The Rise and Fall of Prohibition* (New York: Scribner, 2010), 44.
3. R. Hutton, *Anti Saloon League Yearbook,* 1918.
4. Quoted in Okrent, *Last Call,* 208
5. Andrew Sinclair, *Prohibition, the Era of Excess* (Boston: Little, Brown, 1963), 220.
6. Ibid., 226.
7. Ibid.
8. Roy F. Allen, *Literary Life in German Expressionism and the Berlin Circles* (Ann Arbor, MI: UMI Research Press, 1983), 216–217.
9. John F. Carter, *Atlantic Monthly,* September 1920.
10. Sinclair, *Prohibition,* 181.
11. Denis Brogan, *American Themes* (London: Hamish Hamilton, 1948), 192.
12. F. Scott Fitzgerald, *This Side of Paradise* (New York: Charles Scribner's Sons, 1920), 282.
13. Quoted in John P. O'Neill and Sabine Rewald, *Twentieth Century Modern Masters: The Jacques and Natasha Gelman Collection* (New York: Metropolitan Museum of Art, 1990), 4.
14. Ernest Hemingway, *A Moveable Feast* (New York: Scribner Classics, 1996), 29
15. Quoted in William A. Shack, *Harlem in Montmartre* (Berkeley: University of California Press, 2001), 33.
16. Liverpool Watch Committee Minute Book, June 17, 1919, No. 56, 251–262, 352 1/56, Liverpool Record Office, Central Library.
17. George Grosz, *George Grosz, an Autobiography,* trans. Nora Hodges (New York: Macmillan, 1983), 149.
18. Ibid., 119.
19. Ibid., 113.
20. Ibid.
21. Ibid., 119.
22. Ibid., 149–150.

1921: The End of Hope

1. Quoted in Paul Avrich, *Kronstadt 1921* (Princeton, NJ: Princeton University Press, 1970), 156.
2. *New York Times,* March 31, 1921.
3. Quoted in Avrich, *Kronstadt 1921,* 77–78.

1922: Renaissance in Harlem

1. Langston Hughes, "The Negro Speaks of Rivers," in *Collected Poems of Langston Hughes.*

2. Carl Van Vechten, *Nigger Heaven* (New York: Knopf, 1926), 77.

3. Manning Marable, *W. E. B. Du Bois, Black Radical Democrat* (Boston: Twayne, 1986), 121.

4. Du Bois was to remain editor of *The Crisis* until his resignation in 1934.

5. Quoted in Marable, *W. E. B. Du Bois,* 122.

6. Charles S. Johnson, quoted in Kevin Hillstrom, *Defining Moments: The Harlem Renaissance* (n.p.: KWS, 2011), 38.

7. David Levering Lewis, quoted in Hillstrom, *Defining Moments,* 51.

8. Zora Neale Hurston, "How It Feels to Be Colored Me," in Joyce Carol Oates and Robert Atwan, eds., *The Best American Essays of the Twentieth Century* (New York: Houghton Mifflin, 2000), 405.

9. Ibid.

10. Langston Hughes, quoted in Hillstrom, *Defining Moments,* 182.

11. Aaron Douglas, quoted in Hillstrom, *Defining Moments,* 99. Jamaican-born Marcus Garvey settled in Harlem in 1917, embracing the idea of racial separatism and developing his Universal Negro Improvement Association into a "Back to Africa" movement. In 1923 he was convicted of mail fraud and imprisoned. Though he retained a large popular following, he played little open part in the Harlem Renaissance itself.

12. Van Vechten, *Nigger Heaven,* 15.

13. Ibid., 119.

14. Ibid., 148.

15. Quoted in Hillstrom, *Defining Moments,* 46.

16. Alain Locke, "Enter the New Negro," *Survey Graphic,* March 1925.

17. Hugh Wiley Hitchcock, *Music in the United States: A Historical Introduction* (Englewood Cliffs, NJ: Prentice-Hall, 1974), 207.

18. Van Vechten, *Nigger Heaven,* 212.

19. Ibid, 281.

20. Langston Hughes, *The Big Sea* (London: Macmillan, 1922), 221.

21. Quoted in Wayne F. Cooper, *Claude McKay: Rebel Sojourner in the Harlem Renaissance, a Biography* (Baton Rouge: Louisiana State University Press, 1987), 109.

22. Ibid., 110.

23. Claude McKay, *A Long Way from Home* (New York: Lee Furman, 1937), 55.

24. Hitchcock, *Music in the United States,* 202.

25. Langston Hughes, quoted in Hillstrom, *Defining Moments,* 196.

26. Harry Kessler, *The Diaries of a Cosmopolitan: Count Harry Kessler, 1918–1937,* trans. Charles Kessler (London: Weidenfeld and Nicolson, 1971), entry for February 13, 1926.

27. Willa Cather, *Not Under Forty* (New York: Knopf, 1936), prefatory note.

28. F. Scott Fitzgerald, quoted in Noel Riley Fitch, *Sylvia Beach and the Lost Generation: A History of Literary Paris in the Twenties and Thirties* (New York: Norton, 1983), 183.

1923: Beyond the Milky Way

1. Shapley to Hale, quoted in Marcia Bartusiak, *The Day We Found the Universe* (New York: Pantheon, 2009), 129.

2. Hubble to Shapley, in Bartusiak, *The Day We Found the Universe,* 202.

3. Quoted in Gary Haitel, *The Origins of the Grand Finale* (Bloomington: Indiana University Press, 2014), 11.

4. Werner Heisenberg, "Kausalgesetz und Quantenmechanik" (1931), 182, quoted in Cathryn Carson, *Heisenberg in the Atomic Age* (Cambridge: Cambridge University Press, 2011), 45.

5. Quoted in Jeremy Bernstein, *Secrets of the Old One: Einstein, 1905* (New York: Copernicus, 2006), 171.

6. Philipp Lenard, *Deutsche Physik, 1. Teil* (Berlin: Vorwort, 1938), 38.

7. Oswald Spengler, *Decline of the West,* trans. Charles Francis Atkinson (London: Allen & Unwin, 1926), 92. Translation modified by author.

8. Ibid., 15.

9. Ibid., 103

10. A. Vierkandt, *Die sozialpaedagogische Forderung der Gegenwart* (Berlin, 1920), 20.

11. Werner Heisenberg, "Die Beziehungen zwischen Physik und Chemie" (1953), in Carson, *Heisenberg in the Atomic Age,* 3.

12. G. Doetsch, "Der Sinn der angewandten Mathematik," *Jahresbericht der Deutschen Mathematiker-Vereinigung* 31 (1922): 231–232, quoted in Paul Forman, "Weimar Culture, Causality, and Quantum Theory: Adaptation by German Physicists and Mathematicians to a Hostile Environment," *Historical Studies in the Physical Sciences* 3 (1971): 1–115.

13. Erwin Schrödinger, "Ist die Naturwissenschaft milieubedingt?" (1932), 27–28, quoted in Forman, "Weimar Culture, Causality, and Quantum Theory."

14. R. J. Overy, *The Morbid Age: Britain Between the Wars* (London: Allen Lane, 2009), 47.

15. R. B. Haldane, *The Reign of Relativity* (London: J. Murray, 1921), 5.

16. Ibid., 129.

17. J. B. S. Haldane, *Daedalus or Science and the Future* (London: Dutton, 1925), 3.

18. Ibid.

19. Ibid.

1924: Men Behaving Badly

1. Hugo Ball, "Dada Manifesto," read at the first public Dada soiree, Zürich, July 14, 1916, in Hugo Ball, ed., *Flight out of Time* (Berkeley: University of California Press, 1996), 219.

2. Hans Arp, *On my Way: Poetry and Essays, 1912–1947* (Wittenborn Schulz: New York, 1948), p. 48.

3. Tristan Tzara, "Dada Manifesto 1918," quoted in Mark Polizzotti, *Revolution of the Mind: The Life of André Breton* (New York: Farrar, Straus, and Giroux, 1995), 90.

4. Vaché, quoted in Polizzotti, *Revolution of the Mind,* 42.

5. André Breton, *Entretiens* (Paris: Gallimard, 1952), 56.

6. Breton, quoted in Polizzotti, *Revolution of the Mind,* 105

7. André Breton and Philippe Soupault, "Les Champs Magnétiques Partie III Eclipses," *Littérature* 10 (December 1919): 16. Translation by author.

8. Everling, quoted in Polizzotti, *Revolution of the Mind,* 122.

9. Polizzotti, *Revolution of the Mind*, 123.

10. Ibid., 124.

11. Ibid., 171.

12. Ibid., 175.

13. Ibid., 179.

14. Quoted in Patrick Waldberg, *Surrealism* (New York: McGraw-Hill, 1971), 66–75.

15. Polizzotti, *Revolution of the Mind*, 247.

16. Ibid., 253.

17. Otto Dix, "War Diary" (unpublished), Städtische Kunstsammlungen Galerie Albstadt, Germany.

18. Teresa A. Carbone, *Youth and Beauty: Art of the American Twenties* (New York: Skira Rizzoli, 2011), 96.

19. Ibid., 122.

20. Ibid., 113.

21. Ibid., 114.

22. Ibid., 182.

1925: Monkey Business

1. Quoted in L. Sprague De Camp, *The Great Monkey Trial* (Garden City, NY: Doubleday, 1968), 91.

2. Quoted in Edward Larson, *Summer of the Gods: The Scopes Trial and America's Continuing Debate over Science and Religion* (New York: Basic Books, 1997), 35. The account of the trial I provide here follows Larson's excellent book.

3. Ibid., 45.

4. Ibid., 32.

5. Ibid.

6. Ibid., 72.

7. Ibid., 93.

8. Ibid., 162.

9. H. L. Mencken, *Heathen Days, 1890–1936*(New York: Knopf, 1943), 224–225.

10. Ibid., 177.

11. Ibid., 222.

12. Ibid., 182.

13. *Scopes v. State,* 154 Tenn. 105, 1927.

14. Just Sicard de Pauzole, "L'Avenir et la Préservation de la Race: Eugeénique," in *Prophylaxie antivénerienne* (1932), 201–203, quoted in William Schneider, "Toward the Improvement of the Human Race: The History of Eugenics in France," *Journal of Modern History* 54, no. 2 (June 1982): 268–291.

15. Quoted in Susan Currell and Christina Codgell, eds., *Popular Eugenics: National Efficiency and American Mass Culture in the 1930s* (Athens: Ohio University Press, 2006), 196–197.

16. "Closing Argument, the State of Illinois v. Nathan Leopold & Richard Loeb, Delivered by Clarence Darrow, Chicago, Illinois, August 22, 1924," University of Missouri–Kansas City School of Law, "Famous American Trials: Illinois v. Nathan Leopold and Richard Loeb," http://law2.umkc.edu/faculty/projects/ftrials /leoploeb/darrowclosing.html.

17. Oscar Levy, quoted in Dan Stone, *Breeding Superman: Nietzsche, Race and Eugenics in Edwardian and Interwar Britain* (Liverpool: Liverpool University Press, 2002), 13.
18. Ibid., 20.
19. Ibid., 22.
20. Ibid., 25.
21. Ibid., 27.

1926: Metropolis

1. H. G. Wells, "Mr. Wells Reviews a Current Film: He Takes Issue with This German Conception of What the City of One Hundred Years Hence Will Be Like," *New York Times,* April 17, 1927. Reprinted as "The Silliest Film: Will Machinery Make Robots of Men?" in *Authors on Film,* ed. Harry Geduld (Bloomington: Indiana University Press, 1972), 59–67.
2. *San Antonio Light,* July 1, 1928.
3. Blaise Cendrars, "I've Killed," trans. Bertrand Mathieu, *Chicago Review* 25, no. 3 (1973): 32–36.
4. Lenin, quoted in Richard Stites, *Revolutionary Dreams: Utopian Vision and Experimental Life in the Russian Revolution* (New York: Oxford University Press, 1989), 147.
5. Henry Ford, "The Meaning of Time," quoted in Stites, *Revolutionary Dreams,* 148.
6. Alexei Gastev, quoted in Stites, *Revolutionary Dreams.*
7. Stites, *Revolutionary Dreams,* 202.

1927: A Palace in Flames

1. Anton Kuh, "Wien am Gebirge," in *Die Stunde* 1, 101 (July 4, 1923): 3. Translation by author.
2. Charles Maurras, quoted in Louis Bodin and Jean Touchard, *Front populaire 1936* (Paris: Armand Colin, 1961), 33–34.
3. Charles Maurras, *L'Action Française,* May 15, 1936.
4. Quoted in Wolfgang Huber, "Die Gegenreformation 1933/34," *Neuhäuser,* 2004, 47.

1928: Boop-Boop-a-Doop!

1. Zelda Fitzgerald, "Eulogy on the Flapper," *Metropolitan Magazine,* June 1922, 78.
2. J. B. Watson, *Behaviorism,* rev. ed. (Chicago: University of Chicago Press, 1930), 82.
3. Quoted in Clive Bloom, *Bestsellers: Popular Fiction Since 1900* (Houndmills, Basingstoke: Palgrave Macmillan, 2002), 175–176.
4. Quoted in Joshua Zeitz, *Flapper: A Madcap Story of Sex, Style and Celebrity and the Women who Made America Modern* (New York: Random House, 2007), 211.
5. Harry Kessler, *Diaries of a Cosmopolitan* (London, Weidenfeld & Nicolson, 2012), 284–285.
6. Virginia Woolf, *Collected Essays* (London: Hogarth Press, 1966), 1:320.

7. Quoted in Alison Maloney, *Bright Young Things: Real Lives in the Roaring Twenties* (London: Virgin, 2012), 16.
8. "Neger," *Neues Wiener Tagblatt,* January 9, 1927.
9. Harry Graf Kessler, *Tagebücher 1918–1937* (Frankfurt am Main: Insel Verlag, 1961), entry for February 26, 1926, 482. Quoted in translation in Peter Jelavich, *Berlin Cabaret* (Cambridge, MA: Harvard University Press, 1993), 171.

1929: The Magnetic City

1. Quoted in Stephen Kotkin, *Magnetic Mountain: Stalinism as a Civilization* (Berkeley: University of California Press, 1997), 29.
2. Ibid.
3. Robert Shackleton, *The Book of Chicago* (Philadelphia: Penn Publishing, 1920), 183.
4. Paul O'Hara, *Gary: The Most American of All American Cities* (Bloomington: Indiana University Press, 2011), 6.
5. Quoted in Kotkin, *Magnetic Mountain,* 37.
6. Ibid., 46.
7. Ibid., 81.
8. Ibid., 49.
9. Ibid., 46.
10. John Scott, *Behind the Urals: An American Worker in Russia's City of Steel* (Boston: Houghton Mifflin), 4–5.
11. Ibid., 16.
12. Arthur Koestler, *Arrow in the Blue: An Autobiography* (New York: Macmillan, 1952), 277–278.
13. Stephen Spender, *World Within World: The Autobiography of Stephen Spender* (London: Hamish Hamilton, 1951), 132.
14. Quoted in Ludmila Stern, *Western Intellectuals and the Soviet Union, 1920–40: From Red Square to the Left Bank* (New York: Routledge, 2007), 11.
15. Theodore Dreiser, *Dreiser's Russian Diary,* ed. Thomas P. Riggio and James L. W. West III (Philadelphia: University of Pennsylvania Press, 1996), 67.
16. Ibid., 140.
17. Quoted in Stern, *Western Intellectuals and the Soviet Union,* 105.
18. Ibid.
19. Henri Barbusse, "Le Devoir Socialiste," *L'Humanité,* October 24, 1920.
20. Winston Churchill, *Great Contemporaries* (Chicago: University of Chicago Press, 1973), 55.
21. Ibid.
22. Scott, *Behind the Urals,* 5–6.
23. Kotkin, *Magnetic Mountain,* 182.
24. Ibid., 121.

1930: Lili and the Blue Angel

1. Klaus Mann in *Die Bühne,* 1930.
2. W. H. Auden, quoted in David Clay Large, *Berlin* (New York: Basic Books, 2000), 227.

3. John Lehmann, quoted in Large, *Berlin,* 227.

4. Auden, quoted in Large, *Berlin,* 228.

5. Christopher Isherwood, *Christopher and His Kind,* quoted in Large, *Berlin,* 229.

6. Ibid., 230.

7. Carl von Ossietzky, *Weltbühne,* January 26, 1930.

8. Large, *Berlin,* 237.

9. Stephen Spender, *World Within World,* quoted in Large, *Berlin,* 252.

1931: The Anatomy of Love in Italy

1. "Testament of Michael Schirru," in *"Man!" An Anthology of Anarchist Ideas, Essays, Poetry and Commentaries,* ed. Marcus Graham (London: Cienfuegos Press, 1974), 515.

2. Ibid.

3. Quoted in Piers Brendon, *The Dark Valley: A Panorama of the 1930s* (New York: Knopf, 2000), 72.

4. Booker T. Washington, *The Man Farthest Down: A Record of Observation and Study in Europe* (New York: Doubleday, 1912), 212.

5. Ibid.

6. Speech by Ellison DuRant Smith, April 9, 1924, *Congressional Record,* 68th Congress, 1st Session (Washington, DC: Government Printing Office, 1924), 65:5961–5962.

7. Claretta Petacci, *Mussolini Segreto. Diari 1932–1938 a cura di Mauro Suttora* (Rome: Rizzoli, 2009), 236.

8. Quotations from Christopher Duggan, *Fascist Voices: An Intimate History of Mussolini's Italy* (London: Bodley Head, 2012), 225–244.

9. P. Willson, *Peasant Women and Politics in Fascist Italy: The "Massaie Rurali"* (London: Routledge, 2002), 155–156.

10. Arnaldo Mussolini, quoted in Duggan, *Fascist Voices,* 107.

11. Quoted in Duggan, *Fascist Voices,* 120.

12. Maria Teresa Rosetti, quoted in Duggan, *Fascist Voices,* 205.

13. Edward R. Tannenbaum, *Fascism in Italy: Society and Culture, 1922–1945* (London: Allen Lane, 1973), 264.

1932: Holodomor

1. Miron Dolot, *Execution by Hunger: The Hidden Holocaust* (New York: W. W. Norton, 1985), 1. Dolot is the pen name of Simon Starov, who lived through the forced collectivization and the subsequent famine and later became a language teacher in California. It is impossible to verify the details of his autobiographical and avowedly subjective memoir, but there is no reason to doubt his account, which is generally regarded as reliable, and it certainly describes events and circumstances supported by other historical evidence.

2. Ibid., 2.

3. Ibid.

4. Ibid., 32.

5. Ibid., 56.

6. Ibid., 68.

7. Ibid., 92.
8. Ibid., 137–138.
9. Ibid., 138.
10. Ibid., 140.
11. Ibid., 150.
12. Ibid., 182.
13. Ibid.
14. Arthur Koestler, quoted in Richard Crossman, ed., *The God That Failed* (London: Hamish Hamilton, 1950), 52.
15. Nicolas Werth, Karel Bartošek, Jean-Louis Panné, Jean-Louis Margolin, Andrzej Paczkowski, and Stéphane Courtois, *The Black Book of Communism: Crimes, Terror, Repression* (Cambridge, MA: Harvard University Press, 1999), 159–160.
16. Walter Duranty in the *New York Times,* March 31, 1933.
17. Robert Conquest, *The Harvest of Sorrow: Soviet Collectivization and the Terror-Famine* (Oxford: Oxford University Press, 1986), 306.
18. Archives of the FSB (Federal Security Service), Moscow, 2/11/971/145–147.
19. A. Graziosi, "Lettres de Kharkiv: La famine en Ukraine et dans le Caucase du nord à travers les rapports des diplomates italiens, 1932–1934," *Cahiers du Monde Russe et Soviétique* 30 (1989): 5–106.
20. Dolot, *Execution by Hunger,* 229.

1933: Pogrom of the Intellect

1. Erich Kästner, *Bei Durchsicht meiner Bücher* (Stuttgart: Rowolt, 1946), preface.
2. Hans Karl Leistritz, Erstes Rundschreiben, April 8, 1933, Akte der Deutsche Studentenschaft, Bundesarchiv Berlin.
3. Ibid.
4. Quoted in Helmuth Heyer, "10. Mai 1933 'Ehrentag der freien deutschen Literatur'—zur Bücher-Verbrennung in Bonn," in *Bonner Geschichtsblätter,* 51–52, 2001–2002, 285–328.
5. Quoted in J. S. Medawar and David Pyke, *Hitler's Gift: The True Story of the Scientists Expelled by the Nazi Regime* (New York: Arcade, 2001), 26.
6. Quoted in Marion Sonnenfeld, *The World of Yesterday's Humanist Today: Proceedings of the Stefan Zweig Symposium* (Albany: State University of New York Press, 1983), 221; translation by author.
7. Martin Heidegger, "Die Selbstbehauptung der deutschen Universität, Rede vom 27. Mai 1933," quoted in Victor Farías, *Heidegger und der Nationalsozialismus* (Frankfurt am Main: S. Fischer, 1989), 155ff.
8. Martin Heidegger, "Die Universität im Neuen Reich, Vorlesung vom 30. Juni 1933," quoted in Farías, *Heidegger und der Nationalsozialismus,* 200ff.
9. Benedetto Croce, *Il Giornale d'Italia,* July 9, 1924; translation by author.
10. *Il Mondo,* March 1, 1925.
11. Quoted in John Gordon Garrard and Carol Garrard, *Inside the Soviet Writers' Union* (London: I. B. Tauris, 1990), 1.
12. Ossip Mandelstam, "The Stalin Epigram"; translation by author.
13. Olga Ivinskaya, *A Captive of Time: My Years with Pasternak* (Garden City, NY: Doubleday, 1978), 61–63.

14. Klaus Mann, "Notizen in Moskau," in *Die Sammlung* 2, 2 (1934–1935): 72–83; translation by author.
15. Willi Bredel, "Rede auf dem Moskauer Allunionskongres," *Neue Deutsche Blätter* 12 (1934): 724.

1934: Thank You, Jeeves

1. John Boynton Priestley, *English Journey: Being a Rambling but Truthful Account of What One Man Saw and Heard and Felt and Thought During a Journey Through England During the Autumn of the Year 1933* (London: Harper & Brothers, 1934), 20.
2. Ibid., 28.
3. Ibid., 67.
4. Ibid., 103.
5. Ibid., 197.
6. Ibid., 218.
7. Ibid., 224–229.
8. Ibid., 242.
9. Ibid., 259.
10. Ibid., 272.
11. Max Cohen, *I Was One of the Unemployed* (London: Gollancz, 1945), 11–12.
12. Quoted in Juliet Gardiner, *The Thirties* (New York: HarperPress, 2010), 168.
13. Quoted in Piers Brendon, *Dark Valley: A Panorama of the 1930s* (New York: Knopf, 2000), 169.
14. Cited in the *Times,* May 23, 2006, Law Supplement, 7.
15. John Strachey, *The Coming Struggle for Power* (London: Gollancz, 1932), 245.
16. Martin Stannard, *Evelyn Waugh* (London: Dent, 1986), 1:348.
17. Beatrice Webb, *The Diary of Beatrice Webb,* ed. Norman and Jeanne MacKenzie (Cambridge, MA: Belknap Press, 2009), 232.
18. P. G. Wodehouse, *Thank You, Jeeves* (London: H. Jenkins, 1934), 62.
19. Priestley, *English Journey,* 323.

1935: Route 66

1. Margaret Bourke-White, quoted in Donald Worster, *Dust Bowl: The Southern Plains in the 1930s* (New York: Oxford University Press, 2004), 23.
2. *Kansas City Star,* June 7, 1936.
3. Quoted in Worster, *Dust Bowl,* 23.
4. Ibid., 31.
5. Archibald MacLeish, *Land of the Free* (New York: Harcourt, Brace, 1938), 49.
6. Herbert Hoover, *The Memoirs of Herbert Hoover: The Great Depression, 1929–1941* (New York: Macmillan, 1952), 30.
7. Quoted in James N. Gregory, *American Exodus: The Dust Bowl Migration and Okie Culture in California* (New York: Oxford University Press, 1991), 19.
8. Ibid., 100–101.
9. Ibid., 101.
10. Ibid., 107.

11. John Steinbeck, *The Grapes of Wrath* (New York: Viking, 1939), ch. 18.
12. Ibid., 149.
13. Peter Monro Jack, *New York Times,* April 16, 1939.
14. Joseph Roth, *Briefe 1911–1939* (Köln: Kiepenhauer & Witsch, 1970), 249.
15. Quoted in Roger Daniels, *Coming to America: A History of Immigration and Ethnicity in American Life* (New York: HarperCollins, 1990), 299.
16. Relayed to the author in personal conversation by Herbert Freudenheim.
17. M. E. Yapp, *The Making of the Modern Near East 1792–1923* (Harlow, UK: Longman, 1987), 290.

1936: Beautiful Bodies

1. Heinrich Mann, speech at Konferenz zur Verteidigung der Olympischen Idee, Paris, June 6–7, 1936. Translation by author.
2. Victor Klemperer, quoted in Guy Walters, *Berlin Games: How the Nazis Stole the Olympic Dream* (New York: HarperCollins, 2009), 240.
3. Quoted in Walters, *Berlin Games,* 1.
4. Jean-Jacques Rousseau, *Le contrat social,* in *Oeuvres complètes,* ed. Bernard Gagnebin and Marcel Raymond (Paris: Pléiades, 1964), 3:381–382. Translation by author.
5. Evgeny Zamyatin, *We,* trans. Clarence Brown (New York: Penguin, 1993), 81.
6. Virginia Woolf, *The Diary of Virginia Woolf, Vol. 1, 1915–1919* (London: Penguin, 1979), 13.
7. William Butler Yeats, quoted in Donald J. Childs, *Modernism and Eugenics: Woolf, Eliot, Yeats, and the Culture of Degeneration* (Cambridge: Cambridge University Press, 2001), 17.
8. George F. Kennan, *Memoirs, 1925–1950* (Boston: Little, Brown, 1967), 77.

1937: War Within a War

1. Quoted in Anthony Beevor, *The Battle for Spain* (London: Penguin 2006), 294.
2. George Orwell, *Homage to Catalonia* (London: Secker and Warburg, 1938), 171.
3. Piers Brendon, *The Dark Valley: A Panorama of the 1930s* (New York: Knopf, 2000), 308.
4. Ibid., 308.
5. Ibid., 317.
6. Quoted in Beevor, *The Battle for Spain,* 94.
7. Ibid., 103.
8. The accounts and numbers of the victims follow Beevor, *The Battle for Spain,* 94ff.
9. Beevor, *The Battle for Spain,* 101.
10. Quoted in Paul Preston, *The Spanish Civil War: Reaction, Revolution and Revenge* (New York: W. W. Norton, 2007), 121.
11. Piers Brendon, *The Dark Valley,* 320
12. Quoted in Beevor, *The Battle for Spain,* 147.
13. Ibid., 140.
14. Geoffrey Cox, quoted in Preston, *The Spanish Civil War,* 175–176.

15. Orwell, *Homage to Catalonia,* 155.

16. Quoted in Karl Schlögel, *Terror und Traum* (Munich: Hanser, 2008), 151. Translation by author.

17. Aleksandr I. Solzhenitsyn, *The Gulag Archipelago* (New York: Harper & Row, 1973), 1:378.

18. Quoted in Karl Schlögel, *Terror und Traum.*

1938: Epilogue: Abide by Me

1. Hans Fantel, "Poignance Measured in Digits," *New York Times,* July 16, 1989.

2. Bruno Walter, *Theme and Variations: An Autobiography* (New York: Alfred A. Knopf, 1947), 323–324.

Index

ABOUT THE AUTHOR

Philipp Blom was born in Hamburg in 1970. After some years in Vienna, he moved to Oxford where he obtained a PhD in Jewish philosophy. He has worked in publishing and as a journalist and translator in both London and Paris. He lives in Vienna with his wife Veronica Buckley.